PIPE FITTINGS

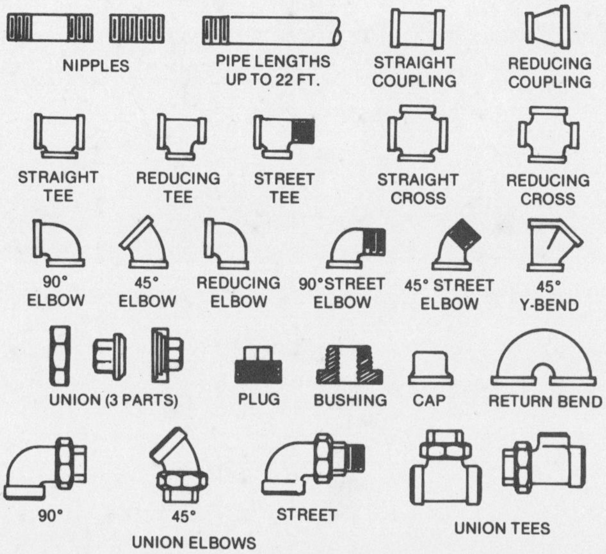

Here are the common steel pipe fittings. Nipples are simply short lengths of pipe threaded on both ends. Reducing fittings join two different sizes of pipe.

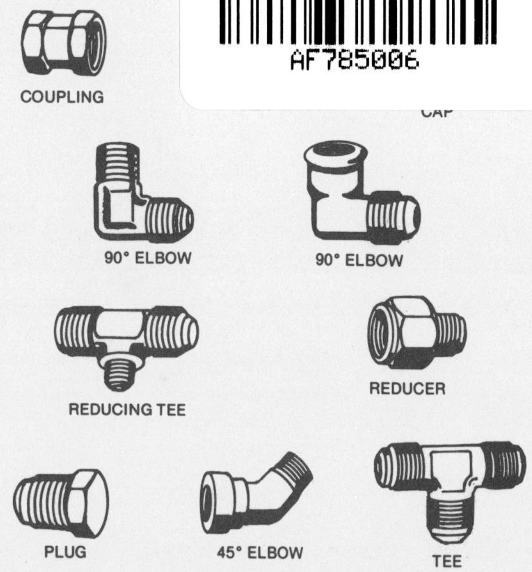

Compression fittings of the flared-tube type are the easiest for the novice to handle when working with copper tubing.

STANDARD STEEL PIPE (All Dimensions in Inches)					
Nominal Size	Outside Diameter	Inside Diameter	Nominal Size	Outside Diameter	Inside Diameter
1/8	0.405	0.269	1	1.315	1.049
1/4	0.540	0.364	1 1/4	1.660	1.380
3/8	0.675	0.493	1 1/2	1.900	1.610
1/2	0.840	0.622	2	2.375	2.067
3/4	1.050	0.824	2 1/2	2.875	2.469

SQUARE MEASURE

144 sq in = 1 sq ft
9 sq ft = 1 sq yd
272.25 sq ft = 1 sq rod
160 sq rods = 1 acre

VOLUME MEASURE

1728 cu in = 1 cu ft
27 cu ft = 1 cu yd

MEASURES OF CAPACITY

1 cup = 8 fl oz
2 cups = 1 pint
2 pints = 1 quart
4 quarts = 1 gallon
2 gallons = 1 peck
4 pecks = 1 bushel

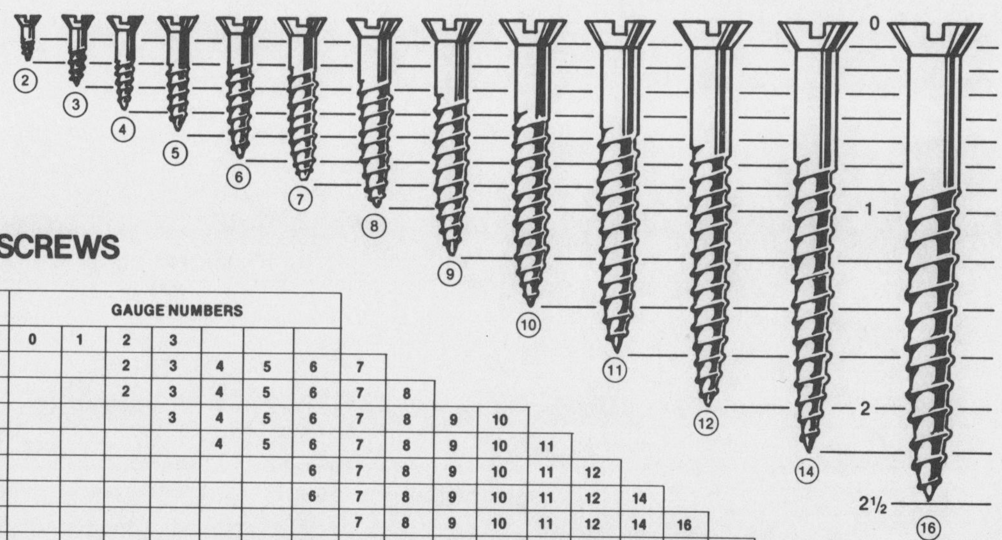

WOOD SCREWS

LENGTH	GAUGE NUMBERS																	
1/4 INCH	0	1	2	3														
3/8 INCH			2	3	4	5	6	7										
1/2 INCH			2	3	4	5	6	7	8									
5/8 INCH				3	4	5	6	7	8	9	10							
3/4 INCH					4	5	6	7	8	9	10	11						
7/8 INCH							6	7	8	9	10	11	12					
1 INCH							6	7	8	9	10	11	12	14				
1 1/4 INCH								7	8	9	10	11	12	14	16			
1 1/2 INCH							6	7	8	9	10	11	12	14	16	18		
1 3/4 INCH									8	9	10	11	12	14	16	18	20	
2 INCH									8	9	10	11	12	14	16	18	20	
2 1/4 INCH										9	10	11	12	14	16	18	20	
2 1/2 INCH													12	14	16	18	20	
2 3/4 INCH														14	16	18	20	
3 INCH															16	18	20	
3 1/2 INCH																18	20	24
4 INCH																18	20	24

WHEN YOU BUY SCREWS, SPECIFY (1) LENGTH, (2) GAUGE NUMBER, (3) TYPE OF HEAD—FLAT, ROUND, OR OVAL, (4) MATERIAL—STEEL, BRASS, BRONZE, ETC., (5) FINISH—BRIGHT, STEEL BLUED, CADMIUM, NICKEL, OR CHROMIUM PLATED.

Look what you'll find in other volumes!

FOR A FAMILY ROOM with a personality all its own, use bold splashes of color, new fabrics and unique materials. Even try zebra-striped closet doors! To learn how, see page 1182 in Vol. 8.

REFINISHING FURNITURE, once a long and tedious process, now is simple and easy. A hand-rubbed finish used to be just that. Now you simply apply a top coat designed to produce such an effect. See page 1208 of Vol. 8

SCUBA DIVING is a thrilling sport. Join the underwater fun. See page 2692 of Vol. 17.

THERE'S A RIGHT and a wrong way to cut firewood—and to stack it, too. Learn how to saw wood, from limbs to big logs, and how to circulate air through a log stack. See page 1229 of Vol. 8.

CONVERT A PORCH into a family room at a reasonable cost, including this attractive built-in wall unit. See Vol. 8, page 1170.

PLYWOOD PANELING can give you the rich effect of exotic woods. See page 2056 of Vol. 13.

THIS PICTURE SHOWS five great family-room ideas. To spot them, see page 1178 of Vol. 8.

FOR STUNNING RESULTS, buy beautiful low-cost prints, then mat and frame them yourself. For complete step-by-step instructions, see page 1264 of Vol. 8.

Popular Mechanics

do-it-yourself encyclopedia

in 20 volumes

a complete how-to guide for the homeowner, the hobbyist—
and anyone who enjoys working with mind and hands!

All about:

home maintenance
home-improvement projects
wall paneling
burglary and fire protection
furniture projects
finishing and refinishing furniture
outdoor living
home remodeling
solutions to home problems
challenging woodworking projects
hobbies and handicrafts
model making
weekend projects
workshop shortcuts and techniques
hand-tool skills
power-tool know-how
shop-made tools
car repairs
car maintenance
appliance repair
boating
hunting
fishing
camping
photography projects
radio, TV and electronics know-how
clever hints and tips
projects just for fun

volume 7

ISBN 0-87851-072-9
Library of Congress Catalog Number 77 84920

MANUFACTURED IN THE UNITED STATES OF AMERICA

contents

VOLUME 7

HANDSOME campaign desk is patterned after the British military desk used by upper-echelon field officers.

Build a handsome campaign desk

For a look of luxury, this reproduction is made from solid cherry and has an authentic-looking embellished leather top

By ROSARIO CAPOTOSTO

SEE ALSO

Antique reproductions . . . Clocks . . . Desk accessories . . . Drawers . . . Finishes, wood . . . Gossip benches . . . Letter racks . . . Staining, wood . . . Study centers . . . Wood finishes

■ THE 19TH-CENTURY British officer's campaign desk is experiencing a revival. The originals had leather tops embellished in hand-tooled gold leaf, metal-bound corners and recessed drawer pulls. They rested on detachable trestles.

PM's version has retained these features, with minor exceptions. Naugahyde and gold leaf are substituted for real leather. An optional top treatment, also illustrated, uses leather-textured Wilsonart plastic laminate embellished with decals.

The desktop is made up in picture-frame form, with a deep rabbet on the inside to permit the "leather" surfaced insert panel to set in flush. This is a simplified and very practical method of inlaying the material. The advantage is that the

MATERIALS LIST—PM'S CAMPAIGN-STYLE DESK

Key	Pcs.	Size and description
A	1	½ X 20½ X 44½" fir plywood
B	2	13/16 x 2½ x 24" cherry
C	3	13/16 x 2½ x 48" cherry
D	1	13/16 x 5⅜ x 46⅞" cherry
E	2	13/16 x 5⅜ x 24" (less width of wood strips that conceal end grain) cherry
F	2	13/16 x 5⅜ x 23-7/16" cherry
G	1	¾ x 22 x 46" fir plywood
H	2	¾ x 1 x 24" cherry
I	2	¾ x 1 x 48" cherry
J	2	½ x 5 x 12-5/16" poplar
K	6	½ x 5 x 22" poplar
L	2	13/16 x 5 x 12-5/16" cherry
M	2	¼ x 11¾ x 21¾" hardboard
N	1	½ x 5 x 20¼" poplar
O	1	13/16 x 5 x 20¼" cherry
P	1	¼ x 19¾ x 21¾" hardboard
Q	8	13/16 x 2 x 25" cherry
R	8	13/16 x 2 x 20½" cherry
S	4	13/16 x 2 x 20¼" cherry
T	4	13/16 x 2¼ x 20½" cherry

Misc. ⅔ yard Naugahyde (Argo's No. AO 577 Russet) or laminated plastic (No. 2935-6 Latigo Leather pattern by Wilsonart); ¼" wood dowels; 4, ¼ x 1" steel rod, Antique brass campaign hardware*: 4, Allison pulls No. 495, and 2, No. 850; 20, Allison "L" Ornament, No. 598; nylon drawer slides*; Mylar gold foil for embossing Naugahyde**; 8 sheets of decals for use on laminate (Meyercord, No. 1539-A); glue, screws and nails as required.

*Nylon drawer slide tape is available at many home improvement centers or from Brookstone Co., 127 Vose Farm Rd., Peterborough, N.H. 03458. Ask for Self Adhering Sliding Tape. The price is $4.25; add $1.55 for shipping.

**Complete kit of campaign hardware, including pulls, handles and corners, may be purchased from Capro Craft, Box 18, Greenlawn, N.Y. 11740. Kit is $14 postpaid; add $2.50 for the roll of Mylar foil.

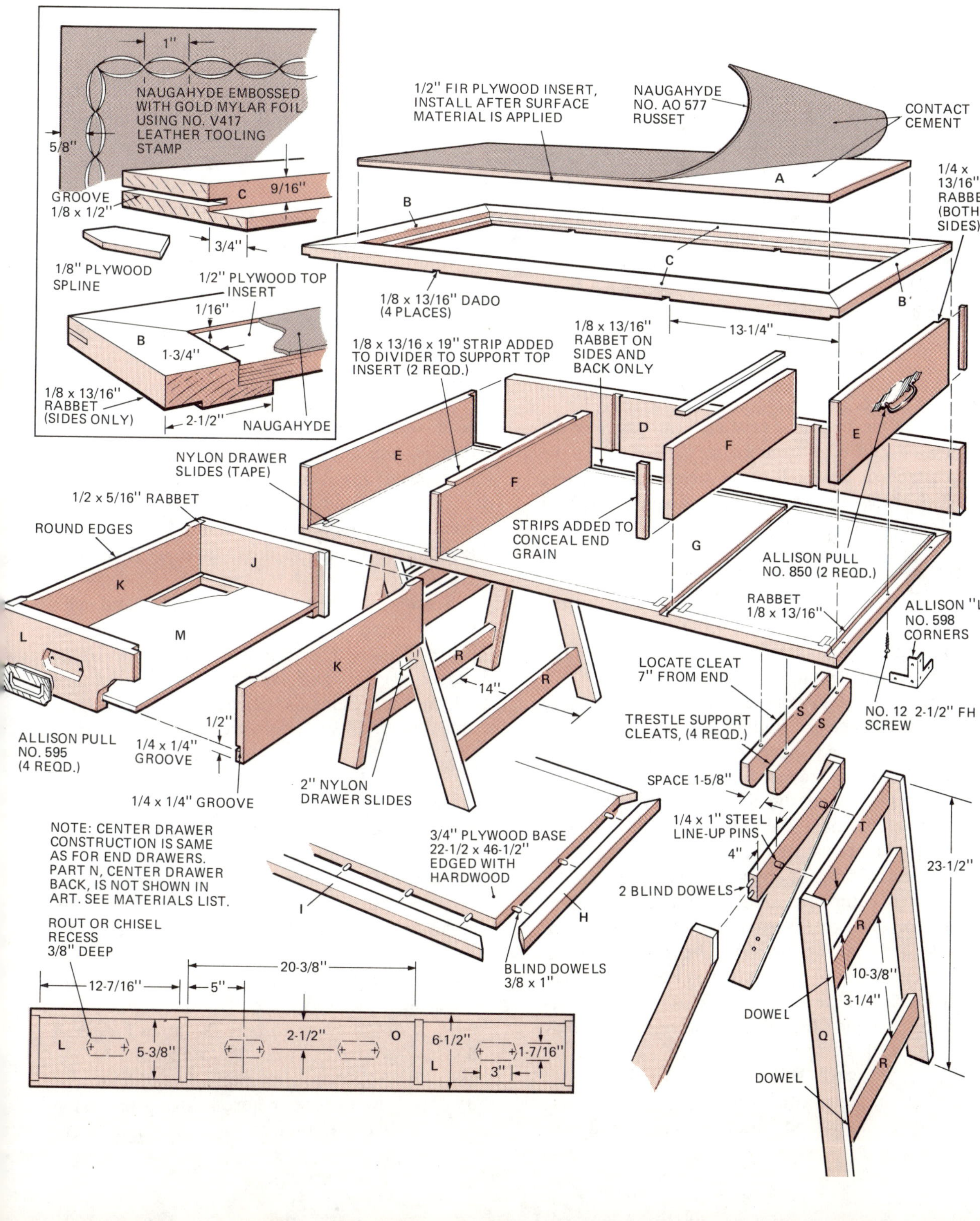

BUILDING THE DESK

1 MITER JIG slides in miter-gauge grooves, makes mitering frame easier.

2 USE fence-riding jig to cut grooves for splines at corners. See drawing.

3 USE hold-down block, auxiliary wood fence for inboard rabbets.

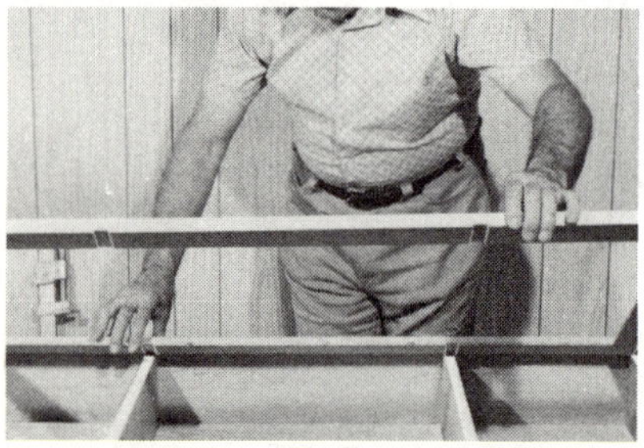

4 JOIN cross members, back to base with screws, glue. Add top, glue, clamp.

5 SIMPLE jig can be used for cutting angles needed on leg tops.

6 USE small nails, with heads removed, to mark dowel-hole centers.

Naugahyde, or plastic laminate, can easily be cemented and edge-trimmed to perfection on the unattached plywood panel before installation. Also, border decorating can be done before final assembly.

getting started

Rip the frame members to width, then cut the deep rabbets. Follow with 45° miter cuts at the ends, then cut grooves for plywood splines at the corners with the aid of the jig in Photo 2.

If you own four miter clamps, use them to glue the frame together. Otherwise, work on a flat board and insert pieces of waxed paper under each corner to prevent gluing the frame to the work table. Clamp the end pieces directly to the work table, insert the sides with splines, then clamp in place with bar clamps.

Carefully sand off any residual glue before the next step: cutting the rabbet around the sides and back of the frame bottom. This is done with a dado head on a table saw. Use a wood facing strip on the saw fence to set the distance between the blade and the steel fence. This permits an inboard cut along the edge of the frame. A hold-down block clamped to the fence, directly over the blade center, will help to maintain proper contact throughout the run.

The ¾-in. plywood bottom panel is edged with ¾-in.-square strips of cherry, joined with blind dowels. Use the same setup for cutting the rabbets and dados as was used for the frame.

The front and back ends of the four cross members are faced with ⅛-in.-thick strips before the final assembly in order to conceal the end grain.

Screws—through the bottom—are used with glue to attach the back board and the four crosspieces. The frame gets glue only, no screws. *If the rabbet joints are well fitted,* glue alone will do the job. When the glue has dried, remove glue lumps and true up all surfaces with a belt sander.

constructing the trestles

The trestles are assembled with blind dowels and glue. Mark the joint locations with a template of thin cardboard.

Use the miter gauge (or radial saw) to cut the top and bottom angles on the legs. The steep angles on the top insides of the legs can be cut on the radial saw with the arrangement shown in Photo 5. Or, make a wedge-shaped guide board to ride against the fence of the table saw.

Use a doweling jig to bore the holes for ⅜x2-in. spiral-grooved dowels. Sand all parts *before* assembly. Apply the glue sparingly and let it air-dry for a few minutes before bringing the parts together. This minimizes parts sliding about.

7 DOWELING jig assures true perpendicular holes and easier assembly.

8 USE paper shims to obtain slip fit when spacing trestle support cleats.

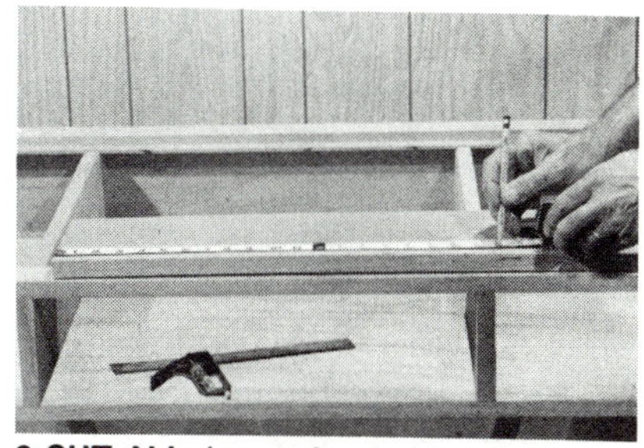

9 CUT ALL drawer fronts from same board to assure pleasing grain.

10 USE AUXILIARY fence with stops, molding-cutter to round drawer-top edge.

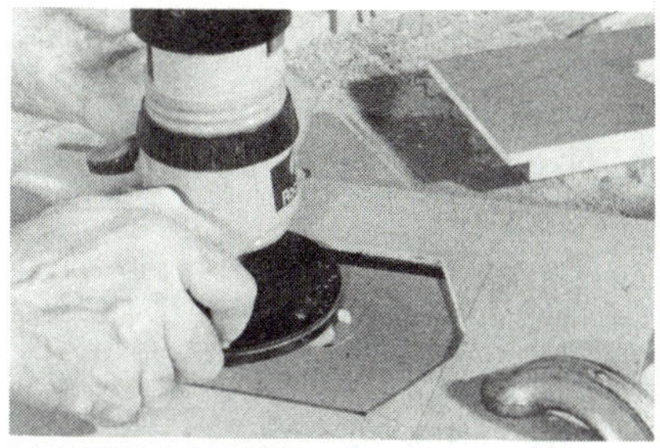

11 WITH ROUTER and template cutout, or chisel and mallet, cut recesses.

12 NYL O TAPE strips on cabinet, drawers, replace drawer hardware.

Some say the best way to handle squeezed-out glue is to let it become almost dry, but *not* brittle. At this point, shave it off with a chisel.

Screw and glue the trestle-support cleats in place, using paper shims between the cross pieces and cleats to obtain accurate alignment for a slip fit.

The trestles are held together in matching pairs with two ¼-in. steel pegs; one end of each peg is secured with a drop of epoxy. If the desk needn't be portable, one screw in each cleat secures the trestles.

building the drawers

First, cut the drawer fronts from a single board. Then, after cutting the other parts to size, run them over a dado head to form the rabbets and grooves. Run a stopped corner round on both sides of the top edges of the drawer sides. This can be done with a corner-round molding-cutter head on the table saw, with a strip of wood with stop blocks clamped to the saw fence, or with a router and rounding-over bit.

The drawer pulls are set into ⅜-in.-deep recesses routed into the drawer fronts. To use the same hardware, make the simple guide shown in Photo 11, from ¼-in. plywood or hardboard.

To assemble the drawers: Use finishing nails and glue to attach a drawer side to a front and a back. Apply glue to the grooves, then insert the bottom. Attach the second side, set nails and fill the holes.

Strips of Nyl O Tape, used instead of conventional drawer-slides, give smooth, easy movement. Cut strips about 2 in. long and apply them to the rear bottom of the drawer sides and to the fronts of the drawer compartments.

making the desk top

Cut ½-in. plywood to fit perfectly into the frame recess, with top surface 1/16 in. *below* the surface of the frame. The Naugahyde will make up the 1/16-in. difference.

The Naugahyde used for this project is available at fabric shops in 54-in. widths, so you'll need ⅔ yard. Be sure to specify Service Quality, which has the proper thickness.

Rough-trim it to overhang about 1 in. on all sides of the plywood. Apply contact adhesive to both surfaces and allow to dry. Naugahyde drys somewhat slowly, so apply the cement to the Naugahyde about a half hour before coating the wood. Use two sheets of wrapping paper as a separator while positioning the material on the wood. Slip out the first piece to allow partial contact, then slip out the other. Use the back of your hand to press the material gradually into place, working from the center outwards. Use a 3- or 4-

INSTALLING THE 'LEATHER' TOP

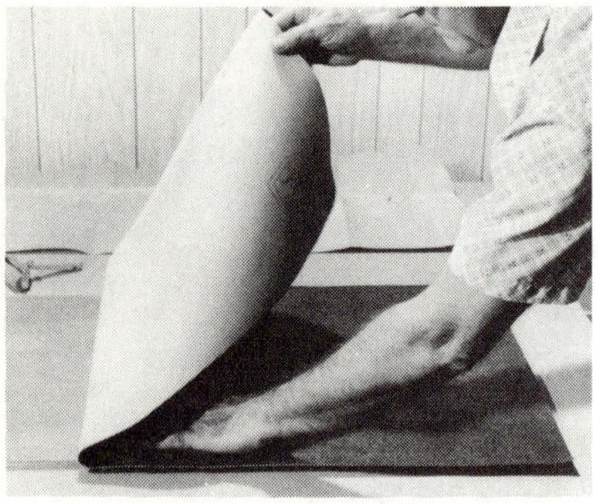

1 USE contact cement to bond Naugahyde to wood; press outward.

2 ALCOHOL lamp, embossing tool, Mylar foil are used for decorative border.

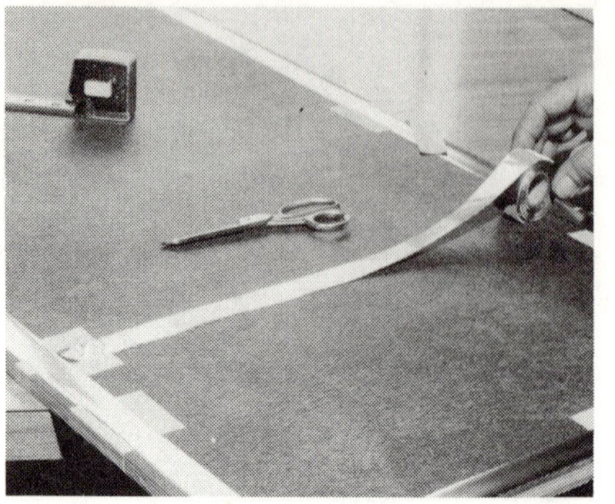

3 AS PIECES of masking tape hold foil in place, butt ends of foil strips.

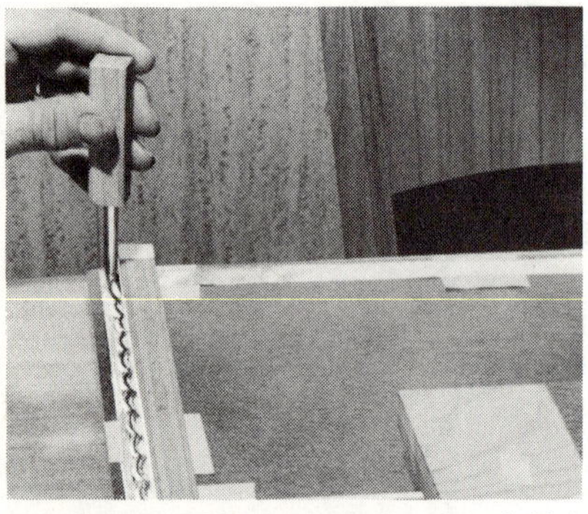

4 SECOND ROW is made freehand. Hot stamp makes up to six impressions.

5 STRAIGHT wood strip guides stamp as you emboss first row of border.

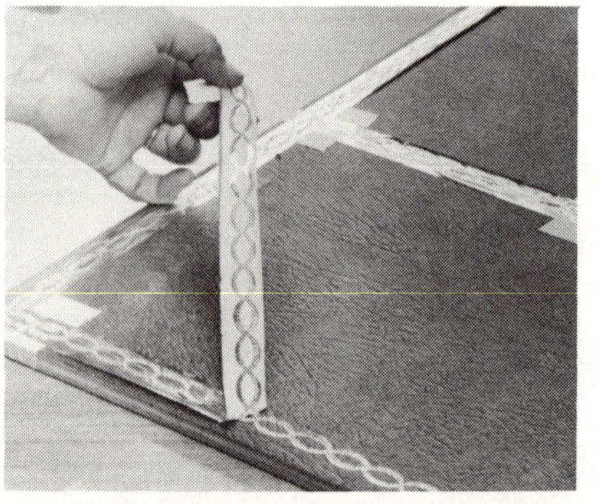

6 AFTER completing series of impressions, peel away foil.

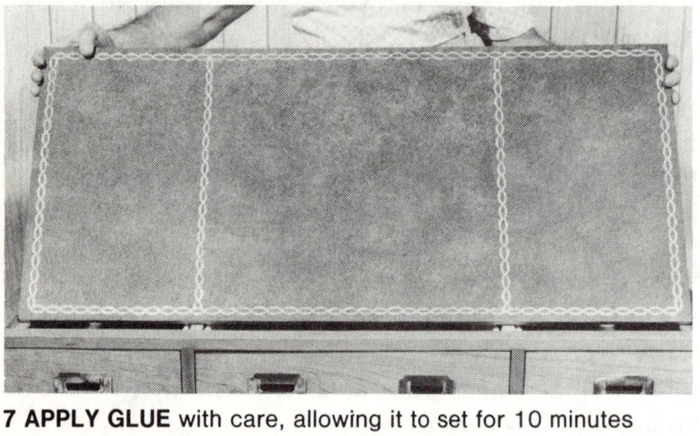

7 APPLY GLUE with care, allowing it to set for 10 minutes before dropping in top and applying weight.

8 SOME OF the nails for hardware should be shortened so they don't collide when driven into top.

in. roller to assure complete contact.

Turn the panel over and use a very sharp knife to trim the Naugahyde flush with the edge of the plywood. The leftover larger piece of material should also be cemented to a scrap board for the next phase.

For the embossing you'll need an alcohol lamp, a decorative leathercraft stamp, a roll of 1-in.-wide Mylar gold foil and some masking tape. Use *only* alcohol to fuel the lamp. Other fuels, and candles, can soil the work with soot. The stamp, No. V 417, is available at hobby or leathercraft shops. If Mylar foil is not available locally, order it by mail (see materials list). To prevent finger burns, make a scrap-wood handle for the stamping tool.

Start by cutting and taping strips of the foil into place, dull side down. Do not overlap the corners; they must butt evenly without spaces. Apply the tape close to the edges so it won't be in

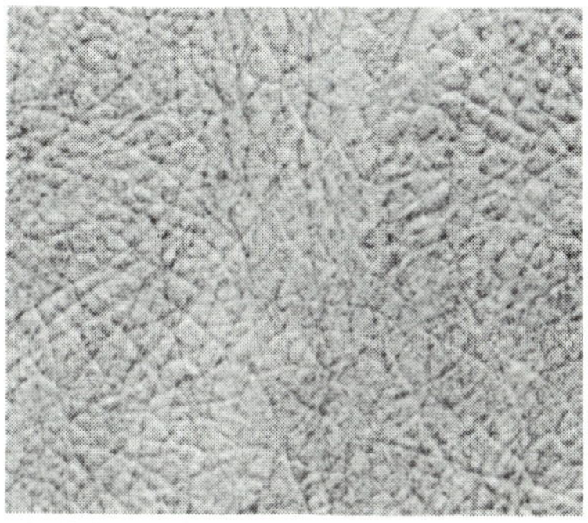

WILSONART latigo plastic laminate has appearance of real leather.

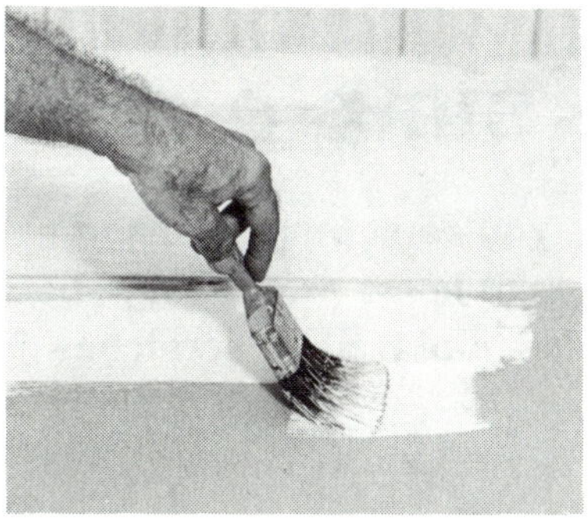

LATEX contact adhesive is applied to both surfaces; let dry until clear.

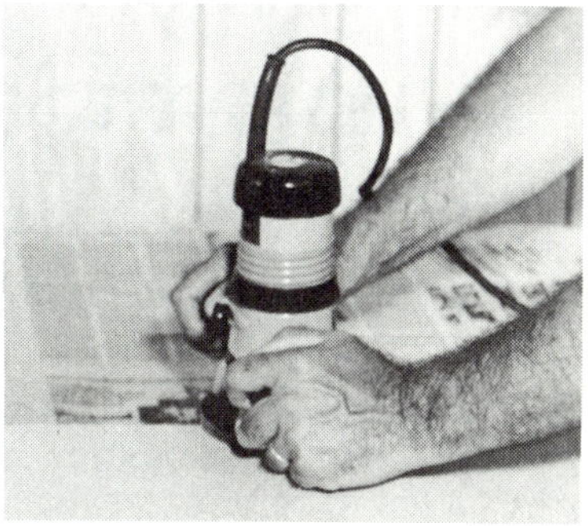

ROUTER with laminate trimming bit is used to remove excess.

Leather-like laminate top

You may prefer a plastic laminate top in place of the Naugahyde. To apply it, first cut the sheet about ⅜-in. oversize on all sides to allow for trimming after bonding. Cut with a fine-toothed saw with little or no set. Next, apply contact cement to both surfaces and allow it to dry. Then bond plastic to the plywood, using Kraft paper as a separator while positioning the laminate.

The water-applied decals (Meyercord, No. 1539-A) won't adhere properly to the textured surface unless you first apply sizing. To do so, brush on a coat of Aqua Podge or a similar latex-based decoupage finish. Allow to dry. Since arranging decals can be tricky, first lay them out in a dry run. Some designs may have to be cut to fit. Apply decals according to instructions, protect with paper and press firmly with a small rubber roller. When the decals have dried, apply another coat of decoupage finish over the top.

the way of the design. The stamp design is crescent shaped, so a double impression, face to face, must be made to obtain the completed design. The first impression, which forms one half of the pattern, is made against a strip of wood which will assure obtaining a straight line of scallops. Tape the guide strip in place so it covers exactly half the foil's length.

The tool makes an impression 1 in. long. To end up with a full loop at the ends of a run, make pencil marks about 1 in. apart on the guide strip. Position the guide accordingly. If the inside cross borders don't divide evenly into full inches, you can make a partial impression by inserting a few sheets of paper between foil and stamp. Or, overlap each crescent slightly to make the pattern fit.

Heat the stamp for 10 or 15 seconds. Set up the scrap piece of Naugahyde with a strip of foil in place and make an impression by pressing the stamp squarely into it. If the tool is too hot it'll scorch both foil and the Naugahyde. Quickly make another test impression. If it looks good, make a series of impressions on the work. Position the tool so both points of the crescent butt up against the guide. Press down firmly and hold the tool in place for about one second each impression. Each heating of the tool should be sufficient for five or six impressions. Don't go beyond this, because an unheated tool will not transfer the gold. Make a test impression each time the tool is reheated.

When the initial row of scallops is completed, remove the guide strip and continue the embossing freehand by matching up the crescent points. When all the stamping is done, peel away the foil.

finishing the desk

Apply the finish *before* installing the top. The prototype was stained with Beverlee's cherry satin stain, followed with two coats of Constantine's Wood Glo clear satin finish. All nonexposed surfaces, including all parts of the drawers, were given a coat of sealer. Heavy staining frequently hides the beauty of wood. For a very light stain, first apply a very diluted coat of sanding sealer (1 part sealer, 5 parts thinner). Sand lightly with 220 paper, then stain.

To install the top, lay in a neat bead of glue, being careful to keep away from the top edges. Put top in place and weight with heavy books. Attach three sections of campaign hardware corners on the four top corners; two each at the lower corners. Note that the close proximity of the nails necessitates clipping some of them short, so they won't interfere with each other. Start the nail holes first, then withdraw and reinsert the clipped nails where necessary.

Avoid these simple darkroom goofs

You can't bring a ruined negative back to life. Here's how to correct the most common mistakes of home processing—before they happen to you and cause such effects as pinholes, streaks and scratches

By CHRISTOPHER CRANDALL

■ DO YOUR NEGATIVES keep coming out of the tank full of pinholes, streaks, scratches and reticulation even though you faithfully follow all of the customary developing steps? The normal reaction is to blame the film (outdated or damaged) or chemicals (exhausted or contaminated). Actually, it could be that your processing technique has some built-in flaws.

The goal of processing your own film is to produce crisp, brilliant negatives and, ultimately, prints of top professional quality. It doesn't make much sense to shoot the original pictures meticulously and then get careless in the processing stage, especially when it may cost you that "once-in-a-lifetime" shot. The following are 15 of the most common goofs, step by step, that are made in home processing.

1. Touching the emulsion. Because film has a frustrating tendency to curl back into a roll, it is a real challenge to your dexterity to get it onto the reel without touching the emulsion (dull) side. Perspiration and skin oils can leave an indelible fingerprint superimposed on the latent image. If you're not sure you can handle film without touching the emulsion, wear a pair of thin cotton gloves such as those sold for the purpose.

2. Bypassing the predevelopment rinse. When developer is poured into the tank, the film temperature drops suddenly and this "shock" can cause reticulation—a network of thin lines that will be reproduced prominently in the print. You can avoid this by first bathing the film for a few minutes in a filtered water bath at the same temperature as that of the developer. (Water has no chemical effect on the film.)

SEE ALSO

Darkrooms . . . Dryers, photo . . . Filters, photo . . . Mountings, photo . . . Photography . . . Prints, photo

3. Using impure water. All tap water contains impurities, some of which can cause adverse reactions in photo chemicals. Ideally, distilled water should be used in mixing solutions, but boiled and filtered tap water works equally well.

4. Measuring carelessly. Only beakers made especially for use in photo processing should be used. Inexpensive plastic cooking beakers tend to be less accurate. The beaker should not be held at eye level while water and chemicals are added, but should be placed on a flat surface. Measure water precisely, or your solution will be too strong or too weak.

5. Mixing improperly. It's always a great temptation to dump powdered chemicals into a jar and just shake vigorously until they dissolve. Gentle stirring with a rod is really the only safe mixing procedure. Violent shaking churns the solution into a froth of air bubbles that settle on the film and cause pinholes.

6. Lack of preparation. Before pouring the developer into the tank, all the chemicals you will need should be mixed and filtered and your equipment should be clean and close at hand. Set the timer for the required development time, *less 35 seconds.* Tanks usually require about this long to empty, so by the time you've drained the tank, the development will be stopped at almost the precise time. (The timer should be started when you begin to pour in the developer, not after the tank is full.)

7. Insufficient agitation. Streaky, blotchy film is the result of inadequate agitation. Fresh developer must reach the film at least every 60 seconds during the development or the solution in contact with the film becomes exhausted. As a result, the film may come out underdeveloped. A greater danger is that the developer may become loaded with halide from the film emulsion and spread unevenly in streaks across the film.

8. Violent agitation. This is the other extreme. It doesn't take much action to create air bubbles inside a tank, and air bubbles cause pinholes. Nikor tanks (stainless steel) should be inverted

HIGH-TEMPERATURE PROCESSING can soften the emulsion to the point where it loses its grip and begins to slip. Result: ugly blotches like these that ruin the negative. Stick to slower, but safer, standard processing, usually at 68° F.

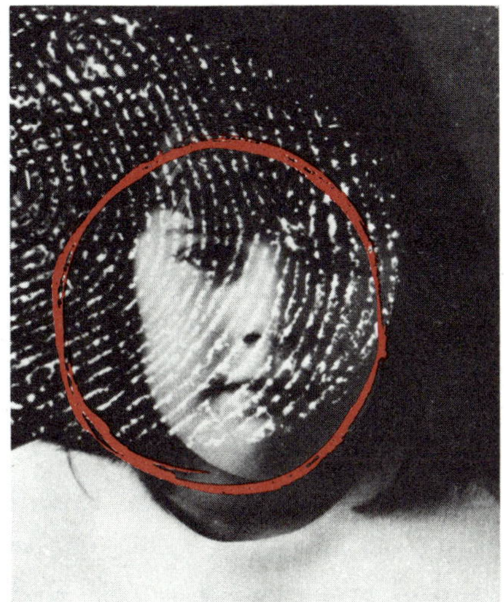

TELLTALE THUMBPRINT on this blowup is a sign of careless handling during the developing. Skin oils will leave indelible prints on the emulsion.

INFURIATING PINHOLES start out as tiny specks in the negative, but look like baseballs when you blow them up, as above. The cause: Air bubbles in the developer. The cure: Use gentle agitation so as not to whip up a froth.

SCRATCHES in the emulsion are caused by rough handling in many ways. Careless sponging ruined what would have been a cute candid shot.

SPOTS LIKE THESE result from improper mixing. Each was caused by a minute granule of undissolved developer crystal. Even so, filtering the solution before use would have trapped the harmful particles and saved the picture.

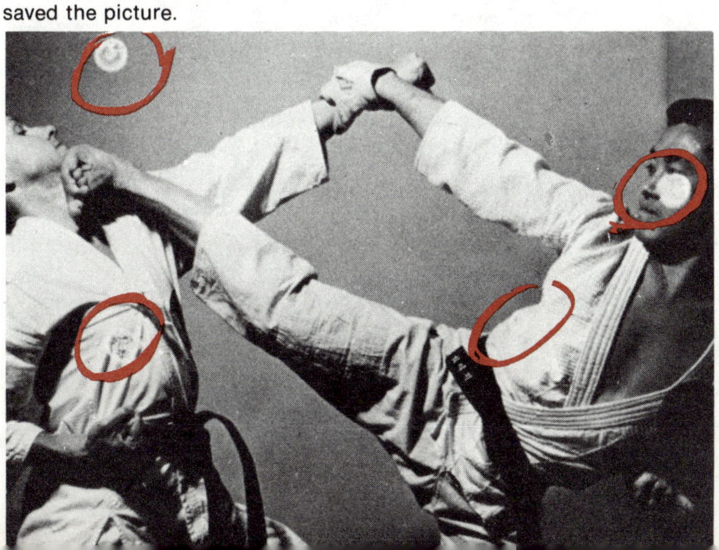

INADEQUATE AGITATION during the development can wreck an entire roll of prize shots. Here streaks are from a halide-loaded developer.

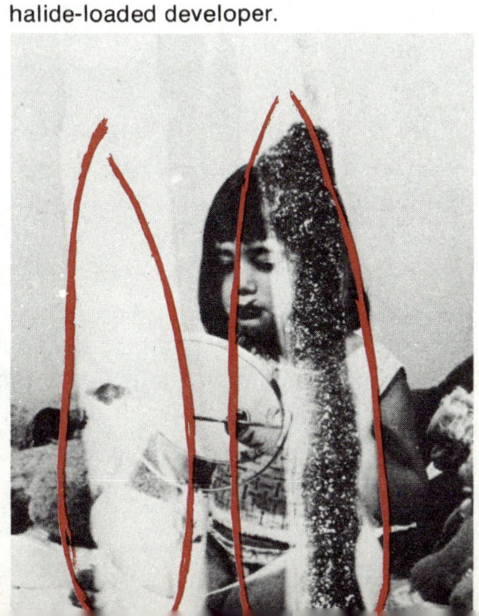

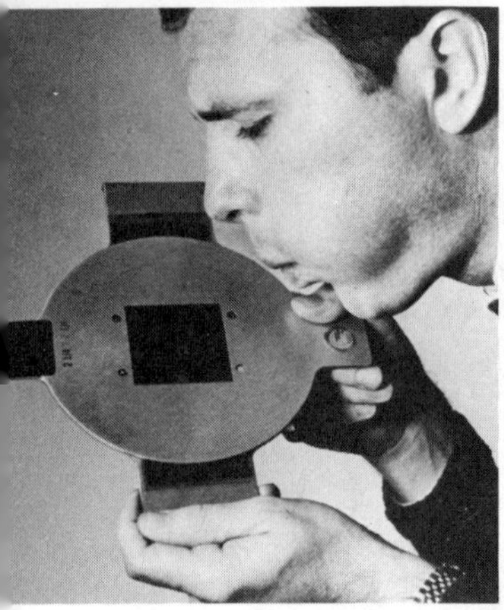

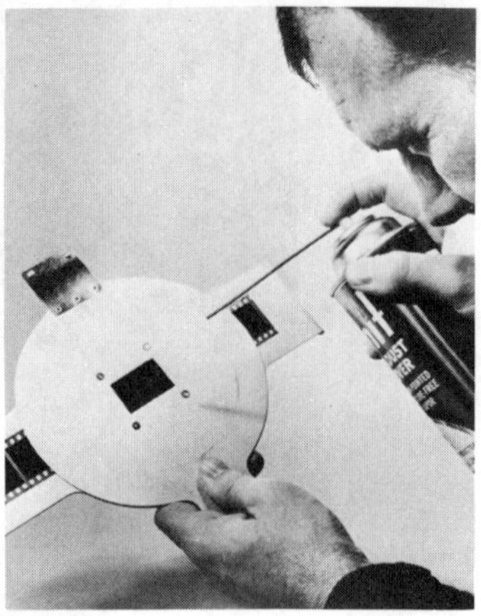

WRONG **RIGHT**

BLOWING IS FINE for starting a charcoal fire, but is no way to remove dust from negatives. Moisture blown onto the surface from your breath will dry as water spots and show up on print. Instead, use a pushbutton can of air. One blast from its jet will safely and effectively whisk away every dust particle.

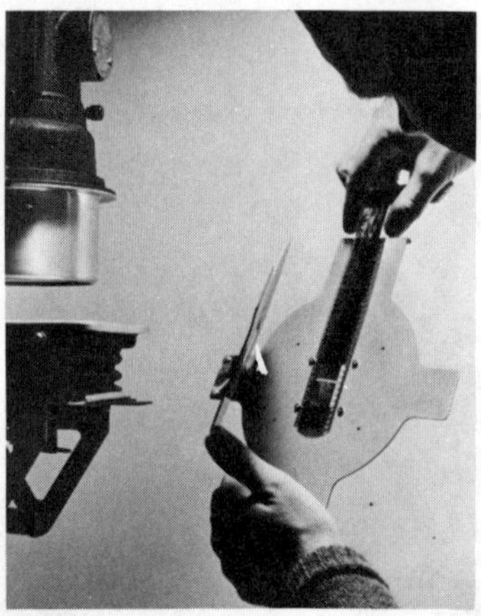

WRONG **RIGHT**

HOLDING THE FILM in your fingers while you are loading it into a carrier, as at far left, is a sure way to get oily prints all over the emulsion; they will show up later on the print. Grip the film at the edges between fingers and bow it slightly so that it won't touch the carrier as you slide it into position.

gently for agitation and slammed occasionally against a flat surface to burst any air bubbles that may have formed. Don't try this with a plastic tank, however. Twirl the rod in a plastic tank three or four times each way for about five seconds during agitation (every 30 seconds with some developers, every 60 seconds with others).

9. Overdevelopment/underdevelopment. There is a solution for both of these problems, but each is tricky and must be performed with care. Overdeveloped negatives can be treated with one of several reducers that absorb silver content in equal amounts from the high, middle and low densities, thereby reducing the visual contrast of the negative.

Underdeveloped negatives are more difficult to improve, especially when they are also underexposed. You simply can't add image detail where none was registered during exposure. The use of an intensifier (silver, chromium, mercury) can add some contrast and occasionally permit you to salvage a negative, but intensifiers have a tendency to stain.

10. Failure to use an acid rinse. Some photographers argue against using an acid stop-bath rinse between development and hypo, claiming that acid causes pinholes. They prefer a water rinse instead. However, those favoring the acid rinse contend that proper agitation during the rinsing phase would prevent gas bubbles from forming and thus eliminate the chance of pinholes.

The purpose of an acid rinse is to stop development immediately by neutralizing any developer that has adhered to the film after the tank is drained. Since water has no chemical effect on film, development can continue during a water rinse, producing overdeveloped negatives. Furthermore, an acid bath helps to remove developer scum and prevents the formation of dichroic fog (red and green stains).

11. Improper fixing. Manufacturers' instructions for using hypo usually say: "Fix two to five minutes." Fixing time will vary from roll to roll. Rather than assume the film is adequately fixed, play it safe by pouring the hypo into a "holding" beaker while you check the film under a strong light. If you spot a milky cast, this is a tipoff that further fixing is required. The image quality of insufficiently fixed film (and prints) will deteriorate rapidly.

There is danger, too, in overfixing both film and prints. Extended "souping" can bleach out most of the image. (Two to three minutes over the recommended time won't hurt.)

12. Using exhausted hypo. Exhausted hypo is loaded with silver thiosulfate compounds that never can be completely removed from films and prints, even with prolonged washing. The results are prominent stains that usually appear long after the films and prints have been processed and dried. Hypo that is being reused should first be tested for potency with Kodak's Residual Silver Test Solution.

13. Careless washing. Films and prints require

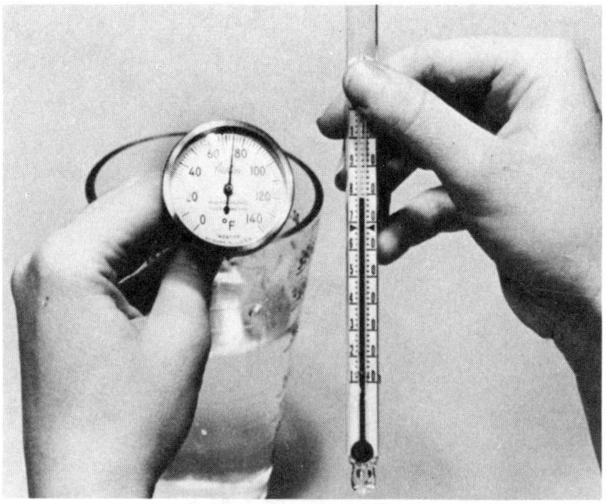

A DARKROOM THERMOMETER should be checked periodically against another thermometer to make sure that it remains absolutely accurate.

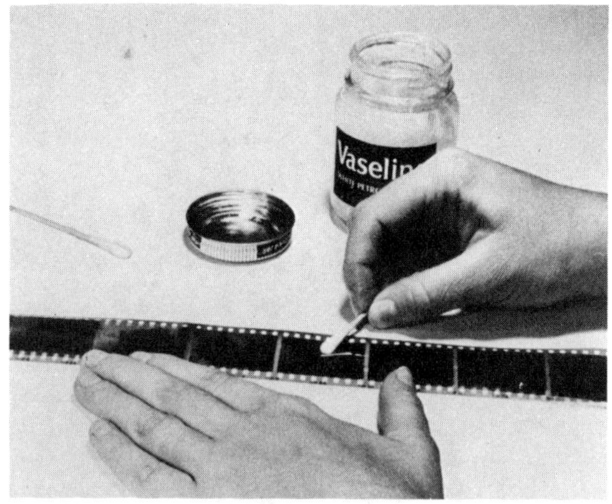

SCRATCHED NEGATIVES often can be salvaged by applying petroleum jelly or a lacquer filler like Edwal's No Scratch to the damaged areas.

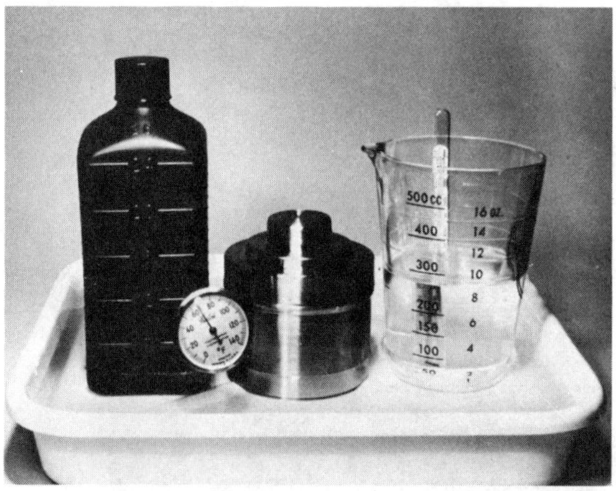

TO KEEP EVERYTHING at the same temperature, put tank and beakers in a tray of water that first has been brought to the correct temperature.

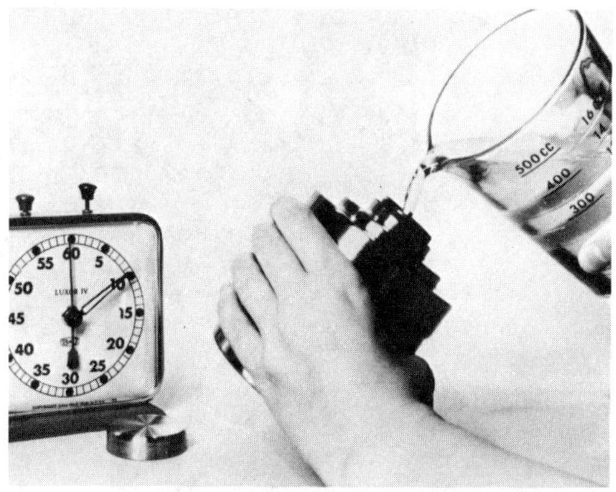

START YOUR TIMER just before you begin filling the developing tank, not after it is full. Tip the tank slightly to prevent air bubbles from forming.

a thorough washing (always in cold water) with *frequent agitation* to remove residual hypo. The flow into the washing tray should be adjusted so there are 12 complete changes of water every hour. Since this is difficult to gauge, try this test: Turn on the water to the flow you intend to use, then pour in a few drops of dye or food coloring concentrate. All traces of the dye should disappear in five minutes. If the dye is still visible after five minutes, increase the flow of water and repeat until the container clears within the set time.

14. Forced drying. Films should never be force-dried by fan, blower heater, hair dryer, or other devices that tend to stir up dust and deposit it on the wet surface of the film. Dust and other foreign matter sticks tenaciously to the film during drying and may even become firmly embedded in the emulsion. Only a second washing or soaking can safely remove such particles, and even this sometimes fails. If you don't have a film-drying cabinet, the bathroom is the next best place to dry film. Run the shower to settle the dust, then hang the film inside the stall.

Film should not be hung for drying directly from the wash. First, treat it with a wetting solution, such as Kodak's Photo-Flo or Edwal's Kwik-Wet.

15. Scratching the emulsion. Occasionally, film picks up particles of foreign matter or scum that resist the wetting agent treatment. Only in this case should a sponge sandwich or chamois be used. Wet emulsion is soft and highly susceptible to damage. A bit of grit or film trapped under the sponge or chamios can gouge an irreparable scratch the length of the film. The less you have to touch the film (wet or dry), the better the results you'll get when you go to the enlarger.

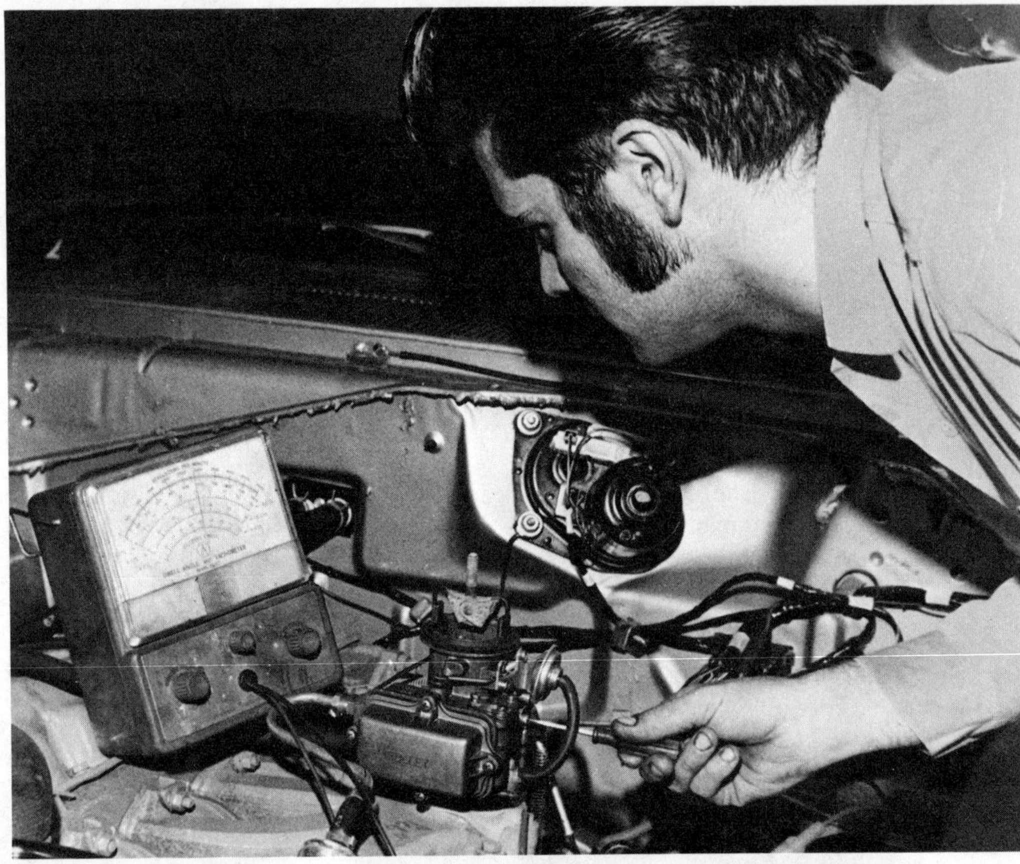

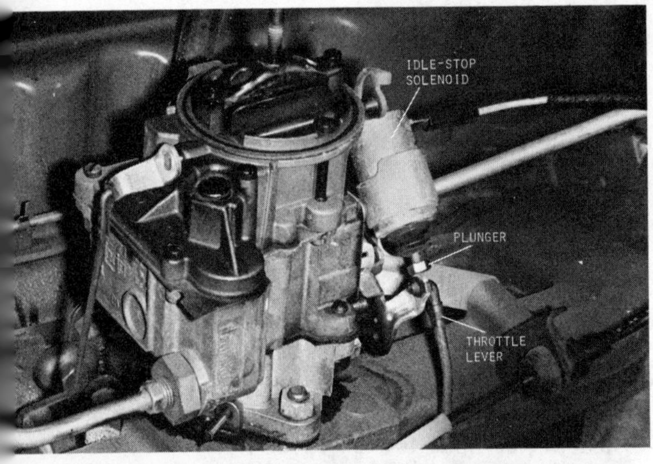

FAST-IDLE AND ENGINE-IDLE speeds should be set, where possible, at the carburetor using a tachometer (top) to meet the manufacturer's specifications precisely. While the engine idles, the plunger of the idle-stop solenoid (above) is against the throttle lever. When the engine is turned off, the plunger should retract. Adjust engine idle by turning the plunger (right).

SEE ALSO

**Carburetors, auto . . . Distributors, auto . . .
Fuel systems, auto . . . Gaskets, auto . . .
Ignition systems, auto . . . Lubrication, auto . . .
Misfiring, auto . . . Sparkplugs . . .
Transmissions, auto . . . Tune-up, auto**

How to stop an engine that won't stop

You switch off the ignition, but the engine keeps chugging and struggling along? For many a driver, that's an unnerving situation—but it's one that is more and more common. Here are the implications, and the solution

By MORT SCHULTZ

■ AN ENGINE that won't start is annoying—but at least it isn't scary. The same thing can't be said for an engine that won't stop when you turn off the ignition key. The continued spasms of chugging have alarmed many a driver.

The condition is commonly referred to as "dieseling," and is also called "run-on" and "after run." Although frightening, it is not harmful. According to Champion Spark Plug Co., "Engineers are pretty well agreed that the condition, so far as research has been able to determine, does not damage the engine."

Still, it isn't normal for an engine to sputter for several seconds after switch-off. Not every car diesels, but the problem is widespread enough to cause concern.

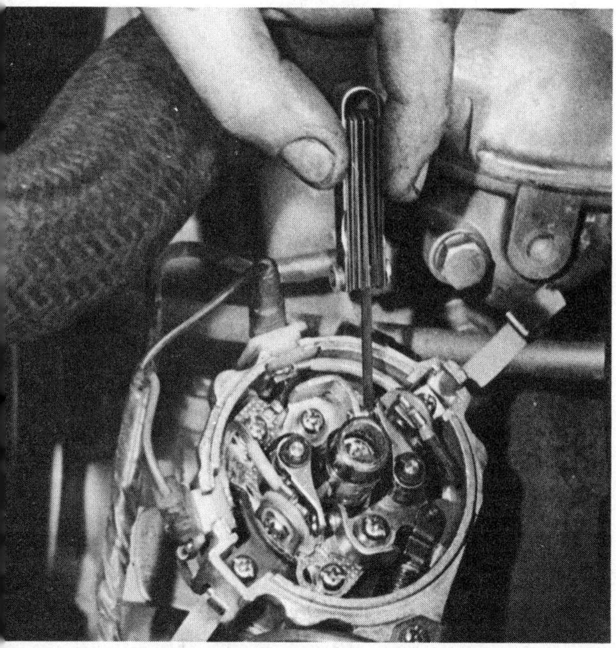

A PROJECT to stop dieseling should include general tune-up procedures. Among the steps to take, if necessary, is setting distributor points using an appropriate size feeler gauge. Then set timing.

Dieseling is ignition in the absence of spark. It occurs when fuel in the combustion chambers (cylinders) is ignited by heat.

The condition comes about when fuel enters the cylinders as the ignition key is turned off, because the throttle plate doesn't fully close. Heat in the cylinders then ignites this unburned fuel.

the wrong remedy

One cause of dieseling, especially in cars without catalytic converters, is the lean fuel mixture required by engines to meet standards of the Clean Air Act. A lean fuel mixture necessitates that ignition timing be set to occur late in the combustion cycle. Late (retarded) timing causes greater heat in cylinders.

There are drivers who think that dieseling can be eliminated by readjusting the fuel mixture to make it richer and advancing ignition timing. This is a bad idea, because engine performance will suffer and emissions will increase.

Idle-mixture screws either have caps over them or are sealed inside the carburetor to dissuade people from readjusting the fuel mixture. Removing the caps or breaking the carburetor seal is illegal unless it's done by a recognized auto mechanic in order to make repairs. In this case, the law states that the mechanic has to install new caps or reseal the carburetor.

Aside from retarded timing, another source of heat that can ignite unburned fuel in cylinders is a rise in engine temperature brought about by a fault in the cooling system. See that the system is clean and the thermostat is functioning properly.

Excessive heat may also be a result of the type of gasoline you're using. More and more engines are able to operate on gasoline with an octane rating of 87 or 88. However, this relatively low octane rating has a higher calorific value than fuel having a higher octane rating; that is, it gives off more heat.

Unburned fuel is more apt to enter cylinders of cars with automatic transmissions than those

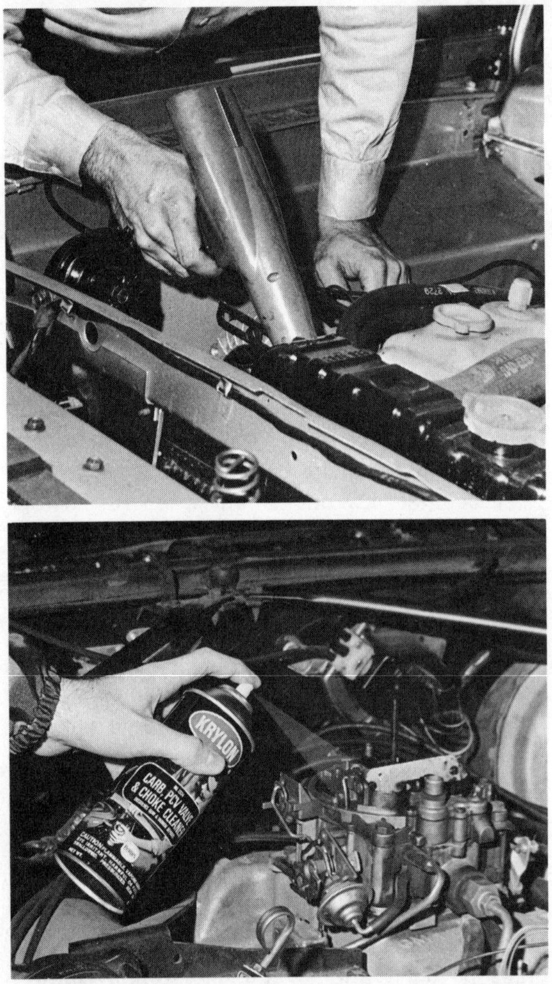

CHECK IGNITION TIMING with a timing light (top) and periodically check and clean carburetor linkage and choke area (bottom). Dirt or damaged linkage could keep the throttle from closing completely and leave the engine more vulnerable to dieseling.

with manual transmissions. Before a driver switches off the ignition key, he normally places the transmission selector lever in PARK or NEUTRAL. This takes a load off the engine and causes an increase in idling speed, which gives unburned fuel a greater chance to enter the cylinders.

driver's-seat repairs

One way to avoid engine dieseling in cars with automatic transmissions is to shut off the ignition with the transmission selector lever in DRIVE. Set the parking brake and keep your foot solidly on the brake pedal as you do.

If a car with a manual transmission has a dieseling problem, stalling the engine will probably stop it. Stop the car. Then, with your foot on the brake and the transmission in gear, release the clutch pedal.

A step taken by manufacturers to prevent dieseling has been the addition of an idle-stop (anti-dieseling) solenoid on some carburetors, especially in cars with automatic transmissions. The solenoid allows the throttle plate in the carburetor to slam closed as soon as you turn off the ignition. This action prevents fuel from entering the cylinders.

When the ignition is turned on, the solenoid drives a plunger against the throttle lever and sets the throttle valve to provide an adequate idling speed. When the ignition is turned off, the solenoid is de-energized and the plunger retracts at once. This causes the throttle valve to spring closed.

set idle speed

The engine idle speed and ignition timing must be set to manufacturer specifications to minimize the possibility of dieseling. Don't confuse engine idle speed, which is also called curb idle, slow idle and hot idle, with the fast idle speed setting.

The fast idle adjustment is made with the engine cold by adjusting the position of the fast idle screw on the fast idle cam. Engine idle speed, on the other hand, is set with the engine at normal operating temperature.

The engine idle speed specification is printed on the vehicle emissions control information decal in the engine compartment and in the service manual for the car. The old days, when every carburetor was set much the same way and a Saturday mechanic could do the job by ear, are long gone. Now you need manufacturer instructions to make the adjustment, if you can make it at all.

In cars that have computer-controlled fuel delivery systems, the engine idle speed adjustment screw is sealed inside the carburetor. The screw is set at the factory and must stay in this position. It doesn't waver in its setting or wear out, so if dieseling results because of an incorrect engine idle speed, the fault lies with the engine computer control system—not with the adjustment screw.

Adjusting engine idle speed, when it can be done, differs from engine to engine. Some cars with airconditioning, for example, require that the airconditioner be turned on while the adjustment is being made. Other manufacturers want the airconditioner off. Some manufacturers require that the carburetor air cleaner be in place. Others want it off. Some manufacturers want the transmission in DRIVE, while others want it in NEUTRAL or PARK. Some want the headlights on, and some want the headlights off.

In many cars, the engine idle speed has to be set using the so-called propane method. This involves injecting propane from a canister into the carburetor to establish the recommended engine idle setting.

The engine idle speed of many cars with idle-stop solenoids is set by turning an idle speed adjusting screw and then setting the plunger of the solenoid. In cars without idle-stop solenoids, the setting is made with an idle speed adjusting screw alone.

check the timing

The ignition timing of most engines is set with a timing light. In cars with distributors that have breaker points, adjust timing after adjusting points.

The relative position of the timing mark specified by the manufacturer in relation to a pointer or index mark allows you to make the adjustment correctly. Normally, the timing light is attached to No. 1 sparkplug cable with an inductive pickup clamp. The other leads of the light are connected to the car battery.

When timing is set correctly, the pulses of the timing light make the prescribed timing mark and pointer or index mark, which align with one another, appear stationary as the engine runs at an idle speed designated by the manufacturer. If the timing mark and pointer or index mark waver, ignition timing is not correct.

To adjust timing, loosen the distributor hold-down clamp and turn the distributor while observing the timing mark setup under the pulses of the timing light. Turn the distributor one way or the other to get the timing mark and pointer or index mark aligned. Then, tighten the distributor hold-down clamp.

overcoming other causes

Remember: Conditions that allow excessive unburned fuel to enter the cylinders and permit an increase in engine heat will cause dieseling. Both fuel and heat have to be present. If you eliminate one, dieseling will stop.

One possibility is a dirty throttle linkage that sticks and keeps the throttle valve from closing all the way when you shut off the engine.

Another condition is a driver who keeps his foot on the accelerator pedal as he turns off the ignition key.

Still another cause is a manifold heat control valve that is stuck in the closed position, trapping hot exhaust gases in the engine. Check to see that the valve moves freely. With the engine cold, find

THE MANIFOLD heat-control valve can be checked for proper operation easily. Turn the counterweight by hand with the engine cold (top). It should move freely. Heat-control valve lubricant (bottom) can help to free up a stuck valve.

the counterweight under the exhaust manifold and try to move it. If it doesn't move, the valve is stuck. Try freeing it with manifold heat control valve lubricant.

If none of the solutions mentioned so far helps to resolve a dieseling problem, it's possible that the cause lies inside the engine. Carbon deposits may be getting red-hot from engine heat and igniting fuel which is entering the cylinders after the ignition is turned off. This is called surface ignition.

However, there's no need to have the engine torn down to get rid of deposits. Unless the condition is particularly severe, using GM Top Engine Cleaner or an equivalent product will usually dissolve deposits. More than one application may be necessary. Keep in mind that of all the causes of dieseling, carbon is the least likely.

How to troubleshoot a differential

By MORT SCHULTZ

■ QUICK NOW—what does the differential do? Not the "differwhat"—the differential, also known as the rear end or rear axle by those who drive rear-wheel-drive cars.

A front-wheel-drive car also has a differential, but you can't legitimately call it a rear end or rear axle since it isn't in the rear. It's up front along with the engine and transmission, and all three are coupled together in an integral unit called the transaxle.

However, most cars on the road are still rear-wheel-drive vehicles, so let's ask the question again: What does the differential do?

If you answer, "It transmits power to a car's wheels by increasing torque from the power train," you're only scratching the surface. This is the least important role performed by the differential.

In fact, if cars traveled only in a straight line,

SEE ALSO
Carburetors, auto . . . Dieseling, auto . . .
Distributors, auto . . . Engines, auto . . .
Lubrication, auto . . . Misfiring, auto . . .
Power-train noise, auto . . .
Steering and suspension, auto . . .
Transmissions, auto

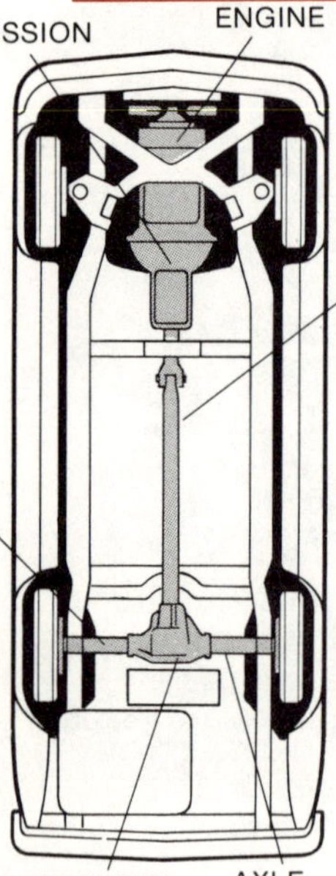

DIFFERENTIAL allows axle shafts to rotate at different speeds in a turn, preventing excessive tire wear. Layout of conventional front-engine/rear-drive car is shown at left.

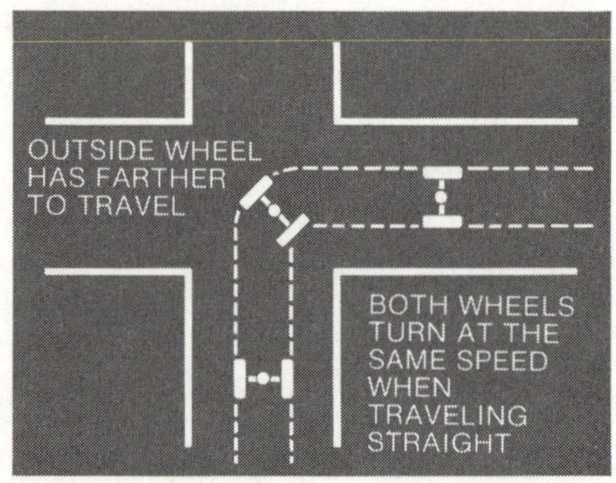

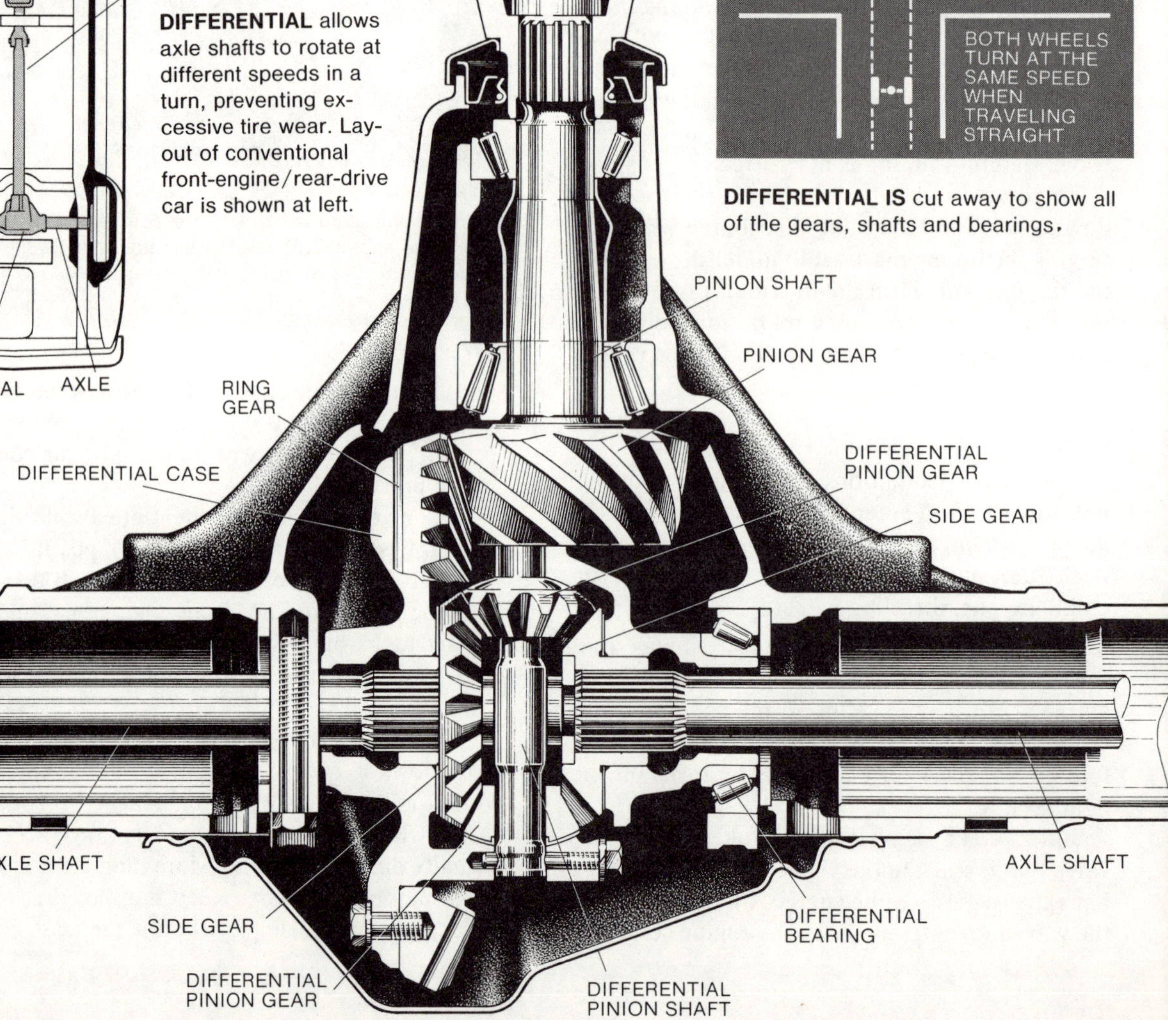

DIFFERENTIAL IS cut away to show all of the gears, shafts and bearings.

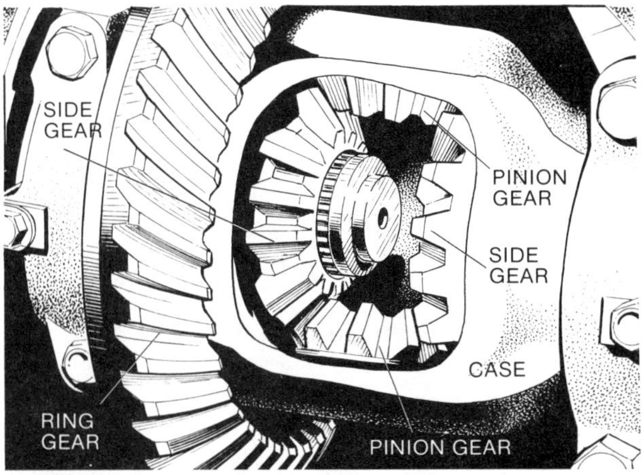

CONVENTIONAL differential, illustrated here, shows meshing of various gears as explained in the text.

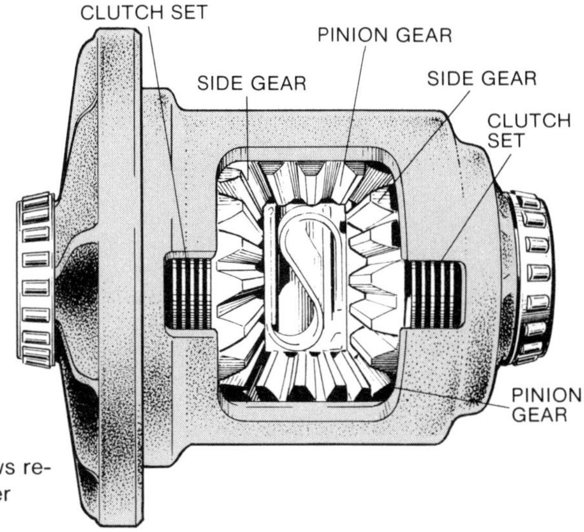

LIMITED-SLIP differential in this illustration shows relationship of the two clutch sets to all of the other components.

differentials wouldn't be needed. Power from the engine and transmission could be applied directly to the wheels through a geared driveshaft.

why it's needed

But cars turn, making it necessary for an outside wheel to travel farther than an inside wheel. If there were no differential, the outside wheel would skid in an effort to keep up with the inside wheel. The car would be hard to control, and you'd be buying a lot of new tires.

So you can bless the differential. It allows wheels to rotate at different speeds during a turn, permitting the outside wheel to catch up with the inside wheel.

In most cars, the rear end is connected to the transmission by a long shaft that revolves. The system consisting of this driveshaft and the differential and transmission is commonly referred to as the final drive.

In other cars, the rear end is connected directly to the engine. There is no driveshaft. This is true of cars having engines in the rear. It is also true, as mentioned before, of cars having front-wheel-drive, but in this case the rear end isn't a rear end, but a differential.

Nuts. Forget semantics. No matter where that differential is located and no matter how it's connected to the transmission, it has the purpose mentioned here. Mechanically, though, it accomplishes these goals in a different way. This article deals with the way it does this in standard vehicles.

conventional or limited-slip

Two kinds of differentials are made for rear-wheel-drive standard passenger cars: conventional and limited-slip. Limited-slip differentials are not used in front-wheel-drive cars and those having engines in the rear.

In a conventional differential, a pinion gear on the end of the pinion shaft (which is the output end of the driveshaft) meshes and turns with a large ring gear that is bolted to the differential case. A pinion is a gear with a small number of teeth that is designed to mesh with a larger gear or wheel.

how it works

The differential case rotates on the axle shafts by means of a bearing between the case and a shaft.

Two side gears, each connected to the differential case and attached to its individual axle shaft, exert power laterally through the axle shafts to the wheels. Other key parts of the differential are the two differential pinion gears. These are held by a differential pinion shaft in the differential case so they mesh with the two side gears.

When the car is on a straight run, the pinion gear turns the ring gear, which causes the differential case and all parts to turn as a unit without any relative motion.

The two differential pinion gears don't rotate on the differential pinion shaft, but they do exert equal pressure on the two side gears, so the side gears turn at the same speed as the ring gear. This allows both axle shafts, and therefore both

TEST MOST limited-slip differentials by trying to rotate wheels (manual transmission in first gear, automatic in park). If unit is okay, it should be very difficult or impossible to budge wheels.

wheels, to turn at the same speed.

When the car rounds a curve, the balance is disrupted. The inner wheel slows down, and the side gear to the inner axle shaft also slows down. The differential pinion gears start rotating on the differential pinion shaft because of this disruption in equilibrium, which allows more speed to be applied to the outside gear and, hence, to the outside axle shaft and wheel.

If the differential case speed represents 100 percent and the inner wheel slows to 90 percent of this speed, the outer wheel would respond by speeding at 110 percent.

A limited-slip differential differs from a conventional differential because of the addition of two sets of clutches, each serving one axle shaft. The purpose of the clutches is to lock the axle shafts to the differential case when either wheel hits ice or mud, which would cause the wheel to lose traction.

Locked in, the "tractionless" wheel can't spin since it cannot turn faster than the other wheel.

Clutches in some limited-slip differentials, such as Ford's Traction-Lok, are not applied at all times, but lock up only when engine torque is applied. This keeps clutch plates from wearing on every turn, which extends their usefulness.

The operation of these torque units is sometimes misunderstood because on surfaces where unequal traction exists, the differential may allow a wheel to spin unless engine torque is applied. An effective way of avoiding this is to engage the parking brake lever two or three notches and accelerate, allowing the differential to lock up. If your car is equipped with a parking brake foot pedal, hold it down using light foot pressure and then accelerate.

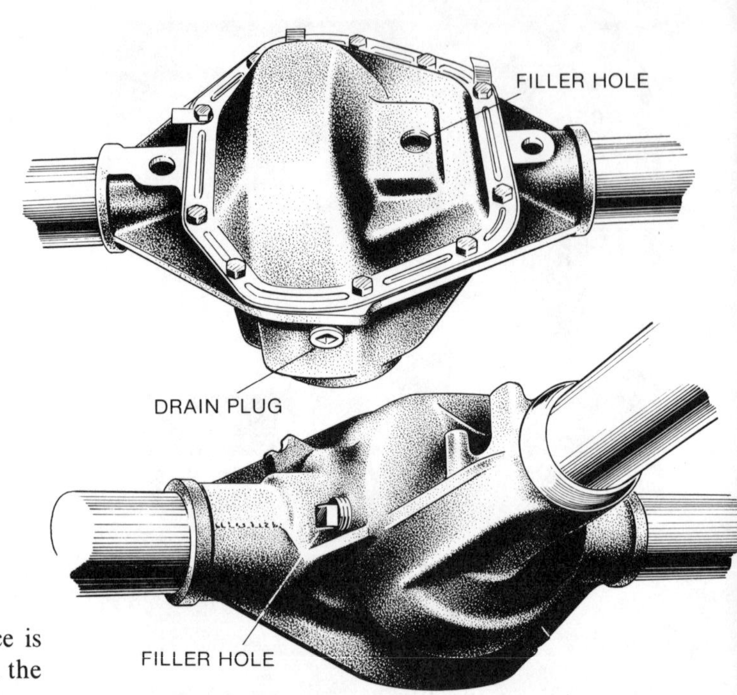

BOTH FILLER HOLES and drain plugs are used on some differentials, as shown at top. Other differentials have only a filler hole, as shown above. When the differential has only a single filler hole, fill and drain it with a special suction tool.

To test the performance of a limited-slip differential not possessing the torque feature, next time the car is on a lift, place an automatic transmission in Park or a manual transmission in low gear. Grip the tire and try turning the wheel.

The differential is in good condition if it is very difficult, if not impossible, to turn the wheels. If either wheel turns easily, the limited-slip unit is not performing properly.

If the car has a limited-slip differential which locks under load (torque) only, a road test is necessary to judge performance. Make the test on a dry pavement, preferably asphalt. Accelerate from a dead stop at full throttle.

Go about 50 or 100 feet and stop the car. Check the pavement for signs of breakaway from both rear tires. If both tires leave marks, the axle is performing properly.

When you buy a new car, a limited-slip differential is normally an option. It's of greatest value if you do much of your driving in mud and/or snow—also on ice.

Whichever differential you have in your car, you can feel pretty good about it. There aren't many assemblies in your vehicle that need less maintenance. All that's involved for most is checking lubricant level whenever the chassis is lubricated.

To check level, remove the differential housing filler-hole plug and insert a clean finger in the filler hole to feel for the lubricant. If you feel the lube, reinsert and tighten the filler-hole plug. If lubricant is needed, add it using an inexpensive syringe.

Important: When checking lube level, make sure the car is level. In many cars, the filler-hole plug can be loosened and tightened with an ordinary open-end wrench. Other differentials are equipped with a recessed plug, requiring a special hex-type wrench to fit the recess.

If from one time to the next, the lube level drops appreciably, watch out. Low lubricant in a differential just doesn't happen. There has to be a reason, and that reason is usually a leak.

Look for a loose filler-hole plug, a leak between the housing and housing cover that indicates loose bolts or a ruptured gasket, or a crack in the housing itself. Loss of lube can also occur because of worn axle-shaft oil seals and a worn pinion shaft oil seal.

Most cars go a lifetime without having to have their differential drained. Others aren't so lucky.

If a differential is ever submerged in water and lubricant is even suspected of being contaminated, drain lubricant at once to prevent differential failure. Also, manufacturers generally recommend that differentials of cars used for towing trailers should have the lubricant drained periodically. Check maintenance instructions in your owner's or service manual.

There are two ways to drain a differential. Some units have drain holes as well as filler holes. Drive the car to get it warmed up. Then, remove the drain-hole plug and let lube pour out.

If your differential has a filler hole only, draining and filling is done with a special suction pump. Clean dirt from around the plug and remove it from the differential case. Draw out old lubricant through the filler plug hole by pulling it into the suction gun. After old lube has been removed, add fresh fluid through the filler plug hole by shooting it into the unit with the suction gun.

The kind of lube you use is important, especially if you have a limited-slip differential. Check manufacturer's recommendations.

If instructions don't call for a multiviscosity lube, keep in mind that viscosity-grade SAE 90 differential lube is generally used where the anticipated temperature will go no lower than minus 10° F. If the anticipated temperature is expected to go as low as minus 30° F., an SAE 80-grade lube will probably be prescribed.

troubleshooting

If something happens to the differential in your car, chances are you're not going to be able to repair it yourself due to lack of experience, special equipment and facilities. But that doesn't mean you shouldn't familiarize yourself with the way differentials signify they're in trouble. Noise is the key.

Any time two gears mesh, there will be a certain amount of sound as the teeth come in contact. This should be a low-decibel sound no louder than normal driving noises from the engine, transmission and tires.

It's only when noise becomes loud that you should begin to worry. If caught early enough, differential noise often can be reduced by readjusting gears to mesh properly.

try a road test

It is sometimes difficult to distinguish differential noise from other noises. The best way is with a road test, as follows:

1. Drive the car an appreciable distance. Noise coming from the differential is loudest when lube is warm.
2. Shut off all accessories.
3. Try to isolate the noise to a particular area. Differential noise is different than noises that come from engine and transmission. Tire noise is a continuous sound that varies with car speed. The sound changes pitch as tires encounter different road surfaces.

In comparison, differential noise is not affected by road surface changes. It tends to fade out below 30 mph. And it often changes pitch between driving and coasting conditions, while tire noise remains the same.

Another way to pinpoint bearing noise is to swerve the car sharply so body weight is shifted to the outside of the turn. Bad bearings will be louder when more pressure is put on them.

It's easy to distinguish automatic transmission noise from differential noise. Run the car under different transmission ranges. If changing the selector position causes the sound to occur at a higher or lower speed, you've isolated the noise to the transmission.

To single out engine or exhaust sounds, run the car and check the road speed at which the sound is most noticeable. Stop the car, put the transmission selector in neutral and again listen for the sound as you rev the engine to the approximate speed where the sound was heard. If you hear it again, the noise is coming either from the engine or exhaust.

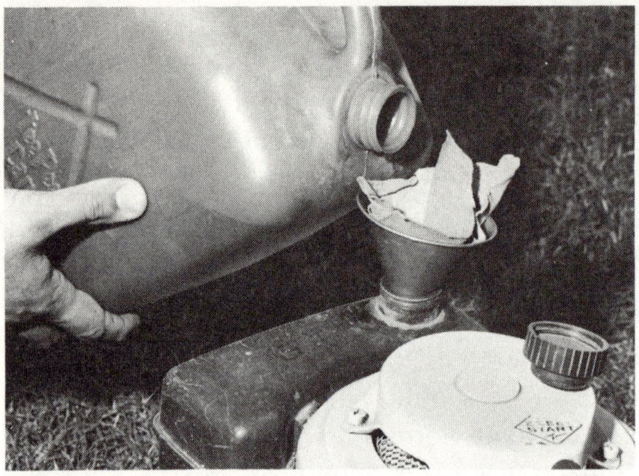

THE CHANCE OF MOWER-ENGINE failure can be lessened by following a procedure used by cautious pilots and experienced mechanics. To keep tiny bits of matter from entering small passages in the carburetor, strain gasoline through a piece of chamois. A small patch in the funnel does the trick.—*Marshall Lincoln, Wickenburg, AZ.*

BUMPERS FOR DOORS and other moving items sometimes are made from short sections of rubber garden hose, but mounting them can be a problem. One solution is to use a plastic toothpaste-tube cap that fits tightly inside the hose. The cap is drilled in the center for a screw.—*Walter E. Burton, Akron, OH.*

PREVENT BALL-SHAPED OBJECTS from rolling about while being glued together in series or patterns with a block of rigid plastic foam. To glue the marbles shown, a guideline was drawn on the foam surface, and then, after epoxy glue was added to each marble, it was pressed into the foam and glued to the preceding marble.—*Burt Webb, Skokie, IL.*

WHEN USING a fast-cutting power sander to smooth a small, flat surface such as the lid of a trinket box, you can avoid accidental overcutting at the edges by surrounding the work with wood. The protective wood border can be made by clamping strips flush with the top surface. —*B. W. Ervin, Kent, OH.*

Build a mini-maxi gateleg table

Folded, this dining table takes only nine inches of space. But it can seat three . . . six or seven . . . or even twelve. So it's perfect backup for parties and big holiday get-togethers. Made with quality plywood, it's attractive yet inexpensive.

By ROSARIO CAPOTOSTO

■ YOU CAN'T BEAT this table for versatility—use it in living or family room or out on the patio when entertaining a group. It'll comfortably seat up to 12 people—then fold away into 9 inches of space after the party.

SEE ALSO
Bridge tables . . . Butler's tables . . . Coffee tables . . . Game tables . . . Hutch tables . . . Legs, furniture . . . Occasional tables . . . Party tables . . . Plywood . . . Snack tables . . . Trays, folding

GATELEG CONCEPT is centuries old—and still a good way to gain extra seating in a hurry when entertaining. This modern unit is easy to build.

V-GROOVES are made on panel edges with shaper. Feed in work from both ends to prevent splintering.

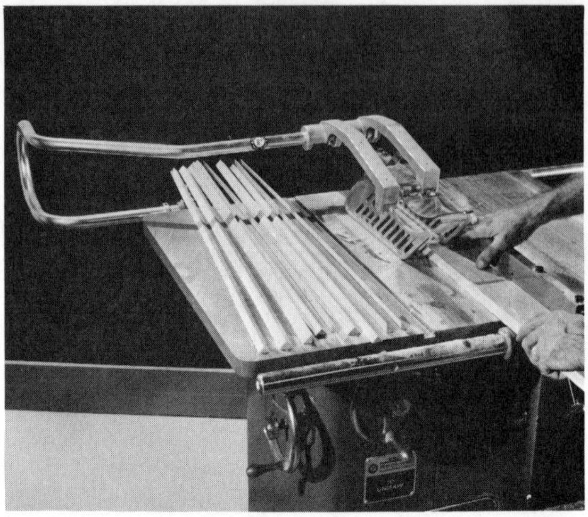

ANGLED INSERT STRIPS are ripped from solid lumber using hollow-ground planer blade, slow feed rate.

EXTREME CARE should be taken when you glue up gatelegs and framing to be sure assembly is square.

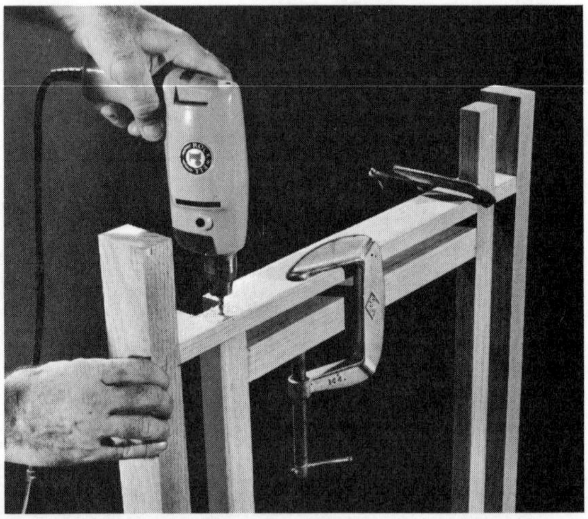

WHEN YOU BORE HOLES for pivot pins, clamp the gatelegs firmly to avoid any chance of movement.

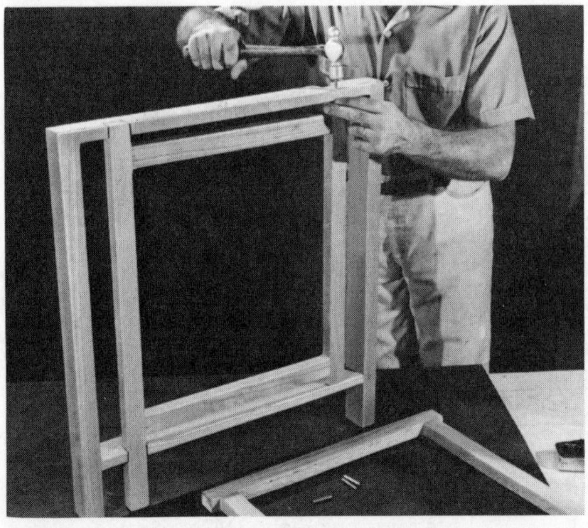

ASSEMBLY is glued and screwed to divider strip. Slight edge-rabbet allows flush seating against hinge.

PIANO HINGE is positioned and screwholes marked so you can drill pivot holes before fastening hinges.

STRIPS are glued to two sides, then passed through shaper to obtain mitered corner on the strip ends.

COMPLETED GATELEG ASSEMBLY, ready to be installed, consists of pair of gatelegs, one leg frame.

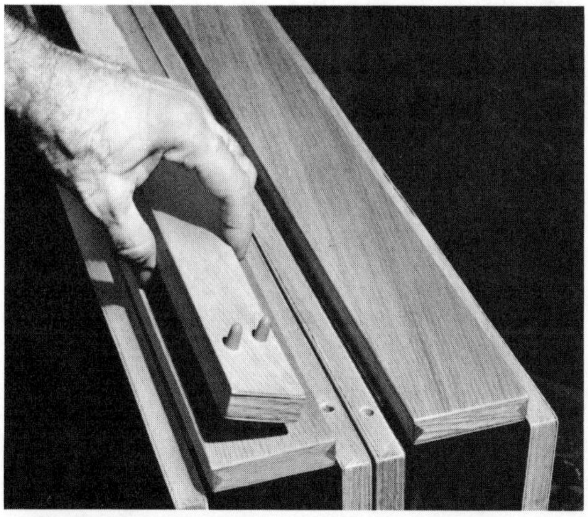

CENTER INSERT STRIP has two projecting pins to hold midsection in place when table is not expanded.

The table shown is of white oak veneer cabinet-grade plywood. This is a high-quality wood and, when finished properly, it will give your table the look of expensive furniture. If you are building yours for family room or patio use where it might be subject to greater abuse, you might consider using fir plywood (A-D) and covering the table entirely with a plastic laminate such as Melamite.

Since the four main tops are cut from two 4x8-ft. panels, lay out the sections so the grain runs parallel to the 36-in. dimension. This will avoid any chance of mismatched grain patterns butting end to end.

Connect each pair of tops to division strips with piano hinges. Recesses for the hinges need not be made on the bottom side of the panels. Instead, do the routing on the top of each frame cross member to take up the thickness of the hinge. Notice that the continuous hinges are spaced; this is essential to provide clearance for the swinging leg units.

precision is a "must"

Construct the gate legs accurately. *If they are out of square full-face or edgewise, they won't operate properly.* If you don't own a drill press, disregard the blind dowel joints indicated in the drawings: instead, clamp the pieces together and bore dowel holes through from the outside with a portable drill. Dowel ends can be left exposed or driven in to allow room for wood plugs cut from the same lumber. Check for squareness after clamping and before the glue sets.

When the outer leg framing is complete, you can bore holes for the pivots. Securely clamp a leg section to the frame and bore ¼ x 1½-in. holes into both ends. Be sure to mark each subassembly so they don't get mixed up. Don't drive in the pins until all parts are sanded and finish-coated.

The pivots are cut from ¼-in. steel rod and one end is ground slightly rounded to facilitate driving. Fit should be snug so they'll stay in place, yet offer a slight resistance so the gatelegs don't swing loosely. Six No. 10 x 1¼-in. wood screws, and glue, secure the leg assembly to the dividing strip. When both sections are completed, butt them together and install a piano hinge to connect the inside table leaves.

Cut an insert strip to snug-fit the void. This filler strip fills the gap while a pair of projecting pins near each end serve to "lock" the two main sections together. The pins can be steel rod or slightly tapered dowels set firmly into the strip.

To expand the table, you simply remove the center strip and extend the desired leaves.

For a finish that brings out all the natural beauty of oak, mix together some raw sienna oil color and natural wood filler. Work the filler well into the open grain, then wipe clean with burlap. Allow to dry for 24 hours; then apply several coats of a clear, semigloss wood finish such as Satinlac, or, if you prefer varnish, McCloskey Heirloom.

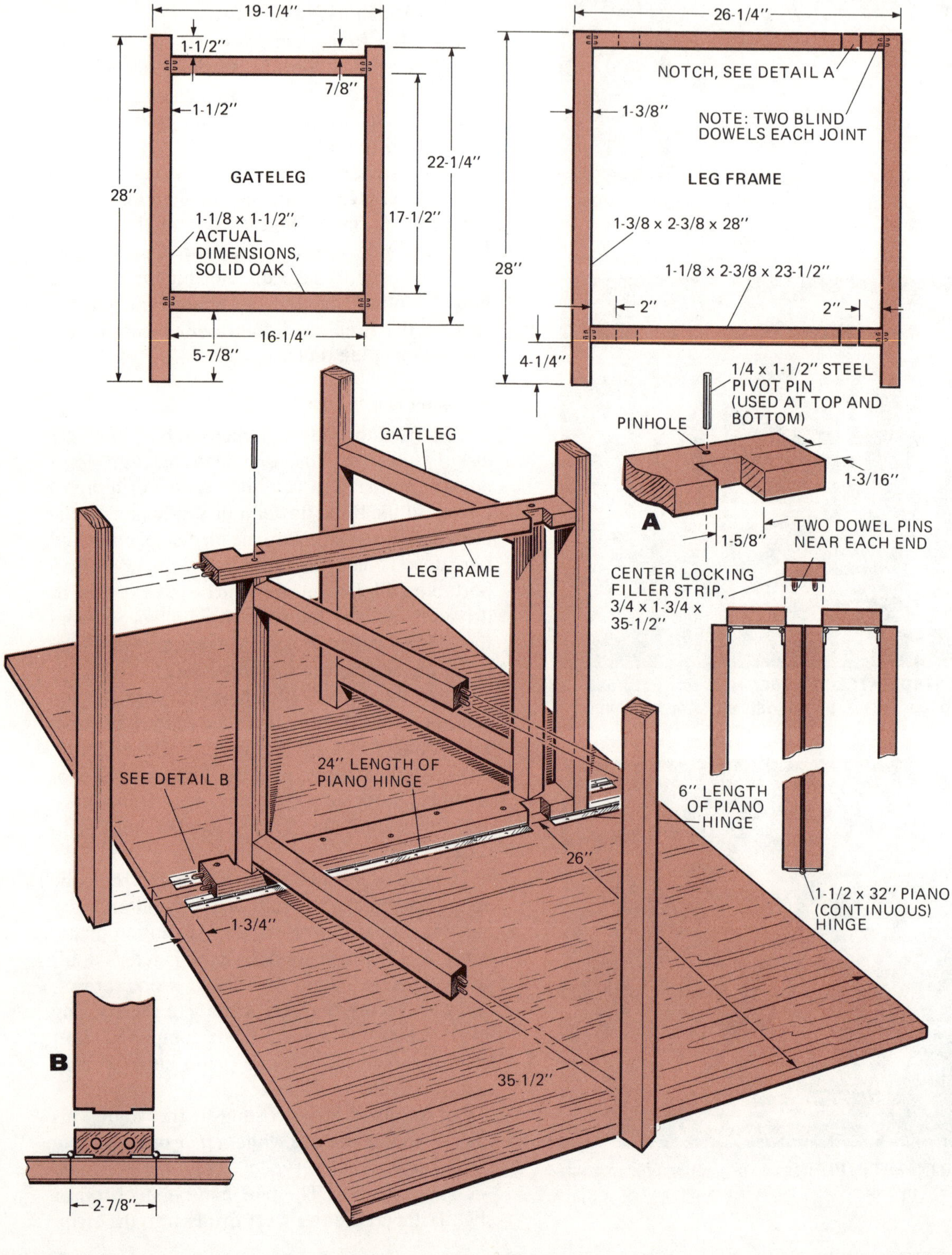

HEAVY OAK TABLE can be used in dining room or kitchen to seat four comfortably, as in large photo. View from below shows details for pedestal and extension slides. Add one leaf for six diners and both leaves for eight.

Build a classic oaken table

By C.E. BANISTER

■ THERE'S SOMETHING REASSURING about eating at a sturdy oak table that you know will be around awhile. Our prototype, crafted from substantial red oak, should last a few lifetimes. The design is at home with almost any decor—traditional or contemporary—and it's functional. It can gracefully accommodate a bois-

SEE ALSO
Bridge tables . . . Butcher block furniture . . . Hutch tables . . . Joinery . . .

SPLINES REINFORCE pedestal's cooper joinery and insure a sturdy table support.

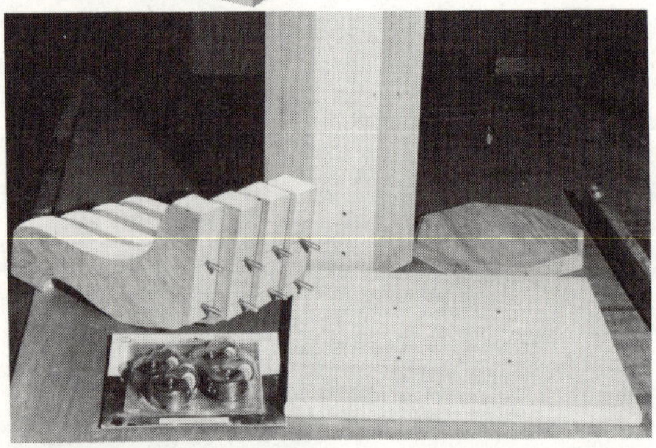

HANGER BOLTS turned into feet will be fastened to pedestal with nuts, washers. Stem-type casters are used.

GLUE UP the stock for the tabletop using dowels. Be sure to alternate grain to minimize warp.

USE JIG that is detailed in plans shown on page 991 to cut a perfect circle with the table saw.

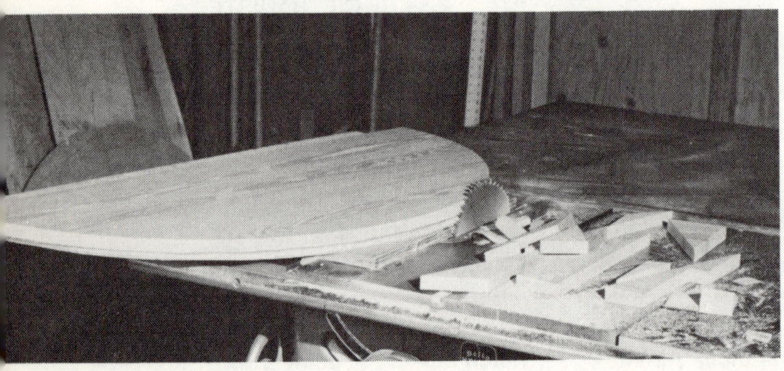

MATERIALS LIST—OAK TABLE

Key	Pcs.	Size and description
A	8	13/16 x 3⅞ x 20″ red oak
B	1	13/16 x 11 x 11″ red oak
C	2	13/16 x 11½ x 42″ red oak
D	6	13/16 x 7 x 42″ (max.) red oak
E	4	13/16 x 2 x 11½″ red oak
F	8	2 x 2¼ x 16⅝″ red oak
G	4	2 x 9 x 14″ (may be glued-up) red oak
H	1	¾ x 16 x 18″ plywood
I	6	½ x 2 x 2½″ red oak
J	8	⅛ x 1 x 20″ hardwood plywood
K	24	⅜″-dia. x 2″ birch dowels
L	1	28″ long (closed) extension slide set*
M	6	16-ga. x ¾ x 2¼″ steel
N	16	birch table pins*
O	1	table lock*
P	4	2″-dia. casters
Q	8	5/16″-dia. x 3″ hanger bolt*, nut, washer nut
R	4	5/16″-dia. x 3″ carriage bolt, washer
S	4	No. 12 x 2″ fh screws
T	24	No. 12 x 2½″ fh screws
U	8	No. 12 x 2½″ fh screws

MATERIALS LIST—CIRCLE-CUTTING JIG

Key	Pcs.	Size and description
V	14	No. 8 x ½″ fh screws
W	2	⅛ x ¾ x 24″ tempered hardboard
X	1	½ x 12″ chest slide support, or cut 16-gauge steel bar to suit
Y	1	¼″ length cut from nail
Z	1	3/16 x ⅝″ stovebolt and teenut
AA	1	¾ x 20 x 24″ plywood
BB	1	½ x ¾ x 22″ hardwood miter bar
CC	1	¼ x 24 x 42″ plywood
DD	1	¾ x 3 x 42″ plywood
EE	1	2 x 2 x 40″ (trim to fit)
FF	12	No. 6 x 1″ fh screws

Misc.: White glue, ¾″ brads to suit

*These items can be ordered from Craftsman Wood Service Co., 2727 South Mary St., Chicago, Ill. 60608.

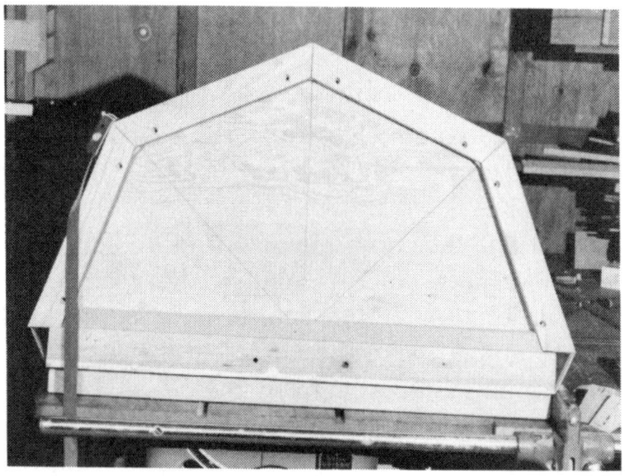

APRON SEGMENTS are splined and glued together. Then they are nailed to jig surface, CC.

SLIDE SUPPORT (H) is fastened securely to the middle member with 3-in. carriage bolts.

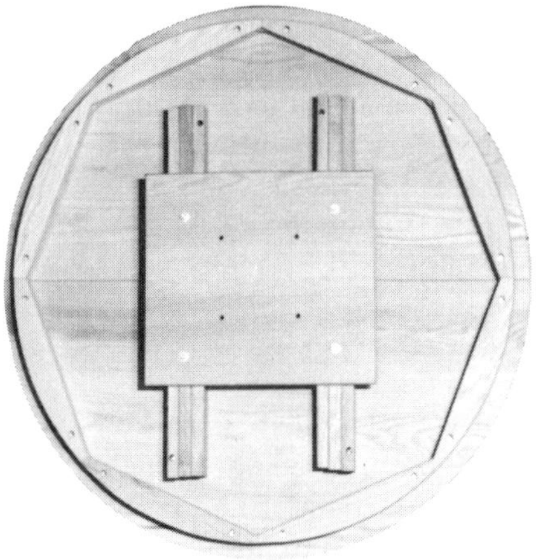

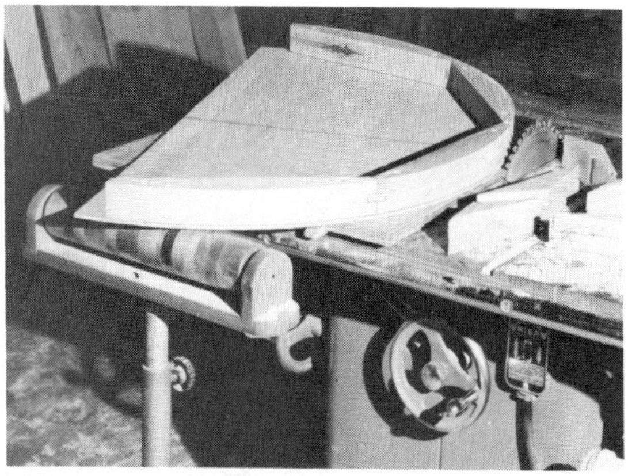

WITH APRON assembly on the sliding jig base, straight cuts on the table saw form a half circle.

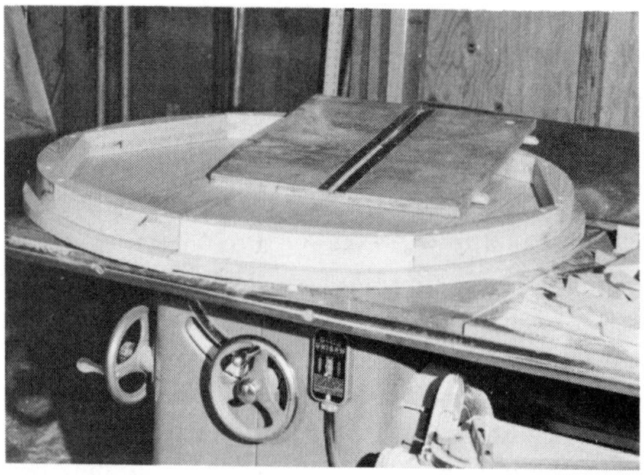

SLIDING JIG base can be used on other projects since it will cut many different sizes.

SPECIALTY HARDWARE, such as extension slides and table lock mechanism, is available by mail.

PINS IN EDGE of the extension leaf make it impossible to install leaf incorrectly. It's a one-person job.

terous holiday party or a quiet candlelit tête-a-tête, along with every meal in between.

Taken one step at a time, the table construction is easier than you would think. We give you all the details for making a circle-cutting jig, which not only simplifies cutting the tabletop and round apron in this project, but will come in handy for circle-cutting tasks in the future.

After gathering all materials (see source for specialty hardware in the materials list on page 988), lay out and cut eight pedestal segments (A) with a table saw. Spline grooves can be cut with a saw blade having a ⅛-in. set. Use ⅛-in. hardwood plywood to make strong splines (J). Run through the assembly dry before gluing and clamping the joints. Belt clamps are ideal, but if you have none, loop ropes around the pedestal, then twist and secure them to serve as clamps.

making the feet

Next, make a pattern for the table feet (G), using the grid in the plans. Trace the shape onto the glued-up oak stock and make the cuts with a bandsaw or heavy-duty sabre saw. Bore holes in the feet as directed by the caster manufacturer. Also bore corresponding pairs of holes in the feet tops and pedestal to accommodate the hanger bolts, which serve to join the two together.

Install the feet and complete the oak table support by making the octagonal base cap (B) and the top cap or slide support (E). Shape the detail around the base cap sides with a ⅜-in. rounding-over bit and use screws to fasten it to the column base. Use hanger bolts to fasten the slide support to the column top.

Carriage bolts can be used to attach the extension slides (L) to the slide support (H). Be sure to counterbore, so that bolt heads don't interfere with spreading and closing tabletop halves.

making tabletop sections

All that remains is to make the tabletop sections and apron. Edge-join the boards (D) for the table halves.

Alternate the end-grain directions to help minimize warping, and strengthen the edge joints with dowels. After the boards have been glued and clamped, make the circle-cutting jig shown in the plans. For a simpler, nonadjustable version, use a nail as a fixed pivot pin. Locate the nail/pivot on the sliding-jig base 21 in. from the table-saw blade for cutting the semicircular aprons.

Now, secure the workpiece to the jig, using screws or nails driven up through part CC. (Do not install fasteners in line of cut.) Position the sliding jig base in the miter groove and align pivot pin on sliding base with hole in jig part CC. Adjust the blade height to ⅛ in. above the workpiece top surface and turn on the saw. Make straight cuts, removing a small amount of waste on each pass. Rotate the workpiece before—not during—each pass. Eventually you get a perfect half circle. Clean up rough spots with a belt sander.

building apron assemblies

To make apron assemblies for the half-circle tops, assemble sections (F) on jig part CC to facilitate gluing and clamping. Once again, you can use band clamps, or rope twisted and secured to provide pressure. Use of spreader (EE), along with jig stop (DD), keeps assembly from collapsing while you set clamps or rope.

After the apron sections are glued, fasten them to the jig with nails from the underside of part CC. Cut to round using same procedure explained above.

leaves with aprons, pins

Before the final assembly, make the table leaves with aprons to match those on the half-circle tabletops. Lay out and bore holes for ⅜-in.-dia. table pins and corresponding holes for the pins. Then install the tabletop lock and metal clips that keep the tops flush.

Apply stain of your choice following instructions on the can. Let dry 24 hours and apply paste wood filler (to fill the open pores). If necessary, tint filler with the stain. Let filler dry until shine disappears; then rub off with a coarse cloth (burlap). When dry, seal with a coat of thinned shellac and finish with a semigloss varnish.

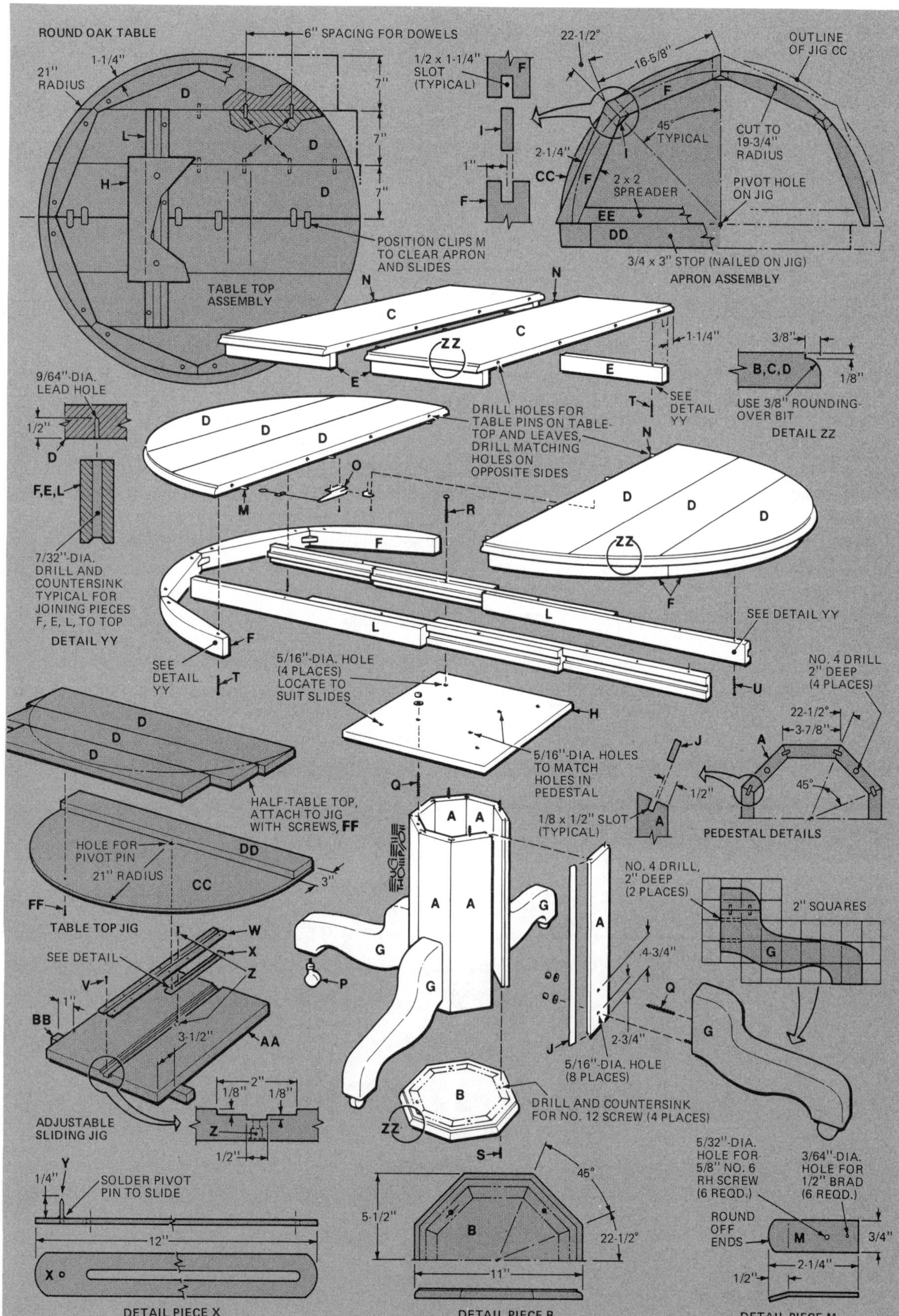
ROUND OAK TABLE
21" RADIUS
1-1/4"
6" SPACING FOR DOWELS
7"
7"
7"
TABLE TOP ASSEMBLY
POSITION CLIPS M TO CLEAR APRON AND SLIDES
1/2 x 1-1/4" SLOT (TYPICAL)
1"
22-1/2°
16-5/8"
OUTLINE OF JIG CC
45° TYPICAL
2-1/4"
CUT TO 19-3/4" RADIUS
2 x 2 SPREADER
PIVOT HOLE ON JIG
3/4 x 3" STOP (NAILED ON JIG)
APRON ASSEMBLY
1-1/4"
3/8"
1/8"
USE 3/8" ROUNDING-OVER BIT
DETAIL ZZ
SEE DETAIL YY
9/64"-DIA. LEAD HOLE
1/2"
DRILL HOLES FOR TABLE PINS ON TABLE-TOP AND LEAVES, DRILL MATCHING HOLES ON OPPOSITE SIDES
7/32"-DIA. DRILL AND COUNTERSINK TYPICAL FOR JOINING PIECES F, E, L, TO TOP
DETAIL YY
SEE DETAIL YY
5/16"-DIA. HOLE (4 PLACES) LOCATE TO SUIT SLIDES
NO. 4 DRILL 2" DEEP (4 PLACES)
22-1/2°
3-7/8"
45°
5/16"-DIA. HOLES TO MATCH HOLES IN PEDESTAL
HALF-TABLE TOP, ATTACH TO JIG WITH SCREWS, FF
1/2"
1/8 x 1/2" SLOT (TYPICAL)
PEDESTAL DETAILS
HOLE FOR PIVOT PIN
21" RADIUS
3"
TABLE TOP JIG
NO. 4 DRILL, 2" DEEP (2 PLACES)
2" SQUARES
SEE DETAIL
4-3/4"
2-3/4"
5/16"-DIA. HOLE (8 PLACES)
DRILL AND COUNTERSINK FOR NO. 12 SCREW (4 PLACES)
3-1/2"
2"
1/8"
1/8"
1/2"
ADJUSTABLE SLIDING JIG
5/32"-DIA. HOLE FOR 5/8" NO. 6 RH SCREW (6 REQD.)
3/64"-DIA. HOLE FOR 1/2" BRAD (6 REQD.)
1/4"
SOLDER PIVOT PIN TO SLIDE
12"
45°
5-1/2"
22-1/2°
11"
ROUND OFF ENDS
3/4"
2-1/4"
1/2"
DETAIL PIECE X
DETAIL PIECE B
DETAIL PIECE M

A graceful dining set

With its colorful cushions and natural mellow finish, this table-and-chair set will add an exciting fresh look to a limited dining area. It's a project that is not as difficult to build as it looks

By ROSARIO CAPOTOSTO

■ THIS CHARMING dining set can be built for approximately $75—about one-fifth the cost of a retail-store version of comparable quality.

Southern (soft) maple is used for all but the tabletop, which is made of ¾-in. birch-veneer, lumber-core plywood and edged with solid maple to achieve a thick look. The coloring and grain patterns of these woods are look-alikes so they can be readily intermixed. I used birch veneer for the top because you'll find that maple-veneer plywood is not commonly available at most lumber-supply houses.

If you haven't worked with southern maple, you're in for a treat. It tools nicely, and while it's known as a "soft" wood, it is more than hard enough for furniture-making.

The table, a modernized version of the trestle style, is not difficult to construct. The cross rail (stretcher) utilizes blind mortise-and-tenon joints and the leg members are put together with cross-lap joints held only with glue.

You shouldn't have trouble making the comfortable swivel chairs. I "engineered" their construction so you can build them with minimal fuss and bother. Note how the turning blanks for the pedestals are made up with 2⅜-in. preformed notches, which would be practically impossible to make with any degree of accuracy or safety *after* the pedestals are turned. Also, rather than call for a steam-bent curved chair back, I used a segmented glued block to obtain a strong parallel-grain structure throughout the curve.

SEE ALSO
Bridge tables . . . Butcher block furniture . . . Butler's tables . . . Centerpieces . . . Chests . . . Cupboards, china . . . Dry sinks . . . Etageres . . . Game tables . . . Hutch tables . . . Lowboys

steps for making the table

1. Start with the understructure. Cut the 5/4 (1⅛-in.) stock for uprights and cross members to size and plane them smooth on the jointer before cutting the cross-lap joints. Removal of stock along the edges after the joints have been made would loosen them.

2. The blind mortise-and-tenon joints for the cross-rail stretcher are next. Form tenons in the rail by making a partial saw cut completely around each end, then remove the waste with a dado head. Then bore a series of holes part way

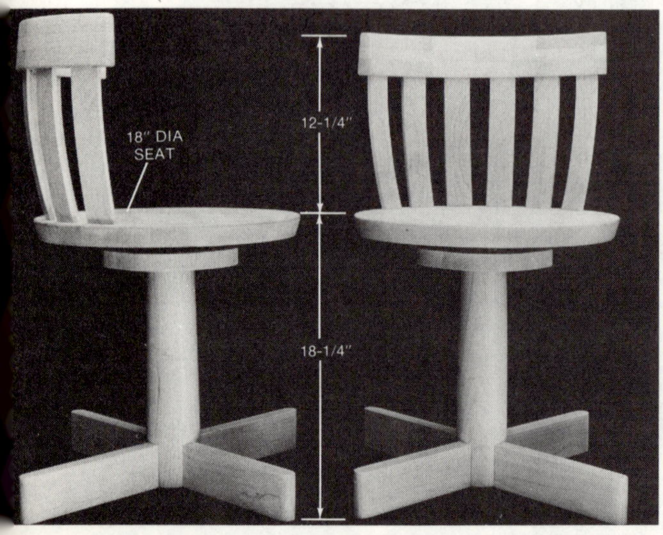

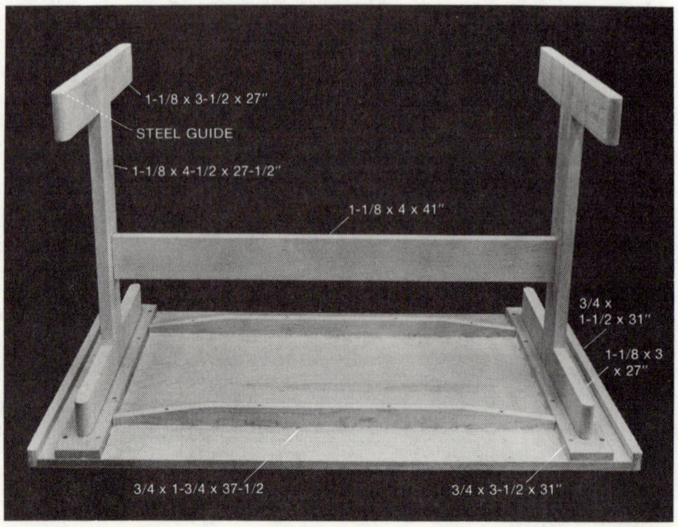

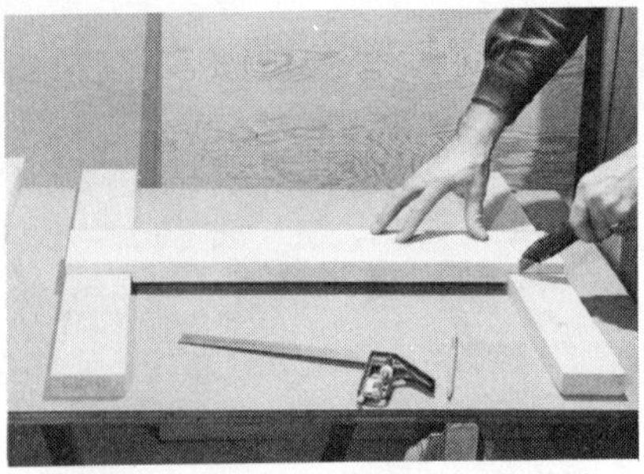

POSITION upright on base, and mark mating half-lap with knife.

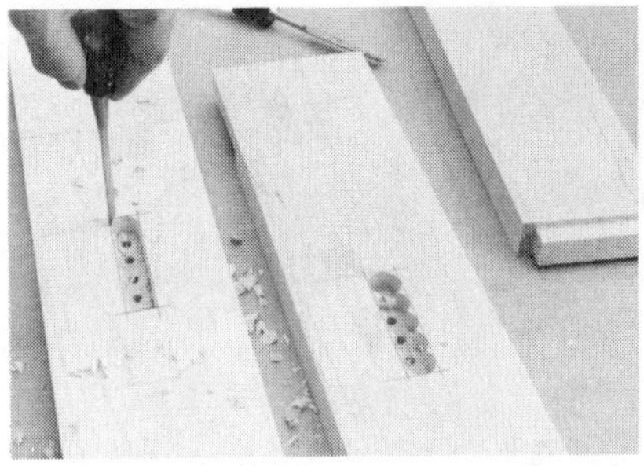

MAKE BLIND cross-rail mortises by boring holes and chiseling out waste.

MAKE REPEATED passes to clear waste after making outside cuts halfway.

MOUNT GLUED-UP pedestal between lathe centers for turning.

APPLY GLUE and tighten lagscrews to secure base to pedestal. Add swivel.

USE HEADLESS brads for slip-proof alignment when clamping chair seats.

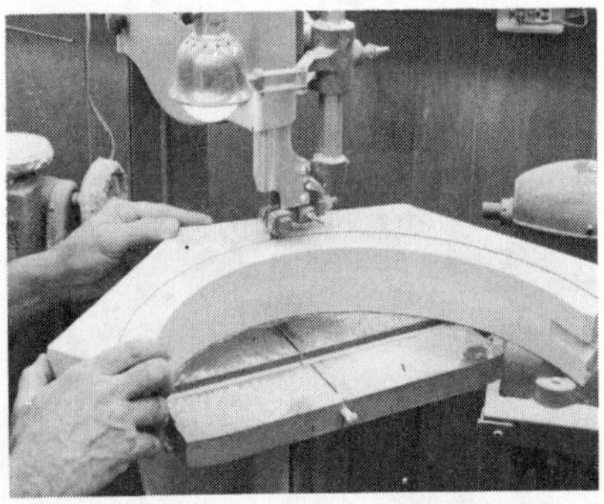

SET BANDSAW table 5°, use sharp blade, saw chair rail slowly.

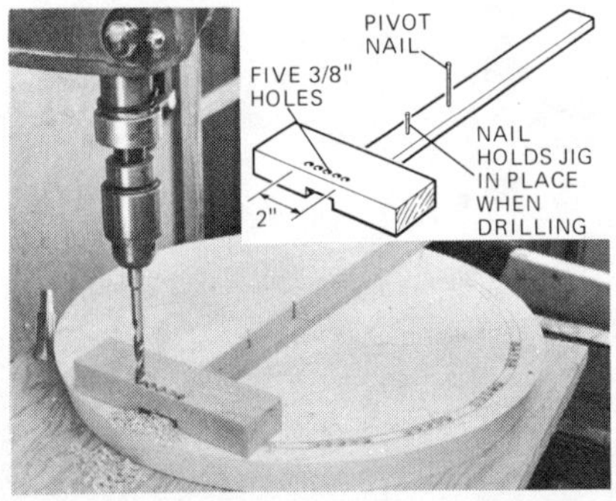

LINE UP slat mortises with pivoting jig and use it to drill series of holes.

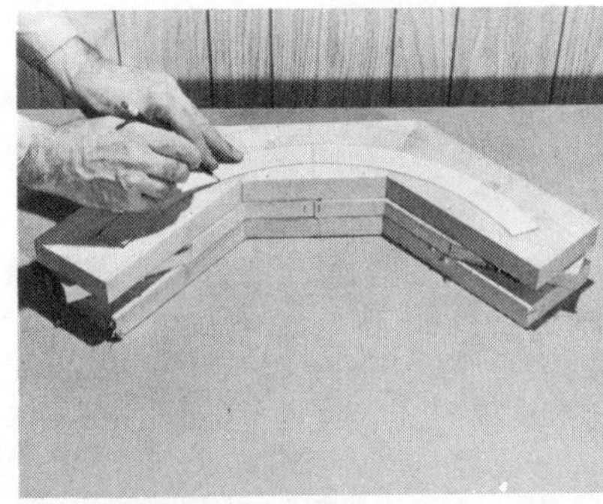

PLACE CARDBOARD template on bottom of back rail; trace for bandsawing.

into the leg members to rough-form the mortise—making sure the drill point does not go through the board—and clear out waste between the holes with a chisel.

3. Finish-sand the parts, then assemble the legs and cross members. When the glue has set, glue and screw the two ¾ x 3½ x 31-in. table-attaching cleats to the tops of both leg sections with 2-in. No. 10 fh screws.

4. Set the tabletop upside down on a pair of horses or other supports and check the surface with a level in both directions. If necessary, shim up the horses to adjust until the top lies perfectly plane. This is important—if the table is glue-assembled while uneven, you may possibly build-in some unwanted twists.

5. Screw one of the assembled legs to the top with 1½-in. No. 10 fh screws in predrilled countersunk holes. Insert the cross rail, secure it with a pair of bar clamps, then screw the other leg assembly to the tabletop. Screw and glue the pair of stiffeners in place.

6. Use concealed nails with heads cut off to help align the mitered edge-facing strips. Install the end strips, glue and clamp. Follow with sides. Round the corners with a block plane, then sand the top.

steps for making chairs

1. Cut a deep notch halfway through each piece of the chair bases to form the cross-lap joints. Round the ends on a stationary disc

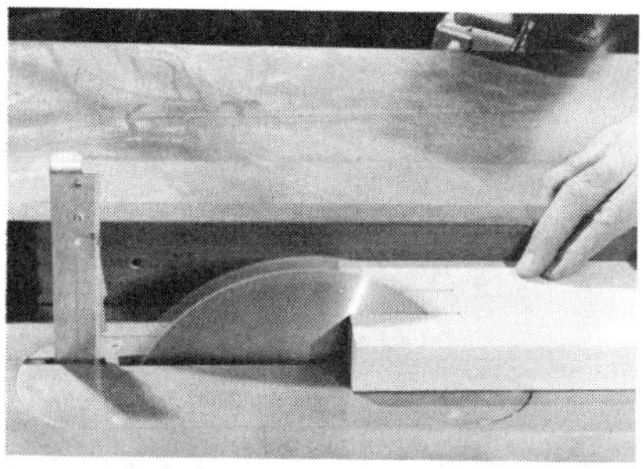

CUT FOUR-WAY pedestal notch before gluing. Set blade high, make two cuts.

JIGSAW WASTE from between saw cuts in two outside members of group.

TEST NOTCHES for fit over base before gluing and clamping pieces.

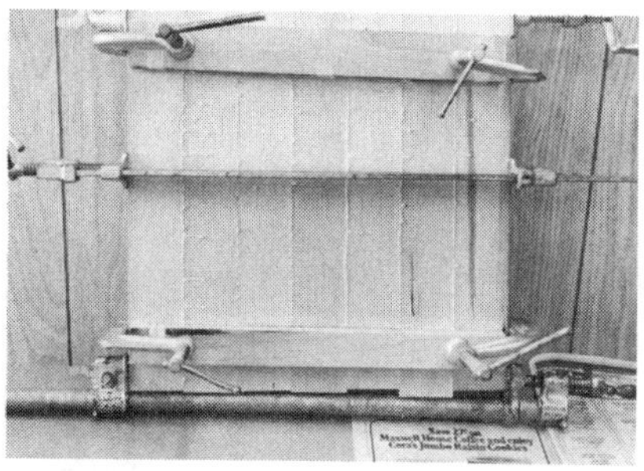

CLAMPED crosspieces keep others flat. Wax paper prevents sticking.

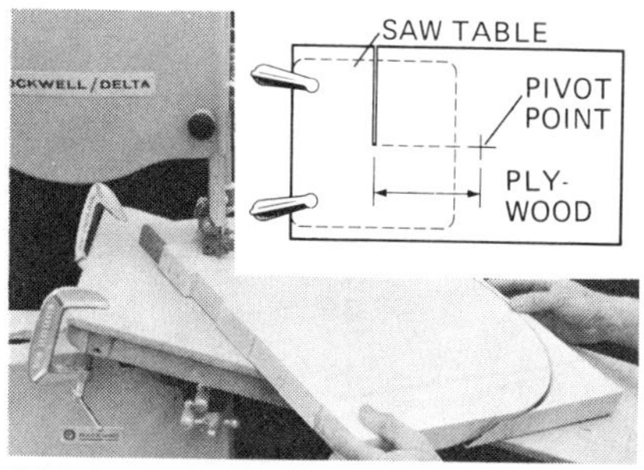

SCREW jig to seat bottom, tilt table 15° to cut perfect 18-in.-diameter.

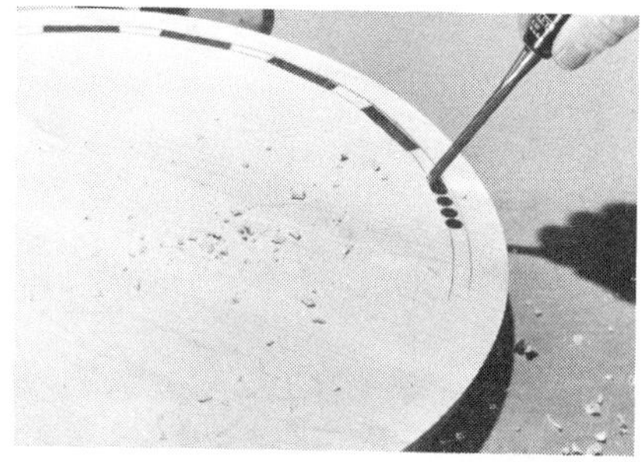

FORM SLAT mortises by squaring up rows of holes in seat bottom with chisel.

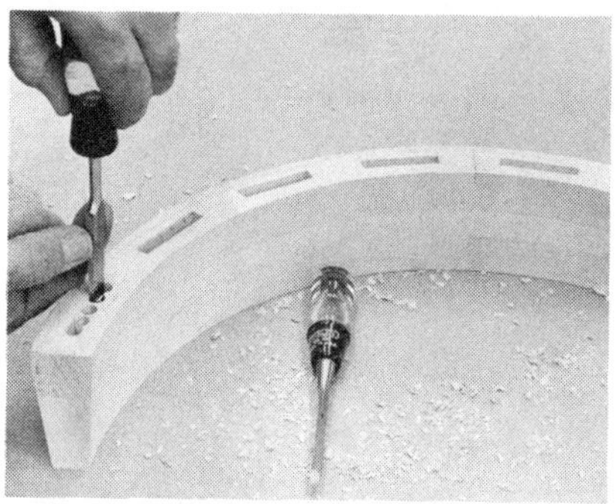

CUT MORTISES in chair-back rail as in seat. Drill holes with brad-point bit.

BANDSAW CURVED slats from solid stock, then drum-sand smooth.

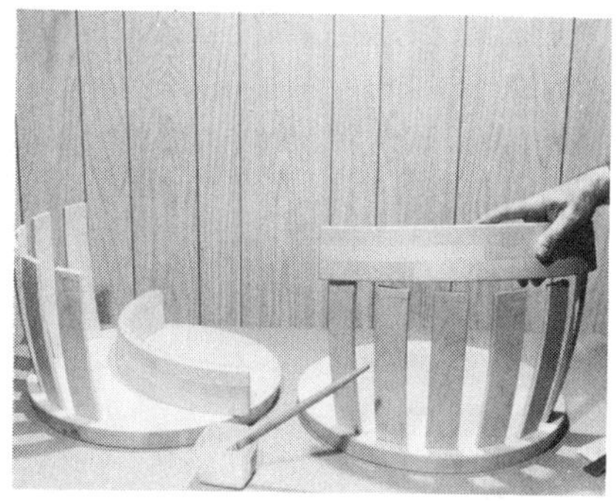

USE TOP RAIL dry (no glue) to hold glued lower ends of slats in alignment.

sander, then glue the members to form the crossed base.

2. Select three lengths of stock to form the turning blanks for each pedestal. Notch the ends of the two outer pieces so they will slide freely over the 1⅛ x 2⅞-in. base section. Insert a few concealed nails without heads for registration, then sandwich the three pieces together. Mark each blank for later match-up with its base. Remove excess glue inside the notches to insure a good fit later.

3. When both blanks have been made up, glue a scrap of hardwood to the notched ends for mounting in the lathe. Bandsaw the four waste corners from the blocks to save a lot of rough lathe work.

4. Use the gouge and skew to turn the slightly tapered cylinder to shape, and use the parting tool at the top to cut the pedestal to proper length. The block at the bottom is cut off by bandsawing at the glue line.

5. The chair seat is next. Select seven lengths of 6/4 (1⅜-in.) stock to make up the seat. Check your rip saw to be sure it is cutting perfectly square. Lay out the pieces so that the annual rings alternately curve up and down. This will counteract any warping tendency. Insert headless brads into predrilled holes so the points protrude about ¼ in. Working on a flat surface, proceed to press the pieces together to form registration brad holes. Separate the pieces, apply glue, then clamp together in this manner: Tape kitchen wax paper

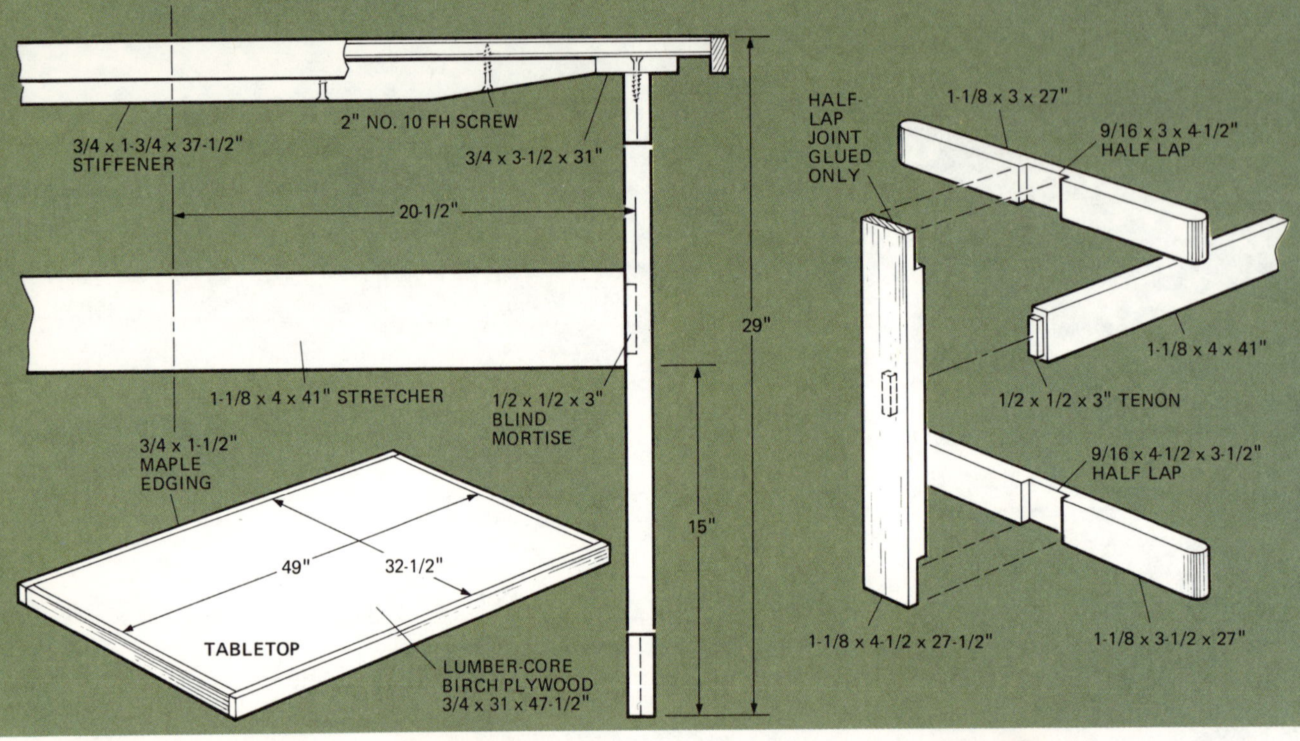
3/4 x 1-3/4 x 37-1/2"
STIFFENER
2" NO. 10 FH SCREW
3/4 x 3-1/2 x 31"
20-1/2"
29"
1-1/8 x 4 x 41" STRETCHER
1/2 x 1/2 x 3"
BLIND
MORTISE
3/4 x 1-1/2"
MAPLE
EDGING
49"
32-1/2"
15"
TABLETOP
LUMBER-CORE
BIRCH PLYWOOD
3/4 x 31 x 47-1/2"
HALF-
LAP
JOINT
GLUED
ONLY
1-1/8 x 3 x 27"
9/16 x 3 x 4-1/2"
HALF LAP
1-1/8 x 4 x 41"
1/2 x 1/2 x 3" TENON
9/16 x 4-1/2 x 3-1/2"
HALF LAP
1-1/8 x 4-1/2 x 27-1/2"
1-1/8 x 3-1/2 x 27"

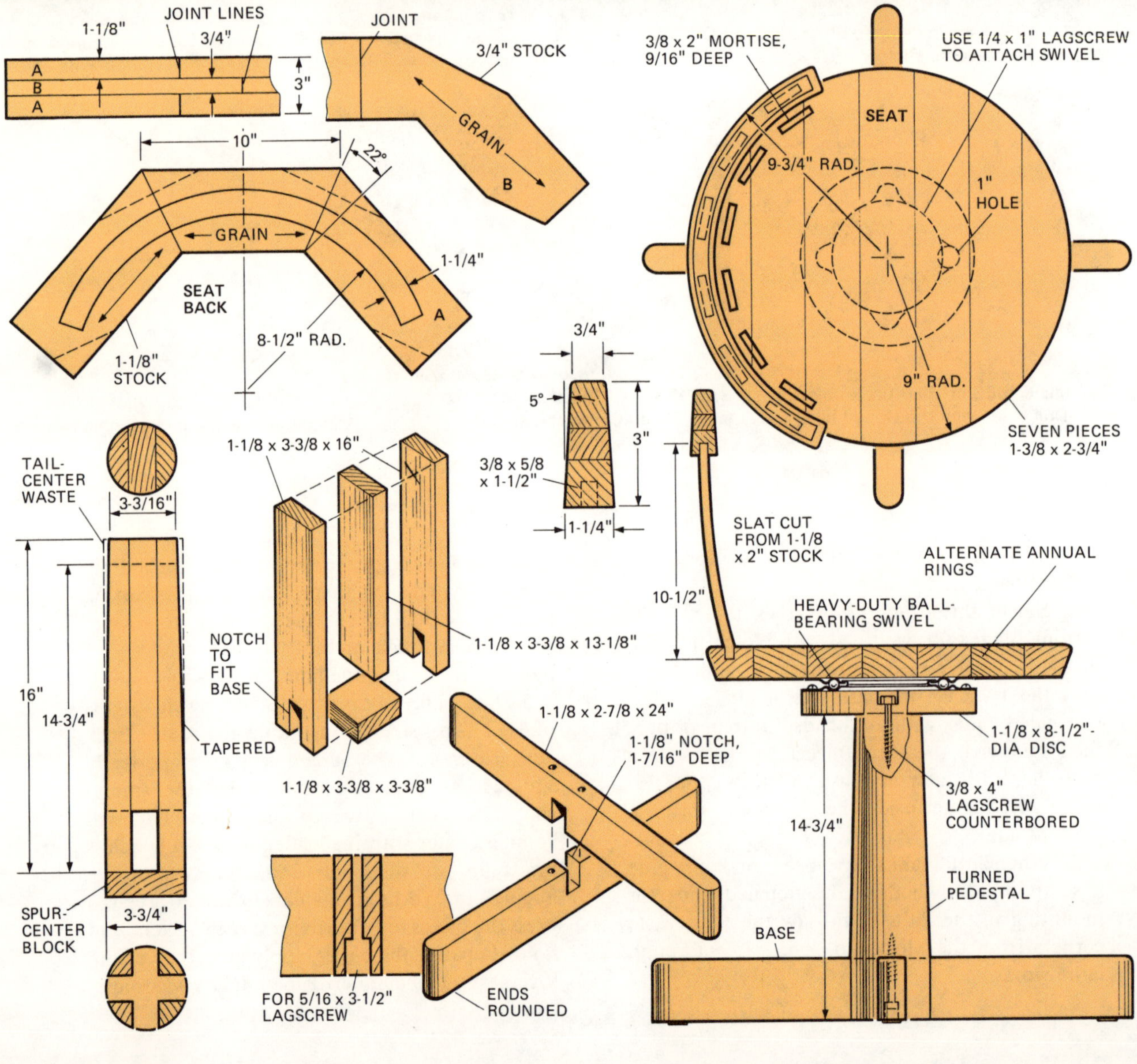
1-1/8"
JOINT LINES
3/4"
A
B
A
3"
JOINT
3/4" STOCK
GRAIN
B
10"
22°
GRAIN
SEAT
BACK
1-1/4"
A
1-1/8"
STOCK
8-1/2" RAD.
3/8 x 2" MORTISE,
9/16" DEEP
USE 1/4 x 1" LAGSCREW
TO ATTACH SWIVEL
SEAT
9-3/4" RAD.
1"
HOLE
9" RAD.
SEVEN PIECES
1-3/8 x 2-3/4"
3/4"
5°
3"
3/8 x 5/8
x 1-1/2"
1-1/4"
TAIL-
CENTER
WASTE
3-3/16"
16"
14-3/4"
TAPERED
SPUR-
CENTER
BLOCK
3-3/4"
1-1/8 x 3-3/8 x 16"
NOTCH
TO
FIT
BASE
1-1/8 x 3-3/8 x 13-1/8"
1-1/8 x 3-3/8 x 3-3/8"
SLAT CUT
FROM 1-1/8
x 2" STOCK
10-1/2"
ALTERNATE ANNUAL
RINGS
HEAVY-DUTY BALL-
BEARING SWIVEL
1-1/8 x 8-1/2"-
DIA. DISC
3/8 x 4"
LAGSCREW
COUNTERBORED
14-3/4"
TURNED
PEDESTAL
BASE
1-1/8 x 2-7/8 x 24"
1-1/8" NOTCH,
1-7/16" DEEP
FOR 5/16 x 3-1/2"
LAGSCREW
ENDS
ROUNDED

to four scrap boards and clamp them to both sides of the bundle using moderate pressure. Apply bar clamps to pull the seven members together. Check that the whole thing is perfectly flat. If necessary, apply more pressure to the clamps on the line-up blocks.

6. The beveled 18-in.-diameter seat is easily cut with a simple circle-cutting jig on the bandsaw. Clamp a board with a partial cut through it (for blade entry) to the saw table. Drive a screw through the bottom of the board so that it is exactly 9 in. from the blade and in perfect alignment with the front edge of the blade teeth. This is very important because if the pivot point is ahead of or behind the teeth, the cut will be eccentric and the work will be spoiled.

You can test the right-angle alignment by trying the cut on some scrap cardboard. When ready, tilt the saw table 15°, start the cut freehand to get the blade into the wood, then stop the saw, insert the screw into the bottom of the seat to provide a pivot.

cut slats freehand

7. The curved slats are cut from 5/4 (1⅛-in.) stock, freehand on the bandsaw. Sanding out the saw marks is easy if you use a 3-in. sanding drum on the drill press. Clamp a scrap of wood on edge and aim it to the center of the drum with just enough space to allow the work to pass through with a snug fit. Keep the work continuously perpendicular to the guide as you push it through. When all the insides have been sanded, move the guide a fraction closer and repeat the operation on the opposite side of the slats. Note that the bottom ends of the slats have a straight portion—be careful not to round them off. Some hand sanding will be required near the flats.

8. The curved back is made up by gluing eight angled segments together. A sandwich is made by stacking three, two and then another set of three blocks, one atop the other. This allows the grain to run as closely as possible in the direction of the curve. The alternating vertical joint lines produce a strong block.

9. The back is tapered in cross section so that it is wider at the bottom. Trace the outline of the bottom curves in the block. Set bandsaw table for a 5° bevel and make both cuts.

10. A simple hole-locating jig is used to bore a series of five overlapping holes in a straight line to form the mortises for the slats. The jig is made to pivot by driving a nail through the stick into the seat center. When the block is positioned where required, a second nail is tacked into the stick to keep the block from moving. A ⅜-in. drill bit is driven through each hole in the block. Work with a spur bit for best results.

11. Use a chisel to clean out the waste and trim the mortises. Because of its shape, the curved back piece does not lend itself so readily to a jig for boring the holes for the mortises. Therefore these holes are lined up and drilled freehand. A slight error here can be tolerated—not so on the seat.

12. When all parts are sanded to completion, test the fit, then apply glue only to bottom ends of the slats and the seat mortises. The curved back is inserted, dry, only to help hold the parts in alignment. When the slats have been glued to the seat, you can proceed to apply glue to the backs. Work upside down, with the curved back resting on a table and the seat elevated and supported on a level plane. Gluing the back in two phases will prevent a messy glue runoff which could drip all over the slats.

putting together the chair

13. Assembly of the chair: First use a hex-head lagscrew and glue to attach the ball-bearing support disc to the top of the pedestal. The hole must be counterbored so the screwhead doesn't project above the surface. Before attaching the disc, bore a 1-in. screw access hole properly located in the block.

Turn the unit over, apply glue and insert the base into the notches in the pedestal. Secure with four hexhead lags. Be sure to counterbore a hole large enough to receive a socket wrench which is required to turn the screws. Attach the swivel mechanism to the disc with lagscrews, then screw the upper section of the swivel to the seat bottom.

The screws are inserted one at a time through the 1-in. access hole in the block which is alternately rotated to reveal each screw-mounting hole. The heavy-duty 8-in. swivel, No. 91 K8, is available from A. Constantine, 2050 Eastchester Rd., Bronx, NY 10461.

14. Finish is optional. I thought it might be refreshing to depart from the usual routine of staining the piece so I applied a coat of sanding sealer followed with two coats of clear satin finish to obtain an interesting high-key effect.

15. Install four steel glides to both table and chair bases.

Seat covers are optional. Shown are oversize shag toilet-lid covers available from Sears. Cut cardboard and 1-in.-thick-foam pieces to fit each seat 1 in. shy all around. Insert foam and then cardboard to retain shape of the cushions.

TABLETOP AND BENCHTOPS are made of clear-pine 2x8s doweled and edge-glued. Pegged stretchers add a great deal of rigidity to the table and benches.

Build a beautiful trestle table

By EVERETT JOHNSON

Simple in appearance but rugged and durable, here is an easy-to-build piece that is sure to become a family heirloom

SEE ALSO
**Coffee tables . . . Desks . . . Game tables . . .
Gossip benches . . . Hutch tables . . .
Picnic tables . . . Sabre saws . . . Woods**

■ SERVING SIX PEOPLE comfortably, as well as offering the rugged good looks of Early American pine furniture, this hand-pegged, trestle dining table is a period piece you'll use and admire for years to come. Its beauty lies in its simplicity, both in design and construction. Best of all, it's made of common clear pine, which means you can get the wood to make it at any lumberyard.

Except for size, the two trestle benches are duplicates of the table, the main difference being the number of pieces required to build up the 30-in. wide top. The 1½-in.-thick stock, which is used for the table and benchtops, is doweled and glued together edgewise, then clamped. When the glue is dry, top surfaces of the built-up members are planed smooth, sanded with a medium-abrasive belt on a belt sander, or by hand, then the top edges are rounded.

The leg patterns for benches and table are similar, and all six legs are sabre-sawed from 1⅛-in.-thick pine. Some lumberyards have 1⅛-in. pine 14 in. wide. Where you can't obtain this width, the stock for the table legs will have to be doweled and glued up like the tabletop. The open mortises in the legs are made 1⅛ in. wide to accept the shouldered ends of the stretchers. The mortises are easily cut with a sabre saw by first boring a ½-in. hole for the saw blade. Cleat and foot members are cut to the sizes given and are attached to the scroll-cut legs with ½-in. dowels.

continued

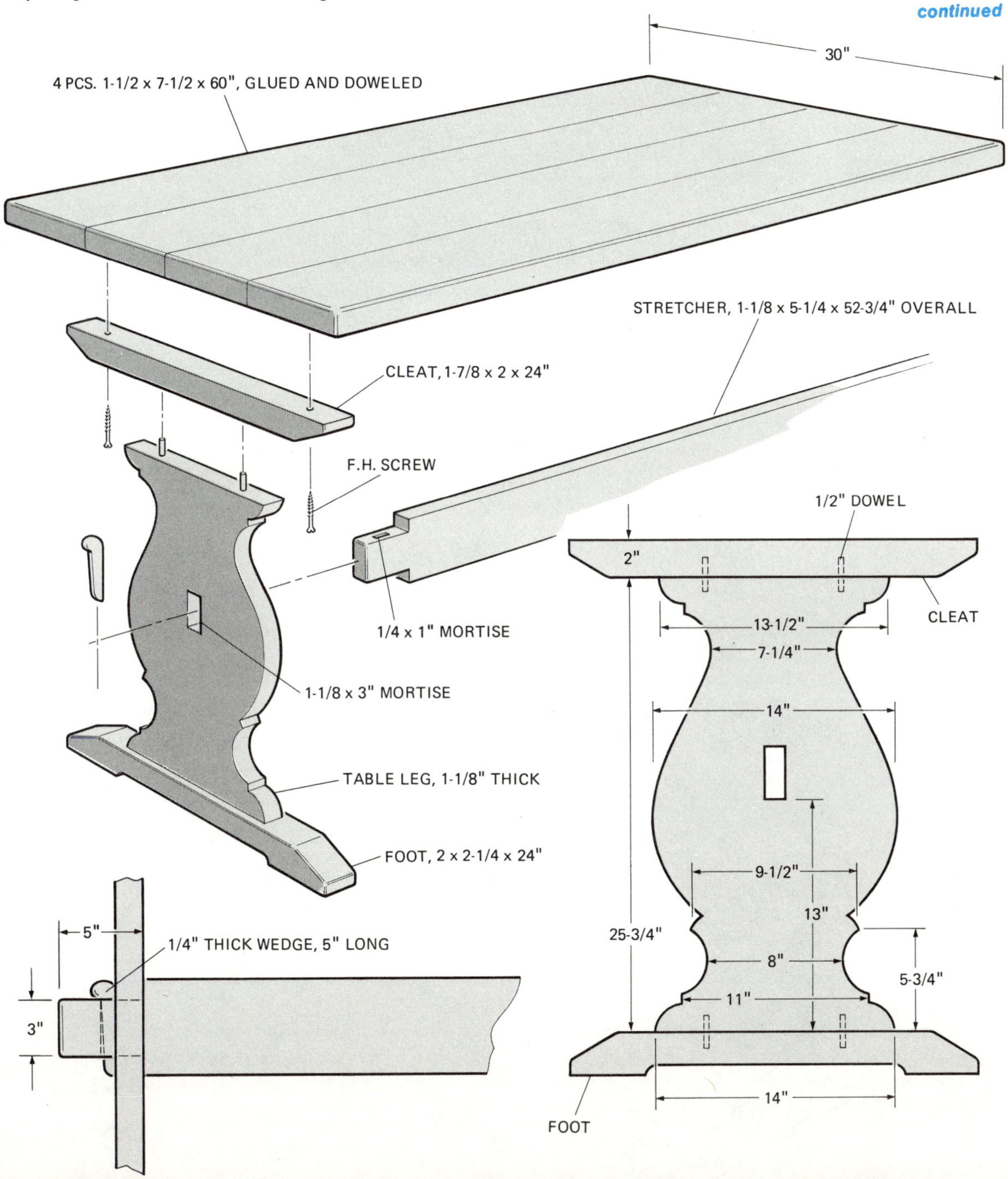

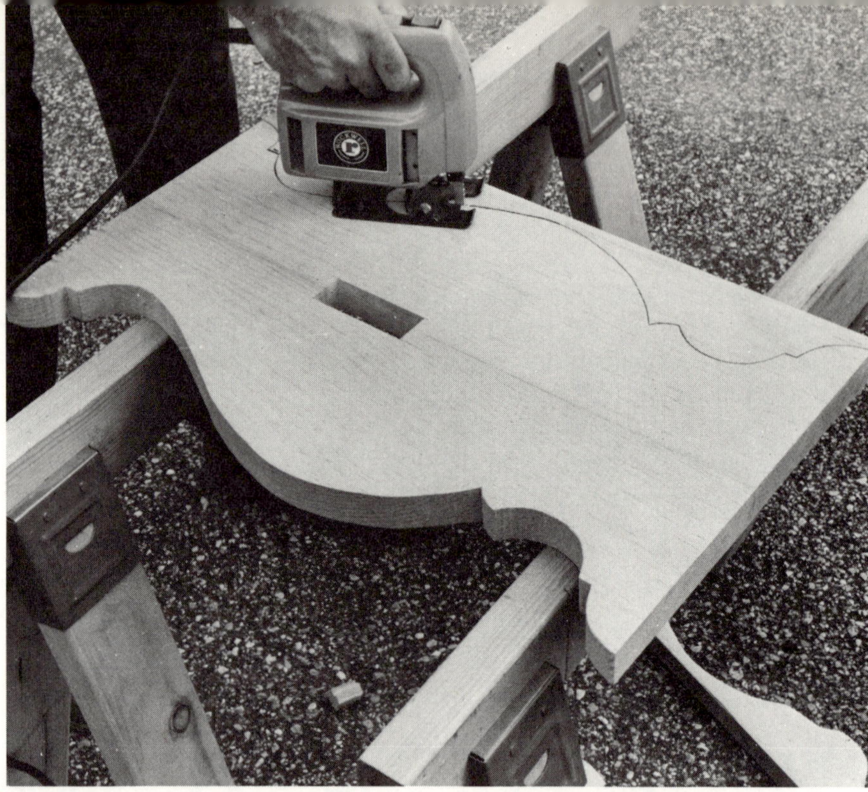

SABRE SAW makes quick work of sawing scrolled table and bench legs. Feed the saw slowly, follow the lines closely, then sand the edges with abrasive blocks.

Counterbored holes in the cleats permit husky screws to be used to anchor the legs to the table and benchtops.

A ¼ x 1-in. open mortise is made vertically in the stretcher tenons for ¼-in. tapered wedges. The mortises are located at a point which will draw the tenon shoulders tightly against the leg when the wedges are tapped in place.

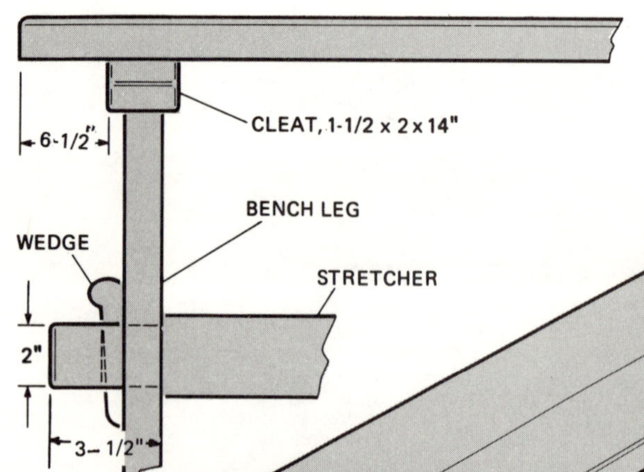

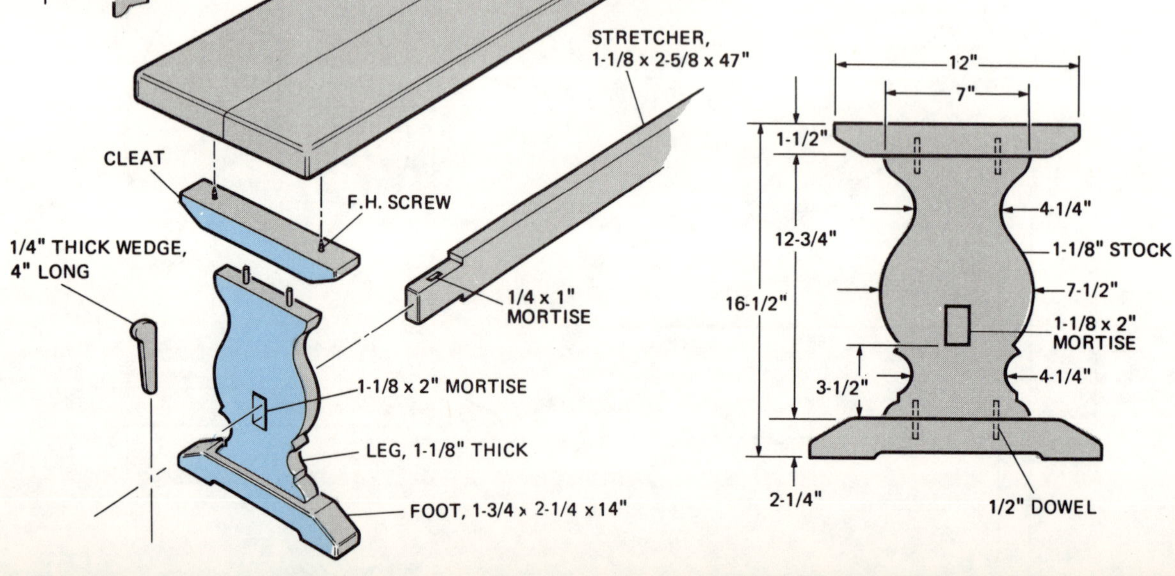

Perfect circles every time

This workshop tool can be very helpful when you are trying to cut and sand perfect wood discs. It is made to fit both your bandsaw and disc sander

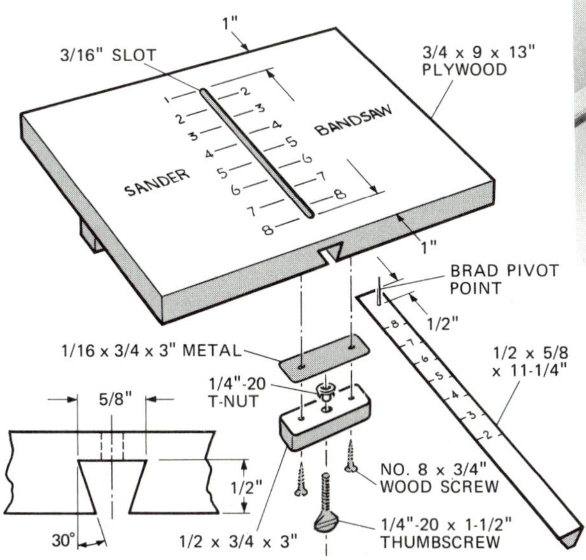

By PAUL D. FIEBICH

■ IF YOU HAVE NEED to cut a number of wood discs accurately and quickly, it will pay you to make this workshop fixture which will handle discs up to 16 in. in diameter. It's designed for use first on the bandsaw and then on the disc sander—first to saw the disc, then to sand it to the exact size. In each case the fixture is positioned by the miter-gauge table groove.

SEE ALSO
Abrasives . . . Bandsaws . . . Belt sanders . . . Bench saws . . . Disc sanders . . . Motors, shop . . . Pad sanders . . . Power-tool stands . . . Shapers . . . Table saws

In use, you set a brad point for the desired radius, lock it and impale the work on the point. Then you place the fixture in the saw-table groove, move it inward until the work touches the blade, clamp it in position with a C-clamp, turn on the saw and slowly rotate the blank. If a number of discs of the same size are to be cut, leave the pivot point undisturbed. If different sizes are needed, simply reset the pivot point for each change of size.

The setup is repeated in switching from bandsaw to sander, except that the brad point is set to the sander calibrations on the fixture. The disc is replaced on the brad, the sander turned on and the fixture moved inward in the groove until the wood disc contacts the spinning abrasive. Here, as before, you clamp the fixture and rotate the disc slowly to produce a perfect circle.

How to fix your dishwasher

SEE ALSO

Appliance repair . . . Appliances . . . Clothes dryers . . . Electrical wiring . . . Heaters, water . . . Kitchens . . . Plumbing . . . Washing machines

WHEN DISHWASHER TROUBLES occur, they are most often caused by washing conditions—water problems, detergent problems, improper stacking of dishes or a combination of these factors. The accompanying troubleshooting charts will help you correct these conditions, as well as common problems of mechanical origin. The illustration on the facing page shows the typical locations of dishwasher com-

PROPER STACKING OF DISHES

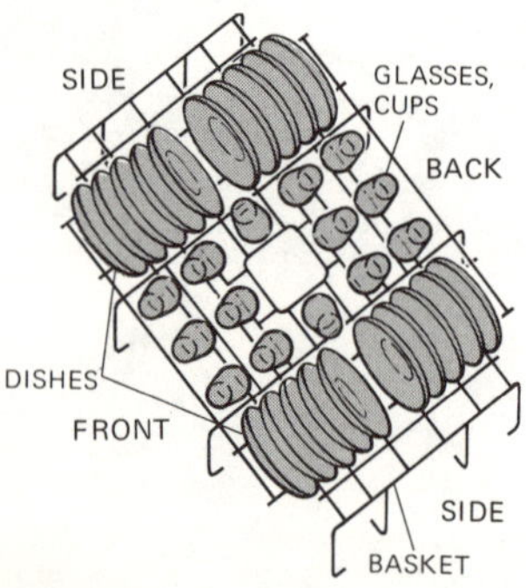

DOOR-LATCH ASSEMBLY

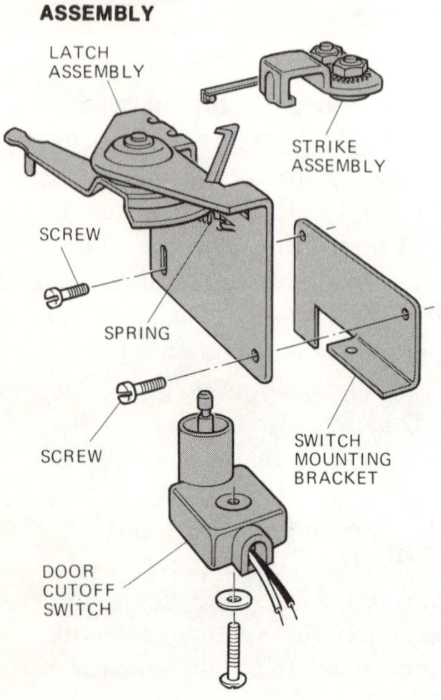

Machine does not operate

POSSIBLE CAUSES	ACTION TO TAKE
1. Door not latched.	Latch door. Make sure handle locks all the way to the right.
2. Door microswitch defective.	Press button on microswitch manually. You should hear a definite clicking noise. If not, replace switch.
3. Latch lever or spring not pressing against microswitch.	Attach door latch to fully depress button or bend or replace spring on microswitch.
4. Timer defective.	Turn on the timer very slowly. It should advance and turn the machine on. If not, replace the timer.
5. Line wires loose or apart.	Check line junction box under machine. All wires should be tight and capped or taped.
6. Blown fuse or tripped circuit breaker.	Check fuse or circuit breaker.
7. Selector buttons not depressed fully.	Press desired cycle button all the way in.

Door will not close

POSSIBLE CAUSES	ACTION TO TAKE
1. Door seal loose or binding inside tank.	Check entire door gasket. All gasket clips or points should be inserted in their proper slots.
2. Door striker.	Shim door striker until door latch catches it and closes very easily.
3. Improper installation.	Remove screw fasteners and let machine spring back, releasing it of any tension. Close door. If no binding, resecure screw fasteners in new position. Also, check level of machine.
4. Door hinges out of adjustment.	Check both hinges. If broken, replace. If out of adjustment, loosen hinge screws. Adjust door until it closes easily, then tighten screws.
5. Bottom service panel.	Check clearance of upper door with bottom service panel. If rubbing or binding, lower the panel or raise upper door by hinges.

ponents. The other illustrations show specific parts and assemblies from dishwashers made by several different manufacturers.

When making electrical checks and tests on a dishwasher or any other appliance, it is important to understand the manufacturer's wiring diagram. This diagram is shown in the instruction manual for portable dishwashers. For built-in models, the diagram can be found either behind the front-door panel or behind the control panel at the top of the door. It may be glued to the machine or rolled up. Since built-in dishwashers are wired directly to the main junction box, and because the combination of water and electricity can be lethal, it is important to use *extreme* caution when making any tests. Know what fuse or circuit breaker controls your dishwasher, and keep it *off* when working under the machine.

Common dishwasher components

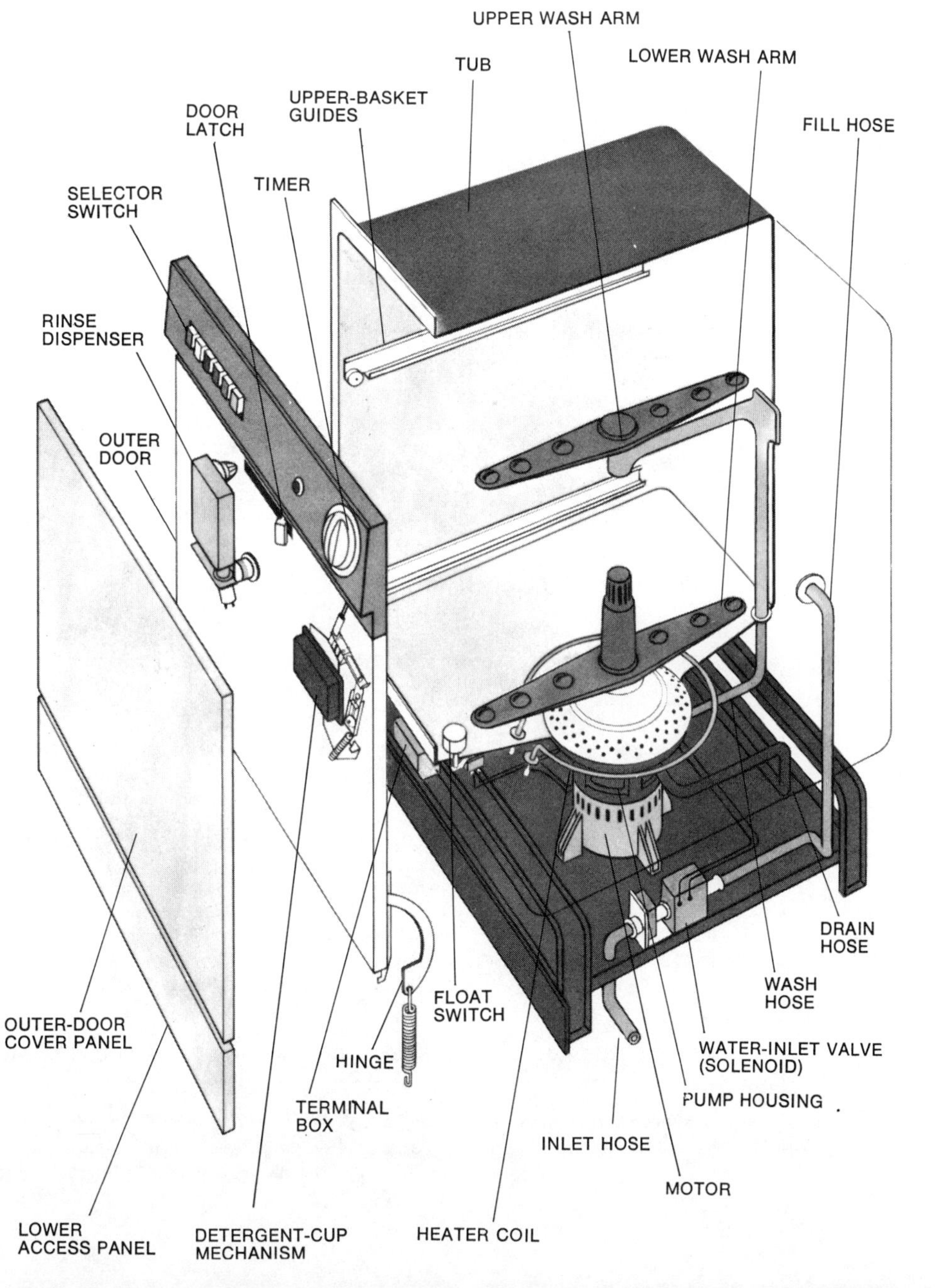

WASH MECHANISM

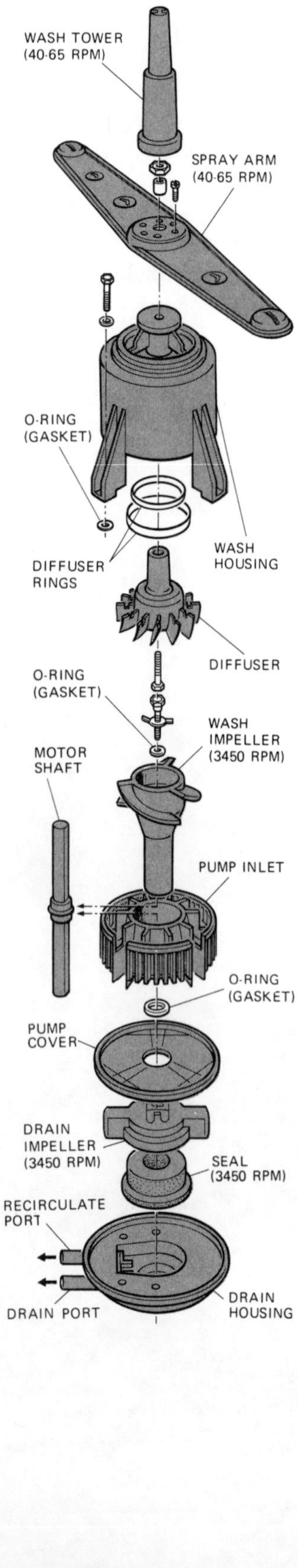

Failure to fill

POSSIBLE CAUSES	ACTION TO TAKE
1. Water valve solenoid.	Turn timer to fill position. Check voltage with 115-v. test light at terminals. If voltage exists but valve won't open, replace solenoid.
2. Water inlet line.	Be sure water valve is in full open position.
3. Float switch (some machines).	Check float-stem position on float switch. It should sit squarely in seat. To test, pick up float inside of tub and let it drop. Definite clicking noise should be heard. Check also for loose or fallen wire from float switch.
4. Pressure switch.	Press rubber diaphragm disc of switch with finger. Definite clicking noise should be heard. If not, replace pressure switch.
5. Water valve assembly.	Filter screen can be clogged. Disassemble and flush line and screen. Check calcium buildup near diaphragm and pin. Replace bad parts if possible. If not, replace whole valve.
6. Low water pressure.	Check flow pressure with screw-on gauge at sink. It must be between 15 and 120 p.s.i.

Water won't shut off

POSSIBLE CAUSES	ACTION TO TAKE
1. Water valve stuck open.	Disassemble and clean. Check valve. If it still hangs up, replace.
2. Water-valve bleed hole clogged.	Disassemble valve and clean bleed hole in solenoid valve with pin.
3. Timer stuck on fill cycle.	Check timer. Fill cycle should last about 60 seconds. If timer doesn't advance, replace.
4. Float switch defective.	Check float switch for internal short. Place 115-v. test lamp across terminals. Depress switch spring; lamp should light. Release switch button; lamp should go out. If not, replace switch. Also, listen for definite clicking sound. If none, replace switch.

Dishwasher does not clean

POSSIBLE CAUSES	ACTION TO TAKE
1. Not enough water.	See section on "Failure to fill" above.
2. Water not hot enough.	Check water temperature. It should be about 150° F. Run hot-water tap in sink before turning on machine or change temperature setting on house hot-water heater.
3. Wash or spray arm clogged.	Check holes in wash or spray arms for blockage by food particles or, possibly, small pieces of broken glass.
4. Not enough detergent or wrong kind.	Adjust detergent to correct water hardness. If water is hard, add more detergent. If detergent is caked in detergent dispenser cup, switch to a more granular brand.
5. Wash arm not turning.	Make sure that no utensil or dish is stopping wash-arm rotation.
6. Dishes improperly stacked.	Restack with space around each piece; avoid any clutter or pile-up. Face soiled sides of cups in top rack toward center of rack.

Water will not drain

POSSIBLE CAUSES	ACTION TO TAKE
1. Pump impeller jammed or broken.	Check impeller blades for pieces of food jammed into them. Clear items and test. If impeller has broken vanes, replace.
2. Pump motor winding defective.	Advance timer to a drain cycle. If motor hums, check for obstacles in impeller. If impeller turns freely and motor still hums, then pump-motor winding is defective. Replace motor.
3. Drain hose kinked.	Check for any sharp bends in the drain hose. Straighten hose and place helical spring (tube bender), a little larger than the o.d. of hose, over kinked area to prevent a recurrence.
4. Drain hose clogged.	Disconnect drain hose from motor housing. Blow through the hose until line clears and reconnect it.
5. Timer stuck in wash cycle.	Check timer. If timer doesn't advance by itself, replace it.

Detergent cup fails to open

POSSIBLE CAUSES	ACTION TO TAKE
1. Detergent left in cup too long, or put in a wet cup causing it to harden.	Use only amount of detergent specified by the manufacturer. Make sure cup is dry. If the detergent still cakes, switch to a more granular brand.
2. Improperly racked dishes or utensils.	Reposition around detergent cup all dishes or utensils that could possibly prevent the cup from opening.
3. White calcium deposits around cup. lid or shaft mechanism (due to hard water).	Clean all calcium deposits around mechanical operating mechanisms of the detergent Use vinegar.
4. Detergent-cup solenoid valve.	Place 115-v. test lamp across both solenoid terminals. Advance timer in fill cycle until test light glows. If solenoid doesn't work, replace.
5. Timer.	Advance timer to positions in the fill cycle that activate detergent-cup mechanism. Place 115-v. test lamp across solenoid terminals. If no voltage is indicated, timer contacts are defective. Replace timer.

Motor will not run

POSSIBLE CAUSES	ACTION TO TAKE
1. Motor hums.	Check for a food particle or piece of broken glass that's jammed in pump impeller. Clear and test.
2. Motor kicked out on overload.	Check line voltage, ±10 percent of 115 v., or binding of the motor shaft. Turn by hand to free shaft.
3. Timer defective.	Advance timer to all wash and drain cycles. Check motor operation on each one. If motor fails to run, replace timer.
4. Motor defective.	Direct-test motor with test jumper. If motor still fails to run, replace it.

DRAIN PUMP

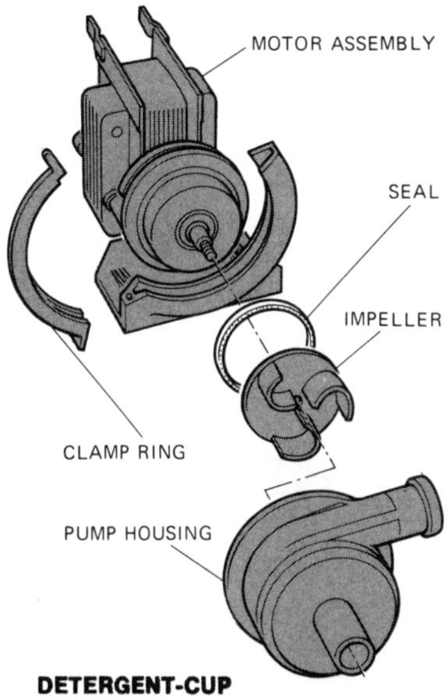

DETERGENT-CUP ASSEMBLY

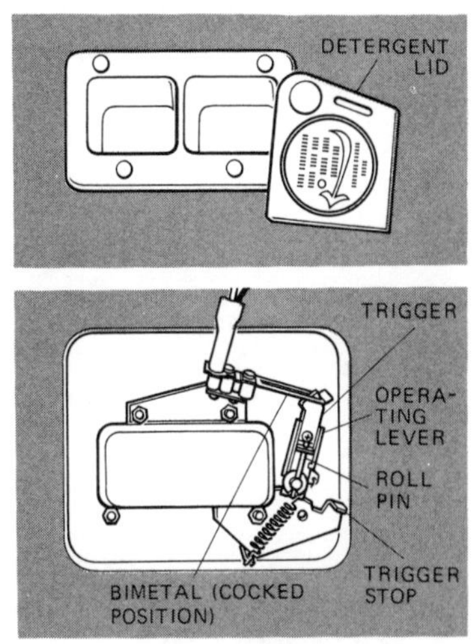

FLOAT SWITCH

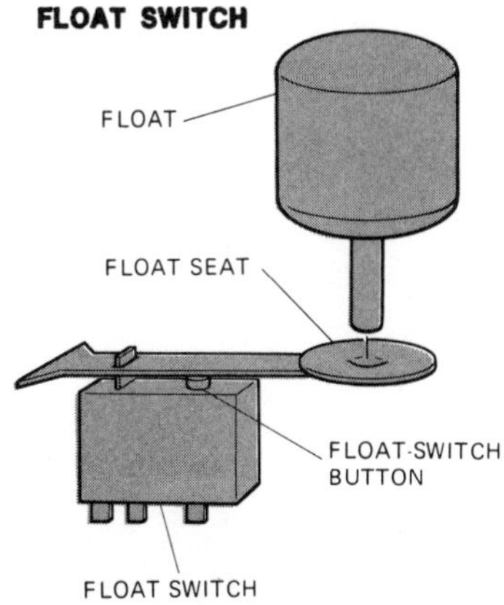

Dishwasher operates when door is open

POSSIBLE CAUSE	ACTION TO TAKE
1. Door switch is shorted.	Replace door switch.

JUNCTION-BOX ASSEMBLY

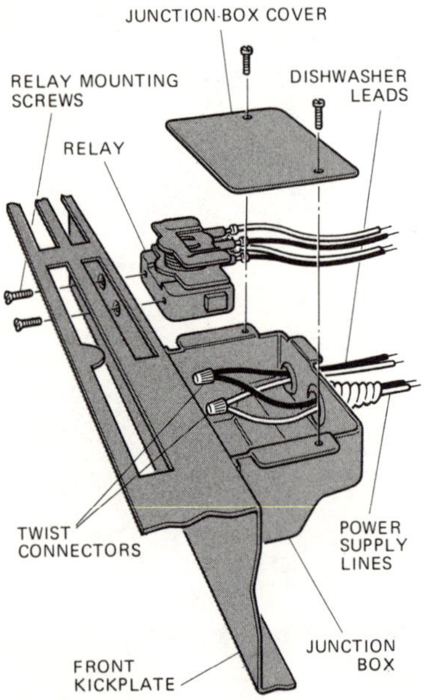

Dishes do not dry

POSSIBLE CAUSES	ACTION TO TAKE
1. Heater element burned out.	Replace heater element.
2. Calcium buildup on heater element.	Clean heater element of all calcium deposits.
3. Wire off heater element.	Replace wire and tighten connections.
4. Water not hot enough.	Check water temperature. It should be approximately 150° F.
5. Water still in dishwater.	Refer to section "Water will not drain," page **1005**.
6. Improper stacking of dishes.	Rack the dishes so that there is air space provided around each and see that they are neither jammed together nor piled on top of each other.
7. Fan motor inoperative (some machines).	Direct-test the fan motor with a test jumper wire. If the motor still fails to operate, replace it.

MAIN-DOOR ASSEMBLY

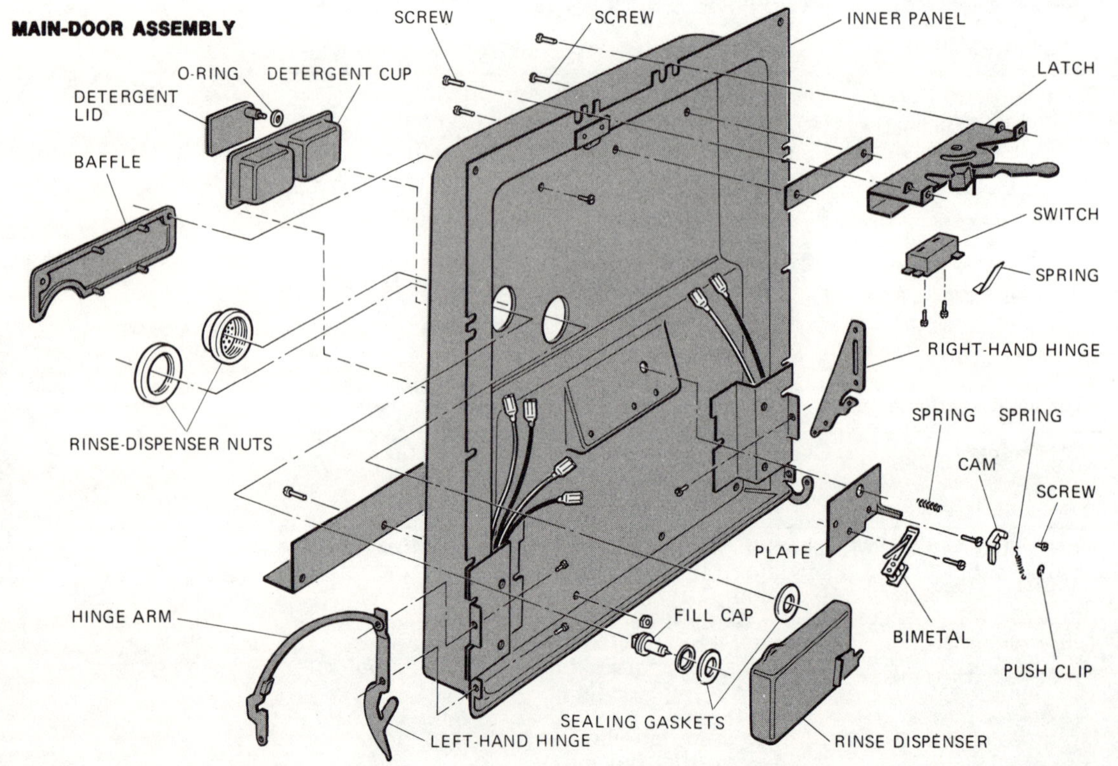

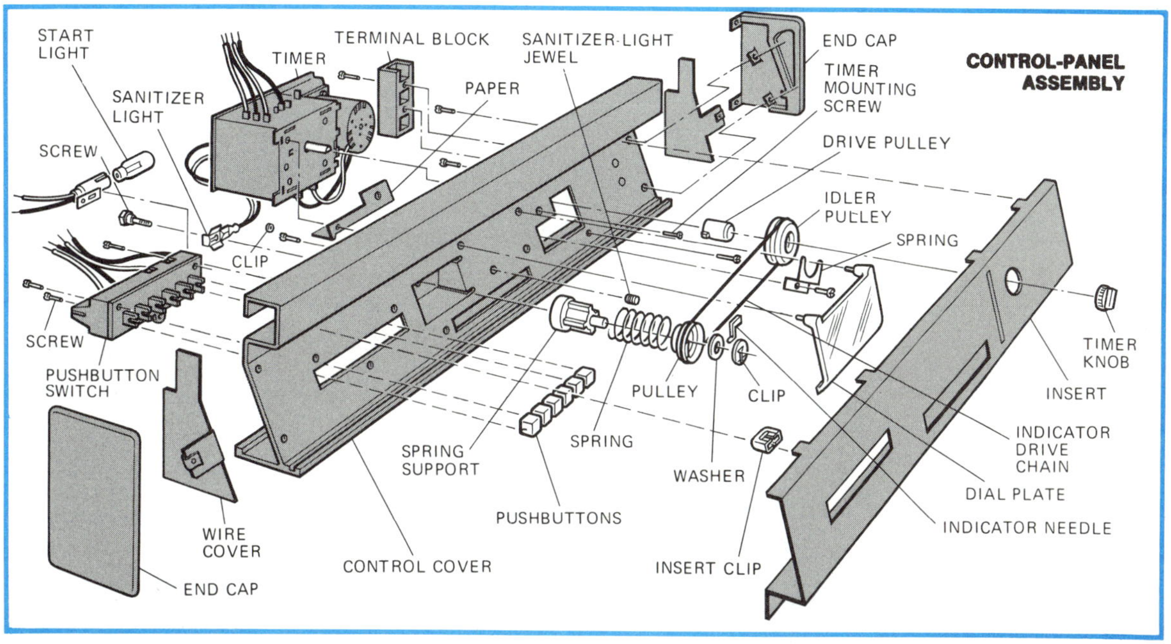

Dishwasher is leaking

POSSIBLE CAUSES	ACTION TO TAKE
1. Door gasket loose or worn.	Check door gasket. It should be clipped in its proper slots. If gasket is torn or flat with no compression left, replace.
2. Door hinges broken or out of adjustment.	Replace broken hinges. Loosen hinges so door sits tight against gasket and retighten.
3. Inlet line fitting.	Check inlet line near water solenoid valve. Tighten compression nut.
4. Motor seal.	Check for water stains or leaks around motor shaft. Replace motor seal.
5. Door alignment.	Check door fit on gasket; it should not bind. See section "Door will not close," page **1002**.
6. Loose hose clamps.	Check all hoses and connections under machine for slippage or water stains.
7. Heating element seals.	Check seals at heating-element holes. If leaking, tighten. If leak remains, replace seals.
8. Nuts, bolts and screws.	Check attachments to tub. Noticeable dripping can be corrected by tightening or caulking the fasteners with putty.

WATER-INLET VALVE

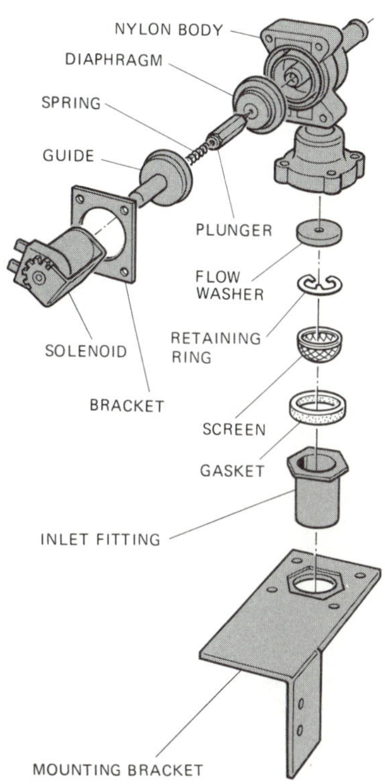

Abnormal water noise

POSSIBLE CAUSES	ACTION TO TAKE
1. Water hammer "thud noise."	Install water-hammer eliminator or pressure reducer (from maker) on inlet line to lower water pressure. Set water heater to 150° F.
2. Water chatter "low-frequency pulsing."	See that inlet piping is at least ⅜ in. i.d. Secure piping to avoid vibration. Set water heater to 150° F.
3. Water flutter "rumble."	Set water heater to 150° F. Install small hand valve in inlet line to cause partial restriction. If valve is already in line, close or open more to adjust pressure.
4. Water whistle "hiss" to shrill whistle.	See answer to No. 3 above and apply the same action.

UPPER-RACK SLIDE ASSEMBLY

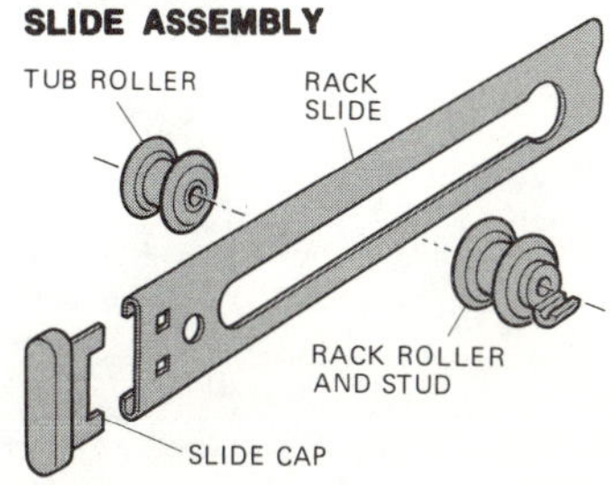

RINSE DISPENSER

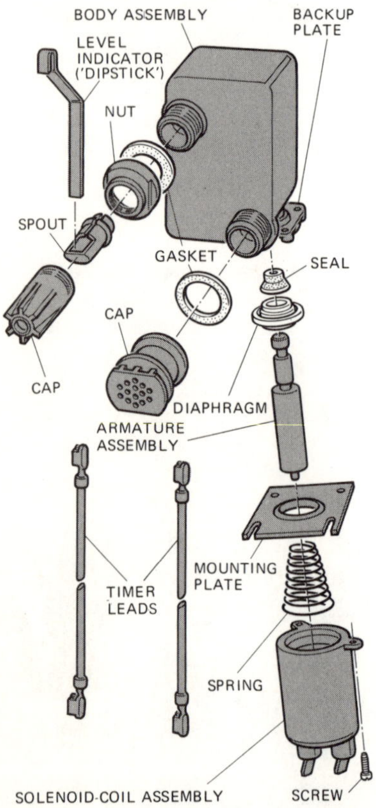

Dishwashing hints

PROBLEM	ACTION TO TAKE
1. Water spots.	Too much detergent. Determine amount by experimentation. Use a rinse conditioner in the final rinse to eliminate water spots.
2. Stains and films.	Caused by water or household plumbing. Use oxalic acid, vinegar or Clorox to remove. Eliminate all silverware and metal to prevent their corrosion from this treatment.
3. Iron film (brown stain).	Wash dishes with full cup of detergent. Omit dry cycle. Use two teaspoons oxalic acid crystals. Wash dishes a second time. Eliminate dry cycle. Wash again with a full cup of detergent. Use dry cycle. Repeat precedure as necessary until stains are gone.
4. Lime film.	Too much detergent with very hard water. Use pint vinegar; run machine through cycle.
5. Coffee, tea and food stains.	Fill detergent cup. Pour 1 teaspoon liquid chlorine bleach over detergent. Operate the dishwasher through a normal cycle.
6. Metallic stains on dishes.	Aluminum abraded into a dish as a result of improper stacking. Remove with household alkali (Drano, lye, washing soda, Clorox).
7. Aluminumware discolored.	Rebrighten with cream of tartar. Fill detergent cup with cream of tartar and let dishwasher go through wash cycle only. Polish aluminumware with soap-filled steel wool pads.
8. Glasses and glassware filming and etching.	Water hardness causes glass to film. Eliminate it by using rinse agents, vinegar or citric acid. Etching cannot be eliminated.
9. Glass breakage.	Due to improper loading. Never wash glasses and cups in the lower rack; the force of water is enough to knock them together or blow them upward out of the rack completely.

DOOR-HINGE ASSEMBLY

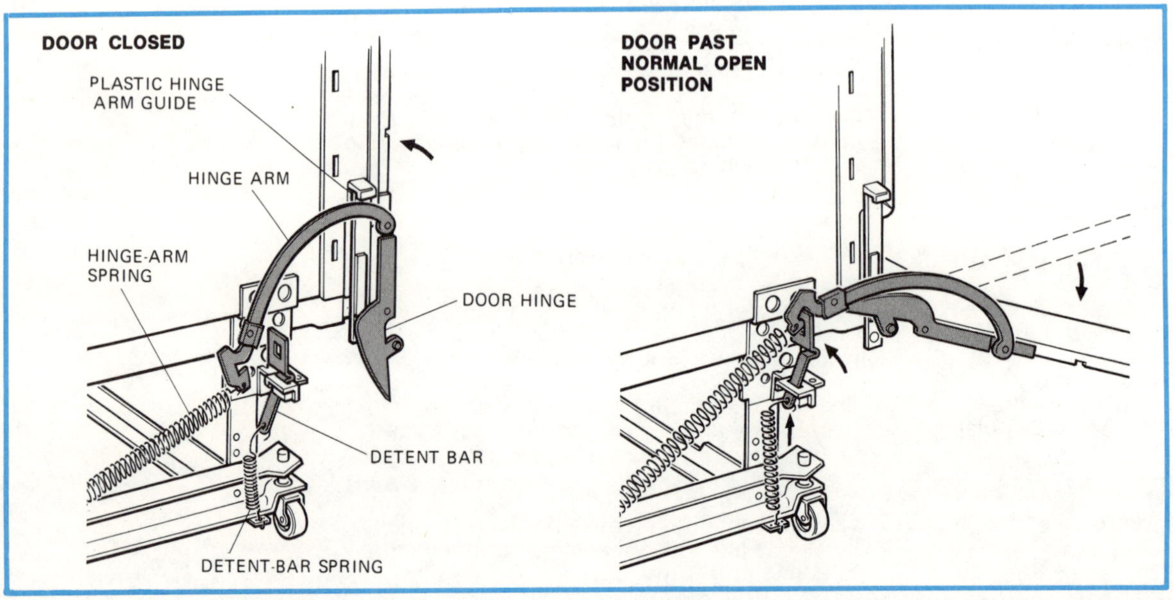

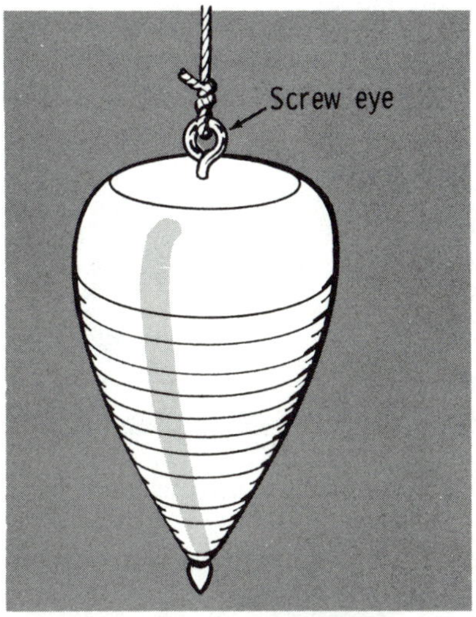

A TOY TOP can be turned into an effective plumb bob by drilling a small hole in the center and driving a screw eye into it. Tie a string to the eye and your "plumb top" is ready for use. A couple of nuts placed over the cord will add weight.

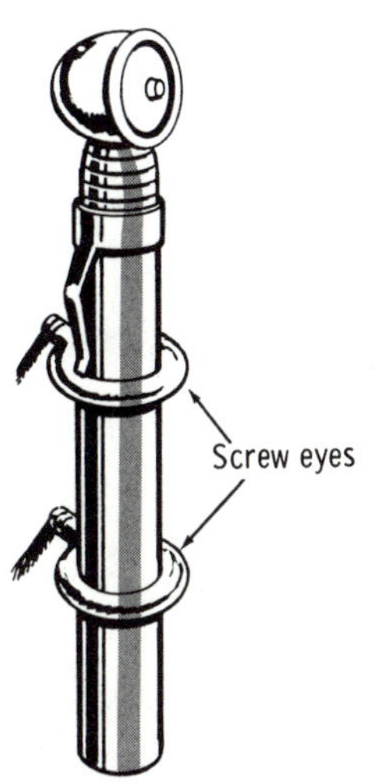

YOU WON'T HAVE to hunt for the pressure gauge to check cold tire pressures at home if you make a simple rack to hold it. Just drive a couple of large-diameter screw eyes into a garage stud. The spring clip will keep it from falling through.

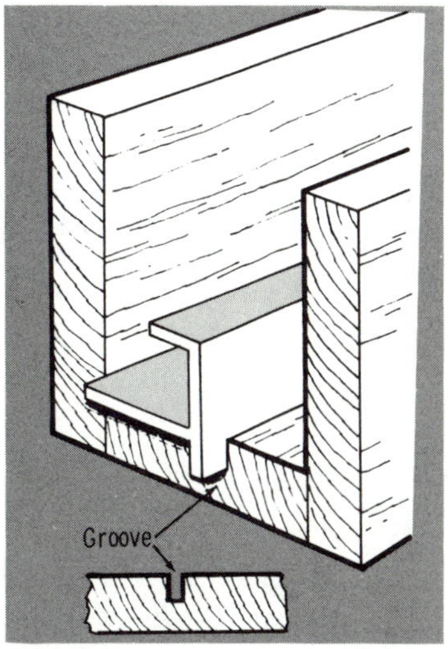

SOME METAL moldings have no flat side so you can't seat them properly in the miter box to cut an exact miter. It will pay you to make a special box with a kerf down the middle, or add a second bottom to an existing box to hold the molding flat.

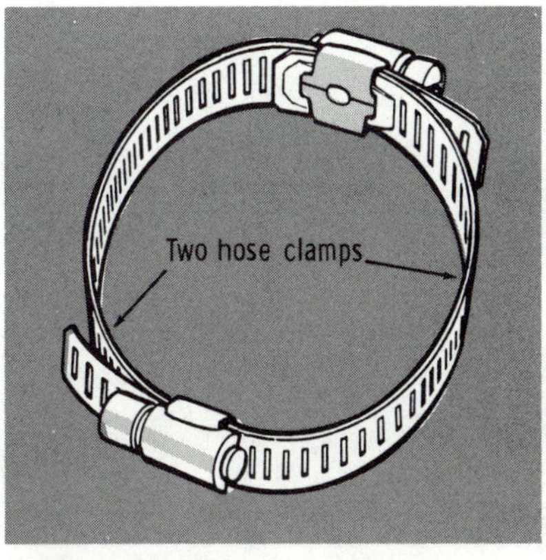

WHEN YOU NEED a large hose clamp and one isn't available, try hooking two smaller clamps together as shown below. Don't forget that you'll have two screws to tighten instead of one.

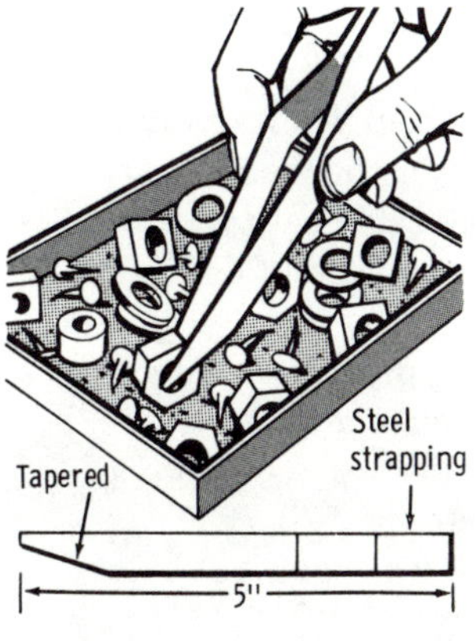

IT'S EASY to cut a finger when rummaging in a box of small hardware. To avoid this, make up a pair of tongs from a steel strip of the type used to reinforce packing cases. Taper ends, smooth edges.

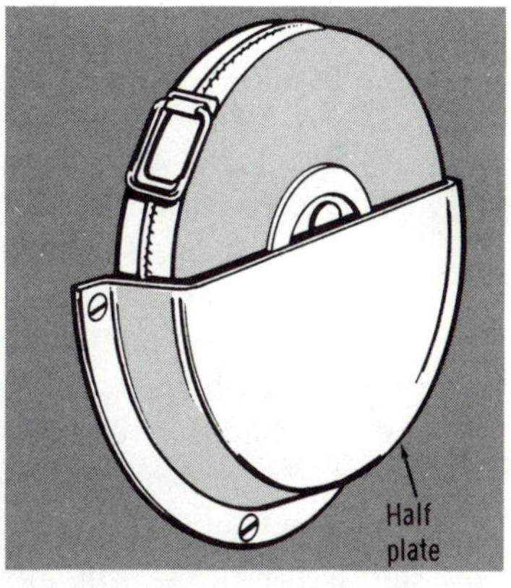

A SHALLOW plastic dish cut in half and mounted on the shop wall provides an ideal storage pocket for your steel measuring tape. Drill holes in the rim and secure it to the wall with three screws.

The fine points of distributor tune-up

By MORT SCHULTZ

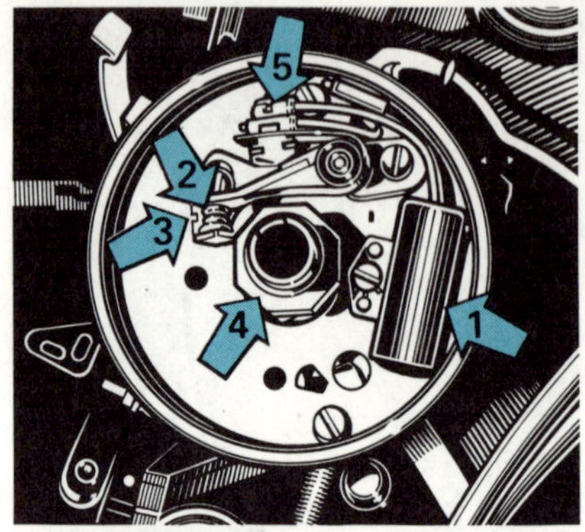

1. DISTRIBUTOR: 1. condenser; 2. points; 3. gap-adjust notch; 4. cam; 5. condenser pigtail, wire terminals.

■ ELECTRONIC IGNITION has come on strong, but there are still many more cars on the road with conventional distributors that use breaker points.

There's a lot more to distributor care than just adjusting point gap, and we'll cover all the maintenance on conventional distributors (Fig. 1) step by step. Servicing can be done with the distributor remaining in the engine, but it should be removed for bench work if a serious problem is revealed. Servicing is done to avoid or overcome such engine problems as hard starting, stalling, missing, and excessive fuel consumption.

1. Remove cables from the distributor towers. Grasp the cable's boot, twist and pull. Do not pull on the cable itself.

As you take each cable from its respective tower, mark the cable and tower with some identifying number or letter. Each cable has to be returned to its respective tower to prevent damage to the engine.

Use clip-type clothespins or pieces of masking tape on which you've written an identifying number to mark cables. To identify towers, apply a piece of masking tape to each.

Remember: The tower and its respective cable must have the same identifying mark.

2. Remove the distributor cap. For the most

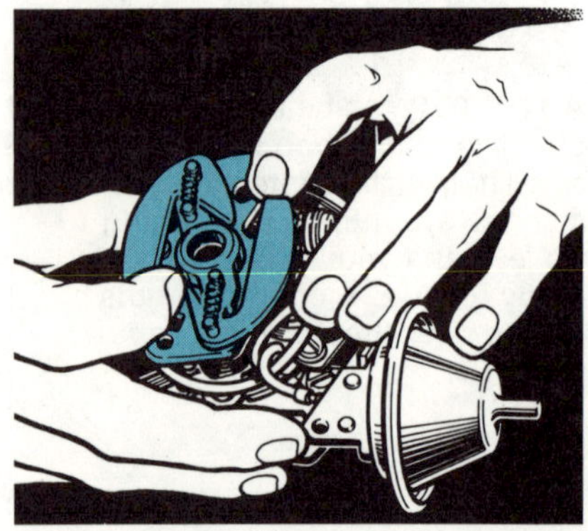

5. TO TEST centrifugal advance unit, spread counterweights to their limit and let them snap closed.

9. CAM MUST not be overlubricated. With cam lubricating wick, do not lubricate cam at all.

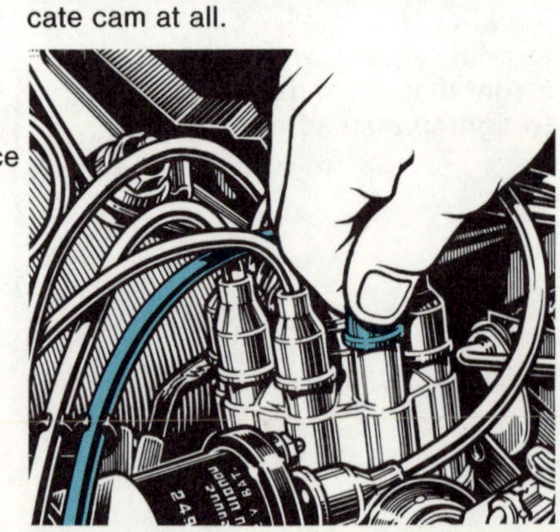

13. SQUEEZE BOOTS as you replace the wires to release trapped air for good connection.

SEE ALSO

Carburetors, auto . . . Dieseling, auto . . .
Electronic ignition, auto . . .
Ignition systems, auto . . . Misfiring, auto . . .
Sparkplugs . . . Stalling, auto . . . Tune-up, auto

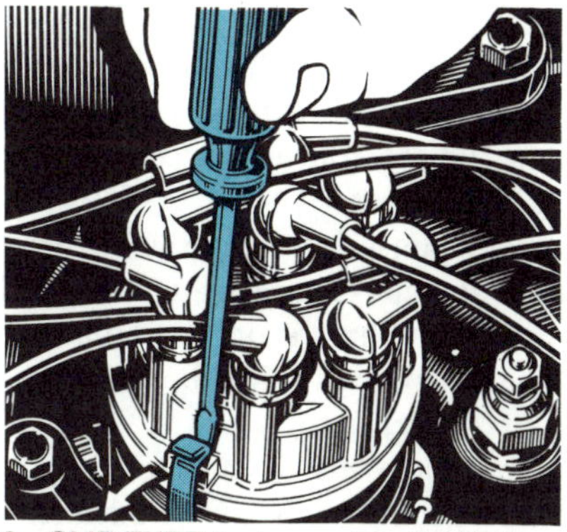

2. CLIP-TYPE fasteners for distributor cap are snapped open to remove cap for access.

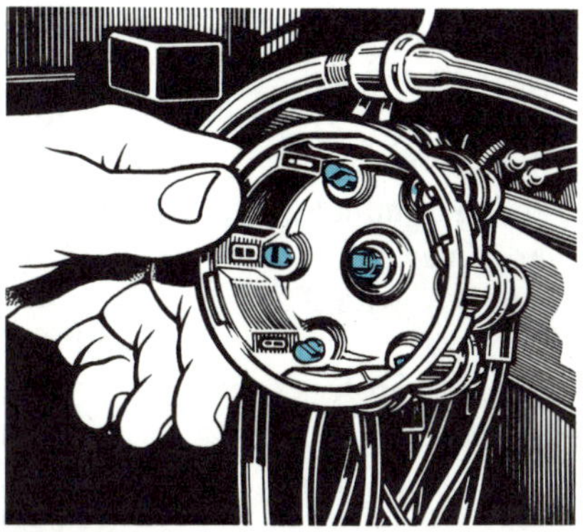

3. INSPECT all terminals and the center contact inside the cap. They must be clean and not worn.

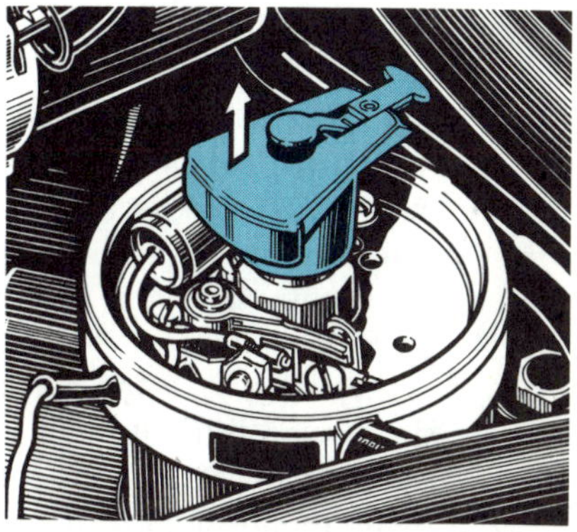

4. DISTRIBUTOR rotor is removed and inspected. Replace if it's cracked or has corroded terminals.

6. CHECK wires: primary lead (1) and condenser pigtail (2). Arrow shows connector for wires.

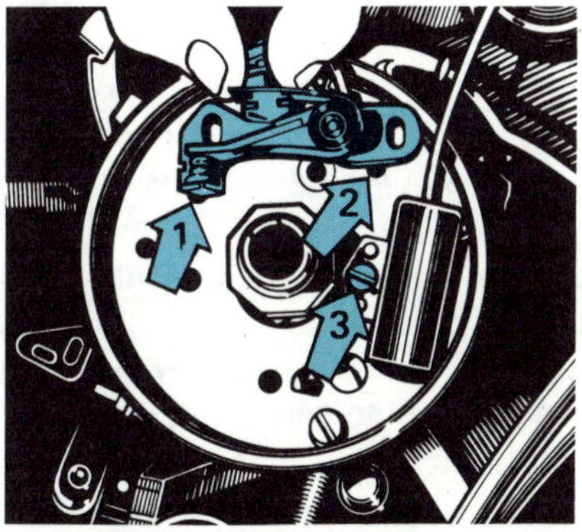

7. REMOVE point assembly held at mountings (1) and (2). Note condenser mounting screw (3).

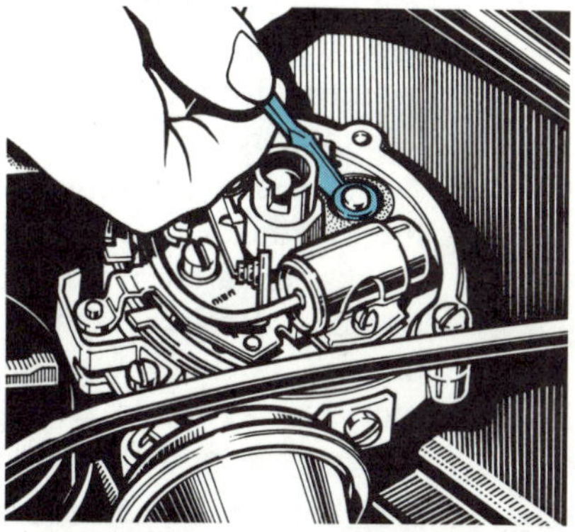

8. TO REPLACE cam lubricating wick, release small lock-type washer with a screwdriver.

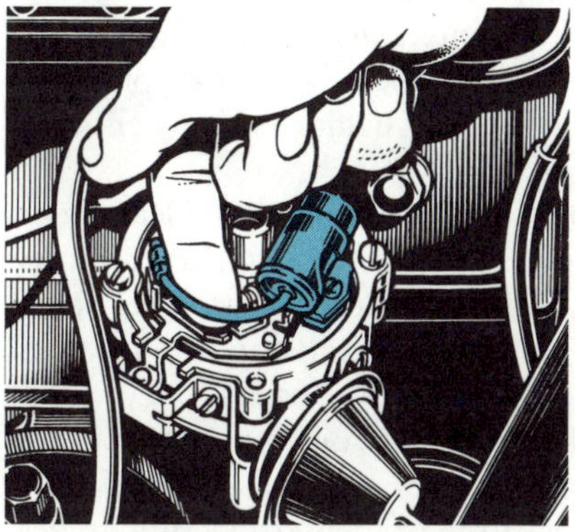

10. CONDENSER pigtail and primary wires should be routed so they don't touch moving parts.

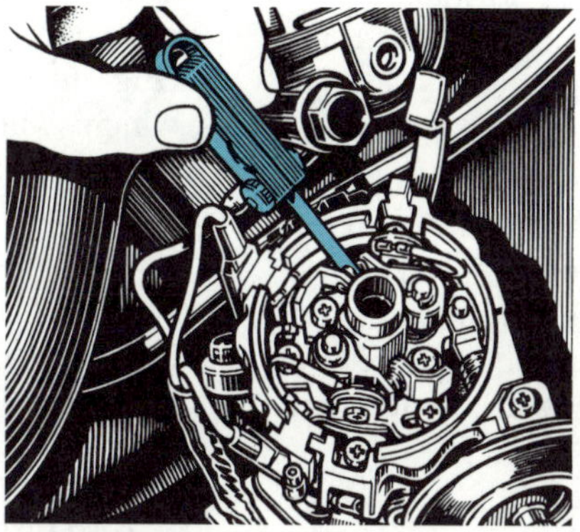

11. FEELER gauge must be held properly for accuracy. This distributor uses two sets of points.

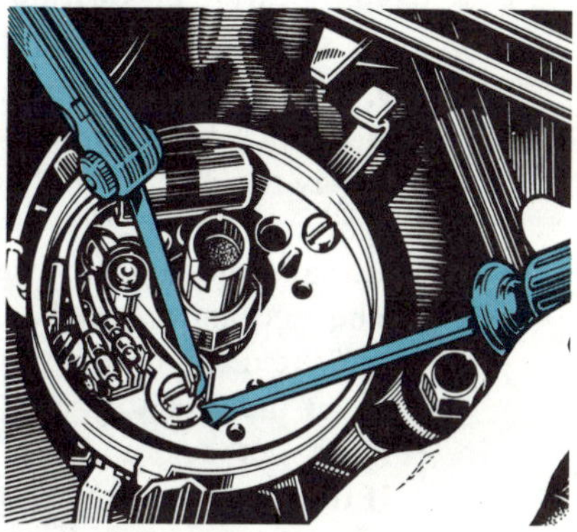

12. POINT GAP is set accurately by means of the adjustment notch in the point assembly.

part, caps are held by either a pair of clips or holding devices having slotted screw-type heads.

If clips are used, insert the tip of a screwdriver behind each clip, snapping the clip off the cap (Fig. 2).

If slotted heads are used, insert a screwdriver into the slot. Turn to disengage the latch.

3. Examine the outside and inside of the cap closely. On the outside look for visible cracks, broken towers and carbon tracks. A carbon track is a trail of soot running along the cap. It signifies a hairline crack.

On the inside look for burned or badly corroded terminals, worn center contact and carbon tracks (Fig. 3).

4. Replace the cap if there is reason to suspect damage. Make sure when buying a new cap that it's the one for your car.

If you replace the cap, lay new and old caps side by side so markings and distinctive features are aligned. Transfer pieces of masking tape with identifying numbers from the towers of the old cap to the respective towers of the new cap.

5. If the old cap can be reused, wipe it clean with paper towels or a clean rag. Polish terminals which are coated with a thin layer of carbon or are slightly corroded by rubbing lightly with a piece of sandpaper.

Clean out each tower. You can use a professional-type distributor tower cleaning tool, which can be purchased in an auto supply store, or a small, round wire brush.

6. Take the rotor from the top of the distributor shaft. For the most part, there are two kinds. One type can simply be pulled off (Fig. 4). The other, which resembles a cap that seems to cover the entire distributor, is held by two screws that have to be removed.

7. Examine the rotor as carefully as you did the distributor. Look for cracks, carbon tracks, breaks, and a burned, corroded or broken metal terminal. Replace a rotor showing even slight damage. Be sure you get the one for your distributor. Not all rotors are the same size although they may be of the same configuration.

8. You may see some sort of cover over the distributor. In some cars this is a radio frequency interference (RFI) shield; it's a dust shield. But it has no bearing on distributor performance. Remove screws and lift each half of the shield off.

9. Find out if the centrifugal advance mechanism is functioning properly. The centrifugal advance is the mechanism, consisting of counterweights and springs, that alters ignition timing by means of centrifugal force as engine speed varies.

The mechanism may be in full view, sitting on top of the distributor shaft. If it is, twist the two parts of the assembly until they are wide apart (Fig. 5). Let them go.

If the parts spring back together, you can proceed to the next step. If not, then the reason for the trouble—whether weak springs, a damaged mechanism or binding distributor shaft or bearings—should be found.

In other distributors, the centrifugal advance is positioned beneath the breaker plate, and you can't get to it. To find out if it's working properly, place the rotor back on the distributor shaft, twist the shaft about 5° in the direction of rotation, and let go. Action should be snappy.

The direction of rotation can be determined by having someone crank the engine for a second or two as you watch in which direction the rotor turns.

10. The spark advance mechanism should be tested to get an idea if it's working. The unit is a vacuum-operated chamber which is usually attached to the outside of the distributor (Fig. 5). It controls ignition timing during acceleration, causing spark to occur earlier.

Place your finger against the rear of the distributor breaker point assembly, pressing against the assembly in a direction which is opposite that of shaft rotation. This causes the distributor point base plate (breaker plate) to turn.

At the same time, hold the tip of your finger tightly against the opening of the spark advance chamber to which the vacuum hose was attached (remove the hose). Release the point assembly. The breaker plate should not move. If it does, replace the spark advance chamber.

Now remove your finger from the opening. The breaker plate should swivel smartly back to its original position. If it doesn't, the cause of the bind (weak spark advance unit or damage to the distributor itself) should be found.

11. Remove the breaker points from the distributor for examination. It is difficult in most cases to get a good look at the points with them still in the distributor.

Loosen the terminal screw on the breaker point assembly and remove the coil-to-distributor primary wire. At this point, let's stop a minute and give that primary wire a very close examination, especially where it enters the distributor housing (Fig. 6). You may spot a potential problem which, when it occurs, baffles car owners and mechanics alike.

A reason for sudden ignition failure, leading to stalling when the car is on the road, is worn primary wire insulation. Exposed bare wires short themselves against the metal distributor housing, which interrupts the flow of current.

Replace a badly frayed coil-to-distributor primary wire.

Also disconnect the condenser pigtail wire between the condenser and breaker points. If this wire is damaged, replace the condenser.

12. There is no need to install new distributor points unless they are needed (Fig. 7). Spread the two points apart and examine surfaces. If points have an overall gray color and/or show slight roughness or pitting, pass a clean fine-cut contact point file between them one time only. Wipe point surfaces with a clean lint-free rag which has been moistened with alcohol.

Cautions: Do not try to file points smooth. The purpose of filing is to remove scale and dirt. Be sure the file is neither greasy nor dirty since contaminants will be passed on to point surfaces.

And don't use emery cloth or sandpaper for cleaning points. Particles will embed themselves, causing arcing and rapid deterioration of point surfaces.

13. If distributor points are severely burned or very rough, replace them with a new set. However, there is usually a reason why points get this way if they have failed within, say, 10,000 miles. Unless the condition is found and corrected, new points may also fail prematurely.

The usual causes for rapid point failure include a weak condenser, weak contact point spring tension, improper point gapping, an overlubricated distributor cam that is tossing lubricant onto point surfaces, malfunctioning voltage regulator, bad resistor, and oil or crankcase vapors that are seeping into the distributor housing and affecting points.

14. If you have to replace contact points, replace the condenser, too. The two work as a team. Unscrew the condenser mounting screw and lift the part out of the distributor (Fig. 7).

15. Wipe the breaker plate clean.

16. Lubricate the cam. Some distributors are equipped with a cam lubricator wick that you should replace with a new one (Fig. 8). Do not relubricate an old wick. You'll cause more trouble than a new one is worth.

Distributors that don't have wick lubricators should have one drop of distributor cam lubricant applied to *one* lobe of the cam (Fig. 9). The drop of lubricant should be equivalent in size to the head of a match.

17. Place the condenser into position on the breaker plate and tighten its mounting screw.

18. Install the breaker point assembly, screwing it securely to the breaker plate.

19. Now, reconnect the primary ignition and condenser pigtail wires, but make certain that the terminal clips aren't in contact with the breaker plate. This will cause a short. Tuck the two wires carefully into the housing, but see to it that they aren't touching any moving parts (Fig. 10).

20. Gap points, using a distributor point (flat) feeler gauge. The purpose of gapping is to bring point adjustment inside the ball park. When the distributor is reassembled and buttoned up, points should be finely adjusted by means of a dwell meter (see below).

To gap points, set the rubbing block of the breaker point assembly on a lobe (raised part) of the cam. You may have to tease the cam into place by having someone in the car crank the ignition in short spurts until the rubbing block ends up resting on a high point of the cam.

You might want to consider the purchase of a remote starter switch, which allows you to crank the engine from beneath the hood. It's a handy device to have around, especially if there's no one available to give you a hand.

In order to gap points, you will need the specification for your distributor. This may be obtained from a tune-up decal which may be pasted somewhere in the engine compartment. You can also get the spec from a service manual or owner's manual.

The gap specification is generally given as a range—for example, .016–.019 inch. If points are new, gap them to the maximum specification (.019 inch). If points are used, gap them to the minimum specification (.016 inch).

Use a feeler gauge that's the same thickness as the specified point gap setting (.016 inch, for instance). Insert the gauge between the points.

Caution: Make sure the feeler gauge is absolutely clean. Hold the gauge straight. Don't twist it. The measurement will not be accurate if you do (Fig. 11).

If you don't feel slight resistance on the gauge as you slide it back and forth between points (if the gauge moves too loosely or rubs hard), points have to be adjusted in one of two ways. One way is by means of an adjustment notch in the point assembly, near a mounting screw. Loosen this screw, insert a screwdriver in the notch, and twist until points open or close to the desired setting (Fig. 12). Keep the gauge in position, testing until the proper gap is attained. Then tighten the mounting screw and doublecheck to make certain the gap is as specified. The point assembly may instead have a point adjustment screw. Insert an Allen wrench in the screw head and turn the screw until the desired setting is attained. Keep the feeler gauge in place, testing as you go along.

21. Finish distributor tune-up by installing the RFI or dust shield, if one is used, and rotor. If the rotor is the type that fits on the distributor shaft without being held by screws, apply two or three drops of SAE 10 or 20 engine oil directly to the inside of the distributor shaft. Make certain no oil drips into the distributor housing.

Reinstall the distributor cap securely and replace cables. Be certain that each cable is inserted into its proper tower.

To seat cables properly, squeeze cable boots as you insert the terminal into the tower to release trapped air (Fig. 13). Make sure cables are firmly seated. If they aren't, arcing may occur, damaging the distributor cap and terminals.

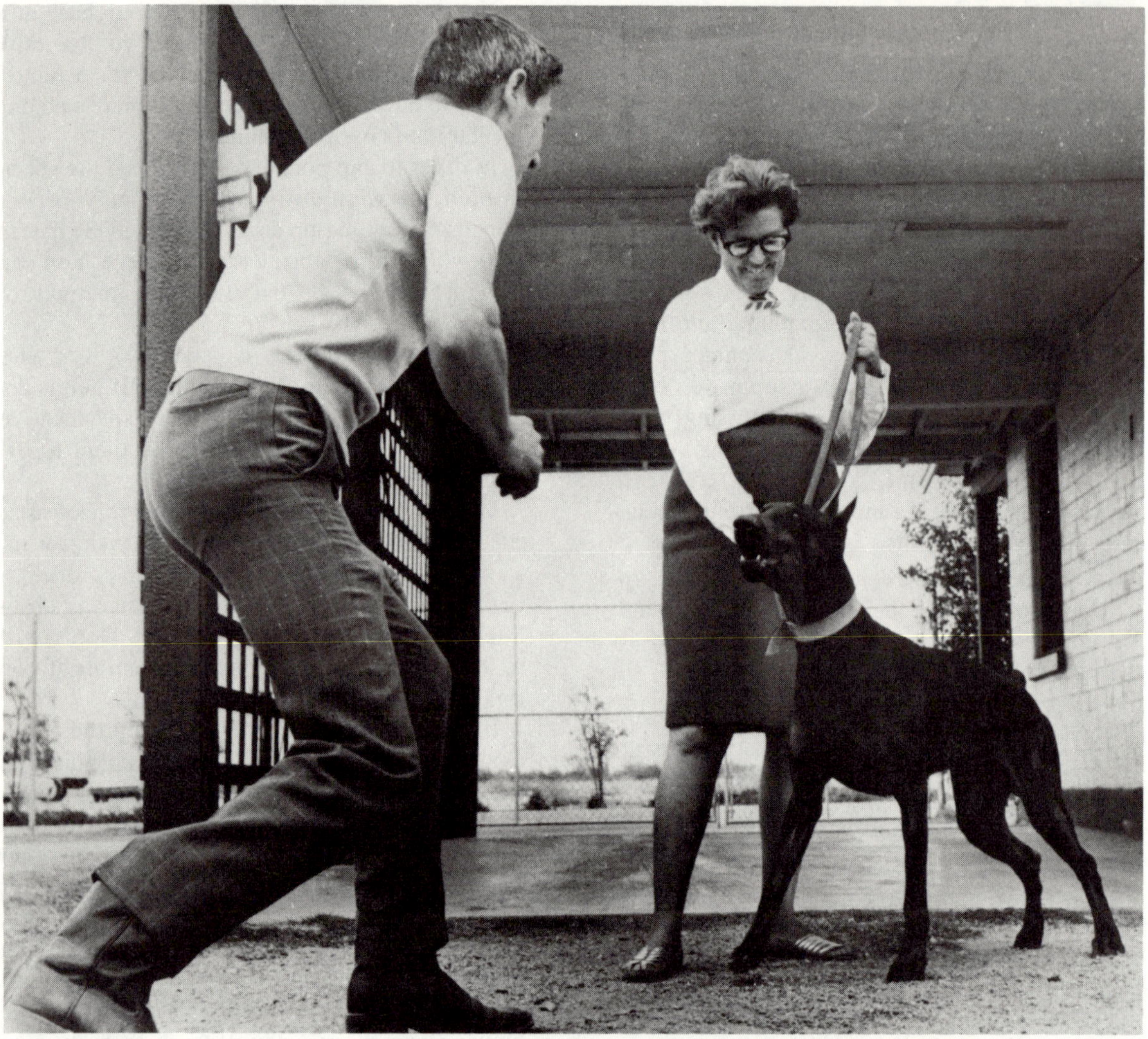

Training a dog entirely on your own usually isn't the best way to do a good job. Hire an expert or take group obedience lessons for both you and the dog. Your dog will become less of a pest and more of a pet

You can have a well-trained dog

By LEE COE

AS THE CRIME RATE soars, many worried citizens are buying dogs for protection. But too often, new dog owners end up with dogs that are not pets, but pests.

To be sure, a dog can be an ideal protector and companion. But where many owners go wrong is in the selection and training of their dogs. As a result, they live with animals that are ill-mannered and uncontrolled, that tug on the leash when walked, jump on neighbors, and occasionally nip a visitor. Such a pet is more a nuisance than it is a companion.

Would the owner be better off with a professionally trained guard dog? Not really. Such dogs—used by the military, police and security

SEE ALSO
Bird feeders . . . Birdhouses . . . Burglar proofing . . . Hunting

agencies—are taught to attack, and to respond only to commands given by their trainer. This can cause unexpected problems.

Consider Duke, a German shepherd assigned to guard duty in an Ohio gas station. The dog took his job so seriously that even after being shot three times by would-be thieves, he pressed his attack until they fled. When police arrived, he refused to allow them to enter the station until his owner came and ordered him away.

Professional dog trainers are well aware of the dangers inherent in giving a guard dog to the average family. Instead, they suggest a well-trained compromise that will be the companion and pet that 90 percent of the new dog owners today have in mind, but seldom get.

One reason for their disappointment is poor selection. Most dogs will instinctively protect what they feel they "own"—your family, house and surrounding area. Size doesn't make much difference. Even the toy breeds will make enough racket to scare most strangers away.

But when choosing a dog, remember that many American canines are overbred. Steadiness and reliability, the most desirable qualities in a pet, are often sacrificed for physical standards needed to win blue ribbons at dog shows.

It's best to deal with the owner of a reputable breeding kennel. He can be worth many times his fee in helping to select the best individual dog for your family, rather than just a fashionable breed.

Remember, protection comes automatically to a dog, whatever the breed. The key is obedience, and that's what the owner has to add, since almost any dog can be taught to obey.

If you start with a pup, he should be taught to *come, sit, stay* and understand the word *no*.

Trainers urge that a dog always be called by his name when given commands. When he responds, a professional praises the dog and occasionally rewards him with a tidbit.

Teaching a pup to sit is simply a matter of holding him by the collar, saying his name, then adding the word *sit* while pushing his hindquarters down.

To emphasize disapproval, the word *no* may be accompanied with a cuff. A rolled-up news-

A WELL-TRAINED dog will remain seated at his owner's foot (left) regardless of the distraction, until released. Instructors combine control with leash and hand signals (center) to teach dog to lie down. Even without leash, disciplined dog will walk beside owner's leg (right).

paper is better than the owner's hand. The point is to frighten the animal, and he may not fear the hand that also rewards him with petting. Never wait to discipline a dog. When he does something wrong, correct him immediately because the dog must associate discipline with wrongdoing.

When a pup is six to seven months old, he's ready for formal training by a professional able to instruct owner and dog to work as a team. Obedience training on an individual basis costs about $25 a week and takes an average of 10 weeks. A cheaper way is to join a group class.

Many organizations such as the YMCA and the American Kennel Club sponsor obedience courses. They usually consist of one class a week for 10 weeks, but such courses frequently cost only one-tenth as much as individual lessons.

John Webb, an Arizona trainer with over 30 years of teaching experience, estimates that about half the owners who attend a group course graduate with an obedient pet. Another 25 percent see a marked improvement in their pet's response to commands. The remainder will note little, if any, progress.

Courses are designed to teach the owner how to train his dog to come when called, walk to heel, sit or lie down on command, and remain in position when told to stay.

Professionals stress that commands must be given in a clear, forceful tone. Orders spoken in a timid way sound like suggestions, and a dog will usually ignore them. At the same time, teachers emphasize that firmness should not be confused with roughness, and they advise owners to use no more force than necessary to get the dog to respond. The first command demonstrated in most group training classes is *heel*. Placing the dog in position at his left leg, the instructor pulls the untrained animal's head up to get his attention while speaking his name and giving him the order *heel*. As he gives the command, the trainer steps forward, moving his left leg first to give the dog the idea of motion. Then he jerks the leash.

Owners following the instructor's example soon find that a quick jerk is more effective than a steady pull which the dog resists. After a few tugs, a dog learns that the tugging will stop if he continues to move forward beside his owner.

At a second session, instructors lead the class through the command *sit*. The owner walks his dog at *heel*. Upon stopping, he gives the command *sit*, and pushes down on his dog's hindquarters. A halt-sit habit means the dog

HAND SIGNALS are a vital part of a dog's training, reinforcing an instructor's verbal commands.

GENTLE TUGS on a leash and a soft push on the hindquarters help a dog understand the order *sit*.

A DOG CAN be more than a pal. Sharpen his protective instincts, and he'll be a loyal guardian for young or old.

must rise before charging off, giving the owner more time to correct him.

Down is an extension of *sit* and is taught next. The pet is placed in a sitting position with the leash coming from under his chin and looped under one of the trainer's feet. The trainer, saying *down*, pushes his foot to the ground, forcing the dog's head to follow. Simultaneously, the trainer puts firm pressure on the animal's shoulders, pressing him down.

Professionals warn that dogs often confuse *sit* and *down* at first, and urge pupils to be patient, and to continue to demonstrate the two commands until the dog has learned what the difference is.

stay is important but difficult

One of the most important orders taught in any class is *stay*. It is also one of the most difficult, and usually requires two persons working together—one holding the leash and the other enticing the dog. After having the dog sit, the owner places his right palm in front of the dog's nose and says *stay*. He then moves away until the dog tries to join him. At this moment, the trainer who holds the leash tugs back so that the animal resumes his sitting position.

If the dog cannot be repositioned, the instructor goes through the drill again until the dog understands the command. Eventually, a hand signal will be sufficient, and the owner can practice without another person.

Probably the most necessary command, the easiest to teach, and the hardest to enforce off-leash is *come*. In group classes, owners place their dogs in the sit position, then walk to the end of the leash—wait a moment—then say the dog's name and the command *come*, at the same time giving a gentle tug on the leash. When the dog responds properly from this position, he may be put on a long leash—a 50-foot clothesline is good—and permitted to wander around. Then he is called by his name and ordered to come.

Dog owners in a group class are always urged to work their pet daily for at least 15 to 20 minutes on a leash. Without day-after-day practice, dogs forget what they've learned. Continual work with the dog in all phases of his training will reinforce his responses until he is considered to be reliable enough to work without a leash.

Owners should also work a dog off-leash in an enclosed area until sure their pet will not run away. And they should always run their pet through the entire command routine before removing the leash.

Even a well-trained older dog should be run through the command series occasionally on a leash to keep his responses from getting sloppy.

But even well-trained dogs can get out-of-hand at times. Overly friendly dogs often jump up on people to show their enthusiasm. This can be easily handled. When the dog jumps up, place your knee firmly against his chest and shove him backwards, saying *no* at the same time. Stepping on the dog's hind toes is equally effective.

strong discipline controls barking

Excessive barking can also be controlled, especially if discipline is begun early, by holding the dog's mouth closed and firmly saying *no*. A dog must bark sufficiently to warn of an intruder, but he should obey his owner's command to be quiet once the alarm is sounded.

If your dog doesn't show enough protective qualities, there are ways a professional trainer can rouse this instinct. But experts caution that this should not be done by the dog owner because he may end up with an overly protective pet who could be dangerous.

Aging dogs can be trained as well as young ones, but it's more difficult. Often, a professional trainer has to be called in to make the older pet socially acceptable, but there is no guarantee this will work unless an owner changes his own permissive personality.

The behavior of a dog often reflects the personality and attitudes of his owner. The choice between a pet and a pest is largely up to you. Today's cute puppy will be tomorrow's 100-pound nuisance to adults unless he's taught to obey by you or a competent instructor. Enrolling yourself and your dog in an obedience class or lessons is the surest way to have a respected—and respecting—pet.

How to repair your doorbell

A malfunctioning doorbell can be a real nuisance for your family and guests. You can repair it yourself with some simple tools such as a circuit tester and a continuity tester

THOUGH A DOORBELL setup is one of the easiest-to-understand mechanical systems in a typical home, a malfunctioning system is often neglected because the average home handyman thinks the service job is beyond his skills. The fact is a do-it-yourselfer easily can determine and correct a faulty system. But you do need an understanding of the basics of a doorbell system and some rather common "tools." The "tools" consist of common household articles like lighter fluid, cotton swabs and fine-grit sandpaper, plus a pocket continuity tester.

You should be aware that there is a difference between a line tester (for 110-v. branch-circuit testing) and a continuity tester. Both testers light up to show whether the part (or system) is working—*but a continuity tester is for low amperage only*. And it must be used with electric current off. Continuity testers range in price from about $2 to $5 at hardware and electrical-supply stores.

The photo below shows the three doorbell components: door button, transformer and chime box. The step-down transformer lowers the household current from 115 v. to a doorbell working voltage of approximately 16 v.—enough to produce a strong magnetic field in the chime box terminal block when the circuit is completed by the doorbell button. A chime box is designed for various tones: chimes, buzzing or ringing, depending on the model.

When the doorbell button is pressed, a circuit

SEE ALSO
**Electrical wiring . . . Home improvement . . .
House numbers . . . Soldering . . .
Testers, continuity . . . Wiring, electrical**

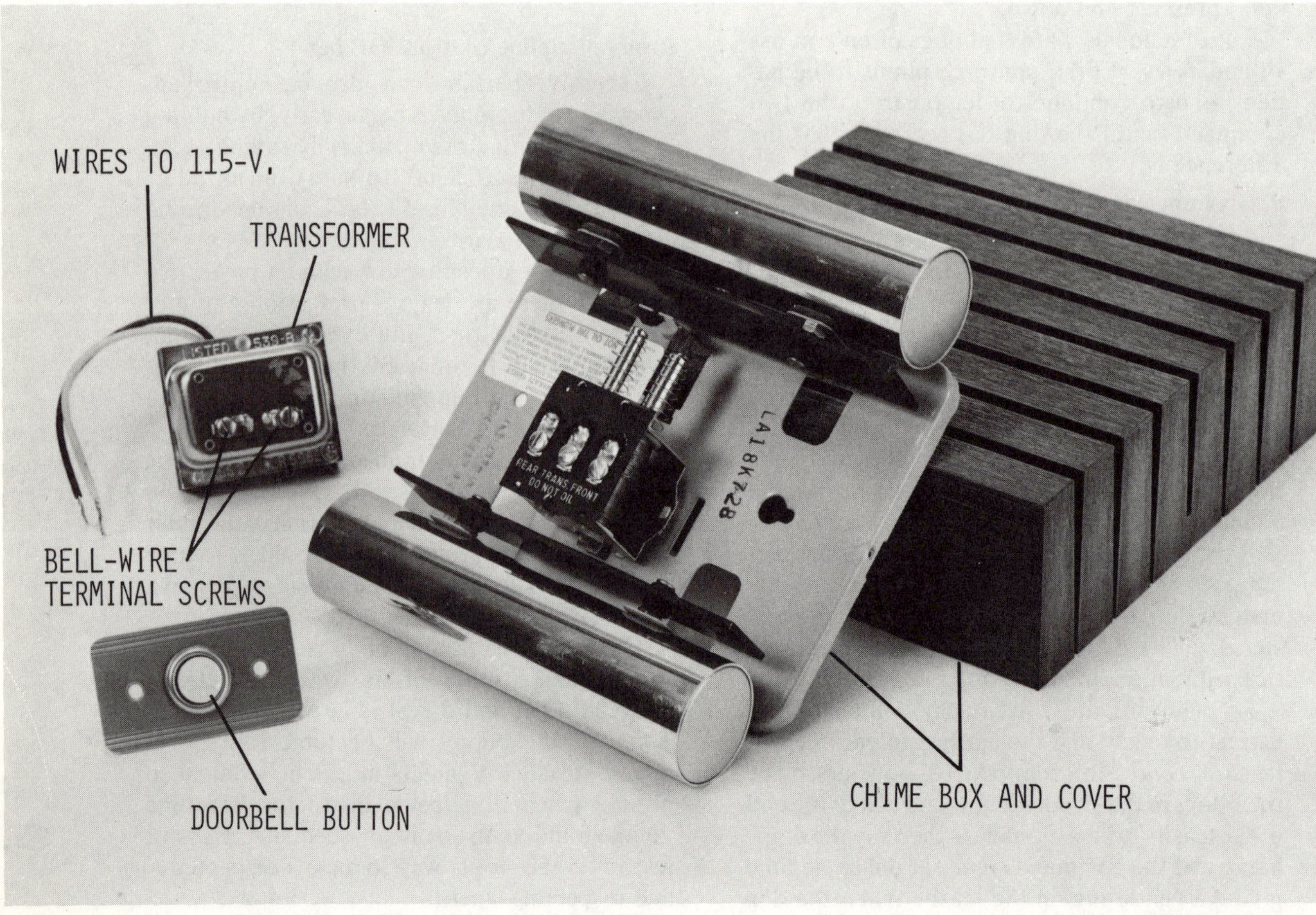

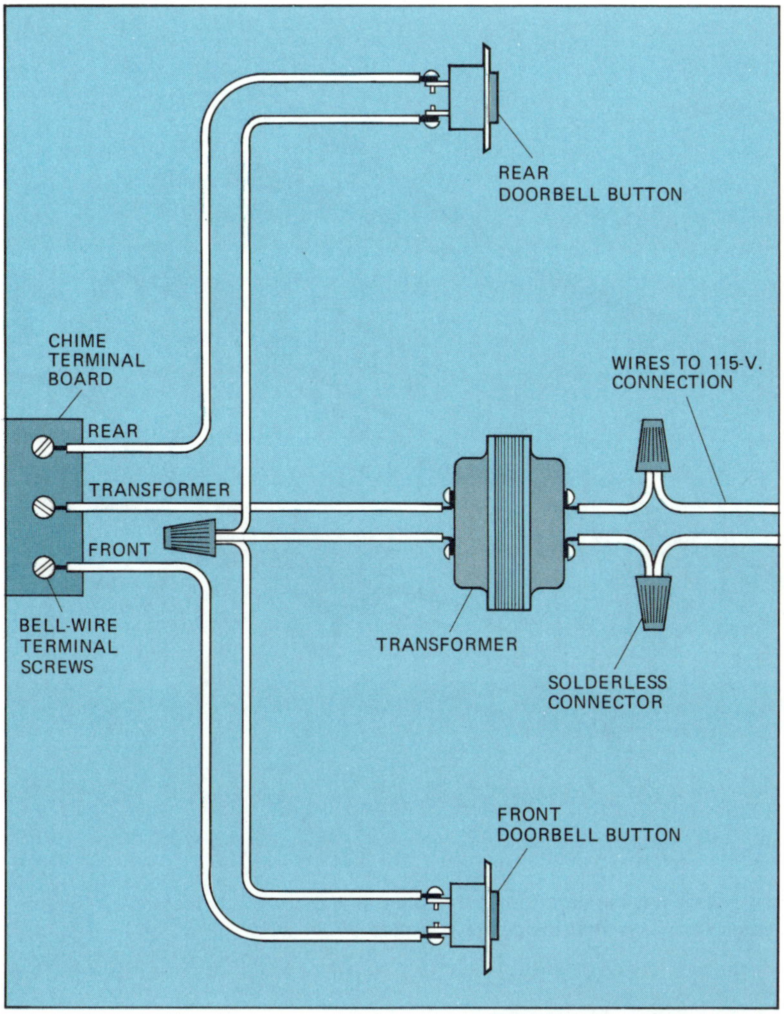

BUZZERS AND doorbells require low-voltage electricity through a transformer hookup. The transformer reduces the 120-v. current to voltage desired. In system at left, front and back door-chime hookup is accomplished by connecting wires as shown. Caution: Make certain that power is off when wiring the transformer to a 110-v.

continued

BASIC COMPONENTS of doorbell/chime system are easier to understand than most homeowners suspect. The system appearing on the facing page is made by Nutone (Model LA-18 with a teakwood chime-box cover).

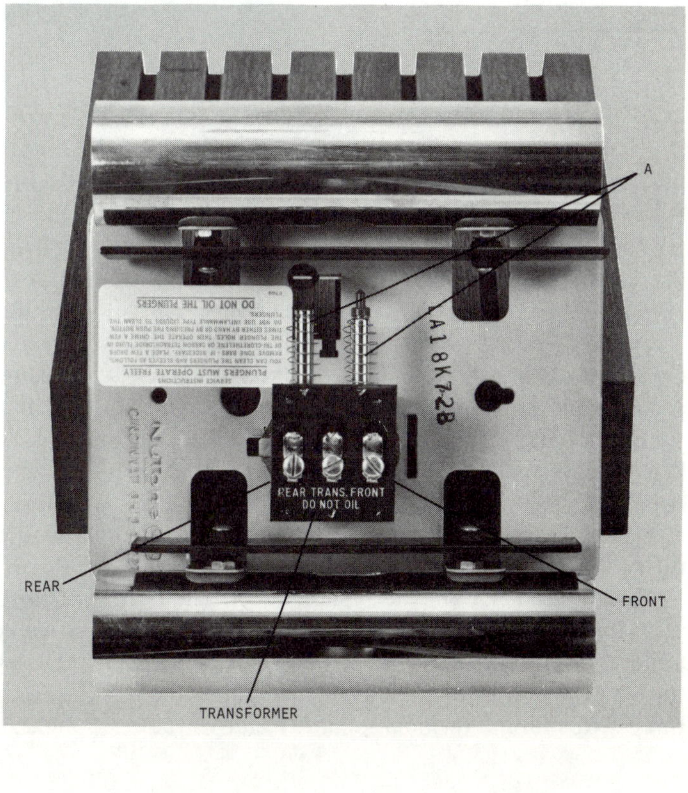

THREE SCREWS on chime-box terminal are easily accessible for making connections. The vertical plungers marked A, directly above the terminal screw board, should *never be oiled.*

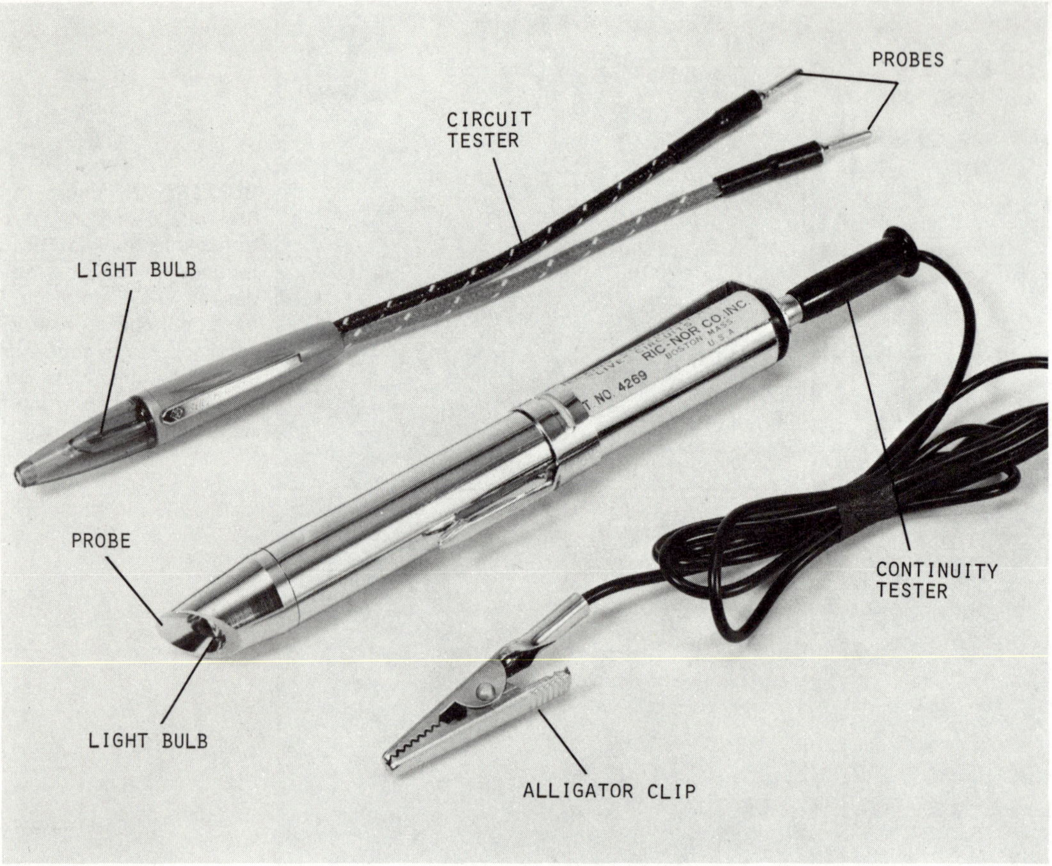

TWO TESTERS that you should always have in your toolbox are circuit and continuity testers. Whenever using the continuity tester *be sure* that the power is turned off.

doorbell repair, continued

is completed at the chime-box terminal board. For example, if the front doorbell button is pressed, there will exist a voltage of 16 v. across the terminals marked *Trans*. and *Front*. This voltage creates a magnetic field in this terminal box which pulls a striker rod through its internal hole, causing it to hit one of the sound bars and produce the sound (something like a "ding"). When the button is released, the circuit is broken, the magnetic field at the terminal board collapses and the spring tension on the striker rod snaps the rod to the other sound bar producing a "dong."

Testing sequence for the system doesn't matter: Most often, however, the problem will be in either the chime box or doorbell button. Remove the cover from the chime box and disconnect the three wires on the terminal board. Remove the two screws holding the electromagnet to the box and carefully lift out the terminal box, striker rods and springs. With a paper clip or nail file, pick the spring off of the striker rod, being extra careful not to stretch or deform it. Using cotton swabs soaked with lighter fluid, thoroughly clean the striker rods and striker-rod holes in the terminal block until they begin to shine. Reassemble springs on striker rods.

A very quick test can now be made of the chime-box terminal board to determine if the windings in each striker-rod hole are intact. Place the tester clip on the terminal marked *Trans*. and the continuity tester probe on either *Front* or *Rear* terminal. If the windings are good, the tester will light. Check both front and rear terminals in this manner. If the tester does not light, the fault is in the chime-box terminal block

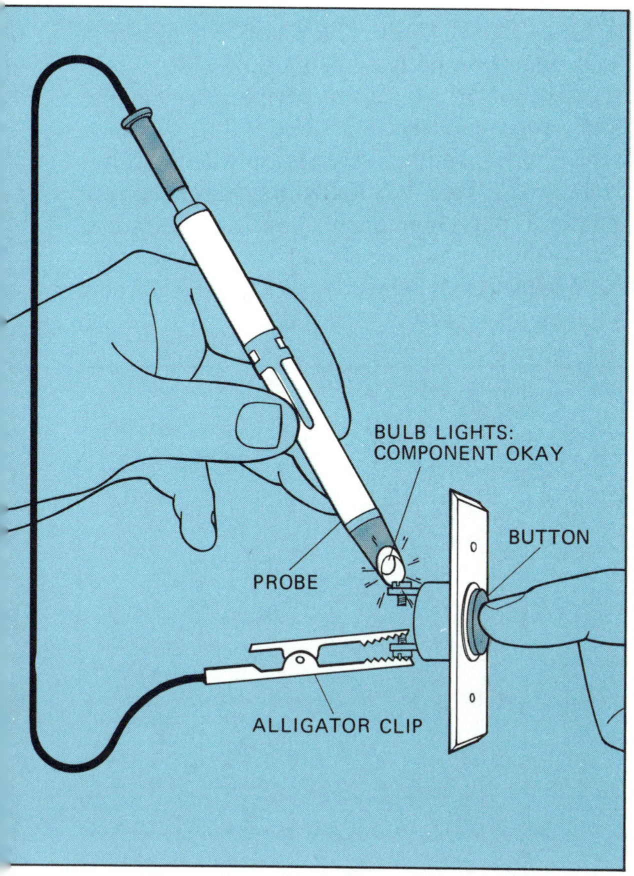

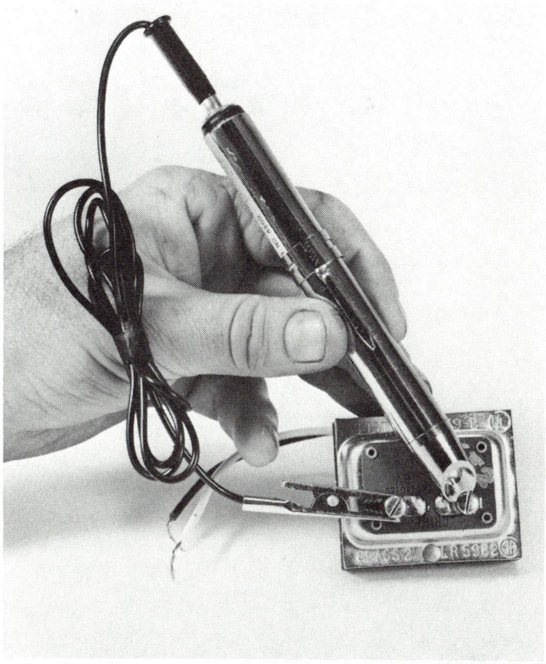

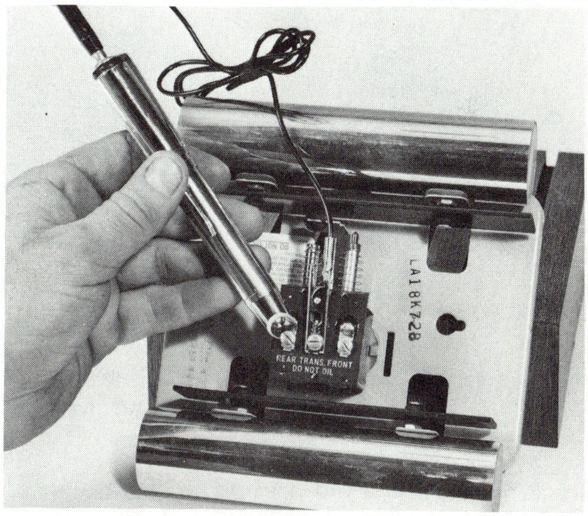

DOORBELL BUTTON is checked by placing alligator clip on one screw, body of continuity tester on second. If tester lights when button is depressed, the button is okay.

TRANSFORMER is checked for continuity by placing alligator clip on one screw, tester probe on the second.

TO CHECK chime box, alligator clip is placed on center screw; front and rear-door terminals are then tested.

and it should be replaced. While the cover is off, it's a good idea to clean up the sound bars with lighter fluid.

To test the doorbell button, remove the two wires connected to the button. Place the continuity tester probe on one screw terminal and the clip on the other. Press the button to close the circuit. If the button is good, the tester will light. A spring(s)-loaded button (the type shown in the photos) cannot be repaired and must be replaced. A copper-strip button (usually rectangular in shape) *can* be repaired. To do it, first disassemble the button. Then, clean the copper contacts with fine sandpaper; also clean the copper in the terminal block of the button. Reassemble and test again. If it still doesn't work, replace it.

Before installing any new or repaired button, clean the bell wire (coming from the hole in the wall).

The last component to check is the transformer. *Caution: At your house service panel, first turn off the power to the transformer.* Next, place the continuity tester probe on one terminal screw and the clip on the other. If the transformer is good, the tester will light. A transformer that tests bad *must be replaced.*

The drawing on page 1019 shows the complete wiring diagram of a two-bell system. If rewiring is necessary, use this as a guide. You are well advised to take the time to read through installation instructions to assure you completely understand them. Although some chime-box mechanisms may differ slightly from the model shown, the test procedures and the repairs will remain the same.

How to hang a door

IT TAKES CARPENTRY skill to hang a door so it swings properly—opening and closing as it should. But the average handyman, armed with knowledge, the right tools and a little common sense, can accomplish the job successfully. Here, we supply the know-how (architectural standards plus techniques). Now it's up to you to supply the common sense and muscle. Once you have hung a door correctly, you have acquired a valuable basic skill.

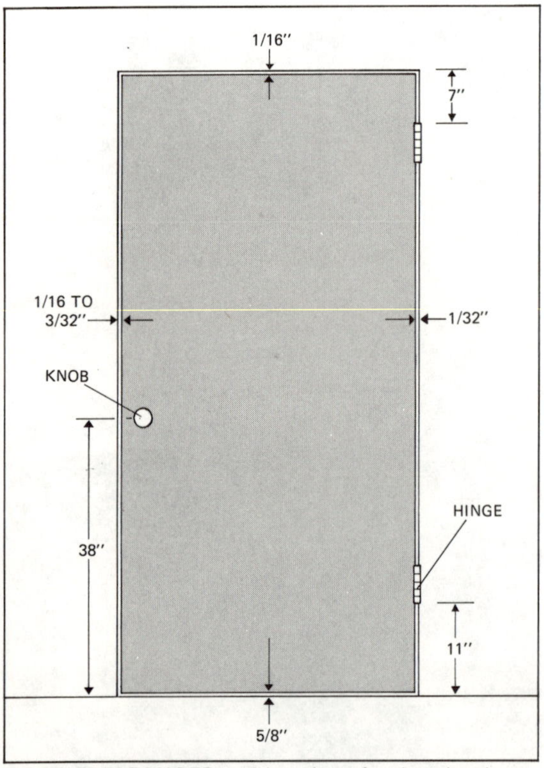

DOOR CLEARANCES and locations for door hardware are standard, as shown. If a third hinge is needed (exterior door), space it midway between top and bottom hinges. On exterior doors, allow clearance at bottom for threshold.

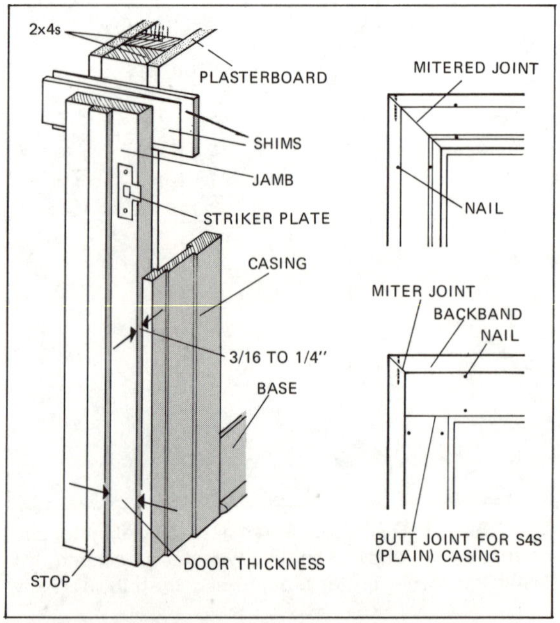

TO SET AN INTERIOR door frame (jamb), wedges or shingles are used between side jambs and the rough opening. When jambs are set flush and plumb, the wedges are driven tightly and jambs are nailed to studs with 8d finishing nails through the shingles. Casings are nailed to the framing studs and the jamb with 8d and 6d nails, respectively. Two types of casings are shown. Use mitered corners on shaped type, 4d finishing nails to hold miters closed tightly.

SEE ALSO

Entryways . . . Hinges . . . Locks, door . . . Security, home . . . Sliding glass doors . . . Winterizing, homes

THERE ARE TWO TYPES of interior doors—panel and flush. Thickness is 1⅜ in. (exterior doors, 1¾ in.) and they come in varying widths and heights. Flush doors have plywood facings, light-weight cores; panel doors have solid stiles and rails with plywood panel inserts.

Cedar shakes over old roof

My asphalt-shingle roof is nearing the end of its normal life and I want to install a cedar-shake roofing. The deck, of boards laid edge-to-edge, seems to be in good condition. Do I need to take off the old shingles or can I lay the shakes over them? Should I replace the felt undercovering? If so, with what?—N.O., Ohio.

I would remove the old shingles—everything right down to the decking—then go over the decking to make sure no boards are loose or cupped. The latter should be replaced and the former nailed securely. Any deck boards that seem deteriorated, rotted, full of knots or otherwise defective due to aging should also be replaced. It's important to provide a solid nailing surface for shakes.

While you can use an ordinary felt undercovering, or liner, this may tend to prevent the underside of shakes from drying. I would, rather, install the "breather-type" liner usually recommended for use under shakes. This should be available through your local building materials dealer, and laid according to the manufacturer's recommendations. If you do the job yourself, be especially careful to avoid splits or hammer dents and make sure you use the right nails.

Unwinding lipped door

I have a grandfather's clock with a lipped access door so warped it can't be closed easily. The door is in one piece, without glass, and has two hinges and a lock. I want to preserve the original, but how can I get rid of the warp?—G.M., Va.

By "warp" you mean the "wind" or twist; that is, if you remove the door and lay it on a flat surface, it will rock when touched on alternate high corners. To eliminate it, run saw kerfs diagonally across the back of the door from low corner to low corner. Space kerfs ½ to ¾ in. apart for a width of 3 to 4 in., depending on the door's size and width. If you have no table saw, try to enlist the help of a friend who has one. You'll have to improvise a guide and then space the cuts by moving the ripping fence after each pass. Ordinarily, the cuts should be run to a depth of ¾ in. or slightly less than the door thickness. As a rule, such cuts will relieve the stresses that produced the wind.

Lay the door on a flat surface, weight it down and rip thin strips that will just drop into the kerfs without wedging. Glue these into the strips and let the glue dry thoroughly. Then trim and sand the strips flush. You can color them to match the old wood by rubbing them with a combination of artists' oil colors.

Shades stay up

Several large window shades in my home won't stay down—they won't catch and hold in any position. The shades are not old, torn or discolored. What's wrong?—Mrs. R. M. Lamb, Chicago.

It is likely that the ratchet ends of the rollers have been filled with lint, or that the springs installed in them have loosened. Take the shades down, brush lint out of the ratchets and use the tines of an old fork to retighten the springs. If no parts are bent or missing, the shades should then work properly.

Veneer lifting

I've stripped a chest of drawers which is veneered. With the remover washed off, some of the veneer has come loose and the edges have lifted. What happened, and what do I do next?—R. Dewey, Tulsa, Okla.

It is quite possible that you dampened the glue under the veneer and, thus, softened it enough to make it let go in places. I'd try lifting the veneer with a sharp chisel, and forcing new glue underneath. Then clamp plywood on top, with wax paper in between, until the glue dries. If blisters result, slit each at its center, force glue through the slits underneath the veneer, and weight until dry.

The best shade tree

What would you suggest as the best shade tree to plant to provide maximum shade?—Ralf Cozzens, Indianapolis.

I'd plant sugar maple. It's a slow-growing hardwood to be sure, but if well cared for, it develops a spreading, symmetrical top and its autumn leaf coloring, in my opinion, is unrivaled. Make sure that you select a well developed, balled specimen and remember to ask your nurseryman for tips on planting it.

Paint peels from plaster patch

A roof leak has led to a plaster patch on a bedroom ceiling. I painted this patch with the same paint that was used originally on the ceiling. Now the paint is peeling. How can I solve this problem?—J.E. Snelling, Denver.

I'm afraid you didn't wait long enough for the plaster to dry thoroughly. This takes time, as much as two months or more, depending on local conditions. Scrape and sand off all the loose paint, wait another month or so, then apply an undercoater or shellac, and repaint it. You'll likely have no further trouble.

How to trim sticking doors

WHEN A DOOR MUST BE PLANED

When a door continues to stick even during dry weather and is hard to open, the only way to fix it is to plane it. Planing is done along the hinge edge of the door since you can't disturb the lock. Take down the door, remove its hinges and support it on edge. A wooden box is a good thing to clamp it to. If you must plane top and bottom, work from edge to center so you won't chip the corners.

■ EVER HAD a door bind so it wouldn't close, or it wouldn't swing over a thick, new carpet? Few homeowners haven't had these problems with doors—particularly binding, for most wood doors swell periodically. Sometimes they expand so much they never shrink back to their former size. When that happens, you have no recourse but to remove the door and plane it. Or you must trim it with a saw if it's binding on a carpet. Not all doors bind because of moisture. Sometimes one won't operate properly because the screws have worked loose in a hinge, allowing the door to droop enough so that it won't open and close the way it should.

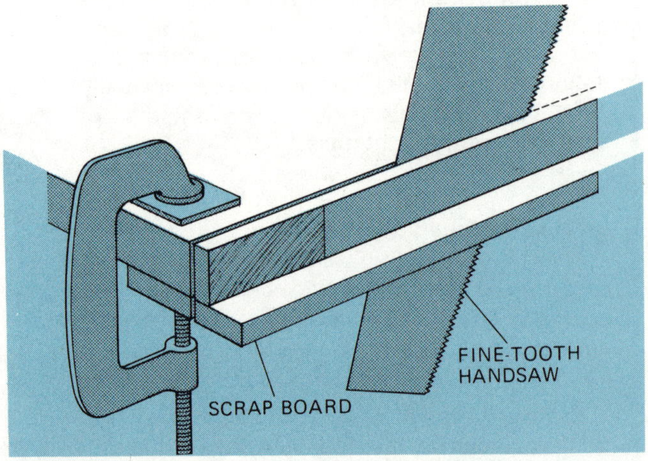

WHEN YOU HAVE TO SHORTEN A DOOR

When a new carpet is thicker than the old and a door drags on it, watch that you don't chip one side when you cut the door. Determine the amount you must take off, and draw a line across the door. Take the door down by knocking out the hinge pins, support it on a couple of padded sawhorses or boxes and clamp a scrap board to the underside of the door. The board not only prevents chipping the thin plywood facing on interior doors but helps keep the saw from running off the line when sawing as little as ¼ in. Use a fine-tooth saw.

WHEN A DOOR NEEDS SEALING

Doors usually swell during prolonged periods of rain, ice and snow. When the top and bottom edges of a door are not sealed, excessive moisture can enter the open end grain and cause the wood to expand and the door to widen. Common shellac is good for sealing the wood against moisture and it dries quickly, but you should wait for a dry spell; you don't want to seal the edges and trap any moisture that may be in the door at the time. Of course, to coat the bottom edge you must take the door down.

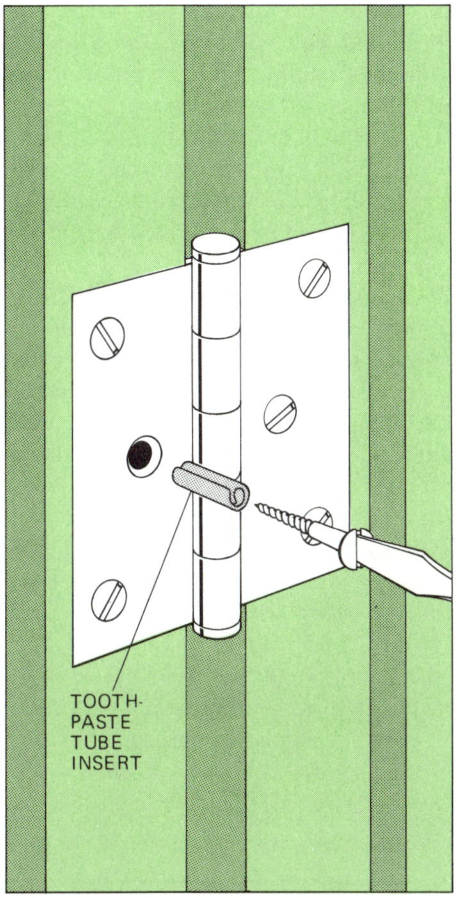

WHEN HINGES WORK LOOSE

Like anything that is used a great deal, a door that is opened and closed frequently puts a strain on the hinges that can eventually cause the door to bind. Usually you will find that a screw or two has worked loose, even to the point where it will no longer hold. When the trouble is found to be an enlarged hole, this hole must be shimmed. Sometimes a wooden matchstick and a little glue will do the trick, but an even better shim is one that's rolled from the soft metal of a toothpaste tube. Like a lead anchor, it will let the screw threads cut into the shim and spread it to fill the hole. Regular plastic screw plugs also can be used to shim an enlarged hole. In this case, the screw makes the plug expand and anchor itself tightly in the hole.

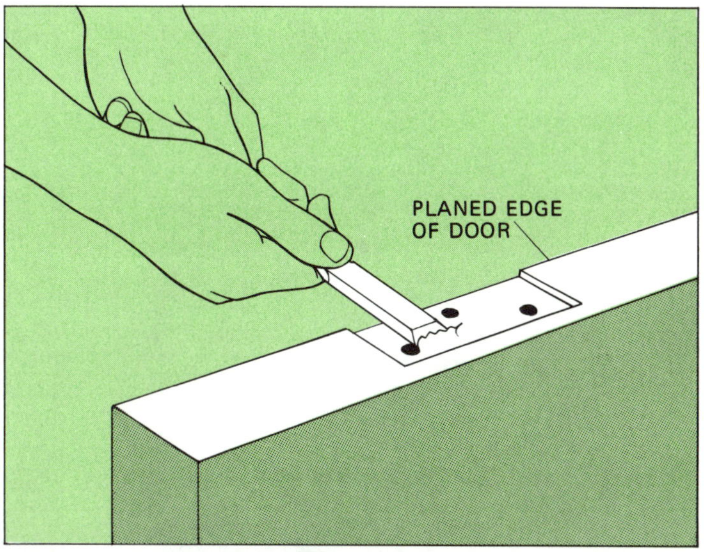

WHEN YOU HAVE TO PLANE OFF A LOT

When you have to plane off more than a little to relieve a binding door, you have to chisel the hinge pockets deeper to compensate for the amount you take off. Try to pare them an even amount. A properly set hinge leaf should be slightly deeper than flush. When the door has been planed enough to close properly, repaint the planed edge.

WHEN A DOOR DRAGS ON ITS THRESHOLD

If you can sand the bottom of a heavy exterior door that rubs on the threshold without removing it from its hinges, it's worth a try. A stunt that often does the trick is to work a sheet of coarse garnet paper under the door as shown above and then move the door back and forth. Little by little it will sand enough off to relieve the rubbing. When the dragging is beyond the sandpaper trick, you'll have to plane it.

SEE ALSO

**Burglar proofing . . . Clamps . . . Entryways . . .
Hinges . . . Locks, door . . . Remodeling . . .
Sliding glass doors . . .
Storm doors and windows . . . Winterizing, homes**

How to make dovetail joints

By ROSARIO CAPOTOSTO

A DOVETAIL with its flared sections is one of the most attractive woodworking joints. Its interlocking parts along with resulting increased gluing surfaces also give this joint great strength.

Laying out the joint accurately is all important and takes careful attention—both with hand and power tools.

laying out the joint

It's best to draw the dovetails on the board, cut them out, then use the piece as a pattern for tracing the outline of the pins on the mating member.

(Note: Although most dovetail joints end with partial pins at the outsides, I've also made the joints ending with partial tails, and have observed no weakness due to the variation.)

Use a sharp, hard lead pencil, or preferably a knife to mark the cutting lines. Make sure both boards are square.

Estimate the number of spaces needed on the first board to accommodate the pins in the second. To do this, first decide the width of the pins; a full pin should equal about a three-quarter thickness of the board. Multiply the pin width by 2½ to find the distance from center to center of the pins. Divide the board width by this distance and you will get the number of pins needed. However, since there are usually half pins (plus ⅛-in. width) at the outside, subtract 1 from the answer you get to allow for them.

Begin by marking off the extra ⅛-in. width of the partial pins on the board that will contain the tails. Depth of the cut-out spaces should equal the thickness of the mating board, so mark off that depth on edges and faces of the dovetail board. Actually, it's best to add 1/32 in. overall to allow for a final flush sanding to size.

To mark off the already determined center-to-center distance of the pins between the ⅛-in. borders, lay a ruler diagonally across the space until the dimension is easily divisible by the number of pins you want. Then with a square at the joint (edge of the board) draw parallel lines to mark the centers of the pins. Continue the lines on the end of the board. (See photos on page 1027.)

On the edge of the board mark off a 5/16-in.

SEE ALSO

Bench saws . . . Clamps . . . Drawers . . . Joinery . . . Miter boards . . . Miter joints . . . Moldings . . . Routers . . . Sanding . . . Shop tools . . . Table saws . . . Workbenches

Computing dovetail joints

CERTAIN PROPORTIONS are best to assure sturdy dovetail joints: 1. Plan the widest point on the pin face to be about three-quarters of the wood thickness. 2. Make the distance from center-to-center of the pins about 2½ times the pin width. 3. The two end pins are usually half the width plus ⅛ in. for strength. 4. Pins and tails can be of equal width, but some craftsmen prefer pins about one-third the width of the wide end of the tail and not less than ¼ in.

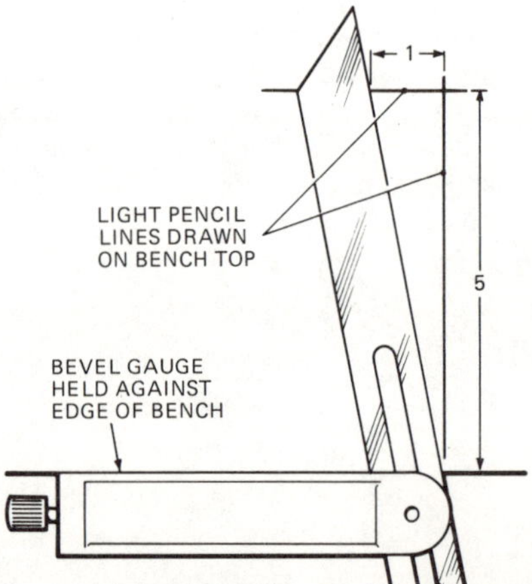

Determine 1° to 5° slope.

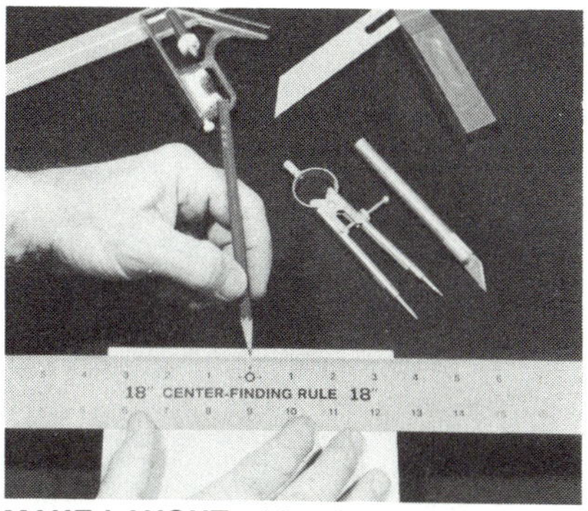

MAKE LAYOUT with ruler, square, bevel square, knife and dividers.

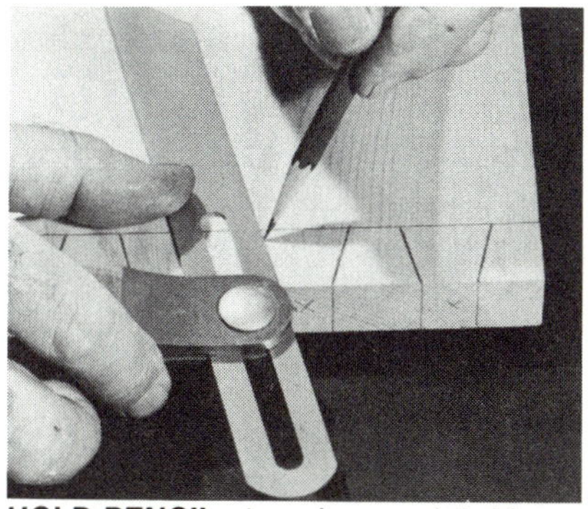

HOLD PENCIL at angle so point rides firmly against straightedge.

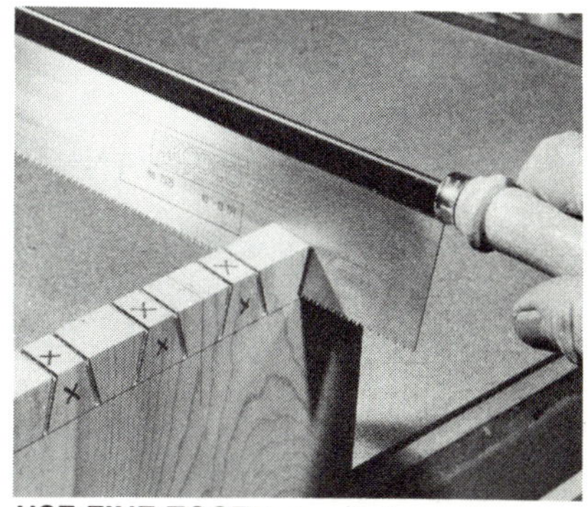

USE FINE-TOOTH dovetail saw to cut joints. Cut on waste side of lines.

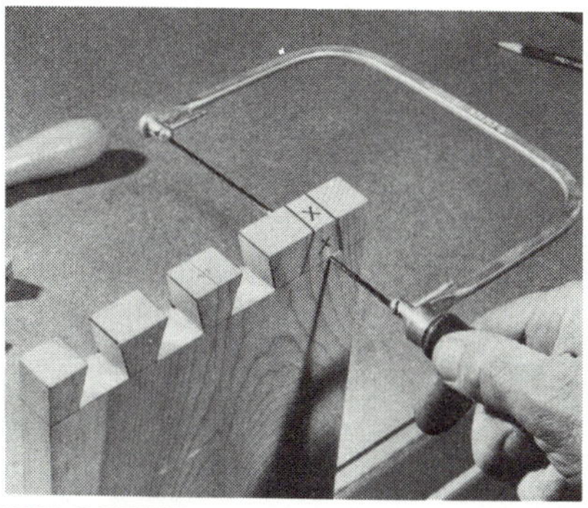

USE COPING saw to make the bottom cut that clears out the waste wood.

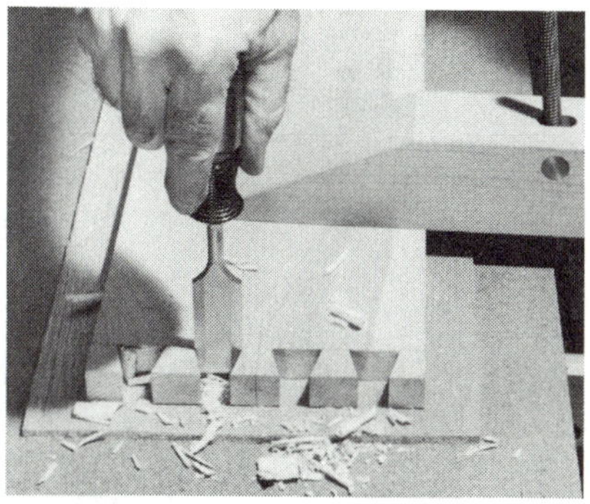

SHARP CHISEL dresses cuts to lines. Clamp and work against a scrap board.

TRACE TAILS with knife to outline pins. With a square carry lines to board face.

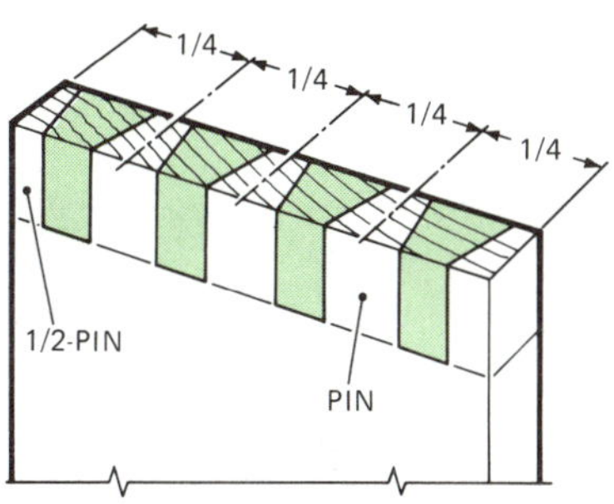

Board divided to make four tails.

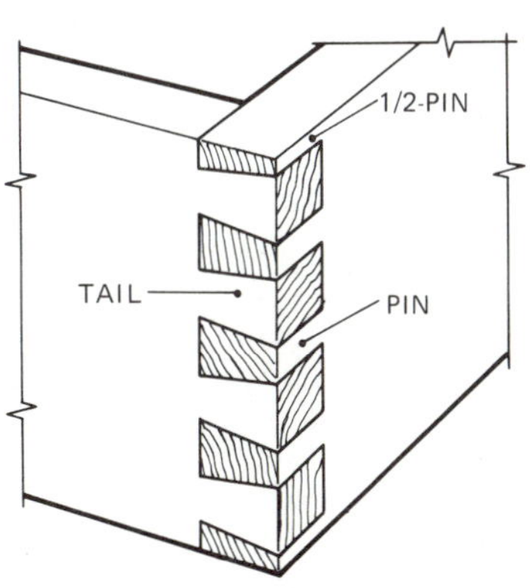

For strength, board with pins is drawer front, tails on sides.

THE FINISHED joint should fit snugly. Note partial tails here.

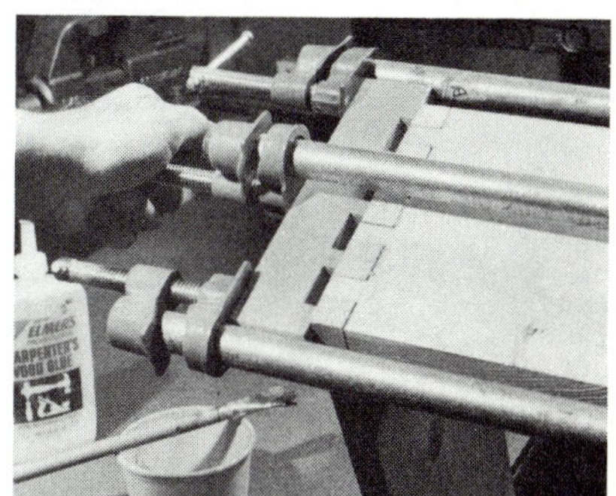

NOTCHED BLOCK bears clamp pressure *only against dovetails* when gluing.

FOR HALF-BLIND doves, cut tails, then saw pins at upward angle.

CLEAR WASTE with chisel and mallet on crossgrain, just chisel on endgrain.

Half-blind dovetails made with router

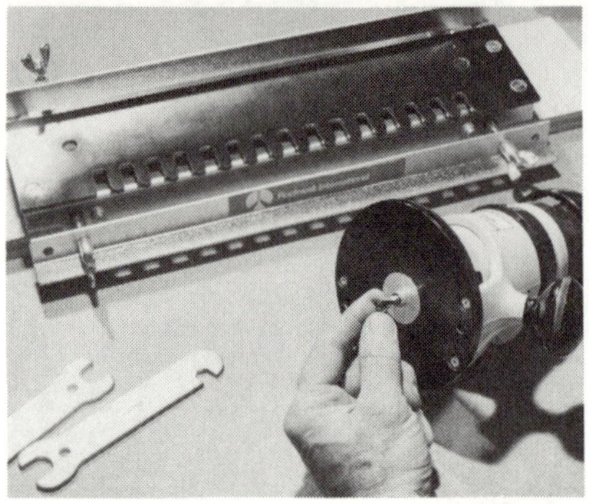

CUT HALF-BLIND doves with a router, template, base guide and dovetail bit.

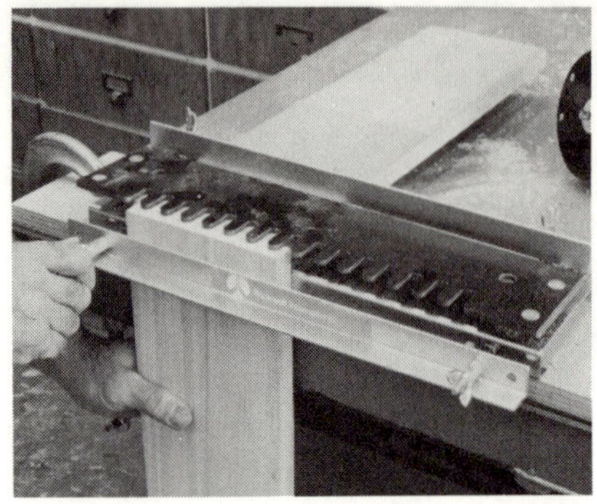

CLAMP SIDE and end member into the template with pieces butting each other.

Single dovetail made with table saw

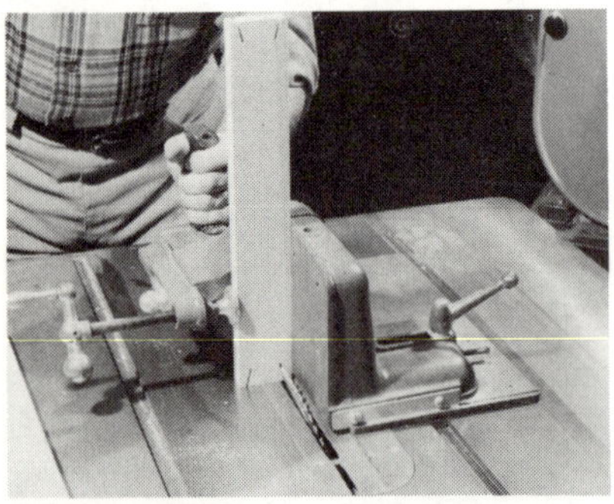

USE TENONING jig to make many cuts. Make first cut, then reverse piece.

TURN WORK perpendicular. Use miter gauge and clamped block to cut waste.

WITH HIGH stop block, set gauge at right, then left angles for pin cuts.

Half-lap dovetail made with radial saw

MAKE TWO straight cuts into each end. Set blade at angle to cut off waste.

REDUCE the face of the dovetail by making repeated passes of the saw.

ESTABLISH cutting lines by tracing them against tail overlap with knife.

width for each pin centered on the centering lines. Then set a bevel square to a 1° to 5° angle (as shown in the drawing on page 1026). Draw the sides of the pin spaces (which are the tapered sides of the tails). Cut out the space for the pins as follows, leaving the tails.

dovetails cut by hand

Secure the piece in a vise and use a fine-tooth back or dovetail saw to cut the tapers. Cut on the waste side of the line, leaving the line exposed.

Cut out the spaces between the pins and finish off with the chisels. This phase will be more tedious because you'll have to work the chisel into the angled bottom corners.

Test for fit frequently. A good joint will require Next use a coping saw to cut across the grain to remove the waste.

Use a razor-sharp chisel—the largest one that fits the opening—to trim the tails. Then clamp this section to the mating piece and use a *knife* to outline the pins.

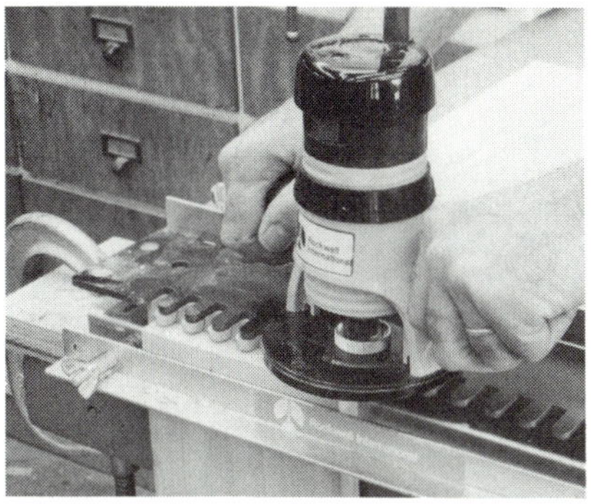

FEED router against template fingers to cut joint parts together.

RESULT: a perfect dovetail that could hardly be duplicated by hand.

ASSEMBLED half-blind routed dovetail. It's excellent for drawers, cabinets.

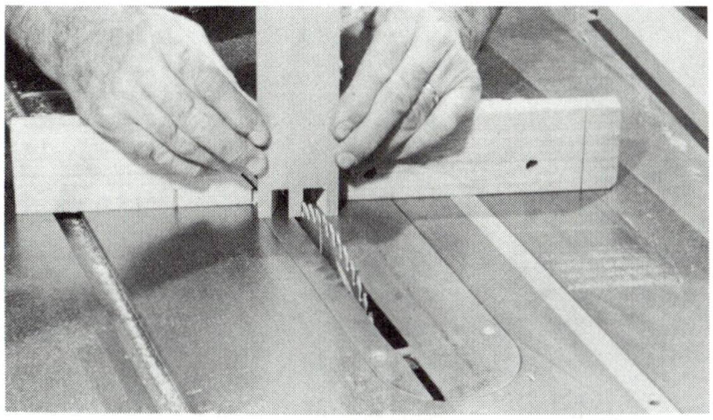

REMOVE THE WASTE between pins by repeated passes over the saw. Keep thumbs out of the blade path!

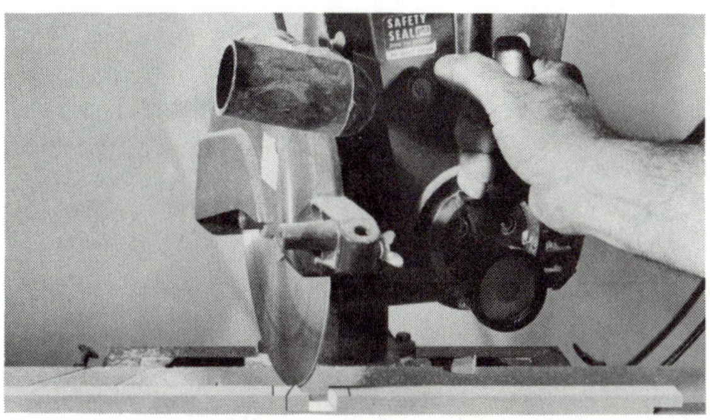

SET THE SAW arm at the required angle. Then raise the arm and make passes with an elevated blade.

light tapping with a hammer (over a scrap block). Apply glue to all surfaces and use a notched block that will bear pressure only over dovetail portions of the joint. Attach clamps. Sand surfaces flush after the glue has dried.

half-blind dovetails hand-cut

A half-blind or lap dovetail doesn't show on the front surface. It is used for drawer fronts or cabinet corners. The procedure for making a half-blind dovetail is similar to that for making a through dovetail. However, the tails are shallower—equal to the amount of the lap dimension of the mating piece; and the pins aren't cut through to the front surface.

Cut dovetails, then place the board on the mating member, set back the required amount from the face. Scribe cutting lines. Pins are not cut through—saw them at an angle for a partial cut. Don't cut beyond the guide lines.

To remove waste between the pins, clamp work to the bench and hold a chisel perfectly perpendicular. Cut a V-notch at the back guide line. Then alternately chisel with and across the grain to remove the waste. Use a mallet when cutting across the grain.

dovetails on table, radial saws

A single through dovetail is used to join narrow-width framing members. A tenoning jig makes cutting the tails on a table saw easier, or you can use a miter gauge. Steps taken to make this joint are shown at the top of page 1028.

Half-lap dovetails are used to join cross members. Steps for making a half-lap dovetail joint with a radial saw are also shown on page 1028.

dovetailing with a router

A router is ideal for making dovetail joints. A guide (collar), dovetail bit and a relatively simple attachment that clamps the mating pieces together in a template reduces the task to its simplest form.

Set up the accessory attachment and insert the guide. Install bit and adjust cutting depth. Clamp butted pieces into the attachment. Run router from right to left to break the front edge of the stock so it won't split at edges. Then, working from left to right, guide it around the template.

Drainage system ends flooding

A hard rain can cause water to pour down your downspouts and flood your foundation. This system solves the problem by carrying the water a safe distance from the house

SEE ALSO

Basement waterproofing . . .
Gutters and downspouts . . .
Home improvement . . . House additions . . .
Plumbing . . . Roofs . . . Sewage systems

IF YOU'RE NOT BOTHERED with water pouring from your downspouts and flooding the foundation of your home, you either (1) live in a desert-like area or (2) have already provided for underground drainage to carry roof water a safe distance away.

Installing a downspout drainage system is a simple job which consists of laying lengths of 3-in. perforated ABS (acrylonitrile butadiene styrene) plastic pipe in sloping trenches 12 to 18 in. deep and tying-in the downspouts with a few simple fittings. The far end of the underground pipe comes to the surface (see drawing) so excess amounts of water from a heavy downpour can bubble up through a grating and spill out onto the lawn. With the perforated pipe resting on a 2-in. bed of gravel or crushed stone, most of the water from a normal rain will seep through before

How pipe joints are 'welded'

1

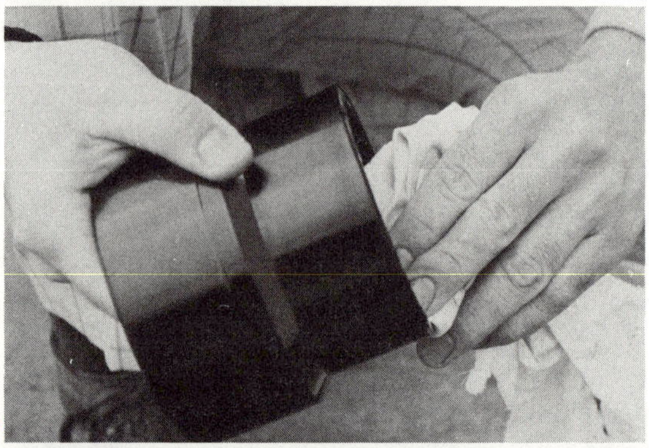
2

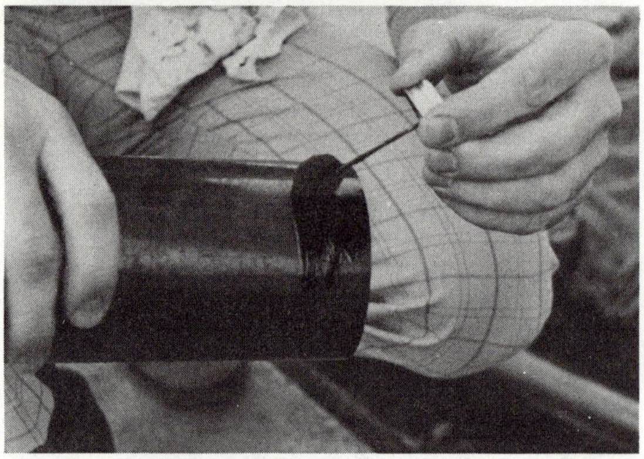
3

TO JOIN PIPE and fittings, burrs on the ends of the pipe are first trimmed with a sharp knife (1). Then both pipe and fitting are wiped clean (2). Solvent is applied to the outside of the pipe and inside of the fitting, inserted and given ¼ turn to spread the solvent (3).

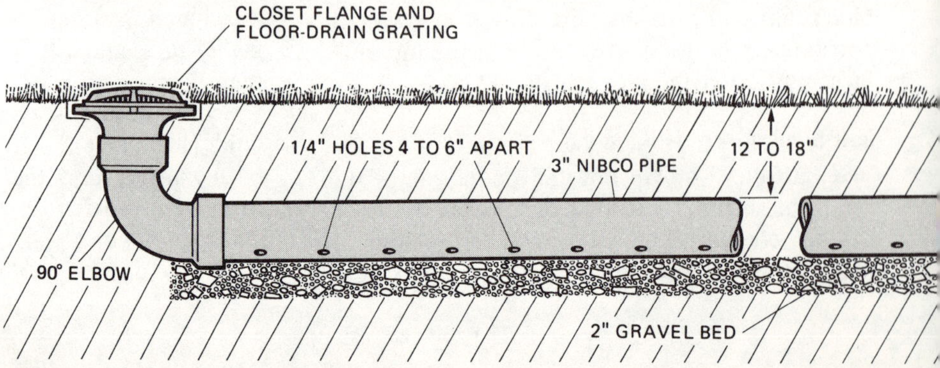

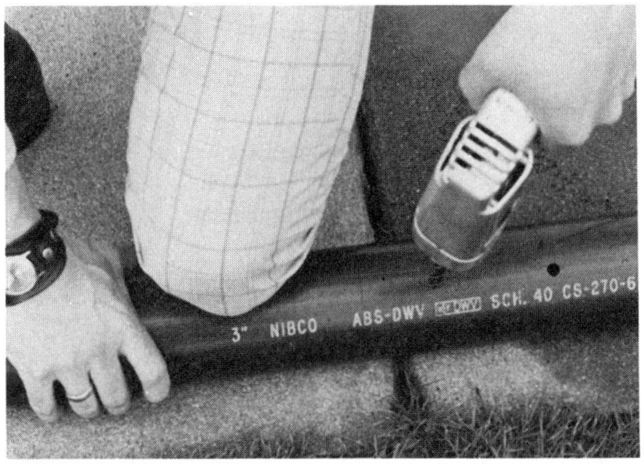

DRILL DRAINAGE HOLES, ¼ in. in diameter, 4 in. apart in the bottom of the pipe.

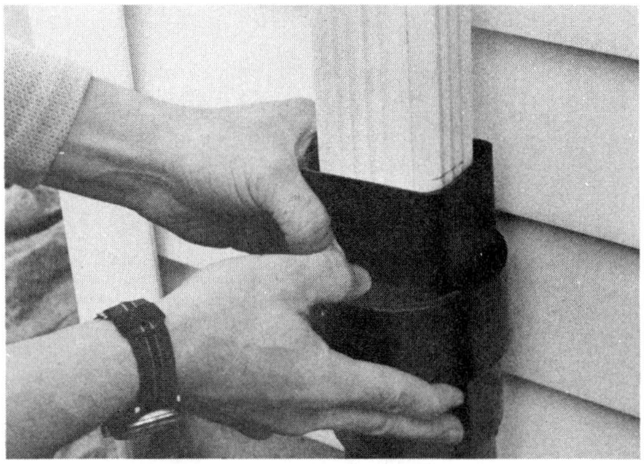

THE DOWNSPOUT is connected to the underground pipe with a fitting that slips over its end.

A NIBCOWARE CLOSET flange is attached to the far end of the pipe to bring the grating flush.

A ROUND GRATING from a floor drain is attached to the closet flange with copper wire.

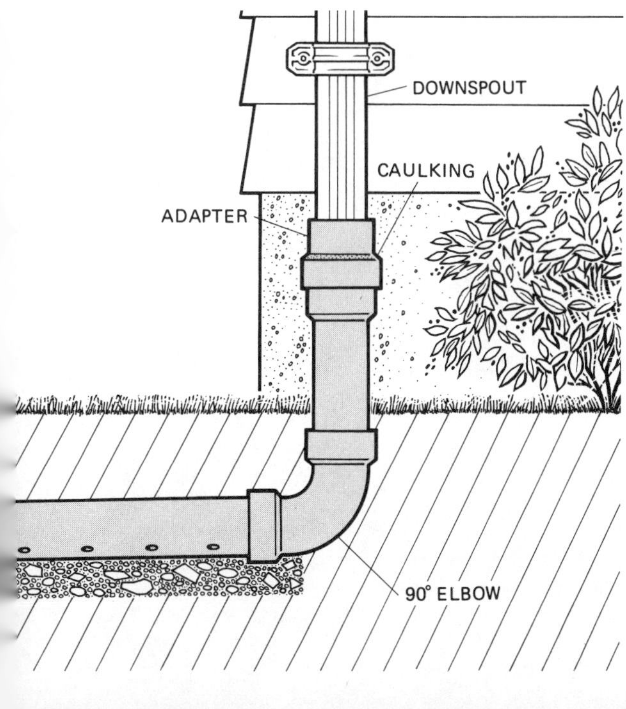

it builds up and will be absorbed by the gravel. By controlling the outflow from your downspouts in this manner, you can eliminate washouts and other damaging effects of ordinary downspout drainage.

Plastic pipe such as that made by Nibco of Elkhart, Ind., is a natural for an underground drain since it can't rust or corrode. Fittings are actually "glued" to the pipe with a cementlike substance called solvent, and the downspouts are connected with special adapter fittings which slide over the ends. Each trench is sloped a minimum of ¼ in. per foot and lined with gravel to provide a "dry well."

To prepare the pipe and fittings for gluing with solvent, first wipe each piece clean to insure a good bond. Apply the solvent to the outside of the pipe and the inside of the fitting, then press both together and give the fitting a quarter turn to spread the solvent evenly. The solvent will set almost immediately. Use the guide markings which you'll find on Nibcoware fittings to assure proper alignment.

How to unclog drains

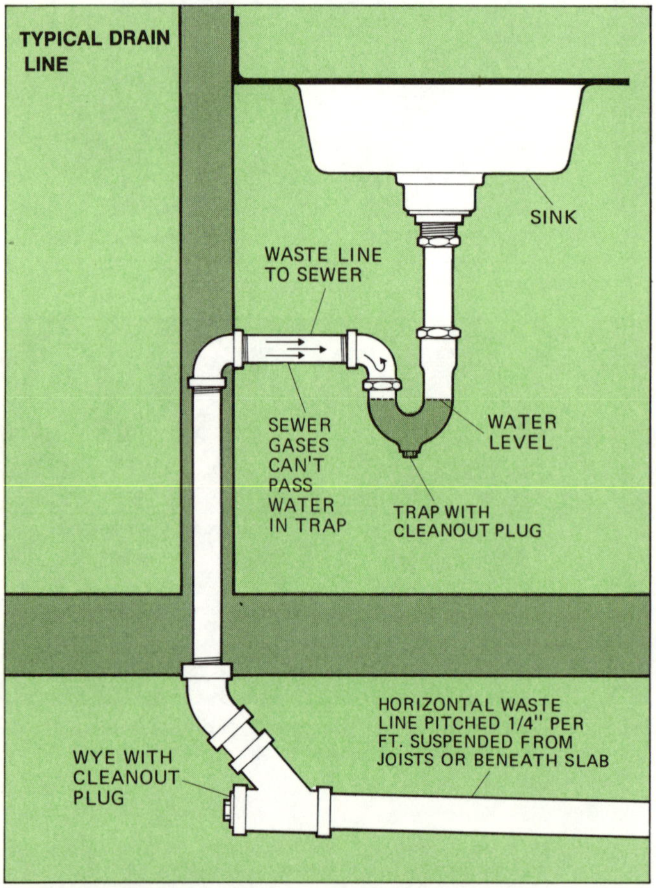

BLOCKED DRAINS—A COMMON PROBLEM

Drain blockage (after dripping faucets) is probably the most frequently encountered home-plumbing problem. The first step to take when a drain has clogged is to check other drains in the house to determine whether the main waste line itself is blocked. A typical drain is shown above. Notice that between the sink basin and waste line horizontal run, there are two places where the line can be cleaned out—at the trap and at the wye. There should also be a cleanout at every angle (turn) in the waste line. The five tools shown at right above will let you handle most emergencies when the obstruction is in the fixture or reachable area of the waste line. If blockage is caused by tree roots outside, your best bet is to call in a pro with his equipment for clearing the line. To free a stopped-up sink (right), plug fixture's overflow vent and use a force cup. Remove stopper, cover force cup with water and stroke with up-and-down motion. Particles drawn up into sink should be removed and operation continued until line is running freely. If this doesn't work, try chemical cleaners; first scoop out all water in sink.

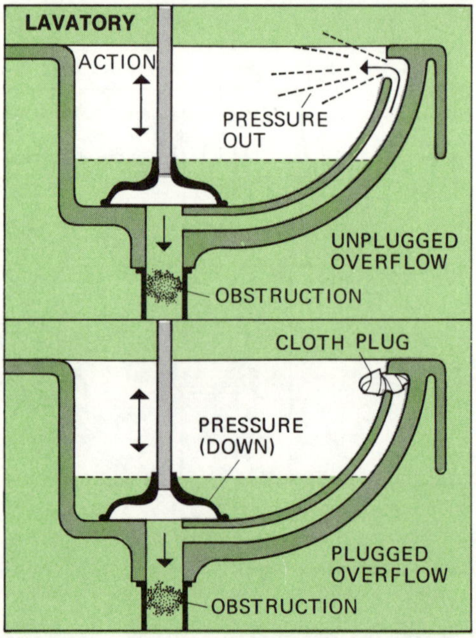

SEE ALSO

Basement remodeling . . . Bathrooms . . . Bathtubs . . . Kitchens . . . Plastic pipe . . . Plumbing . . . Sewage systems

CLOGGED TOILET

If just one toilet is clogged, it means that the problem is in the toilet itself and not in the drain line. Generally, a number of energetic thrusts with the force cup will free the obstruction. If this fails, try removing the obstruction using a bent wire coathanger or toilet auger. (Removal of the obstruction is better than pushing it along where it may clog further along the line.)

The toilet auger is a flexible wire encased in a metal tube. When the handle is cranked the flexible wire is forced out of the tube and into the trap. Though a good tool for clearing toilet obstructions, its effectiveness is limited by length—usually 3 to 4 ft. If auger won't reach the obstruction, try using a drain and trap auger. If this fails, the toilet will have to be removed so clearing of line can be accomplished.

WHEN ALL ELSE FAILS

If you've tried all methods without success, the obstruction is in the main sewer line. In this event, a professional is required; he has the tools and the specialized know-how for clearing clogged lines (usually tree roots) with a minimum of fuss and inconvenience for the family.

CHEMICAL CLEANERS

To avoid clogged drains, chemical cleaners should be used at the first sign that water drainage is slowing down in fixtures. Make certain you read and follow the manufacturer's instructions on the container, paying particular attention to the safety precautions (and antidotes). When using chemical cleaners, wear rubber gloves, protect your eyes and make certain you *never use a force cup immediately after using chemicals;* your skin can be severely burned by liquids that may splash back. Give cleaner time to do its job (following maker's instructions), then flush out drain with cold water.

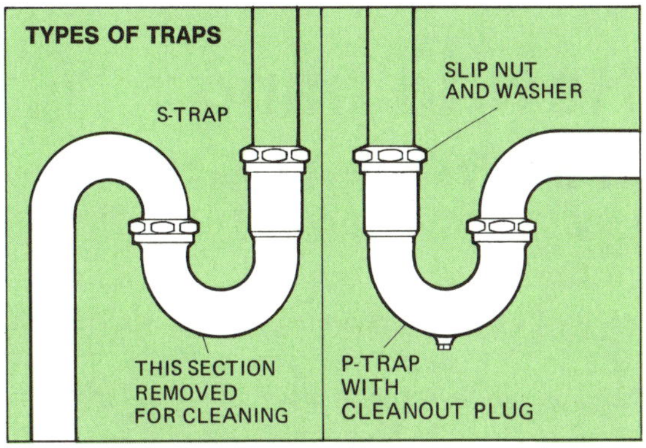

CLEANING OUT THE TRAP

The primary function of the trap in a waste line is to prevent the odor of sewer gases from entering the house via the fixture. Water, which is always in the trap, prevents this from happening. If the force cup or chemicals won't clear the line, the third step is to clean out the trap. S-traps must be removed entirely for cleaning by loosening two slip nuts. However, most traps have a cleanout plug at the bottom. Here, simply place a pail beneath the trap and back out the cleanout plug. Then the obstruction usually can be washed out with tap water or snaked out with a drain auger. When line is clear, *carefully* replace the plug or slip nuts. They have very fine threads that are easily stripped if not started right. At this time, check washers on the slip nuts for resiliency. If they show signs of wear, they should be replaced.

GENERAL FACTS ABOUT CLOGGED DRAINS

By conscientiously performing a few maintenance chores every few months, you can probably avoid clogged drains to begin with (except for root problems in the main sewer line). Periodically back out the clean-out plug (or remove S-trap) and flush out all sludge, hair and the like. Make certain you have a pail handy as you remove the plug—remember it is always filled with water. Second, periodically use a chemical cleaner. One type of "clogging" occurs in winter only: Freezing. Here, you must first locate the frozen section of pipe—usually in an unheated attic or crawl space. If water lines are in an outside wall, in some cases the freezing will be where you can't directly reach it. Here, heat applied lower on the line will eventually reach and thaw out the frozen section. Apply heat to pipes using flameless heater, hair dryer, or warm air from the exhaust outlet of a vacuum cleaner. If you use a propane torch, keep flame moving and remove flame from pipe every few minutes or steam might develop to explosive pressure.

How to hang traverse rods

■ PUTTING UP new drapery rods so they stay is a job all homeowners face at times, whether they're moving into a new home or switching over to today's bold, new drapery hardware. Since the popular trend is to stack the draperies back off the glass, you won't always find a stud where you want it. If you do, you're lucky, but chances are you'll be faced with attaching the brackets to a hollow part of the wall. You can't drive plain screws into the plaster; they won't hold. The answer is a Molly fastener which is designed to hold anything securely to a wall without a stud.

Plan to place brackets for the rods above the casing, or at least 4 in. above the glass and an equal distance from the ceiling.

GLASS WIDTH	STACKBACK SPACE	ROD WIDTH
20″	20″	40″
26″	22″	48″
32″	24″	56″
38″	26″	64″
44″	28″	72″
50″	30″	80″
56″	32″	88″
62″	34″	96″
68″	36″	104″
75″	37″	112″
81″	39″	120″
87″	41″	128″
94″	42″	136″
100″	44″	144″
106″	46″	152″
112″	48″	160″
119″	49″	168″

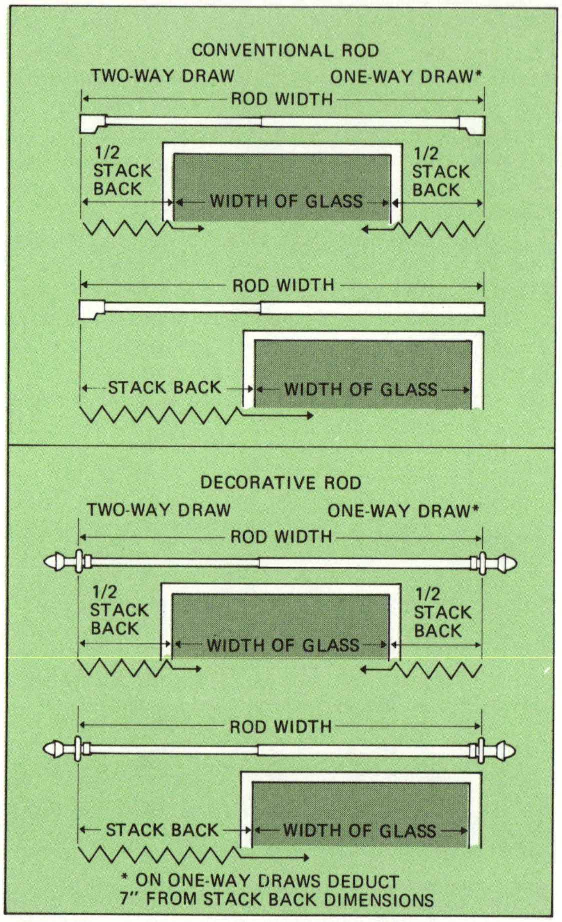

How to find the right rod length

With a draw treatment, it's best to have the draperies stack back over the window frame and wall, uncovering all the glass. To do this you must know the amount of wall space needed for the open panels before buying and installing the traverse rods. Use the chart at the left to find the correct rod length. Begin by measuring the glass width of your window. Say it's 38 inches wide. The chart shows you'll need 26 in. of wall for stack-back. So you add 38 and 26 in. and you'll see that you need a rod 64 in. long. The drawings above illustrate where the stack-back will be located. Stack-back is the amount of space occupied by open draw draperies. Space will vary depending on panel width, pleat spacing and fabric bulk. Since windows have two sides, you divide the stack-back distance in half (in this case 13 in.) to see how far the rod should extend beyond the glass. If you use one-way draperies, add the full 26 in. to one side

SEE ALSO
**Bolts . . . Fasteners . . . Screws . . .
Storm doors and windows . . . Windows . . .
Winterizing, homes**

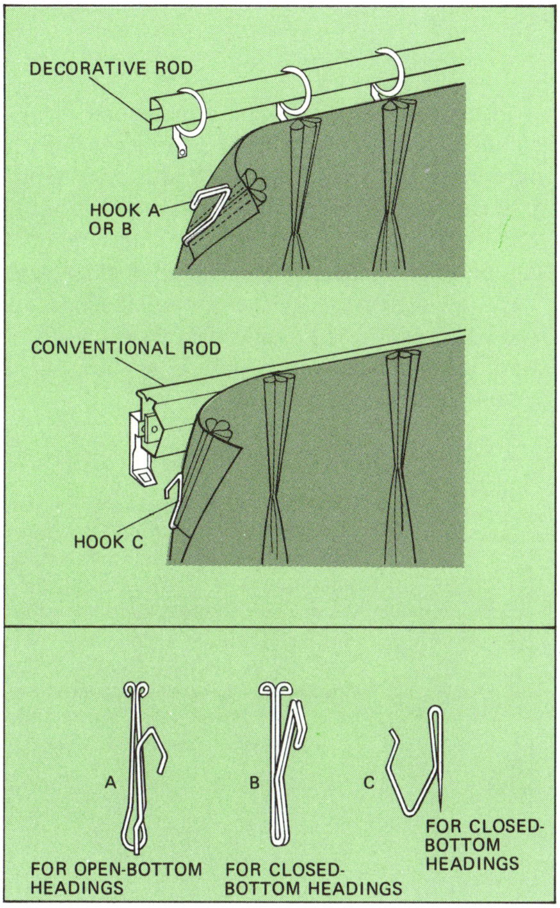

Selecting proper drapery hooks

The right drapery hooks can mean the difference between tip-tilt headings and those that stand properly erect. Always important, your choice of hooks is vital to the proper appearance of draperies hung on decorative traverse rods. At each window you will need one hook for each drapery pleat, plus four for returns and overlaps. On a decorative rod, the heading covers the pendants and falls just below the bottom of the rings. On a conventional rod, the heading extends to cover the rod. Thus hooks for conventional rods must be longer from the top of the hook to the top of the shank than hooks used for decorative rods

Ways to anchor brackets securely

Correct fastening devices are a must for proper installation of drapery hardware. Wood screws 1¼ in. long threaded the full length of the shanks are suitable for attaching brackets to studs. If wood studs can't be located or bracket-location falls between studs, Mollies (hollow-wall anchors) should be used as shown below. They are inserted in holes drilled through plaster or dry wall, tapped flush with the surface to embed the points and finally pulled up tight on the back by turning the screw that comes with the anchor. When mounting the modern, lightweight drapery rods on the wall, you can use plastic screw anchors. These easy-to-use tapered sleeve-type plugs are tapped in place in undersize holes drilled right through the plaster. Then simply find a full-thread wood screw of the proper size and turn it into the plug. As you turn it in, it spreads the split plastic sleeve and anchors it securely in place

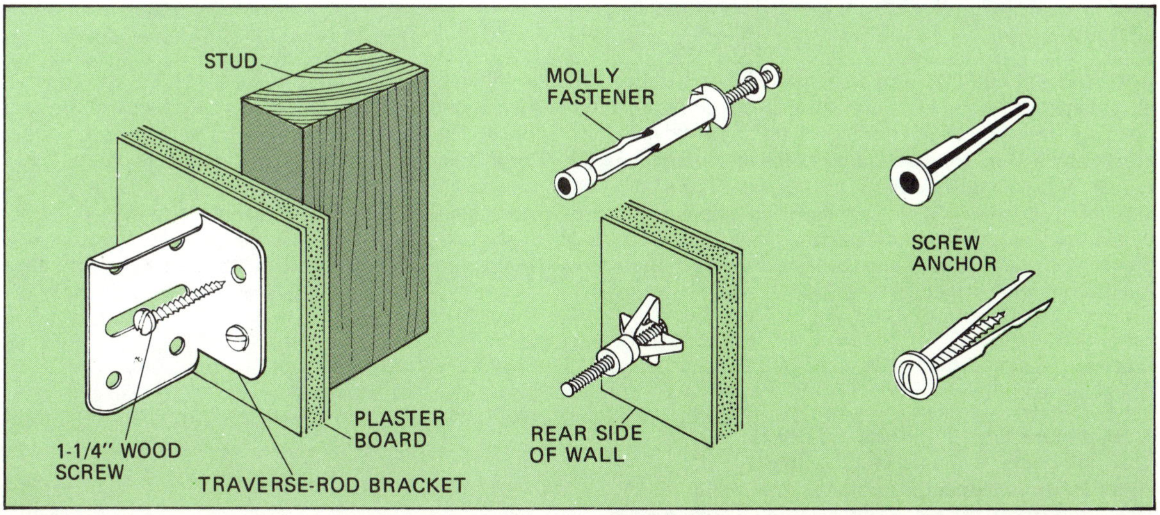

How to make drawers

THOUGH MANY do-it-yourselfers mistakenly think that making a drawer is beyond their abilities, no great mystery surrounds the task. The two keys to good drawermaking—whether using sophisticated joinery techniques or constructing the simplest drawer—are: 1. accurate measurements, and 2. perfectly square cuts.

Whether you are building a drawer from a working drawing or taking dimensions from a cabinet, study the drawing or cabinet carefully to determine the exact height, width and depth. Use the same kind of wood for drawer front as was used on the cabinet; drawer sides and back can be of less expensive nonwarped clear pine. The drawings on these pages give all the basics of good drawer construction. Study them carefully. Additional drawer know-how is spelled out in accompanying captions.

THREE MOST COMMON DRAWER FRONTS

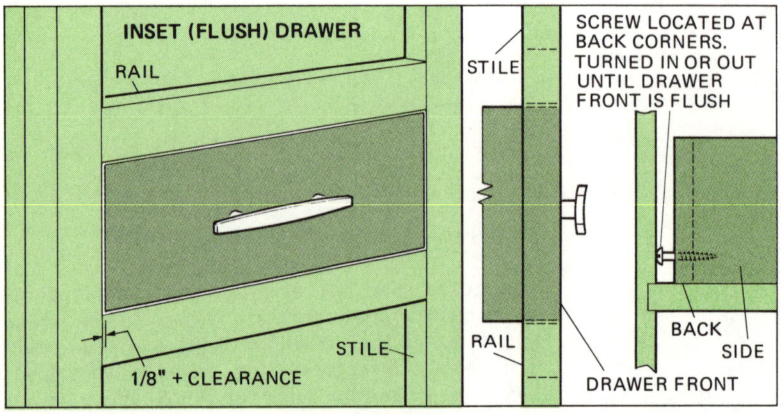

AN INSET flush drawer should have uniform clearance around the opening on all four sides. The usual clearance is ⅛ in. When laying out the drawer, carefully determine the length of the sides so that the drawer front will be perfectly flush with the stiles and rails. A pair of screws in the back corners will aid in aligning the drawer front if drawer is too short.

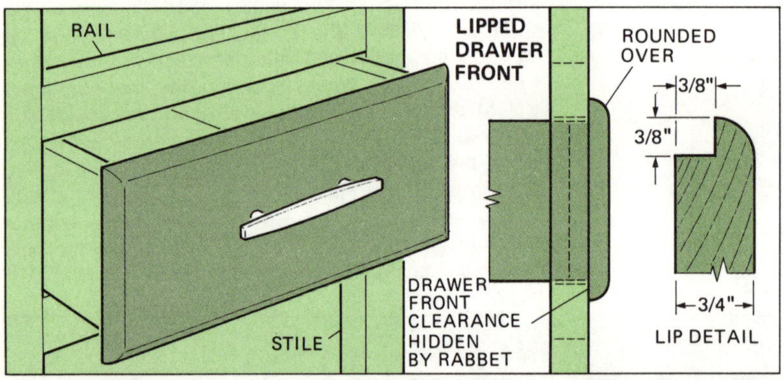

ROUNDED OR LIPPED fronts are most commonly used on kitchen cabinets. The advantage of this type front is that the lip conceals the gap between drawer and opening—thus, the ⅛-in. clearance mentioned above is not as critical. The lip is created by a ⅜-in.-sq. rabbet around the inside edges of the drawer front. This rabbet can be made with a router in one pass, or on a table saw in two passes. The remaining edge is usually rounded off with either a shaper or a block plane and belt sander. If you prefer a contemporary look, omit the rounding off step. A lipped drawer front can also be created by fastening ⅜-in. quarter-round moldings to the outside of each of the drawer edges.

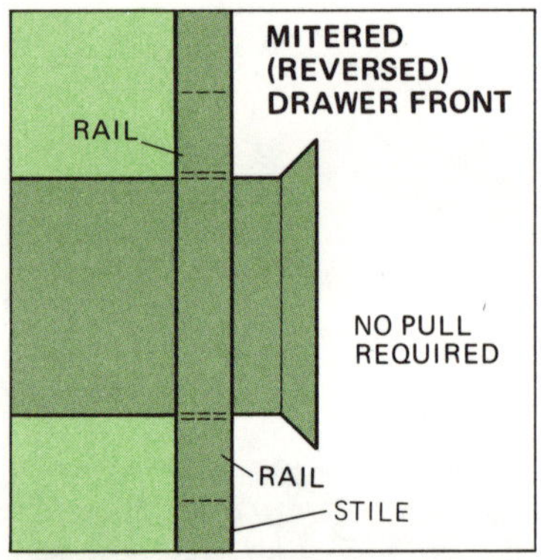

MITERING ON THE inside edge of a drawer front calls for careful cutting. After setting the table-saw blade to the desired angle, adjust the rip fence to leave a feather edge as shown. Cut ends of the front first (across the end grain), then make cuts with the grain. For safety, attach a wood face to your rip fence.

SEE ALSO

Cabinet furniture . . . Chests . . . Desks . . . Dovetail joints . . . Fasteners . . . Joinery . . . Miter joints . . . Modular furniture

TYPICAL DRAWER JOINERY

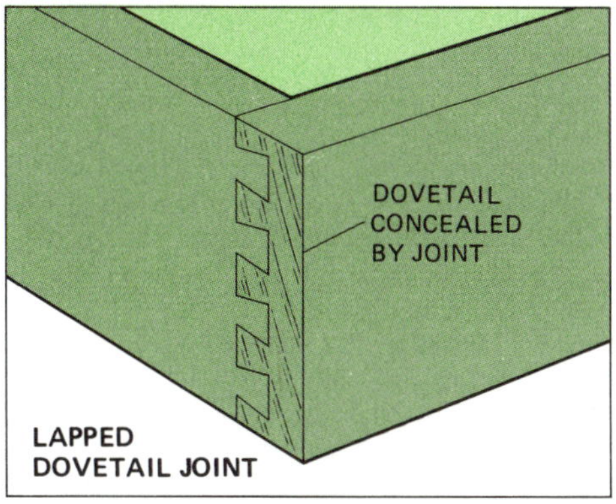

THE DOVETAIL JOINT is the strongest you can use in drawer-making. A well-made dovetail joint will, literally, hold without glue—a fact old world craftsmen prided themselves on. Today the joint is made using a router equipped with a dovetail bit, and a dovetail template; instructions for use are packed with the template. Once you are familiar with the template, the joints are rather easy to make; to be safe, first perfect your technique on scrap wood.

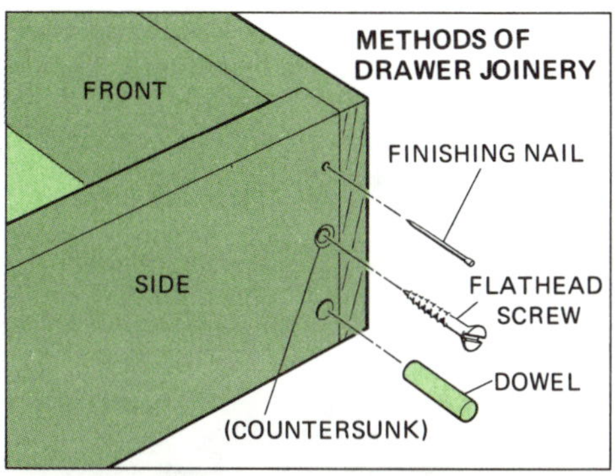

UNLESS YOU are faithfully reproducing a period piece with nonglued dovetail joints, the chances are you will assemble your drawers using one of the three fastening methods shown. Regardless of which fastener you use, glue should be liberally applied to mating surfaces of pieces to be joined. For maximum strength, fasteners should be installed parallel to the drawer front. Thus, pull on a drawer creates a shear action on a fastener. This gives greater resistance to pull-out than if fasteners are installed perpendicular to front.

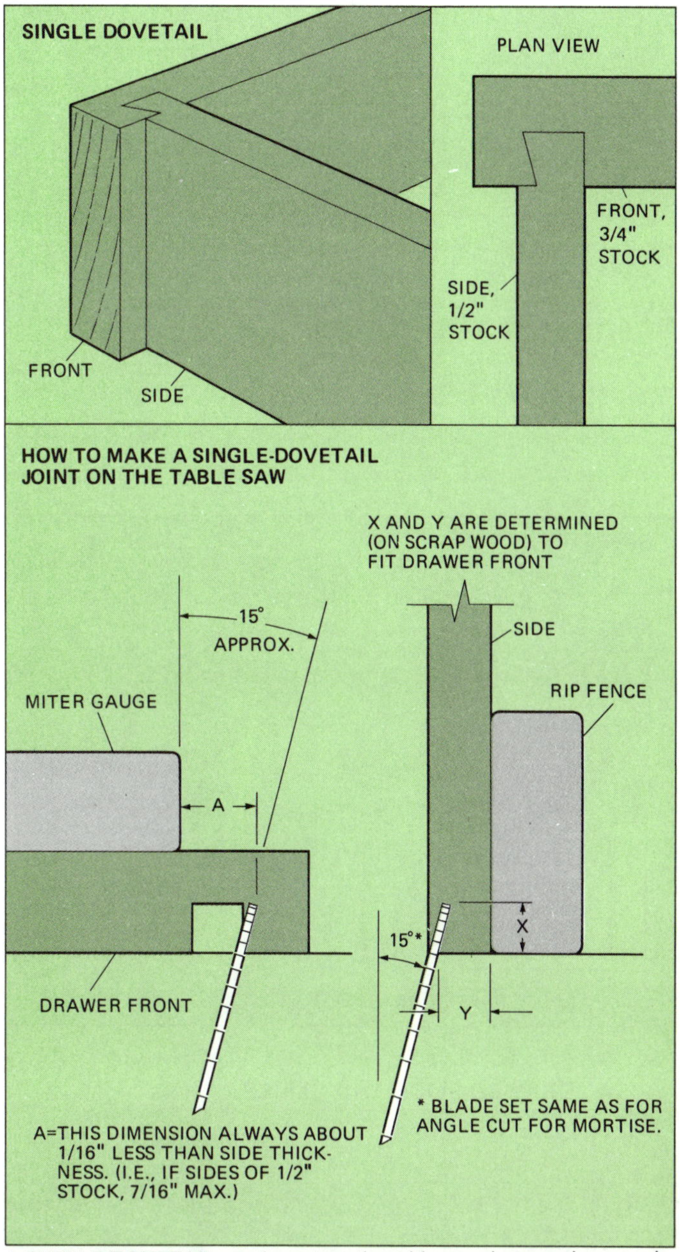

A SINGLE-DOVETAIL can be cut on the table saw, but requires much care and laying out prior to cutting. Make test cuts on scrap lumber of exactly the same size and dimensions as will be used in drawer construction. Try all test cuts and fits before putting the blade to the project materials. First cut the dado about one-half the depth of the front. Then set the saw blade to about 15° and make the cut shown above left. Without disturbing the blade setting, make the mating angle cuts on the drawer sides. The blade can then be set at 0° and the triangular pieces cut out of the sides. Note: X and Y are determined on scrap wood first.

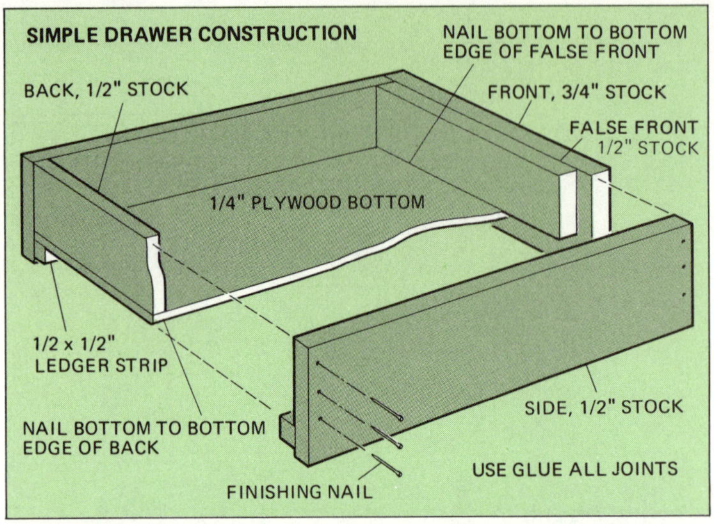

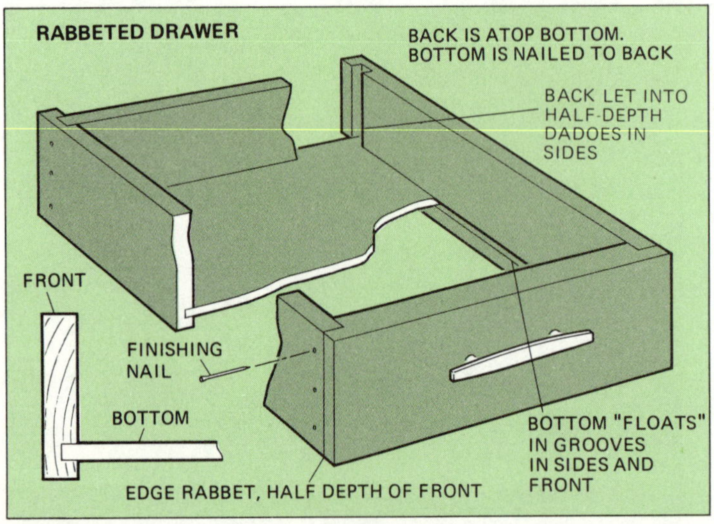

THE DRAWER at left can be entirely constructed using hand tools only. After determining drawer-front dimensions, subtract thickness of sides and bottom. Assemble false front to front with glue and brads. Then cut the sides, back and bottom. Use ½ x ½-in. strips to make the ledger strips upon which the bottom rests. These are placed so top surface of bottom will be snug against bottom of false front and back. To assemble the drawer, apply glue, and nail sides to front as shown. With drawer on workbench, apply glue and install the back. Next, flop drawer, position the bottom on drawer frame and secure it with one nail. Before driving a second nail, check the drawer assembly with a square. Holding the drawer square, drive two more nails through bottom into back and false front. To finish assembly, using glue and brads, install the ledger strips beneath bottom on both sides. Recheck with square. Let dry.

A COMBINATION rabbet-and-fastener assembly provides a strong drawer. Here, you simply edge rabbet the drawer front to half the depth of the front and to a width equal to thickness of drawer sides. Test-fit the drawer dry (using brads). When you're satisfied with outside dimensions and squareness, the drawer can be permanently assembled using glue and fasteners.

TYPICAL DRAWER SLIDE AND GLIDES

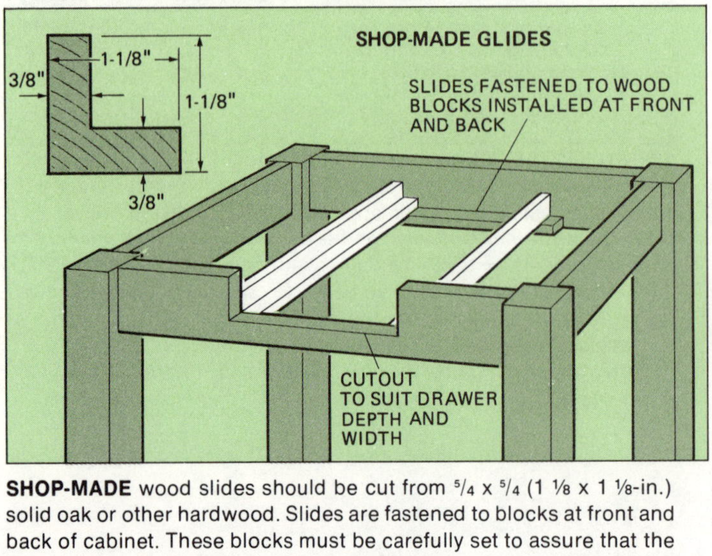

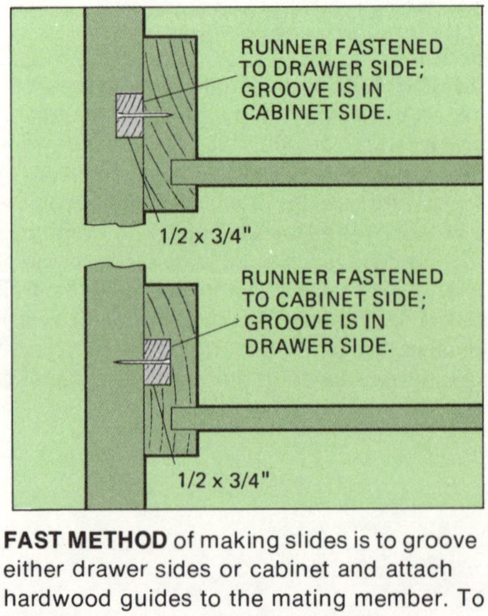

SHOP-MADE wood slides should be cut from $^5/_4$ x $^5/_4$ (1 ⅛ x 1 ⅛-in.) solid oak or other hardwood. Slides are fastened to blocks at front and back of cabinet. These blocks must be carefully set to assure that the drawer front is parallel to the cabinet front. For ease of operation, spray the slides at regular intervals with silicone.

FAST METHOD of making slides is to groove either drawer sides or cabinet and attach hardwood guides to the mating member. To keep the cabinet sides from binding, it is a must that they be straight and unwarped.

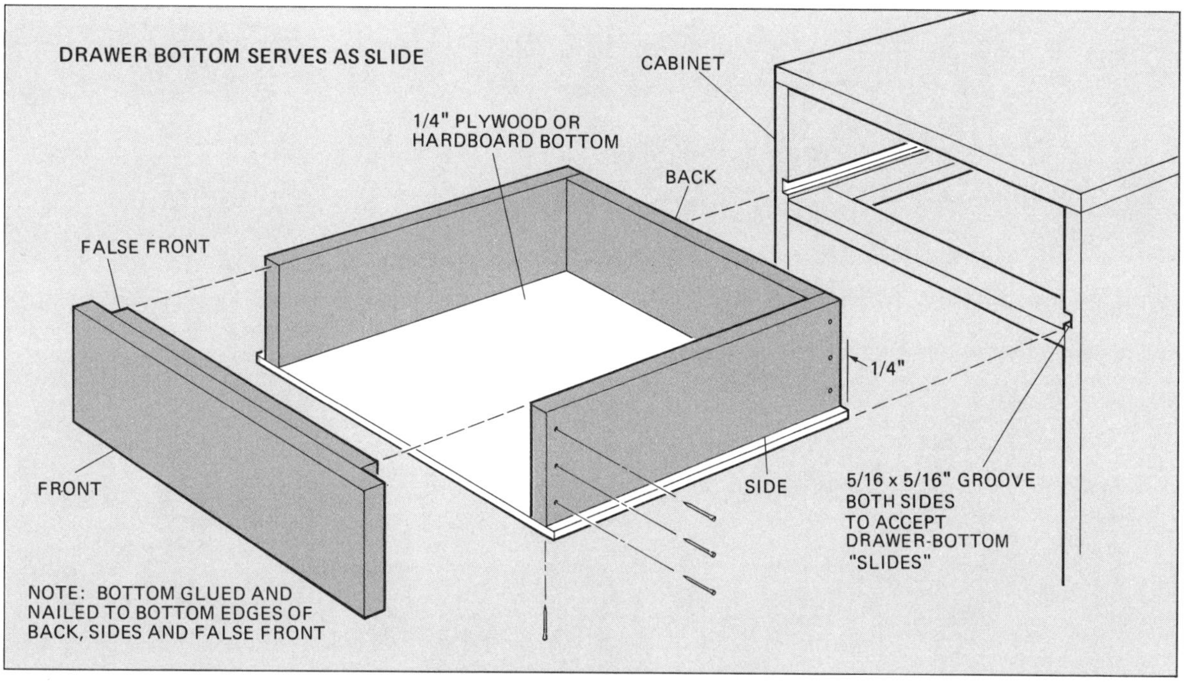

A GOOD STUNT—when drawer appearance is not of primary concern—is to build in runners merely by extending the drawer bottom on both sides. This creates slides which ride in corresponding grooves that are cut in the cabinet sides. In this case, it is best to use ¼-in. hardboard for the drawer bottom. For troublefree sliding, keep the grooves clean and spray them periodically with silicone to prevent sticking.

COMMERCIAL SLIDES are available in bottom and side-mount styles (both shown at right). The bottom-mount type is easiest to install; version shown in drawing is screw-fastened to drawer bottom (at center) as well as to cabinet rail and cabinet back. Less expensive types feature a single roller fastened to the back of the drawer.

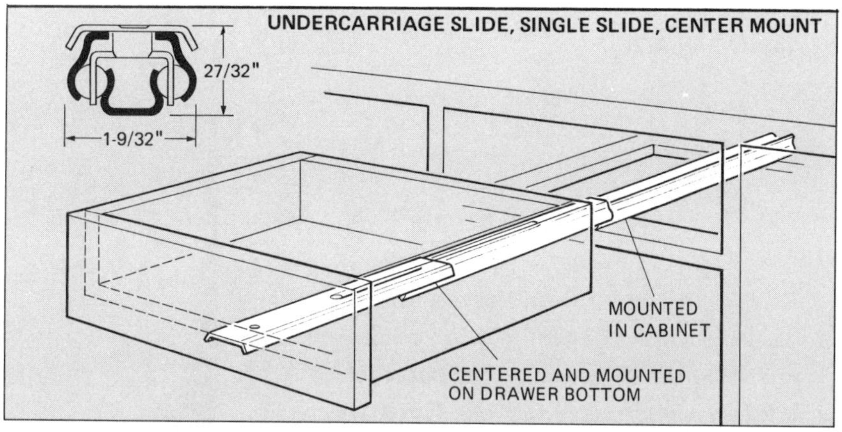

SIDE-MOUNT hardware at right can be used to add a drawer beneath a countertop; units operate the same as side-mounts installed in a cabinet. When using factory-made slides, clearance for hardware must be made when building the drawer (drawer must be narrower). Whether using side or bottom-mount slides, always read the maker's instructions before you begin laying out your drawer.

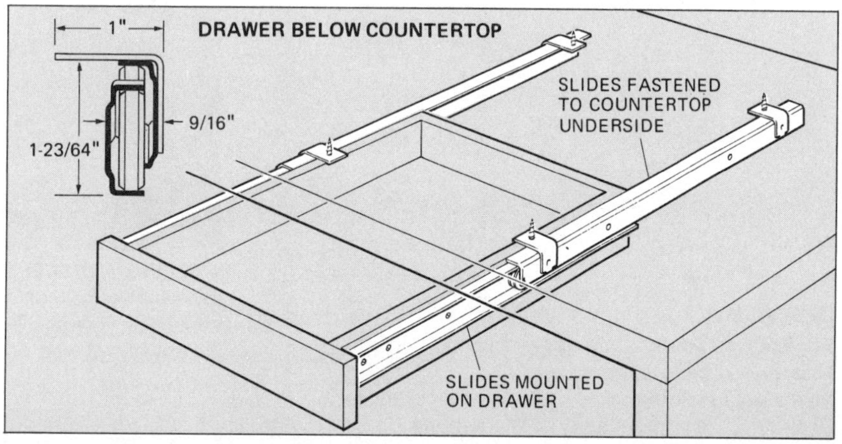

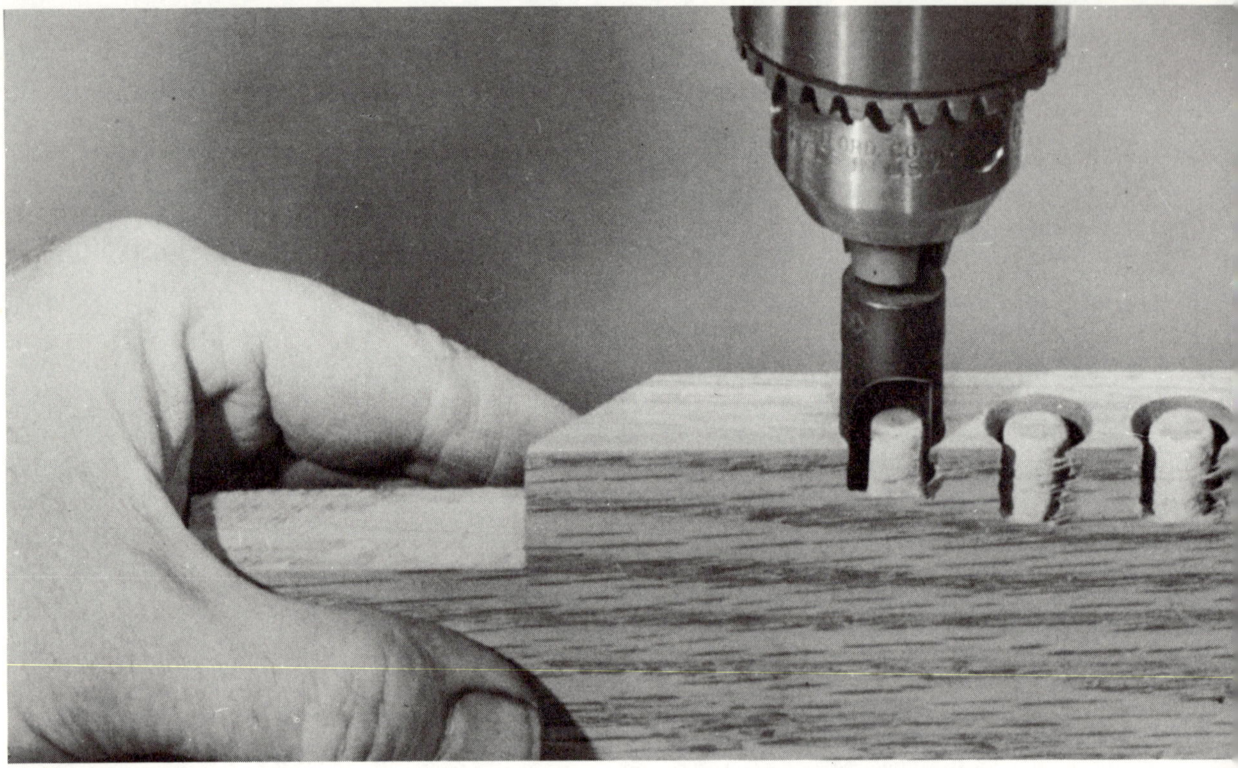

Get the most out of your drill press

By MANLY BANISTER

Don't sell your drill press short! It can be the most versatile tool in your shop—once you've learned to exploit its potential with a few simple accessories. Here are a dozen or so ideas to remember

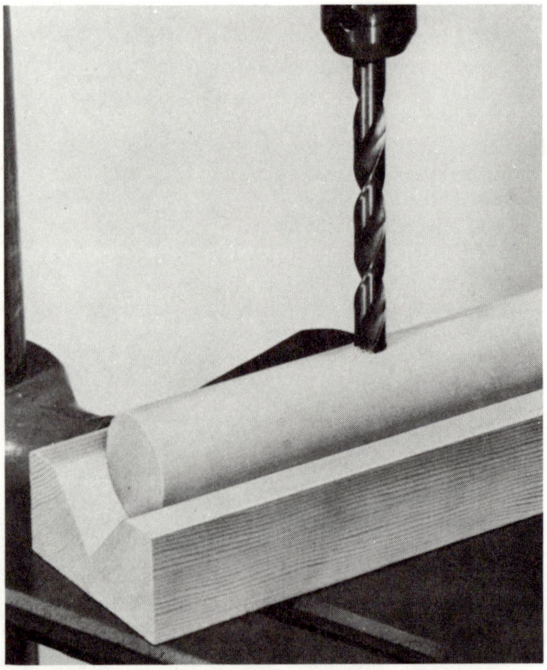

DRILLING A DOWEL. When a hole must be drilled transversely through a dowel, take time to make a V-block on your saw from a short 2x4 scrap. It will cradle the dowel, yet won't mar it in the slightest.

SEE ALSO
Angles, compound . . . Angles, drilling . . . Clamps . . . Motors, shop . . . Power-tool maintenance . . . Power-tool stands . . . Screws . . . Workbenches . . . Workshops

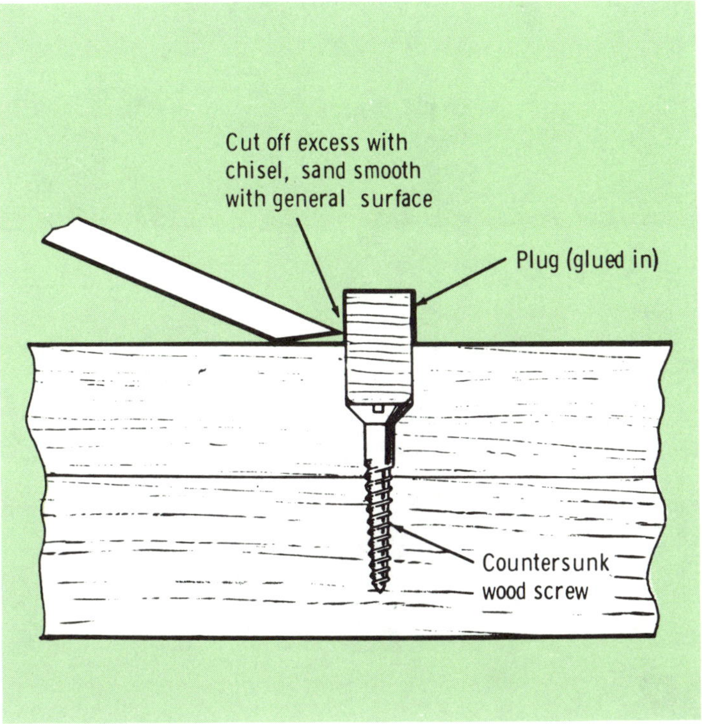

CUTTING SCREW PLUGS. A handy drill-press accessory is a plug cutter. This is a tool for making wooden plugs which are used to conceal screwheads in counterbored holes. Plugs differ from dowels in that their grain is crosswise so that they can be chiseled off flush after being glued in place. The thing to remember in using a plug cutter is to bring it down as far in the wood as it will go. This tapers the plug so it will fit the hole tightly when tapped in place. Note the direction of the grain shown at the left.

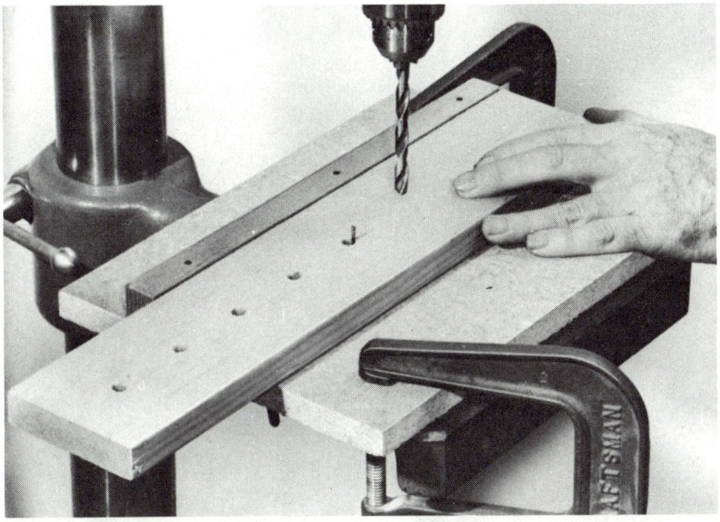

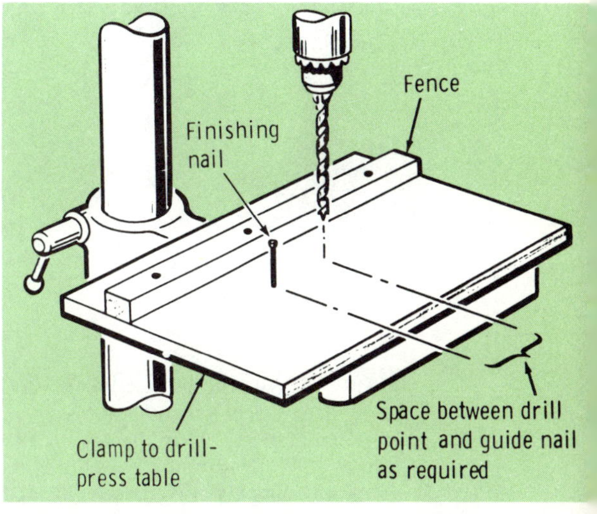

DRILLING EQUALLY SPACED HOLES. Where a row of holes must be drilled exactly the same distance apart, you can do it in jig time with an auxiliary plywood table that's clamped to the drill press and fitted with a nail-on fence. The work is placed against the fence and the first hole is drilled. Then the work is shifted and the second hole is drilled. The bit is left in the second hole so the work can't move and a finishing nail is driven in the first hole. As each new hole is drilled, the work is slipped over the nail for the next hole. The nail automatically spaces each hole identically.

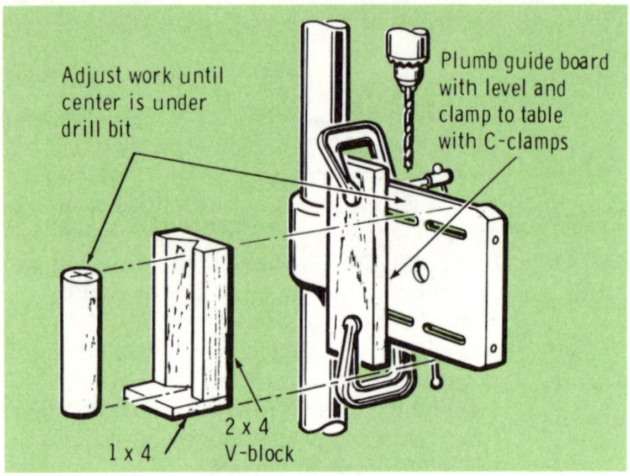

END DRILLING DOWELS. If your drill-press table tilts, the setup at right automatically centers the work under the bit when you want to end-drill round stock. A stop nailed to the end of the V-block lets you stand the work on end to hold it securely for drilling.

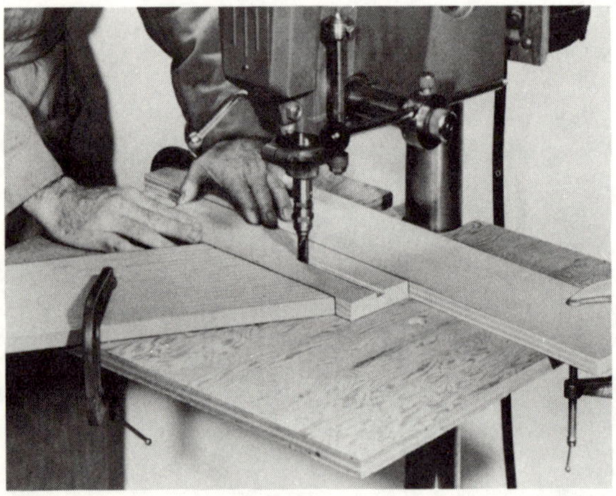

DRILL-PRESS ROUTING. With a fingerboard forcing the work snugly against a fence of an auxiliary table clamped to the drill press, open and blind grooves can be accurately made with a router bit in the chuck. Here the drill press is run at its highest speed for a smooth cut. Limit each pass to a ⅛-in. cut, feeding the work from the left side, against the direction of rotation of the cutter.

GAINING DRILLING DEPTH. When there's plenty of drill left, but you've reached the end of the quill, you can still complete the hole when there's but an inch or so to go. Simply turn off the motor, leave the bit in the hole, raise the work on a block and continue drilling.

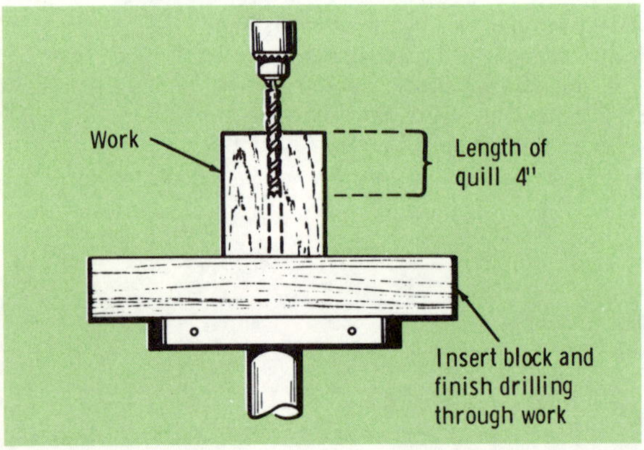

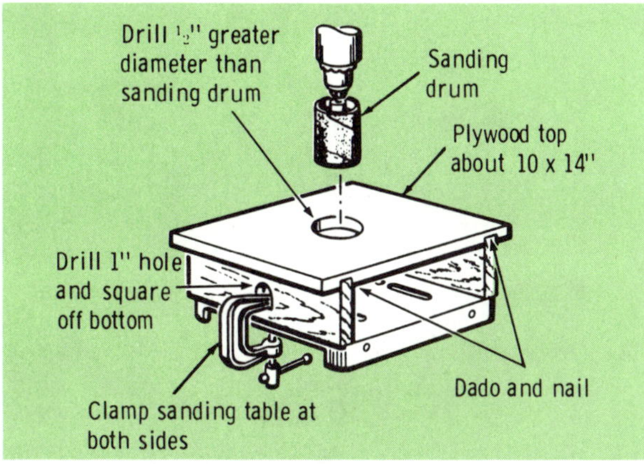

USING ALL OF A DRUM. Using a sanding drum in a drill press always means you have to clamp a board with a hole in it to the drill-press table so the drum can be lowered below the work level. However, if the board is elevated as shown, you'll be able to distribute abrasive wear evenly over the full length of the sleeve.

"SAWING" WITH A DRILL PRESS. The fastest way of cutting discs and large holes up to 8-in. in both wood and metal is with a flycutter. If you're cutting a hole, position the cutting bit to face in; if cutting a disc, turn the bit to face out. Regulate the drill speed by the size of the hole—the larger the hole, the slower the speed. Always clamp the work to be safe.

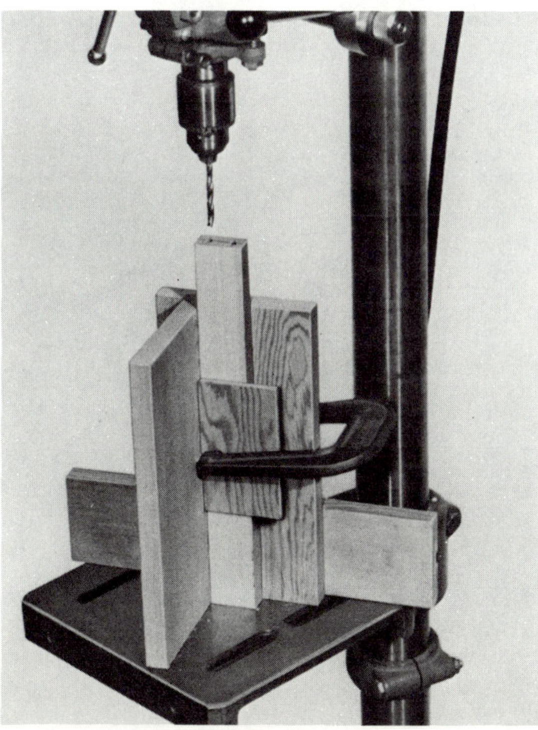

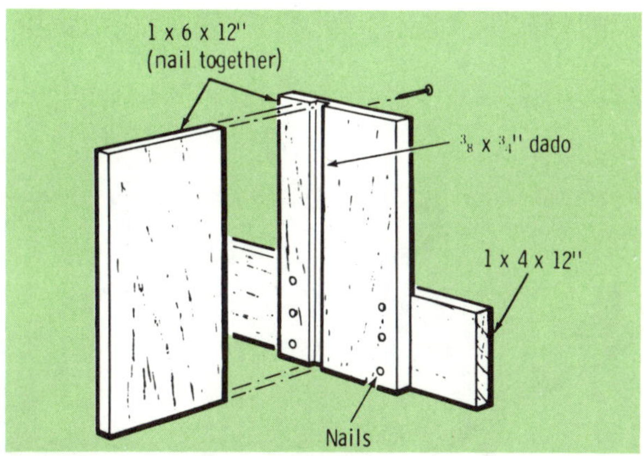

DRILLING FOR DOWELS. Holding slender work vertically for drilling dowel holes in the ends is no problem with this T-shaped jig made to stand on the drill-press table and slide along a wood clamp-on fence. Work is placed in the corner of the jig and clamped. The jig must stand perfectly plumb.

A STUNT TO REMEMBER. When drilling bar stock, you should always play it safe and clamp the metal in a vise. You'll also wind up with a clean-cut hole and you won't have the problem of "grabbing" when the drill breaks through if you make it a practice to place a hardwood block under the work when clamping it in the drill-press vise, as shown at right.

MAKING THE CENTER OF RODS. A smart way of spotting the exact center of cylindrical stock is to lay the rod in a couple of V-blocks as shown in the photo. Then with the drill press turned on and the bit lowered to barely touch the metal, pass the work under the bit.

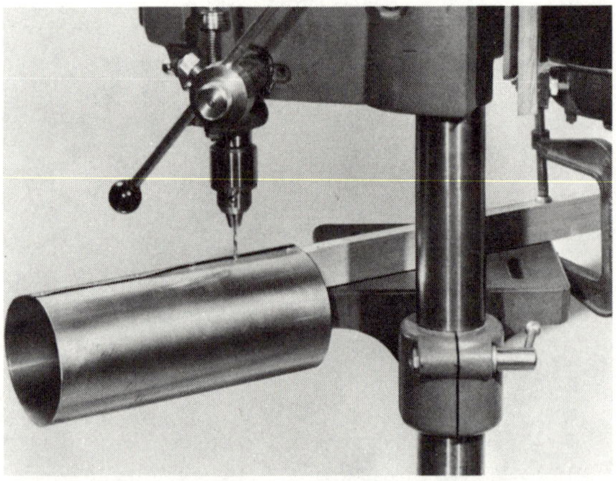

OUTBOARD DRILLING. A backing block is what you need when it comes to drilling through the side of a sheet-metal pipe, the side of a can or the face of a band. Round the top edge of a short 2x4, swing the table to one side and clamp the block to it so it's under the drill bit.

COMPOUND-ANGLE DRILLING. How do you drill two-way holes for splayed stool legs? You can't miss with the auxiliary table detailed at the right. In use, a block along the back of the work props it up 15° in one plane, while the table tilts it 15° in the other plane.

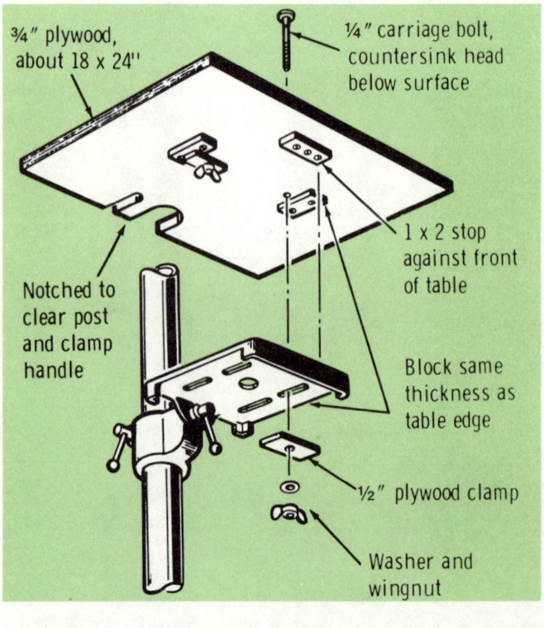

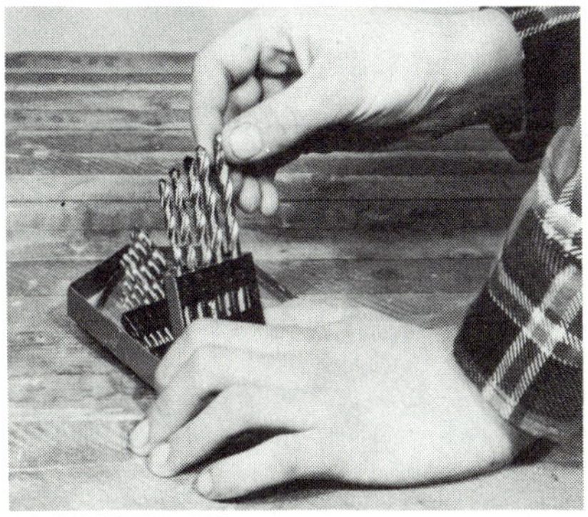

PROTECT BITS by storing them in a metal case. This one holds 23 drills.

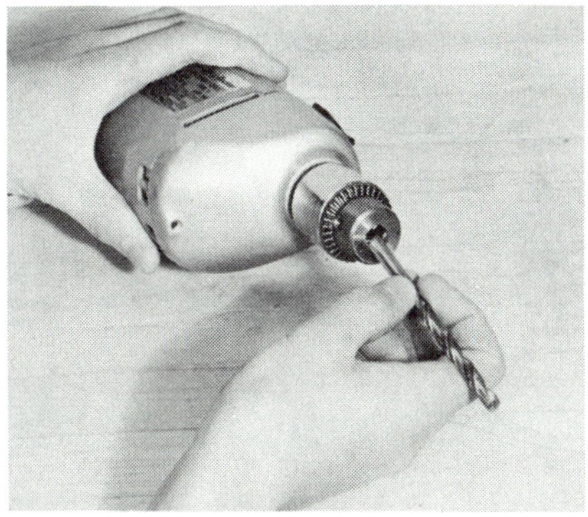

BIT IS fully inserted into Jacobs chuck, aligned so *all three jaws* hold it.

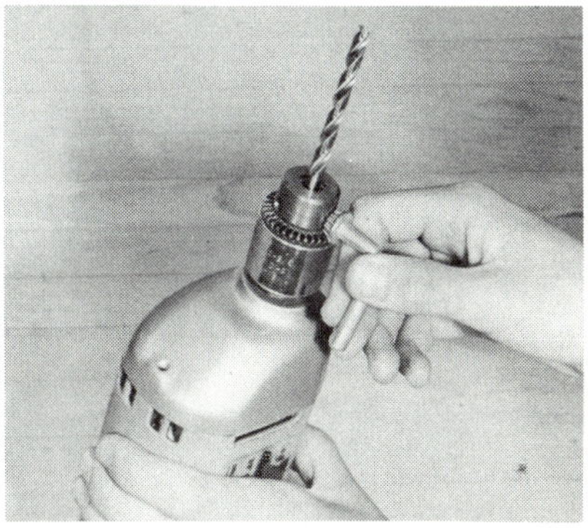

NEXT, use chuck key that comes with the tool to tighten bit securely.

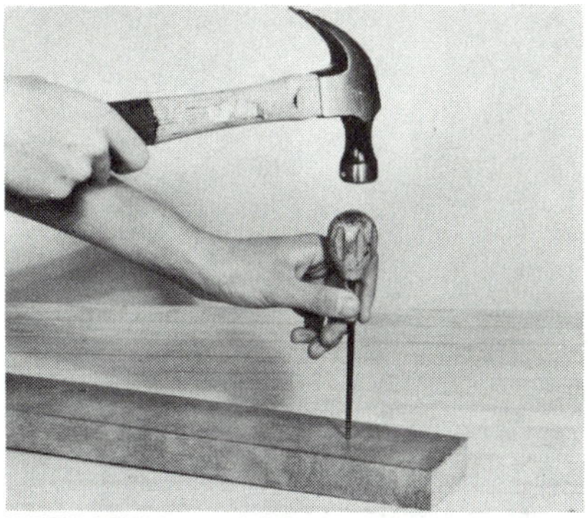

KEEP BIT from drifting as drill is started by indenting with an awl.

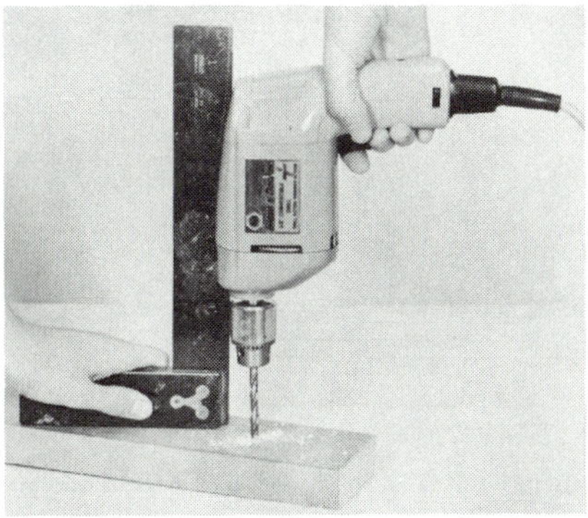

TO MAKE SURE drill is perpendicular to work, use square on front and side.

USE countersink when installing flathead screws so heads will be flush.

ROSETTE SINKS are available in a variety of diameters for countersinking.

Portable drill basics

By HARRY WICKS

■ A PORTABLE electric drill is generally the first power tool a fledgling craftsman should buy. Besides boring accurate holes, a drill can be used to countersink, counterbore, sand rough surfaces smooth, stir paint—and a lot more.

The most-commonly purchased drill is the ¼-incher; that is, a drill whose chuck will accept bits up to ¼ in. in diameter. But give some thought to buying a ⅜-in. drill instead. It will handle all tasks that a ¼-in. drill will while giving you greater bit, thus boring, capacity. Because of this increased capacity, the ⅜-in. drills come with motors that provide greater torque; you will find that most of them have speeds in the 300-to-1200-rpm range.

Since various types of material call for different drill speeds, take a look at the variable-speed models that most makers offer. With one of these you can drill safely in most materials.

A desirable feature is the ability to reverse chuck rotation. A drill with this feature quickly becomes a power screwdriver when fitted with a screwdriver accessory.

SEE ALSO
Angles, drilling . . . Motors, shop . . . Portable drills . . . Power-tool stands

Look what you can do with a portable drill

By HARRY WICKS

DRILL, BUFF, POLISH, sand, scrape, cut, mix, grind—you name a shop job and it's a pretty safe bet there's an accessory around that will let you handle the task with your portable drill. In fact, when you consider the tremendous variety of jobs—besides boring holes—you can do with a drill, it becomes apparent why the portable drill is the most purchased power tool.

freeing both hands

With many accessories, you must have both hands free to handle the work while the tool does

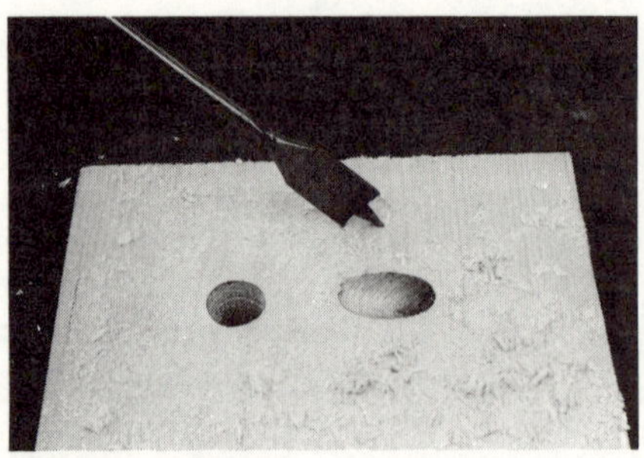

SPADE bit is perfect for drilling straight or angled holes in most woods.

BIT CASE from Sears holds 29 bits, lists sizes and decimal equivalents.

FOR EXTRA-SMALL holes, chuck a brad into drill after nipping off its head.

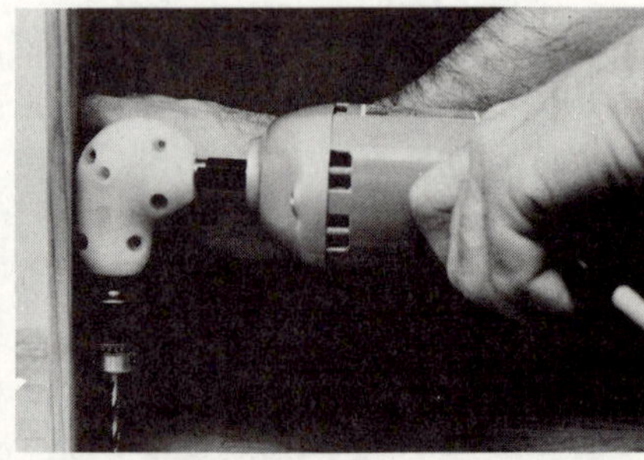

RIGHT-ANGLE attachment gets you close to a corner, also helps polishing.

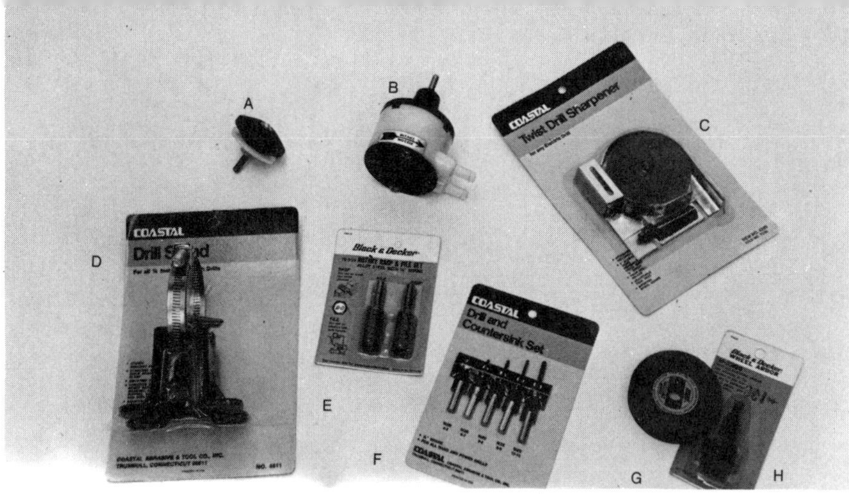

INCREASE DRILL VERSATILITY with: A, mower blade sharpener; B, water pump; C, low-cost drill sharpener; D, bench stand; E, rotary rasp-file for quick wood removal; F, bits with built-in countersinks; G, grinding wheel, and H, an arbor for use with certain types of drill accessories.

THIS ACCESSORY pack includes ½, ¾ and 1-in. spade bits, ¼-in. masonry bit and Phillips-head and slotted screwdrivers for easy job on screws.

CARBON AND high-speed twist bits can be sharpened with this tool. It accepts 11 most common sizes.

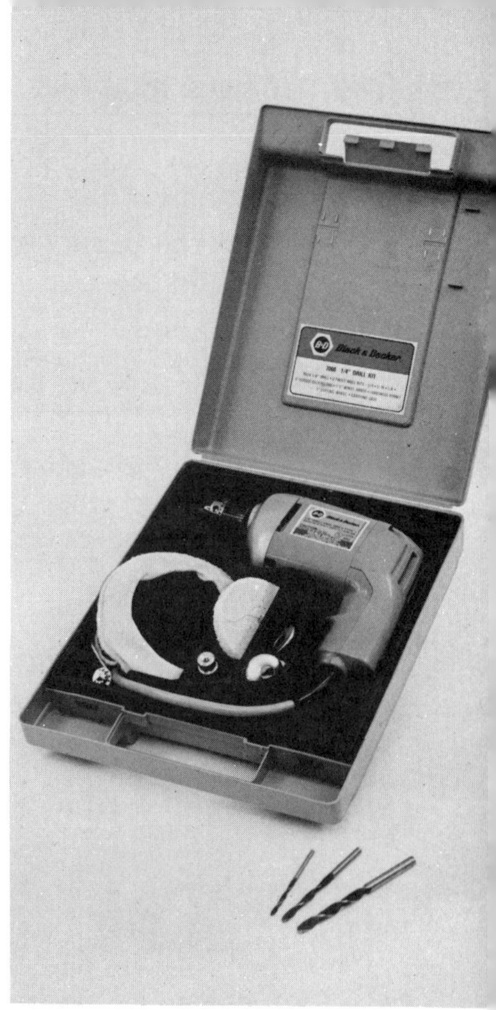

DOUBLE-INSULATED ¼-in. drill kit has three bits, rubber backing pad, polishing pad, arbor, lamb's-wool bonnet and a convenient plastic carrying case.

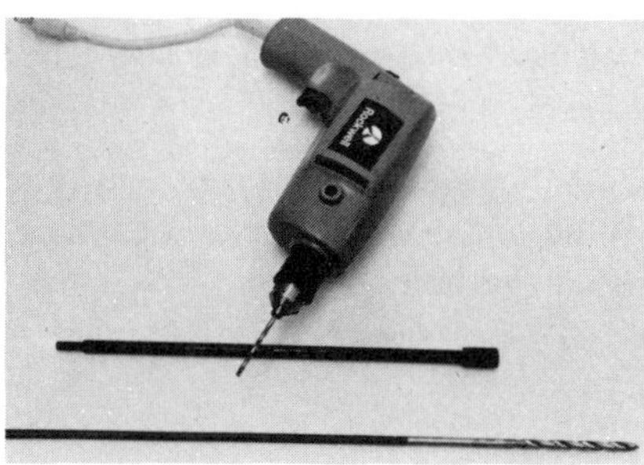

ELECTRICIAN'S 18-in. bit and 12-in. extension help deep drilling.

ADJUSTABLE hole saw cuts many sizes. Use slow speed and moderate pressure.

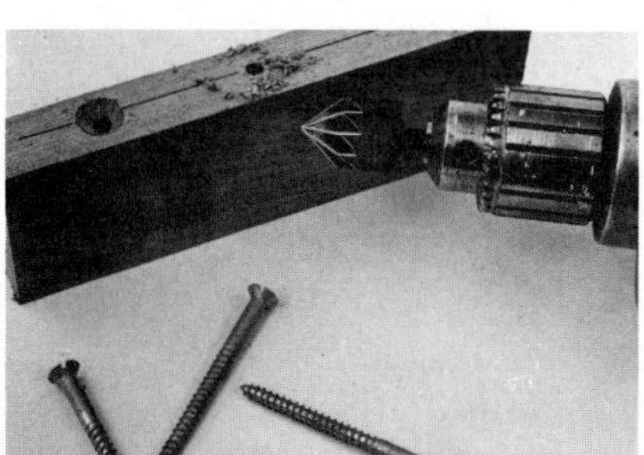

COUNTERSINK can be used in wood, plastics and composition materials.

DOWEL-PLUG cutter is best used in a drill with a maximum speed of 3000 rpm.

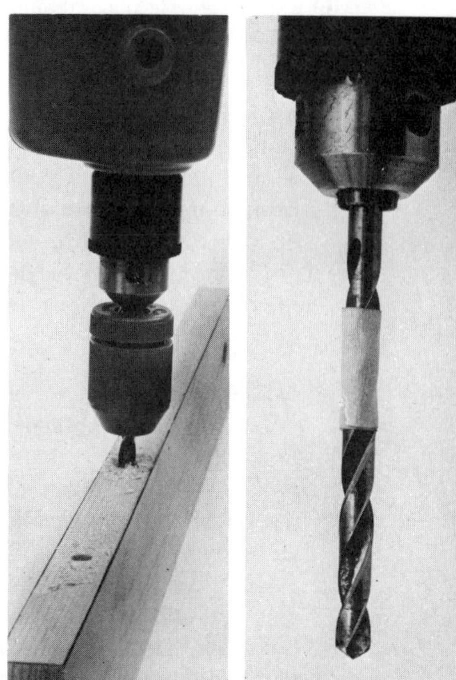

COMMERCIAL drill stop limits bit travel; masking tape (right) is a guide.

For shaping, carving and cutting

ROTARY RASPS come in many shapes and sizes and should be used at high speeds. They're for carving, shaping and milling operations in soft materials and plastics and work especially well on fitting into different shapes in wood.

SURFORM drum from Stanley has a sharp cutting edge at each hole.

QUICKLY and neatly, Surform takes off stock. Both hands steady drill.

DRUM SANDERS handle curves well; they come in a variety of diameters.

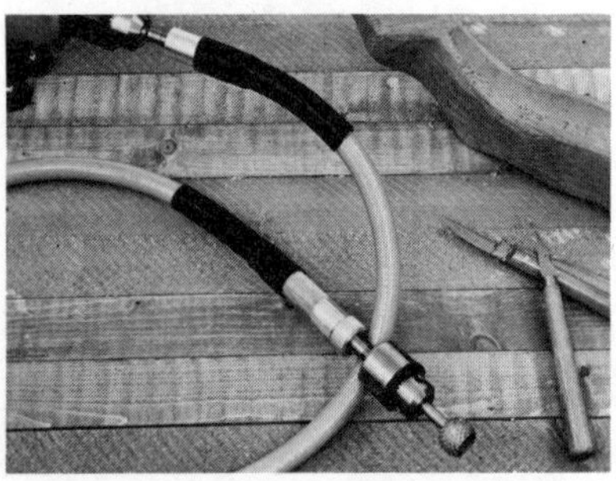

FLEXIBLE SHAFT adds flexibility to your sanding and polishing operations.

METAL sanding disc is okay for first smoothing of rough, flat surfaces.

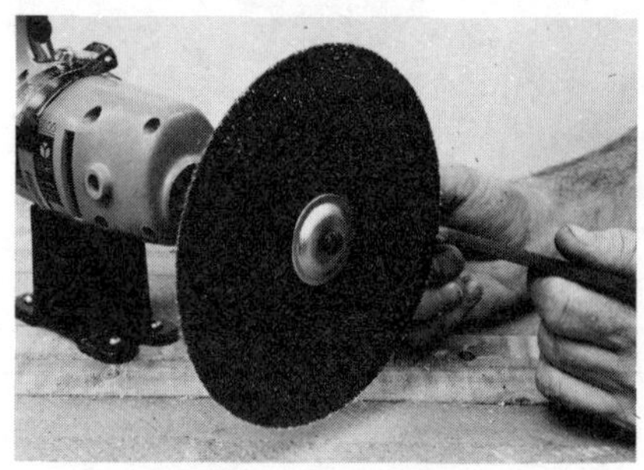

ZIPPIDI-DO disc cuts through many materials including this metal file.

its job. Several makers offer horizontal drill stands for bench-mounting; these sell for about $4 and are a must if you want to get more use from your drill. Vertical drill stands, on the other hand, are intended to convert a portable drill into an accurate and reliable drill press at a fraction of the cost. You can have this convenience for $20 or so.

accessories for drilling

Besides the high-speed twist bits that you probably got with your drill when you bought it, you ought to treat yourself to a full set of power (spade) bits. The larger-diameter ones come with step-down ¼-in. shanks. Thus you can drill up to 1⅜-in. holes with a ¼-in. drill. For 1½-in.-diameter and larger holes, you will have to use a hole saw. There are two types—nonadjustable and adjustable. A typical adjustable one is shown on page 1039. The adjustable type gives a choice of hole sizes, but be aware that it does not bore holes as neatly as the single-size, rigid-type hole saws do and some sanding may be necessary to clean out the hole.

shaping with a drill

Several manufacturers now offer various accessories for shaping and milling with a drill. Of all drill accessories available, I think these are the least desirable. Remember that most wood shaping is best done at high speeds—30,000 rpm with a router, for example. In a drill, you will probably work with a speed somewhere around 2000 rpm. You pay for the difference in quality of work. The cuts will be much rougher and not as accurate.

Tools labeled rotary rasps and files work best when used in a drill mounted in a vertical drill stand. Before using any rasp, make certain you read the manufacturer's instructions carefully concerning speed and use, both for safety and better performance.

smoothing operations

For fast, easy stock removal on rough work, you can't beat Stanley's Surform drum for curved surfaces or a metal disc rasp for flat work-pieces. These tools come with many cutting edges spaced about their work surfaces; thus it's best to stop periodically and clear the tool to keep it from clogging.

To sand various woods and metals, your best bet is to fit a rubber backing pad on an arbor and mount sandpaper discs of suitable grit. This type sanding is undesirable when finish and grain will show because of swirl marks, but it's perfect for fast stock removal and for preliminary sanding of metal.

Though not shown, a good sanding device is the Sand-O-Flex Wheel manufactured by Merit Abrasive Co. This is a wheel fitted with short strips of sandpaper. As the wheel revolves, the flapping strips quickly smooth round or odd-shaped workpieces.

To make your drill a screwdriver, consider buying an attachment like that one shown below. But if you own a variable-speed reversible drill, you can make it a screwdriver by simply buying the driver bits.

Other accessories

DRILL MOUNTED in horizontal drill stand frees both hands to hold work for job such as polishing.

For those tough drilling chores

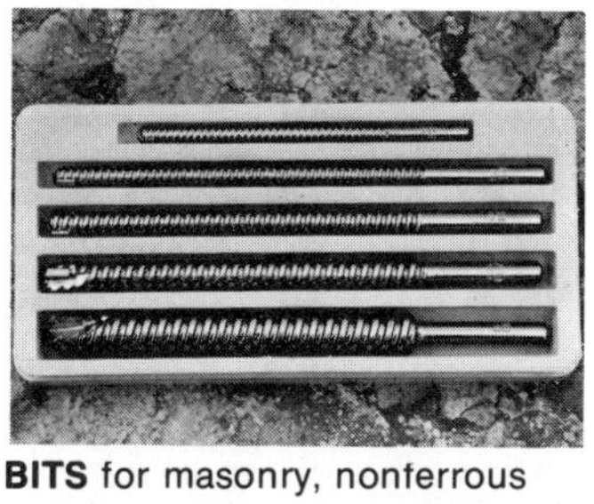

BITS for masonry, nonferrous metals use tungsten-carbide tips.

WITH SPECIAL bits, variable-speed drills drive screws quickly, easily.

IN VERTICAL stand, the tool becomes a drill press. Here, cup brush is chucked.

FOR MORE holding power, drill hole in mortar joint, not brick.

THIS SCREWDRIVER attachment lets single-speed drill drive screws.

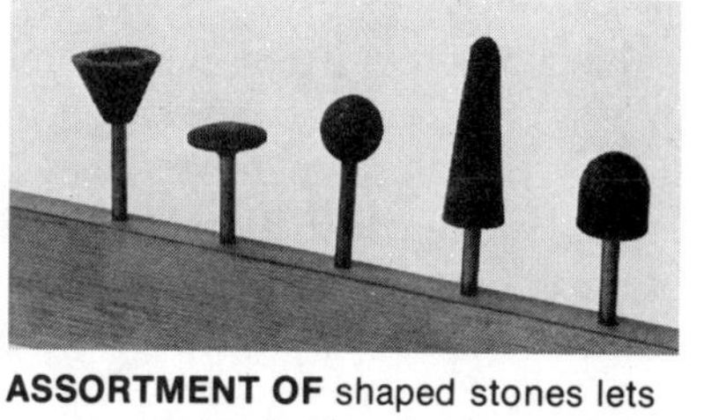

ASSORTMENT OF shaped stones lets you do most grinding, finishing jobs.

TO DRILL ceramic tile use slow speed; cool bit with water.

SPECIALLY shaped bit bores chip-free holes in sheet acrylics.

FAST, complete mixing of paint is assured with powered homogenizer.

This "antique" colonial dry sink has roomy drawers and storage space. Use it to display your indoor plants

By WAYNE C. LECKEY

Build this colonial dry sink

SERVING ORIGINALLY as a place to wash and to store a porcelain water pitcher and bowl, the charming colonial dry sink of yesteryear continues to be a graceful and useful piece of furniture some hundred years later.

Today it provides a perfect place to display your indoor plants; it has two roomy drawers felt-lined for silverware and there is ample storage below for linens behind two raised-panel doors.

We built the little beauty you see here for about $45 from common pine which you can buy at any lumberyard. Its authentic design makes it a collector's item, and its simple construction makes it a natural for the home craftsman to duplicate.

The ends require pieces which measure 17½ in. wide. Since you can't buy pine this wide, you will have to glue and dowel several 1 x 8 (¾ x 7½ in.) boards together. With the possible exception of the doors, the ends are the only members you will have to build up. The wide pieces for the sink top, shelf, bottom and back are cut from plywood. Both ends are worked as right and left-hand members when you run the dadoes across the inside, cut the rabbets for the plywood back and rip the set-back edges at the front. The latter is done on your table saw to assure a straight cut. Here the work is ripped ¾ in. in from the edge for a distance of 25⅝ in., then backed off and the stopped cut is finished by hand. Notice that the ¼-in.-wide rabbets along the rear edges are made ¾ in. wide for a distance of 7 in. down from the top.

SEE ALSO

**Chests . . . Cupboards, china . . . Dining tables . . .
Drawers . . . Hinges . . . House plants . . .
Planters . . . Servers . . . Staining, wood . . .
Wood finishes**

The scroll design at the top of the ends is cut with your sabre saw, then both inside and outside edges are antiqued (distressed) by rounding and sanding.

When you have the sink top and bottom plywood members cut to size, you can glue them in the dadoes of the solid-pine ends. Use long clamps if you have them and check the assembly with a square before setting it aside.

While the glue is drying, make the scroll-cut member for the back. This is cut from a 1 x 10 pine board to rest in the ¾-in. end rabbets previously made and has a rabbet cut along the bottom edge to fit over the sink top. Round and sand the edges of the scroll as you did the ends and then glue and nail the piece in place, driving the nails from the back.

Next, make the framework for the front. This is a separate unit made from ¾-in. pine strips to fit flush with the ends of the cabinet and even with the top surfaces of the sink top and bottom. Butt, dowel and glue the joints; if you have clamps, use them to pull the joints together. When the framework is completed, glue it to the cabinet.

Now you can add the scroll-cut base to the front and ends. Rip a board long enough to make the three pieces, rabbet one edge so it will lap the base and bevel the outer edge as shown. The pieces are mitered at the front and sawed off even at the back. Attach the members with glue and screws from the inside.

A ¼-in. back is added to the cabinet next. Notice that it has "legs" at each side which continue past the sink bottom. The legs provide support for the base members at the rear corners. After the back is glued and nailed in place, add glue blocks to these inside corners.

Now you can make the slanting front piece. It is rabbeted along three edges to lap the front frame and the cabinet ends, and is shorter than the overall length of the cabinet. Cut the top edge as indicated, round the edges as before and glue in place.

The drawers ride on rails installed along each side of the openings. They are cut on the table saw from 2 x 4 stock and rest on a cleat glued and nailed to the cabinet back. The outer rails are glued and screwed to the cabinet sides. The center rails (actually two rails in one) are glued at the front and nailed to the cleat at the back. Notice that the rails project 1/16 in. into the opening on each side. Follow typical drawer construction when you make the drawers and take dimensions directly from the cabinet. The drawer fronts are rabbeted all around so they will lap the openings.

Unless you happen to have a shaper and a set of regular sash cutters, it will be almost impossible for you to duplicate a factory-made raised-panel door in which the panel sits in a groove and the molded, mortised members are undercut to fit perfectly at the corners. The best a home craftsman can do is to assemble simple frames of ¾-in. stock, butt-glue the joints and use a portable router to run the rabbet on the back for the panel and to shape the molded edge on the front. The overall effect is practically the same and few will notice any change. The main difference is that the cutter will leave a rounded inside corner instead of a square one.

Another way to make the doors is to run the stock like picture-frame molding and simply miter the corners. However, this makes a somewhat less authentic-looking door.

The raised panel is a simple thing to run on your table saw by tilting the blade and passing the work through on edge. Then the shallow shoulder cut is made with the work flat on the table and against the fence. A ⅛ x ¾-in. flat molding holds the panel in the frame and covers the joint. As with the drawers, the doors are rabbeted all around so they will lap the openings.

Appropriate hand-wrought hinges should be picked for the doors. You'll need the kind which are offset to accommodate the door lip. White porcelain knobs carry out the colonial feeling.

If you plan to use live potted plants in the sink which require watering and tending, you should fit the top with a shallow sheet-metal tray.

To finish your dry sink, first sand the wood until you are satisfied with its smoothness. You can start with a medium grit and finish with a fine-grit paper. (If you prefer an early American

The rear view shows how the back panel is cut to provide "legs" that support the corner glue blocks

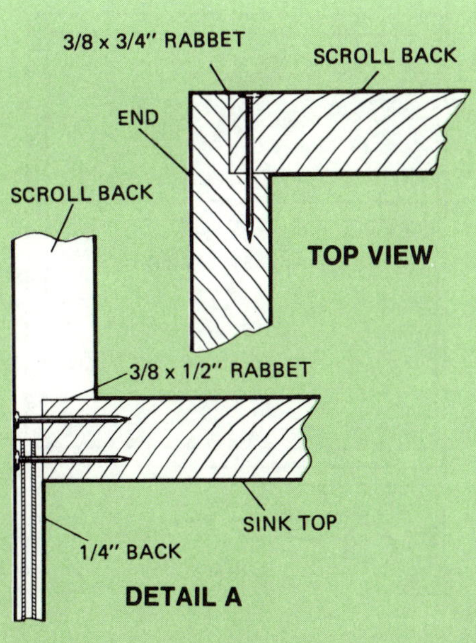

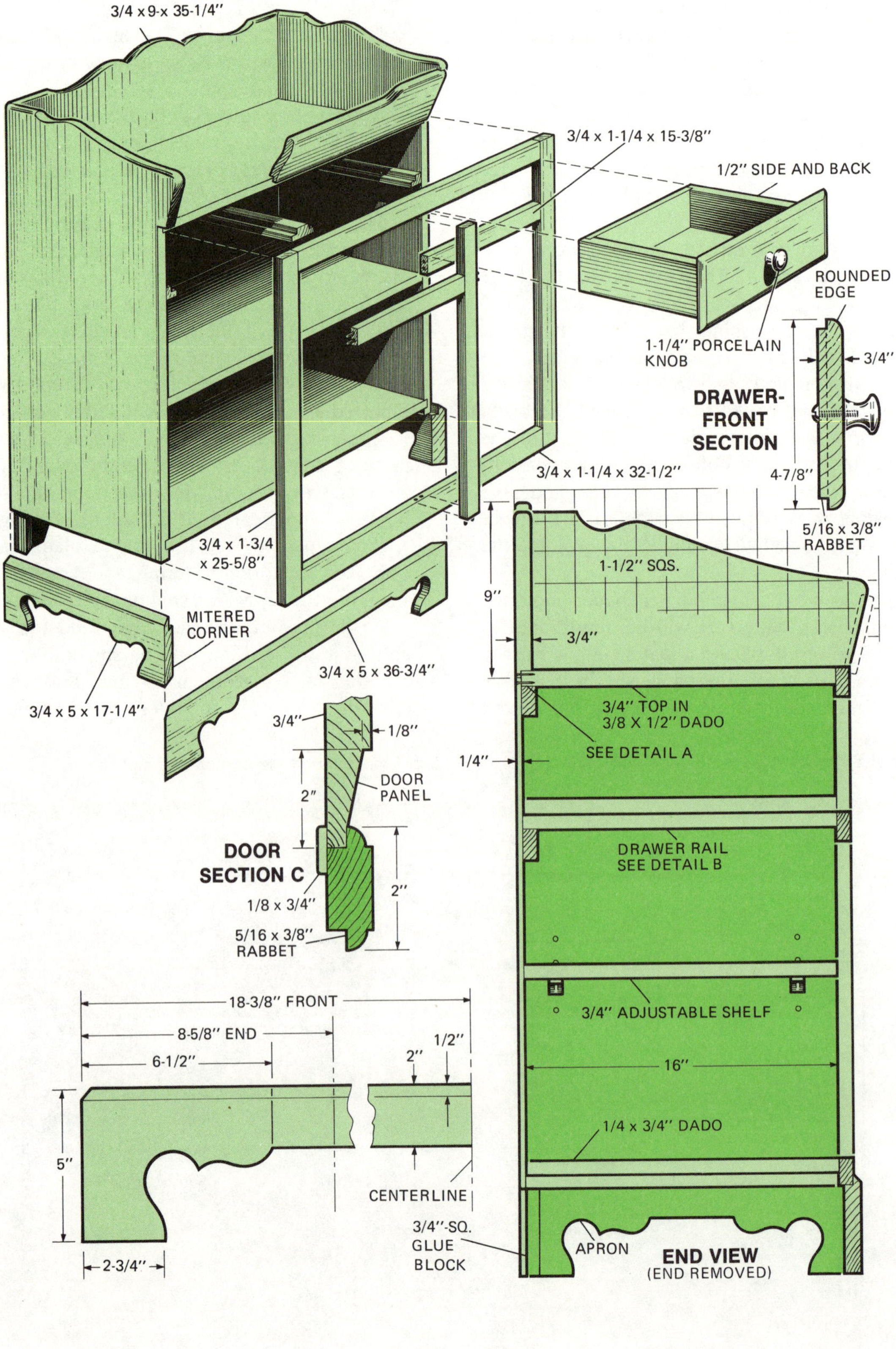
3/4 x 9 x 35-1/4"
3/4 x 1-1/4 x 15-3/8"
1/2" SIDE AND BACK
ROUNDED EDGE
1-1/4" PORCELAIN KNOB
3/4"
DRAWER-FRONT SECTION
4-7/8"
5/16 x 3/8" RABBET
3/4 x 1-1/4 x 32-1/2"
3/4 x 1-3/4 x 25-5/8"
1-1/2" SQS.
9"
3/4"
MITERED CORNER
3/4 x 5 x 36-3/4"
3/4 x 5 x 17-1/4"
3/4"
1/8"
2"
DOOR PANEL
DOOR SECTION C
1/8 x 3/4"
2"
5/16 x 3/8" RABBET
3/4" TOP IN 3/8 X 1/2" DADO
SEE DETAIL A
1/4"
DRAWER RAIL SEE DETAIL B
3/4" ADJUSTABLE SHELF
16"
1/4 x 3/4" DADO
18-3/8" FRONT
8-5/8" END
6-1/2"
2"
1/2"
5"
CENTERLINE
2-3/4"
3/4"-SQ. GLUE BLOCK
APRON
END VIEW
(END REMOVED)

"primitive" look, *don't* oversand the wood.) After the sanding has been completed, wipe off all sawdust.

For a natural or stained finish apply the color stain you prefer, following directions on the can label. Allow to set for approximately 15 to 20 minutes and then—using a clean rag—wipe off all excess, rubbing *with* the grain. Allow the piece to dry overnight (24 hours). If desired, the piece can be antiqued by blending in burnt umber with a rag. (This, too, must be allowed to dry for 24 to 48 hours.) To finish, apply two coats of McCloskey Heirloom semigloss varnish. Allow 24 hours drying time between coats. After approximately three weeks, rub lightly with double-O steel wool saturated with Butcher's Wax and buff to a sheen.

Antiquing hints: Use burnt umber—direct from the tube—to simulate any surfaces that will be exposed to the most dirt accumulation over a long period of time (in corners or crevices, for example). And always blend the burnt umber into the mating stain so that there is no visible "line" or joint.

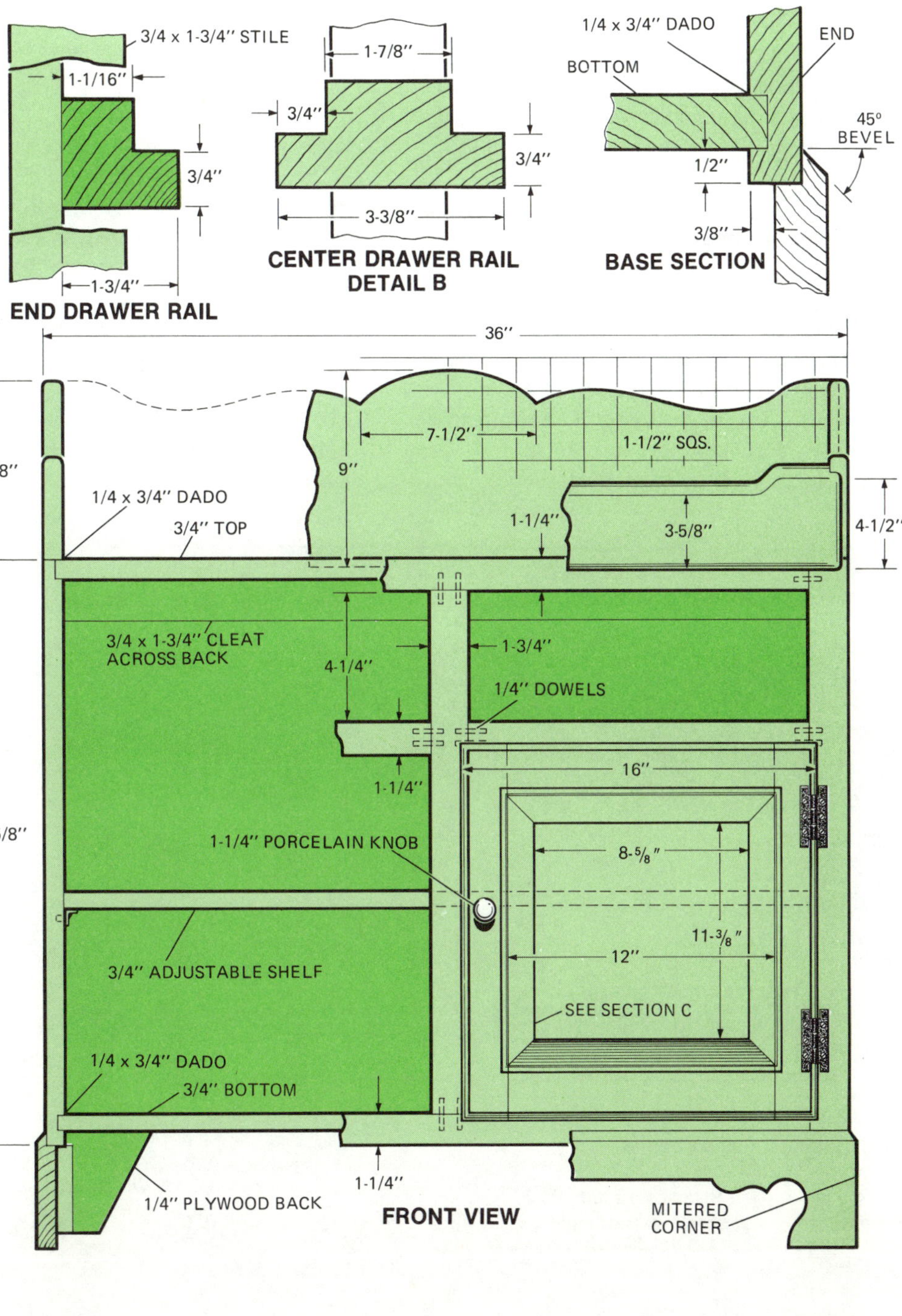

Build your own fruit and vegetable dryer

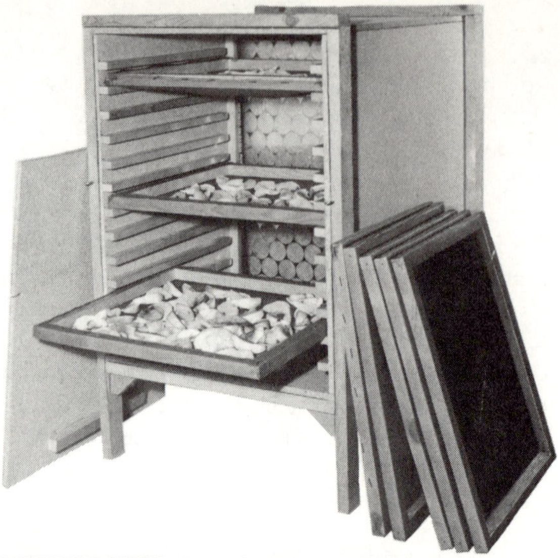

INTERIOR VIEW shows how trays slide in and out. Two furnace filters at rear filter air from blower.

■ AN OLD AND satisfactory method of preserving food is by drying. This dryer uses a fan and two 300-watt heaters to maintain a temperature of about 120° F. and will dry a load in about 12 hours. Electrical consumption is low so the cost of drying a load is only about 22 cents.

To dry vegetables or fruit, you simply spread the food out in a single layer on screen-covered trays and then shift the trays from top to bottom during the drying period.

The dryer cabinet is made of ⅜-in. particle board and wood strips glued and nailed together. The front panel is held in place by two screw eyes that act as catches in the panel slots.

A small blower is attached to the underside of the cabinet to force air through the dryer. The two 300-w. heaters are mounted in the air outlet of the blower to heat the airstream. The cabinet is divided by two furnace filters.

The air safety switch, located at the blower outlet, is actuated by the airflow and insures that the heaters will not operate unless the blower is providing air. The switch assembly is located after the blower and heater are installed. Bend the vane and locate the assembly so the airstream will raise the vane to actuate the switch. Be sure the switch opens when the vane falls. In the off position, the vane rests against the heaters. A thin sheet of aluminum is attached to the inside of the rear panel to reflect radiant heat.

Do not paint or finish the inside of the cabinet as this may taint the food.

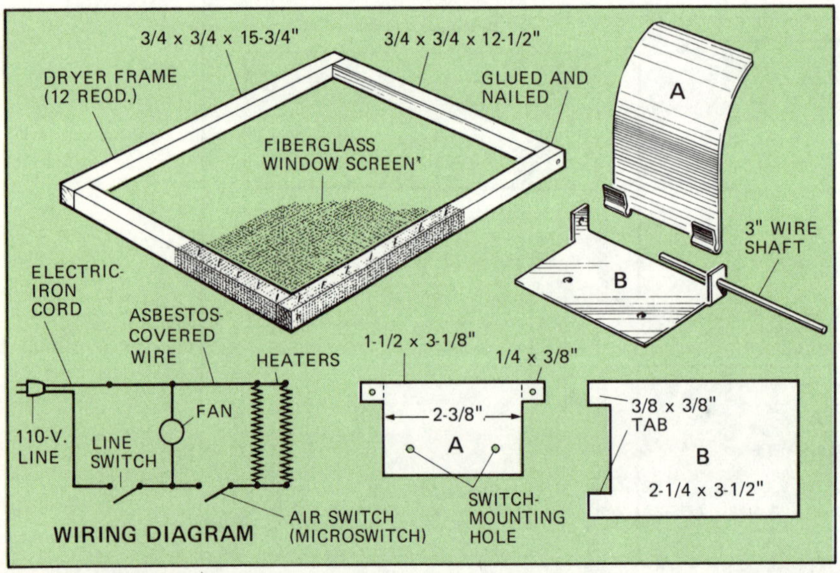

By R. S. HEDIN

REAR VIEW, back removed, shows blower and heaters. Switch is in "on" position.

SEE ALSO

Benches, potting . . . Cold frames . . .
Gardening . . . House plants . . .
Shears, gardening . . . Strawberry barrels . . .
Transplanting . . . Vegetable gardening

USE ⅜-in. particle board (not plywood) for drying compartment, and fiberglass window screen (not metal) to cover the food trays. Note air vent at top of door.

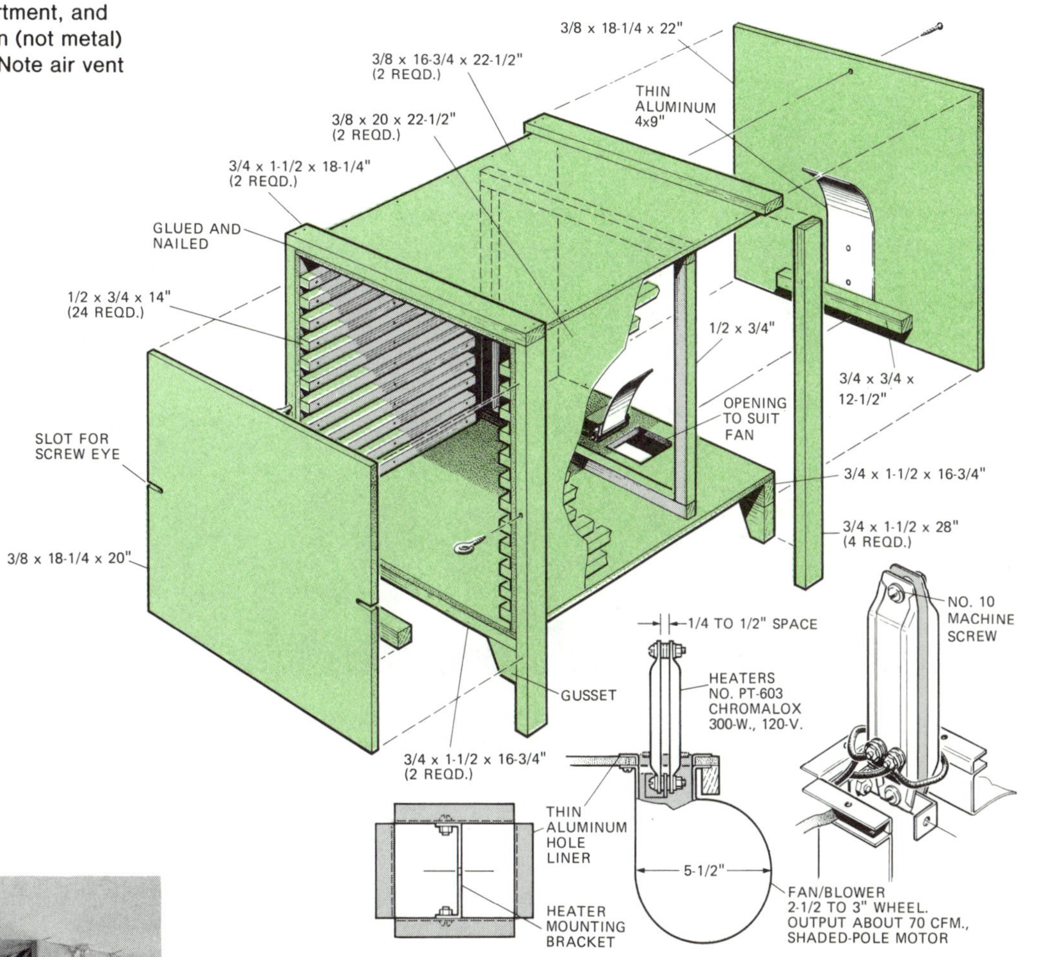

BLOWER should have about 70-C.F.M. output. This one was from copier.

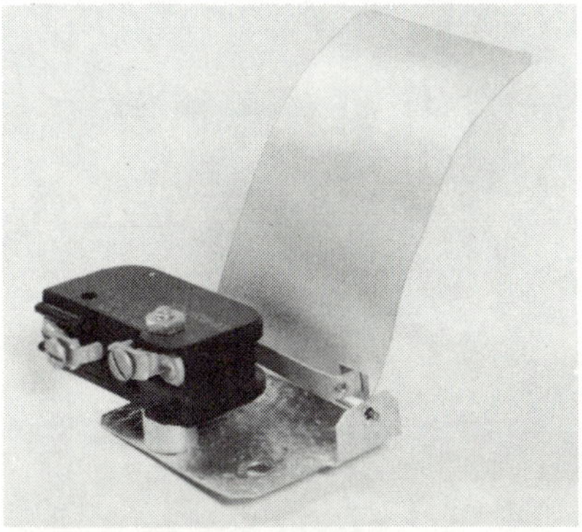

ACTUATING arm of air switch is bent to contact curved vane at hinge flap.

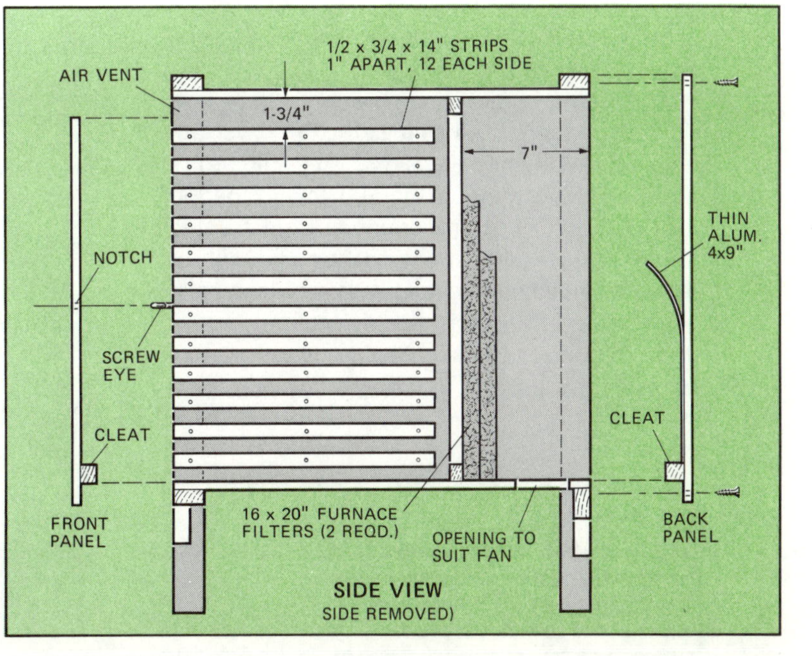

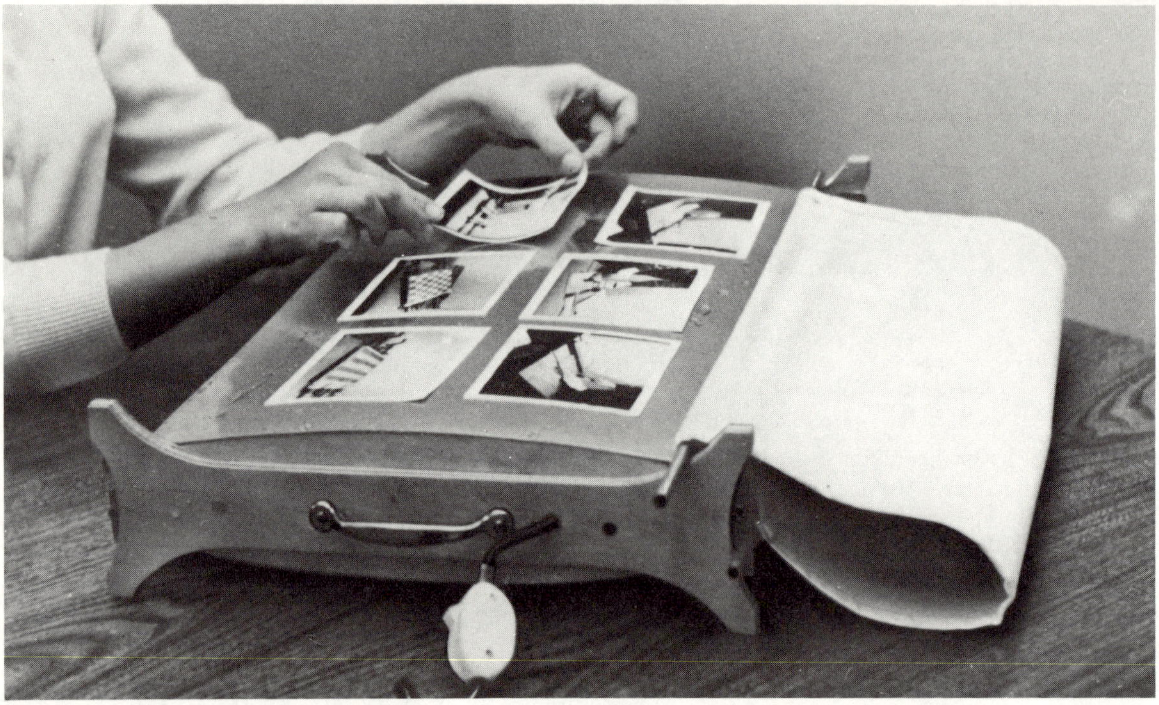

An inexpensive photo print dryer

By JAMES A. JOYNER

■ IF YOU'RE TIRED of waiting hours for your prints to dry on a ferrotype plate, you can build this electrically heated dryer and have them ready in a fraction of the time. The double-sided design provides drying surfaces on both sides. Wet prints are laid out on metal sheets and held flat by canvas retaining strips hooked over the ends and pulled taut. There's room for two 8x10s on each side or four 4x5s.

The frame is made of plywood scrap. Two sidepieces serve both as legs for the dryer and hooks for stretching the canvas over the prints. Screwed to the frame are metal sheets to conduct heat. These can be thin aluminum, stainless steel or galvanized—almost any sheet metal will do. Reynolds aluminum is readily available at hardware stores in 1/16-inch sheets. You can size the dryer to take ready-made cookie sheets or stock ferrotype plates.

SEE ALSO
Cutting boards . . . Darkrooms . . . Developing, photo . . . Lightboxes . . . Mountings, photo . . . Photography . . . Prints, photo . . . Slides, photo

Supported inside the frame is the heating element from an old space heater. Wired in series with the coil is a bimetallic thermostat from an electric coffeemaker to keep the heat constant. If you can't scrounge these items from around the house, replacement heating coils and thermo-

HEATING COIL inside the dryer is strung through glass or porcelain insulators of the type used to anchor radio antennas. Be sure that the coil doesn't sag and touch the metal drying plates at any point.

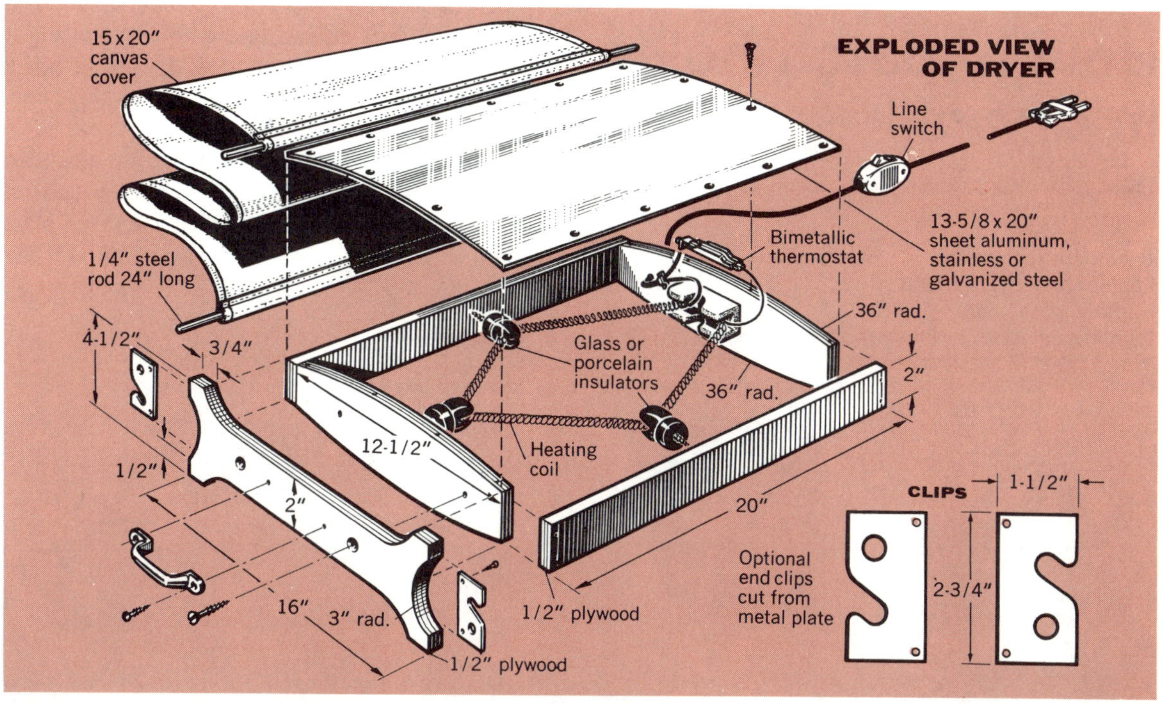

stats can be purchased at electrical appliance stores. Measure the length of coil you need, then buy one as close as possible to this length. A coil can be stretched or shortened slightly to adjust its length, but don't cut off much or you will change its electrical resistance.

String the coil through insulators as shown. The ends are connected to screws on a large porcelain fuse holder serving as a terminal block. Any similar insulated terminal block will do. One lead of the power cord is connected directly to one end of the coil on the block. The other is attached to the thermostat, which is connected to the other end of the coil.

The canvas covers are held in place by metal rods. Have your wife sew pockets in the ends to hold the rods. The rods can be hooked over the legs or, for a neater arrangement, you can make the metal rod holders shown in the drawing above. In use, the dryer is loaded one side at a time in the flat position, then it's stood upright during the drying period.

FUSE HOLDER serves as insulated terminal block for fastening the ends of heating coil. Note how the tubular thermostat is mounted against one of the metal drying plates with a small clip bent from metal strap.

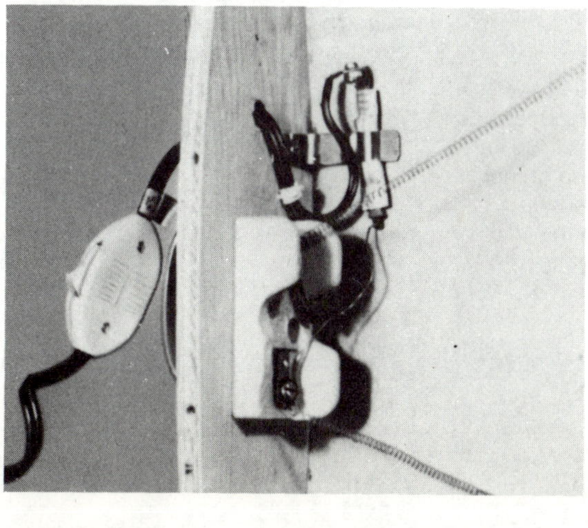

IN UPRIGHT POSITION, dryer is well ventilated and both sides receive heat evenly. Screen-door handles at ends facilitate turning and carrying it. The line switch in the power cord is within easy reach for convenience.

How to patch holes in drywall

SEE ALSO

Basement remodeling . . . Family rooms . . . Fasteners . . . Hardboard . . . Home improvement . . . Nails . . . Painting, interior . . . Plasterboard . . . Tapes, repair

■ THE USUAL WAY to repair a hole in drywall involves enlarging the hole by cutting it back to the centers of the closest studs. Then a large patch is nailed to the studs and the joints are concealed with tape.

Using the method shown, however, you can repair the same hole (in a wall or other *vertical* surface) simply and quickly with a smaller plasterboard patch. Doing it this way eliminates the joint tape step.

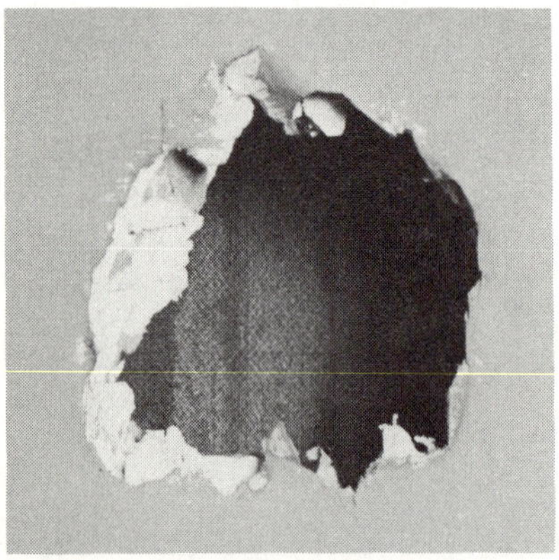

1 This doorknob-size hole is a disturbing but common sight in drywall houses where children and teenagers live.

2 Use a keyhole or sabre saw to cut damaged area into a square or rectangle. Watch for pipes or wires behind wall.

3 Cut a plasterboard patch 2 in. larger than the hole on each side. Centered on the back of the patch, mark an area ¼ in. smaller than the hole on each side. Score the lines with a knife; cut through the paper and *slightly* into the plaster.

4 Snap and peel paper backing and plaster from borders. Leave center plaster attached to front border paper.

5 Sand only the outer edges of the paper with 120-grit abrasive until they taper as much as possible. This will assure invisible joints.

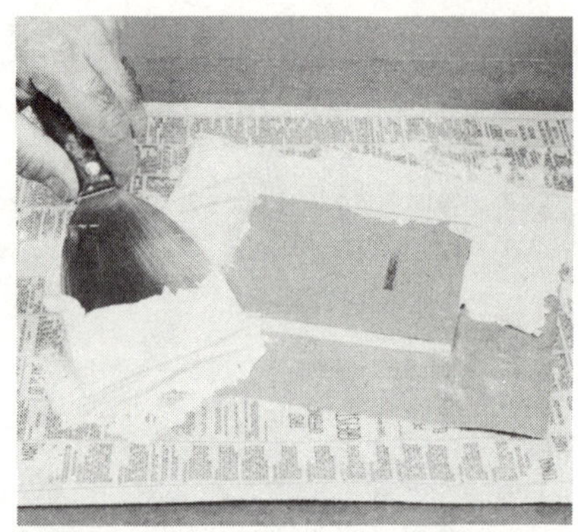

6 Apply joint compound to the back of the patch. Make sure you put a heavy deposit around inside corners.

7 Position the patch, then carefully press it into the damaged area.

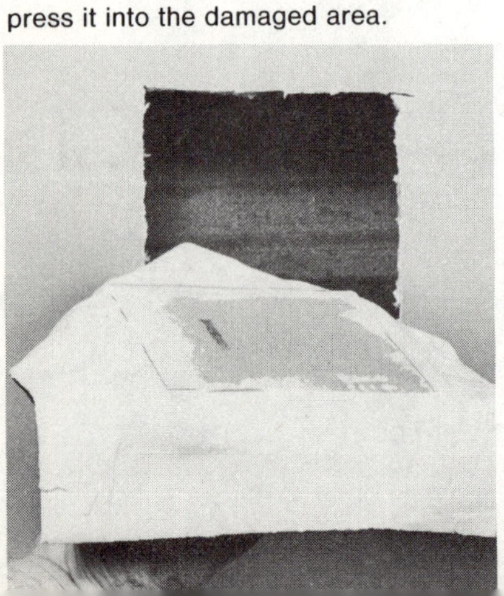

8 Using a 4-in.-wide, flexible drywall knife, go over the patch and squeeze its paper edges flush with the wall. Be sure to work over the entire surface of the joint, so the compound around the patch will adhere properly to the wall.

9 Let the initial coat dry 24 hours. Sand smooth. Apply a thin coat. When dry, sand this coat, paying attention to the edges. Prime and paint.

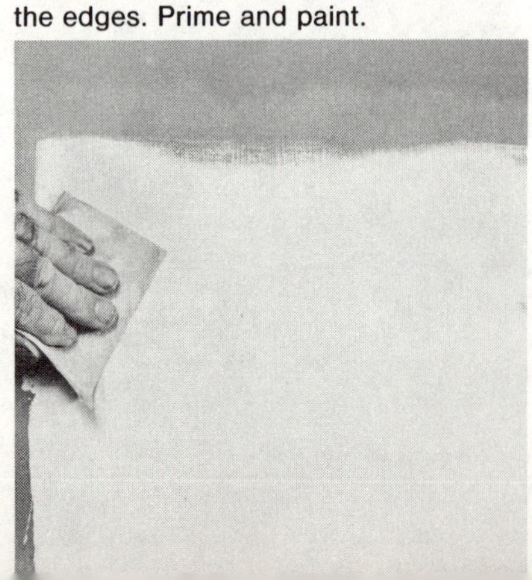

Toy dump truck

By DAVE ACTON

■ WHAT LITTLE GUY wouldn't think his dad the greatest ever when surprised with this all-wood dump truck? It actually dumps with a turn of a crank, and it's built to take a beating.

Start work with the chassis and cut, notch and bore the two rails at one time. Bore both front axle blocks together so the holes align, and assemble the 8½-in. long square "tube" in which the rear axle turns.

Space the two rails 6½ in. with a 1-in. dowel at the front and the axle tube at the rear. Glue the axle blocks in the notches at the front and add the cab's floor and steering wheel. Single wheels are glued to the front axle; dual wheels to the rear.

Assemble the cab so it straddles the rails and floor. Make it complete with seat and bore a hole in the floor, seat and back for the winch cord. I used screws in counterbored holes, then capped the heads with short pieces of dowel glued in the holes and sanded flush. Make the ends of the hood fit between the rails and cover them with ¼-in. pine. Drill for 1-in.-dowel headlights and for a ¼-in. radiator cap.

Inside width of the dump body should be 6⅝ in. so it fits over the rails and pivots freely on a dowel at the rear. The tailgate should also swing open freely. Finish with nontoxic paint or varnish, or let it remain as bare wood.

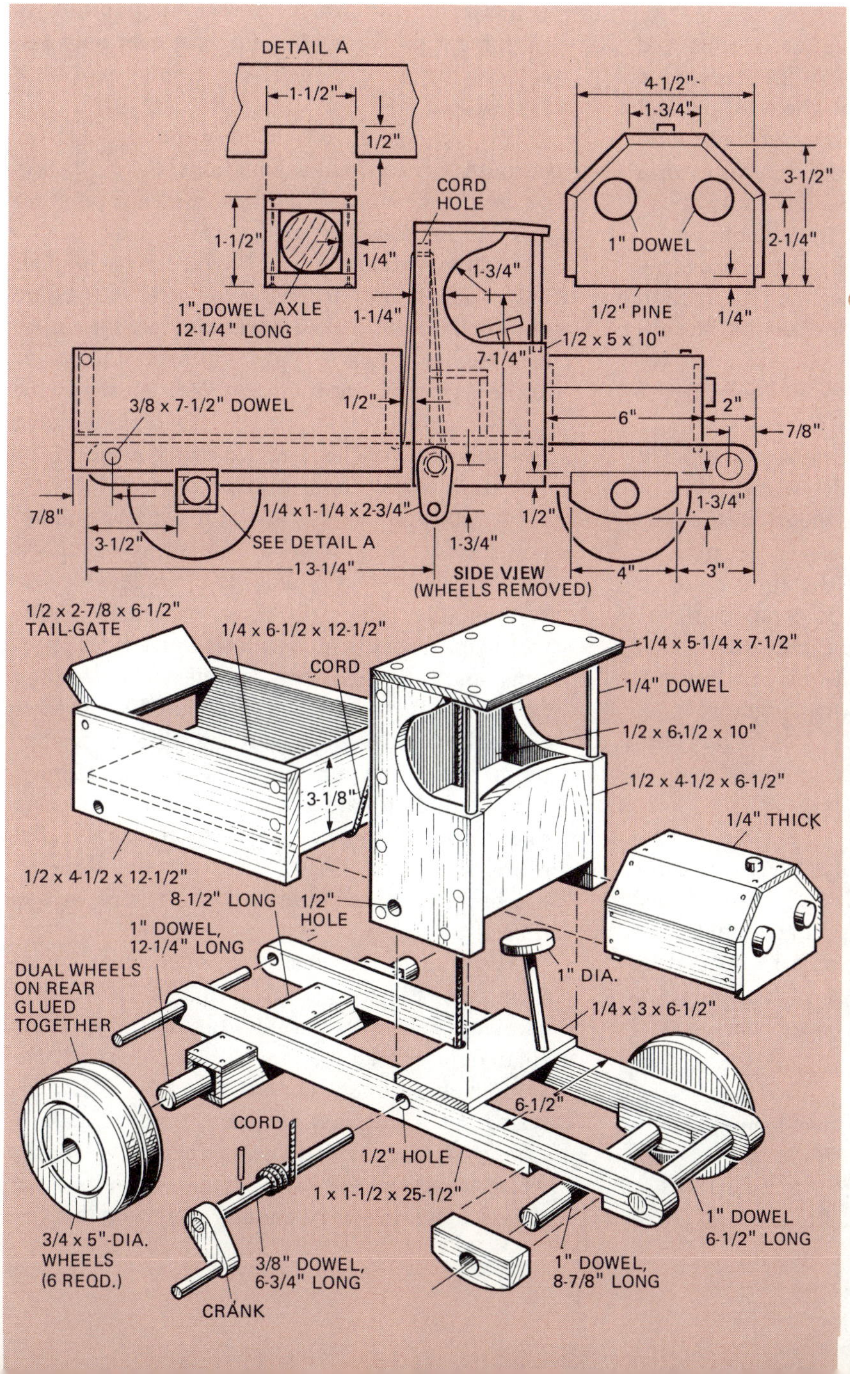

SEE ALSO

Children's furniture . . .
Gifts, Christmas . . .
Kites . . . Miniature houses . . .
Toys . . . Weekend projects

Basics of home wiring

■ FUSES BLOW frequently. The lights dim and flicker. The television picture wobbles and shrinks. The toaster and iron heat slowly—or not at all. The range won't heat and company is on the way for dinner.

Sound familiar?

These are the signs of inadequate wiring, and the signs should not be ignored. With inadequate wiring—and experts claim that about 90 percent of homes are inadequately wired—you not only get poor service from appliances, but you run a serious risk of fire. You are loading electrical circuits with more power than they can handle.

Inadequate wiring is just part of this scenario. Electrical remodeling completes the picture, and it includes wiring a new switch or outlet, installing new lighting, adding new circuits to power new appliances or provide more to your present ones.

The good news is that you can handle most of these inadequate wiring problems and add improvements yourself and save plenty in the bargain. There is nothing mysterious or difficult about electricity if you take the time to learn what it's all about. But don't be deluded: If you are careless, electricity can be the deadliest hazard in your home. You can *completely* remove this danger by following just one simple rule:

Disconnect the power before you make any electrical repairs or improvements.

how housepower works

The electric utility from which you buy power distributes it through a series of sub-stations. Each station steps down the original voltage until it reaches a transformer on a pole near your home. At this point the power is at 2400 volts.

SEE ALSO
Checkers, outlet . . . Doorbells . . .
Extension cord reels . . . Fluorescent lamps . . .
Lamps . . . Lighting . . . Post lamps . . .
Soldering . . . Testers, continuity . . .
Wiring, electrical . . . Yard lighting

From the transformer, electricity is supplied to you and your neighbors as either 115- or 230-volt service. Or it may be at 120/240 volts. The actual voltage which reaches your home may vary slightly because of loads on the power line. For example, during heavy use of airconditioning equipment there may be periods where only 110 volts or less are supplied. The result could be a "brown-out."

The National Electric Code stipulates that for purposes of electrical calculations, 115/230 volts be used, and you will find this reference point on this and the following pages.

All homes should have 230-volt service, and all brand-new homes are wired for it. If your home doesn't have 230-volt service now, ask the utility company to install it. They will bring the power to the service box at their cost. You must pay for any wiring changes inside the house. If you have 230-volt service, check to see if it is 60 amps or 100 amps. Most codes require 100 amp service; 150 or 200 amp service is best if you drive many power tools and appliances. The utility company can help with details on this upgraded service.

Imagining pictorially how electricity works will help you in troubleshooting electrical problems and repairs. Think of electricity coming from the transformer as a smoothly flowing river between two high banks. At the service entrance the river is divided into a number of small streams (individual circuits). Each time you plug in an appliance or snap on a switch, you use part of the water from one of these streams. You can use no more water than is in the stream at one time.

At the head of each stream, where it is divided from the main river, is a dam (fuse) by which you can stop the flow of water. Just ahead of these small dams is a larger dam (main fuse) which can completely stop the flow of water at once. In analyzing the wiring in your home, you are making sure that there are enough streams to supply water to all the appliances you use, and to see that the streams carry enough water for the job.

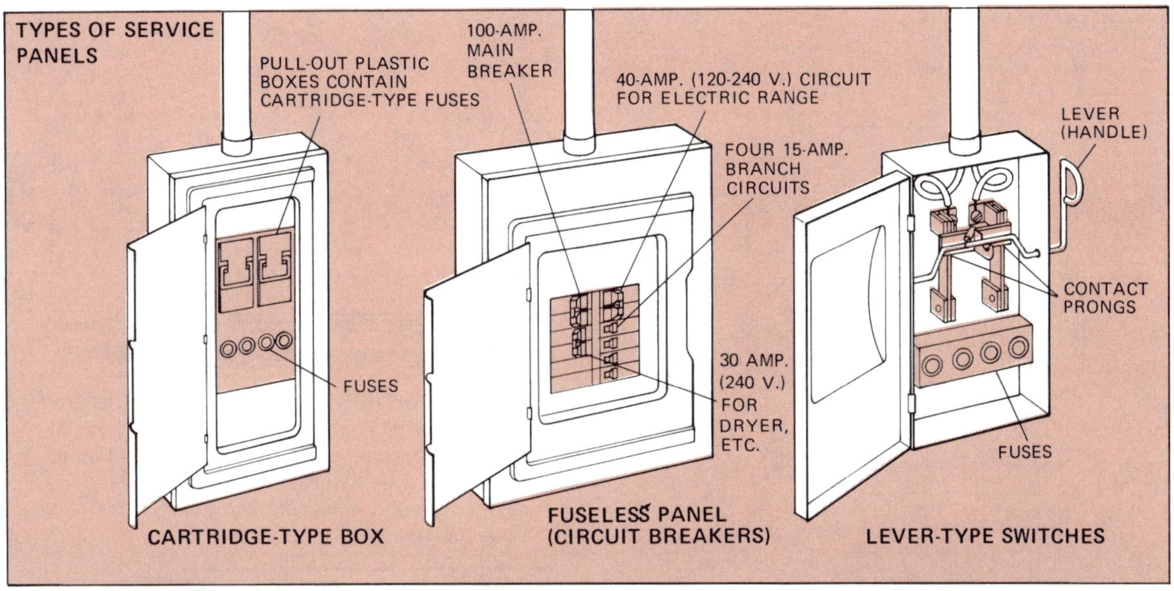

IN CARTRIDGE-TYPE BOX (service-entrance panel), the power is shut off by pulling out both of the cartridge cases. The main fuses (cartridge-type) are housed inside this box. The fuses below the main fuses serve branch circuits throughout the house.

FUSELESS service entrance panels are equipped with circuit breakers that handle the main source of power and individual branch circuits. To shut off all power, the main breaker is moved to the OFF position. Circuit toggles control individual circuits.

KNIFE-TYPE SWITCHES are made in several varieties. They usually are found in older wiring systems. To cut the power, move the lever handle to OFF. If the box has fuses in it, each fuse controls one circuit.

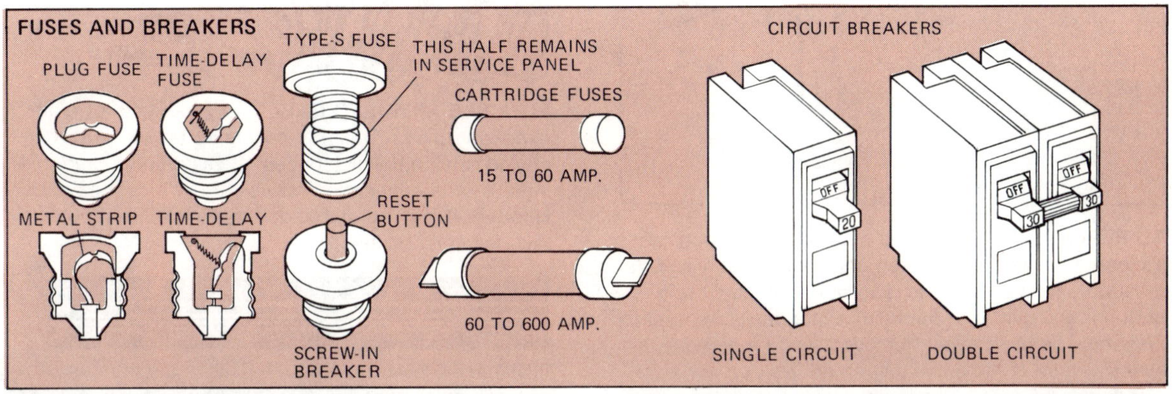

FUSES AND BREAKERS are designed to prevent fire hazards. If a line (circuit) becomes overloaded because its capacity is exceeded by current demand, the fuse controlling that line will "blow." This breaks the link with the main fuse, and the line goes dead. Cartridge and plug type fuses always must be replaced with new fuses. Circuit breakers trip a switch to the OFF position when the line becomes overloaded. You simply flip the toggle to ON to restore the power. Before reactivating a circuit breaker that has tripped, turn off the equipment on that circuit to prevent a surge of power along the line.

This description is oversimplified, of course, but it may help you visualize how electrical circuits are connected and work.

electrical tools and products

A basic electrical tool kit doesn't need to be elaborate or costly. In fact, you probably have many of the necessary tools. The basic kit can be expanded as you get into specialized electrical projects. Tools and products you need include:

Straight slot screwdrivers, Phillips head screwdrivers, a hammer, utility knife, long nose pliers, and a voltage and/or continuity tester. You'll also need fuses, if your electrical service entrance isn't on a circuit-breaker system, wire nuts, electrician's tape, and wire strippers.

Nice to have, but not essential, are a fish tape, lineman's pliers, a fuse puller (if system is fused),

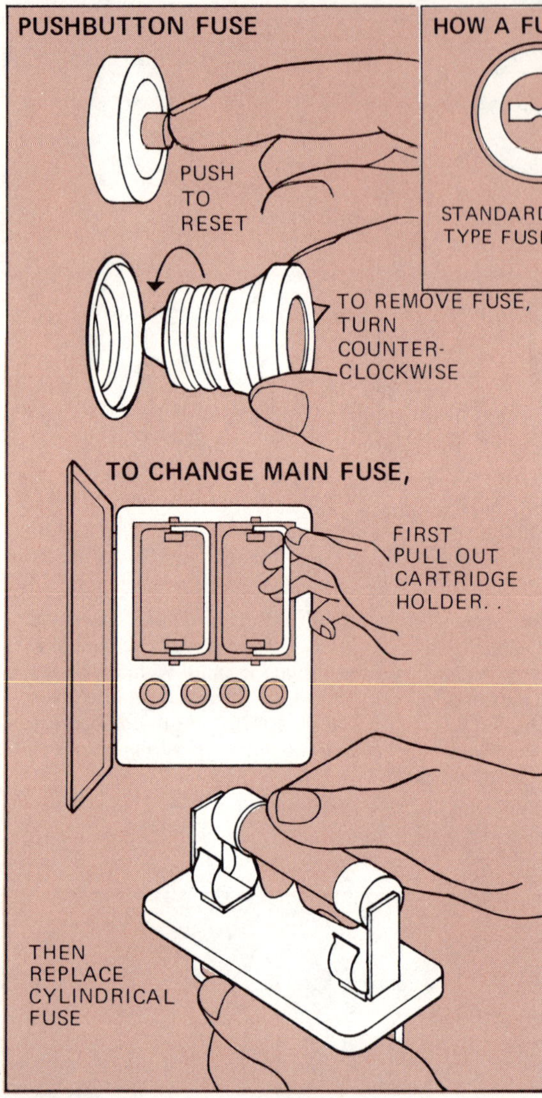

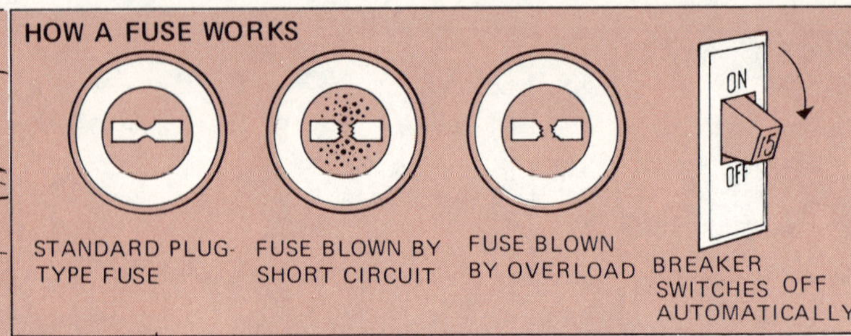

TO REPLACE A FUSE, stand on a dry spot (such as a piece of plywood) and keep one hand behind you. A resettable screw-in fuse is reactivated by pushing a button in the center of the fuse. A standard plug-type fuse must be unscrewed, removed, and replaced with a similar fuse of the same amperage. Do not use a higher-rated fuse—even temporarily. The amperage rating is stamped on the bottom metal contact of the fuse. A cartridge-type fuse is replaced by pulling the plastic box housing. If the contacts are corroded, clean them with steel wool and apply a daub of petroleum jelly to the metal ends. This will help deter corrosion.

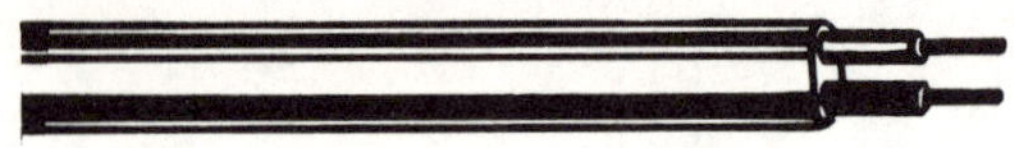

PLASTIC-SHEATHED CABLE—INDOOR. This product is used for all types of circuits indoors. It is flat, with a tough, flexible outer jacket. It is easy to pull and strip, especially where the wire has to be "snaked" through walls and floors. It has solid-copper conductors.

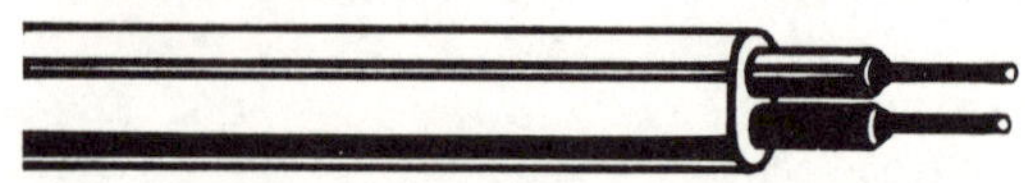

PLASTIC-SHEATHED CABLE—DUAL-PURPOSE. This cable is made for indoor and outdoor use and underground. It requires no conduit and is flat in shape. Manufactured to resist moisture, acid, and corrosion, the cable may be run through masonry units and between framing.

FLEXIBLE ARMORED CABLE may be used for either exposed runs on wall and ceiling surfaces, or for concealed runs in hollow spaces of walls, floors, and ceilings. It is recommended for use in dry locations only. However it may be embedded in wall or ceiling plaster. Use steel boxes.

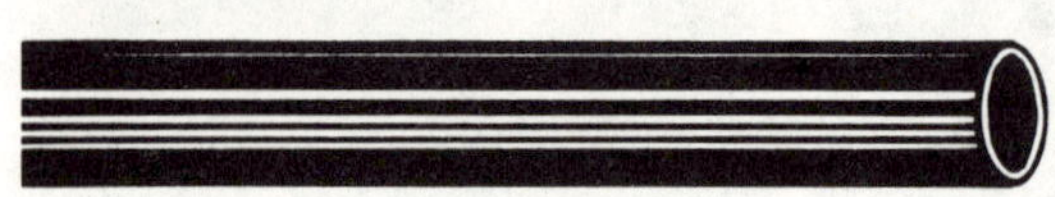

RIGID THIN-WALL CONDUIT. This is the most expensive and most generally accepted type of wire covering because it gives greater protection to the wires. It also grounds the entire system for added safety. It may be used inside and outside and through masonry units—except cinder block.

a quarter-inch portable electric drill, spade bits, masonry bits, and an extension attachment for the bits. The fish tape, bits, drill, and extension are used to run wires between walls and through floors when you're adding new circuits.

electrical emergencies

Usually when the power fails the problem is at the utility company. Once the problem is solved there, the power comes back on.

Occasionally the power may go off because a circuit in the house has become overloaded with appliances, lights, tools. What happens is a fuse pops or a circuit breaker trips at the main service panel or at a separate service panel elsewhere in the house. The fuses or circuit breakers are designed to blow or trip to prevent electrical fires due to overloading.

THREE-WIRE CONNECTIONS for either an additional fuse panel or safety switch are installed this way. The power take-off lugs, available in most entrance panels, permit partial extensions of existing wiring without installation of a larger entrance switch to handle the electricity.

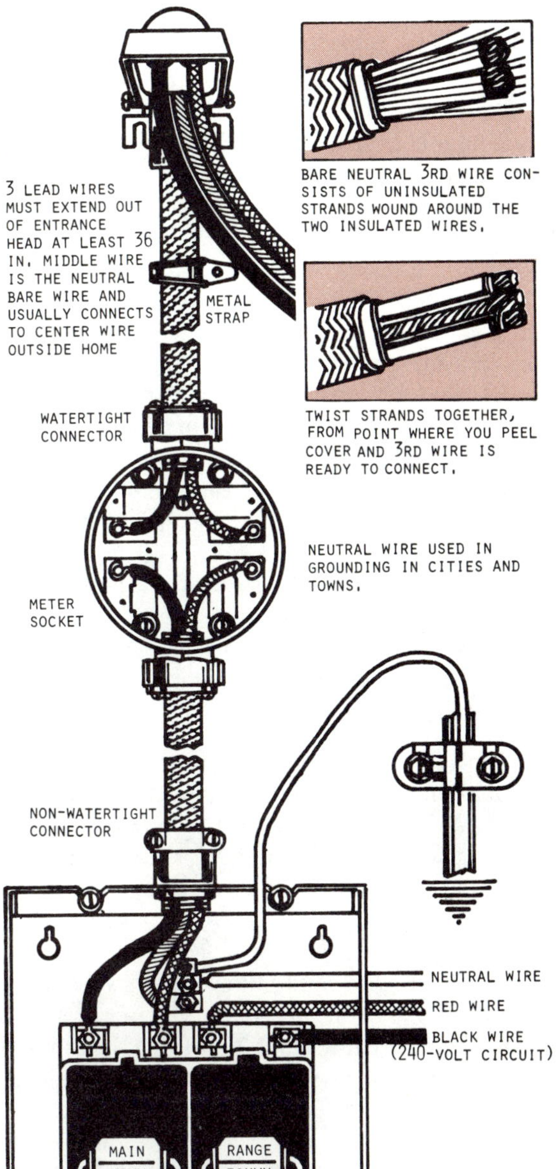

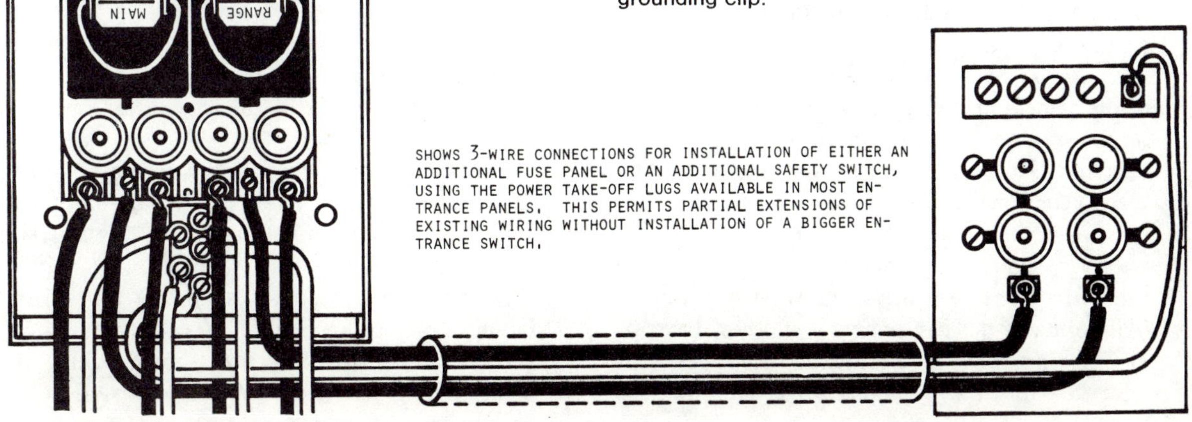

If the fuses in your home pop often, or the circuit breakers trip frequently, chances are the system is not large enough to handle the power demand. Consult the utility about this; the service usually is free.

When the power fails at your house, and the utility company is not to blame, follow these steps:

1. If the floor below the service (fuse) box is damp, place a wide board or piece of plywood on the floor under the entrance and stand on it. It's a good idea to have such a board stored near the power entrance for emergencies. The wood isolates you from the damp flooring and protects against electrical shock.

2. If the house is on a circuit-breaker system, snap the toggles of the breaker to the "on" position. You may have to do this a couple of times to restore the power. If so, the toggle is faulty and should be replaced.

3. If the house is on a fuse system, put one

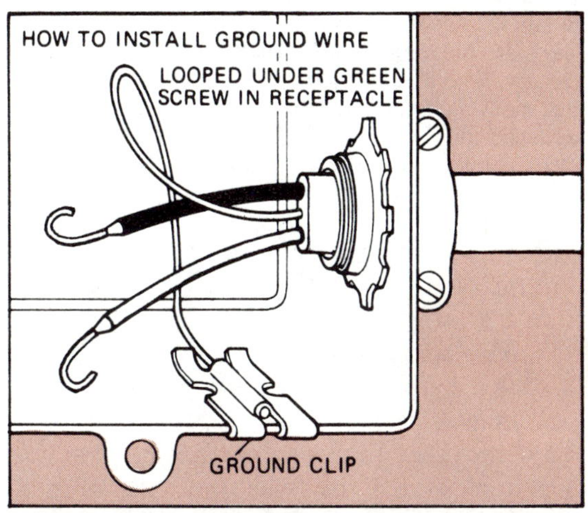

GROUNDING IS REQUIRED if you are using nonmetallic cable. The ground connects from a green screw to a ground clip mounted on the junction box. The screw is on the receptacle. Loop the wire around it, turn down the screw, and tie off the wire in the grounding clip.

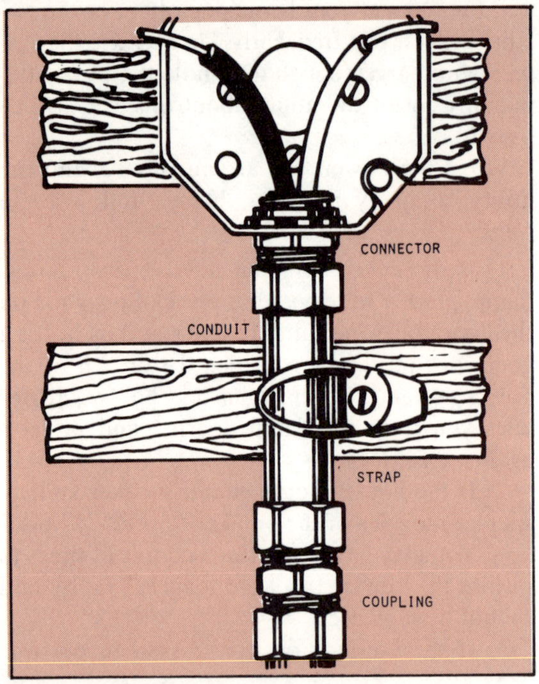

WHEN INSTALLING thin-wall conduit, the empty conduit is first fastened in place before the insulated wires are fed through. For bends, use a conduit bender. Smooth any cut edges with a metal file. Conduit must be supported with a hanger every 6 ft. on exposed runs and every 10 ft. on concealed runs. Conduit couplings are available.

hand in your hip pocket or behind you and turn out the blown fuse with your other hand. If the fuse is a cartridge type product, use a fuse puller to remove and replace it.

Many appliances—especially washers, dryers, and ranges—may have a separate fusing system built into them. They may be receiving power but still won't work. If this is the case, try pushing the "reset" button on the appliance. It will be marked as such and usually is located on the main control panel of the appliance.

Some electric ranges have a fuse system. This fuse usually is located in the top rear of the oven compartment or under one of the rear elements on top of the range.

Caution: Always replace a fuse with a new fuse of the same amperage. The amperage is stamped on the conductor at the bottom of the fuse: "15," "20," or "30." A smaller fuse size may cause the fuse to continually pop; a larger fuse size may not pop when the circuit is overloaded.

If you live in an older home, there may be more than one central power service entrance. This often is the case where a clothes dryer or electric range has been added. More power is necessary for these appliances, so a separate fuse system (usually a circuit breaker) was installed to handle the extra load. If changing fuses and tripping circuit breakers at the main power entrance doesn't restore power, be sure to look elsewhere for another fuse box or circuit breaker. The trouble may be in this power entrance.

wire sizes are important

Different sizes of electrical wires carry different amounts of electricity. Each size is designated by a number, and the smaller the number, the larger the wire. Generally, most lighting circuits are wired with No. 14 wire. Most appliance circuits are wired with No. 12 wire and sometimes with No. 10 wire.

Wire offers resistance to the electricity passing through it. The larger the diameter of the wire the less the resistance. Resistance creates heat, and the more resistance, the greater the heat. When you draw too much current through a small wire by plugging in too many appliances, you generate considerable heat—enough, in fact, to create a fire hazard. The insulation melts off the wires.

While the National Electrical Code permits the use of No. 14 wire in lighting circuits, some local codes demand that No. 12 be the smallest wire used. The additional capacity of No. 12 is an extra margin of safety.

These specifications refer to copper wire. If aluminum wire is used, always install one size larger—No. 12 and No. 10. The wire will be designated with the letters CO-ALR for 15- and 20-amps and CU-AL for higher power ratings. Always make sure that the terminals of switches, outlets, and other fixtures are so marked. Mixing copper wire with aluminum terminals—or copper terminals with aluminum wire—can set up corrosion and cause trouble. Also, make sure terminal screws are especially tight on aluminum wires. Aluminum tends to expand and contract, which loosens the screws and therefore causes poor electrical contact.

When buying wire, keep this formula in mind: 0 to 4 gauge wire for transformer to service entrance hookups; 6 to 14 gauge wire for electrical circuit hookups.

Wires have different colored insulation for a purpose. Black and colored wires (usually red) are "hot" or power wires. They carry current. White wires are neutral or ground wires. Green wires also are ground wires. The present wiring in your home follows this color coding, and when you install new wiring, you should follow the color code. It will make the job go easier.

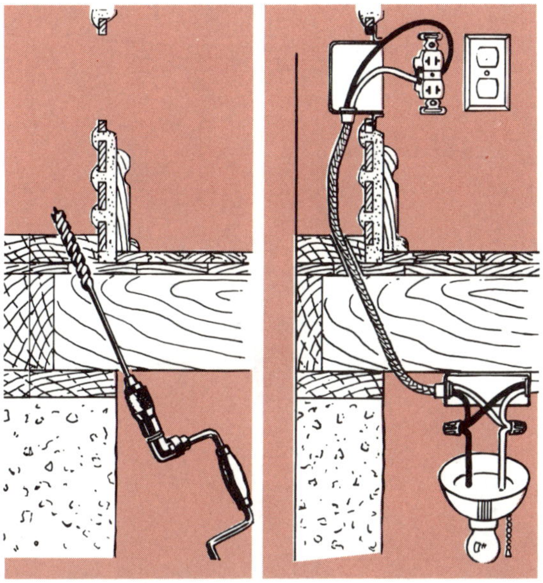

TO RUN A WIRE through a floor, first select the outlet site and cut an opening through the wall covering. Bore a diagonal hole up from the basement or crawl space. Then push a short length of fish wire up from the lower level with wires attached, and pull the wires through to the outlet opening. Use armored or sheathed cable.

The National Electrical Code also has a formula for determining how many circuits are needed in a home. First, find the square footage of your home, using the outside dimensions of the foundation. Include the area of each floor in use, and also the areas like the basement and attic which may not be in use now but might at sometime in the future.

The code calls for a minimum of 3 watts available for each sq. ft. of space. This means that a standard 15-amp. circuit delivering 1725 watts can serve 600 sq. ft. If you divide the total square footage of your home by 600, you will find the minimum number of lighting circuits required.

Note that this figure is *minimum,* and refers to lighting circuits only. If you are to have ample wiring with some room for growth, divide the square footage by 400. Thus, if your home is 2400 sq. ft., you should have a minimum of four lighting circuits, but six circuits would be much better.

In addition to the lighting circuits, the code also requires that you have at least two appliance circuits, each rated at 20 amps, and wired with No. 12 wire. No lights are included in these circuits, which are intended for small appliance outlets only. The circuits must serve the kitchen, dining room, laundry, family room, and breakfast area, where you use most of the appliances.

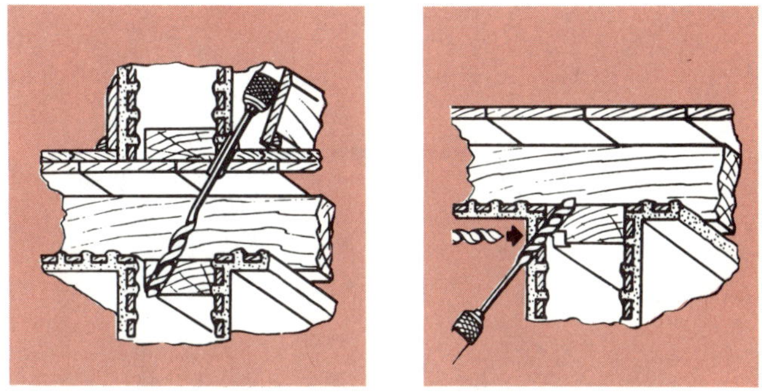

USE THESE TRICKS to fish a wire through floors and ceilings. If you can get into the room above, remove the baseboard and drill a diagonal hole downward. Then drill a hole upward from below. Special auger bits help bore holes for fishing power wires.

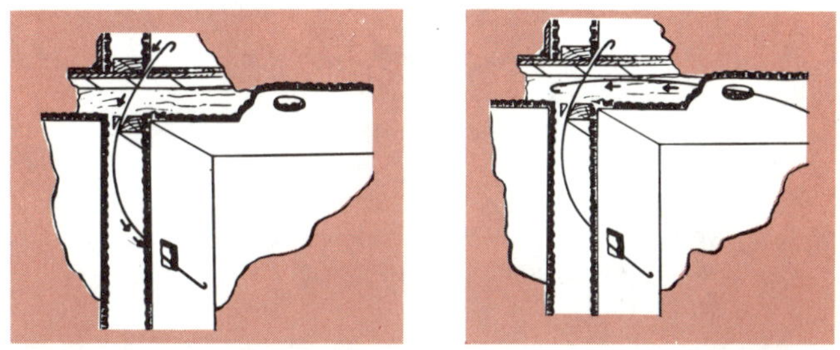

PUSH THE FISH WIRE, hooked at the ends, through the hole on the second floor. Pull one end out at the switch or outlet opening. Then push the wire through a ceiling outlet. Fish until you hook the first wire. Electrical fish wires are made in several lengths; 12- and 20-ft. are best.

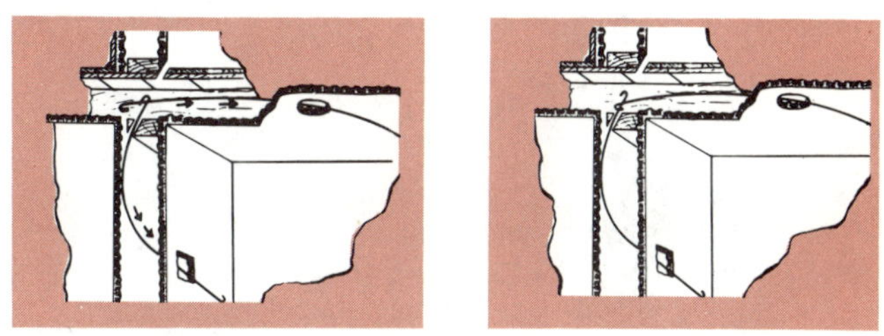

PULL EITHER WIRE until both are hooked. Then pull both wires until the hooks meet. Finally, pull the shorter wire through the switch outlet. When the hook from the long wire appears, attach the cable and pull it through. Make sure the cable is attached tightly to the fish wire.

Both of these circuits must extend to the kitchen.

In determining adequate wiring for your home, a good rule of thumb is to figure an appliance circuit for each 500 sq. ft. You also should keep in mind the areas of heavy appliance use, such as a workshop, laundry area, etc. In a home of 2400 sq. ft., five appliance circuits would assure good safe wiring.

planning for new wiring

Draw an electrical diagram of your home, first because you should have a chart of the circuits for handy reference, and second, to use in determining whether or not your wiring is adequate.

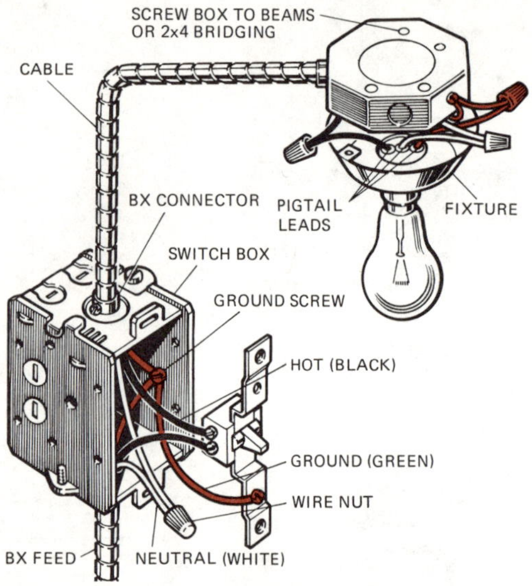

HERE'S HOW to install a fixture switch. Be sure that you connect black wires to black wires, white to white, and ground to ground from switch to the fixture.

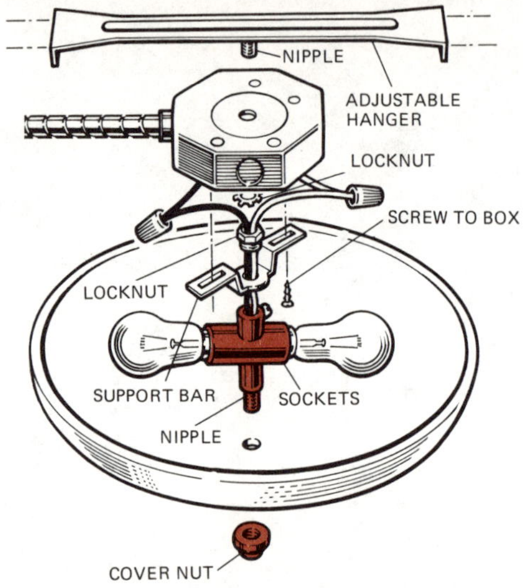

A TYPICAL FIXTURE is assembled this way. The hanger spans the joists and supports the assembly. It is adjustable so the assembly is easy to install between framing members. If a hanger isn't used, the box is screwed or nailed to the joist for support.

Begin by counting the fuses in the service box to find the number of circuits. Then learn what lights and outlets are on each circuit.

One way to do this is to turn on all lights, then unscrew the fuses one at a time. Note which lights go out. Check wall outlets the same way by

A THREE-WAY SWITCH that controls a fixture from two points is wired this way. The box connections will be easy if you study this diagram before you start. For strength, wrap the wire nut connections with plastic electrician's tape.

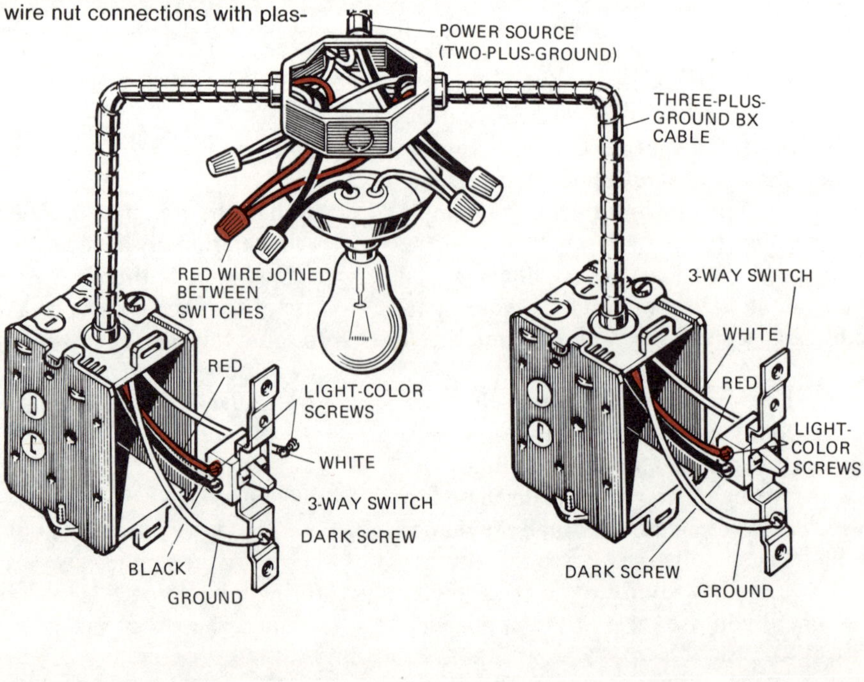

plugging table lamps into them.

Draw a plan of each floor, locating all lights, outlets and switches. Use colored pencils to join the outlets and lights on each circuit. Finally, number each circuit, and tape the numbers near the corresponding fuses in the service box.

Now survey the chart and answer these questions:

• Do you have at least as many circuits as required by national or local codes?

• Do you have enough circuits for really good wiring?

• Are there at least two appliance circuits?

• Are there individual circuits for such heavy-duty appliances as electric ranges, water heaters, the furnace, air conditioning, clothes dryer?

You may have to slightly rework your initial plan. If so, here are several rules to follow:

1. Plan a wall outlet for every 12 ft. of wall in the house. For convenience, have at least three in each room, more if the room is large.

2. One lighting circuit might include two small bedrooms and a bathroom, or a large bedroom and a bathroom or walk-in closet.

3. Don't put all the lights on one floor on one circuit. If that fuse blows, you're out of light.

4. Living room and kitchen lights can be on one circuit since the power demand isn't too great.

5. Dining room and hall lights may be put on one circuit, along with a powder room.

6. One appliance circuit should start in the kitchen and have outlets in the dining room and breakfast or family rooms. Another appliance circuit should serve the kitchen only.

7. Plan separate appliance circuits for the laundry and workshop areas.

8. Plan separate circuits for individual major appliances. Some of the appliances may require 230 v. instead of 115 v.

Now plan the changes you want to make, along with the new circuits. Check the service box. Does it have empty fuse sockets or unused panels for circuit breakers? If not, you can buy an additional service box which can be mounted alongside the present one. There usually are lugs in the present box from which you can wire the service to the new box. Simply knock out the lugs with a punch. Also check the use to which you are putting your present circuits. If you are overusing some of them, plan to cut them in half, providing two circuits and two fuses or circuit breaker toggles.

At this point, you can make a diagram of the house as it will be after you have made the wiring changes. Plan your work in easy steps, and make a list of the materials you will need for the job.

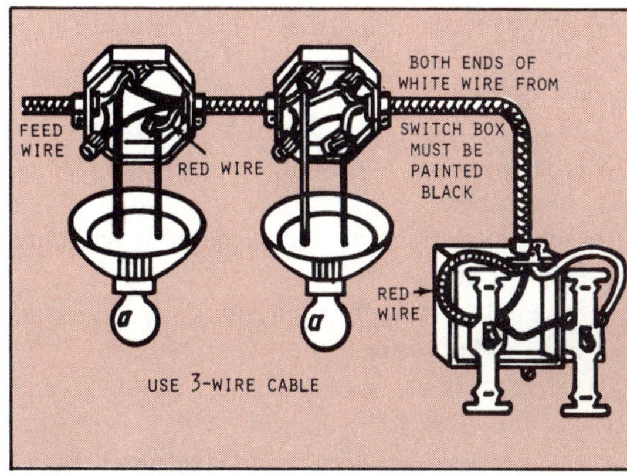

WHEN 3-WIRE CABLE is required (specified "14/3 With Ground"), the white wire from the switch must be painted or somehow tagged "black" at the switch and at the outlet. This code lets you know that the wire is "hot."

wire buymanship

Most electrical codes permit three kinds of wire. Most retailers sell all three kinds:

Flexible armored cable, sometimes known as BX, is good for rewiring a home because of its flexibility. It is easy to run through existing walls. It cannot, however, be used in damp locations, outside, or underground. And some local codes do not permit its use anywhere.

Plastic sheathed cable is very flexible and excellent when you must "snake" wire through existing walls. However, care must be taken when working with it not to damage the plastic covering.

Thin-wall rigid conduit is the most acceptable type of wiring system. Wires are threaded through it. Most new work is done with conduit, and many communities require it because it does the best job of protecting the wires it carries, and because the entire system is grounded. It is difficult, however, to use in remodeling work.

Wire is known by *type* and is stamped as such. Type AC cable is used where codes specify that the wires must be metal-clad. Type NM cable is the plastic sheathed cable described above. Unless it is otherwise specified by local codes, Type NM cable should be used indoors under dry conditions. Type UF cable may be used underground or in wet and corrosive areas. Do not expose UF cable to sunlight.

In rewiring your home, or remodeling the wiring, your big buy in wire will be Type NM with two- or three-wire configurations. Conductor sizes will include No. 14, No. 12, and, probably No. 10. The cable will have a ground wire—usually bare without insulation.

The color codes on Type NM will be:

• One black, one white, and one bare wire in two-wire cable.

• One black, one white, one red, and one bare in three-wire cable.

• One black, one white, one red, one blue, and one bare in four-wire cable.

Heater cords are specified as Type HPD and HPN. Type HPN is the best buy; HPD is asbestos lined and is now being taken off the market.

Type SPT is lamp cord. You know it by its shape: a groove runs down the center of both wires so the wires may be split. The wires also are stranded, not solid, as in Types NM, UF, HPN, and so forth. Wire usually is sold by the roll: 25-, 50,- and 100-ft.

working with electricity

"Work safe" are the key words in making any electrical repairs or improvements. Note the following precautions before you start any job:

1. Do not work on any switch or outlet until you have disconnected the circuit by tripping the circuit breaker or unscrewing the fuse.

2. When working at the service box, pull out the main fuse, completely disconnecting the box from the incoming power lines.

3. Double-check your work before restoring the power to the circuit.

Take time to study the service box. Note that wires come in from a transformer. The wires are black, red, and white. Each of the colored wires carries 115 v. The white wire is neutral.

The black and red wires are connected to the main fuses or circuit breakers, while the white wire is connected to a copper bar, which is grounded to a cold water pipe. If you pull the main plastic fuse box out, you will find in it two red fuses that look similar to shotgun shells. When the box is pulled out, all electricity is shut OFF. When it is pushed back in place, the current is ON. Some service boxes have just a toggle that is switched to turn the power on and off.

Each of the individual fuses or circuit breakers is connected to the main fuse. If the wiring is visible, you can see that the connection is made with a black wire. A white wire connects each individual fuse to the grounding bar.

You may find several lugs or big screws near the fuses. These are the points at which you attach the wiring when you install another service box. Many service boxes have what appears to be a second main fuse, usually marked "Range." This is the fuse for a 230-volt circuit, and both incoming hot wires are connected to it, while only one of the incoming wires is connected to the other main fuse. If you live in an older home, the "Range" circuit may be in another service box near the main service box.

adding new circuits

If you have enough empty fuse sockets for additional circuits, follow this procedure when wiring a circuit to the service box:

1. Pull the main fuse to turn off the power.

2. Select a "knock-out" plug near the fuse to be used and knock it out with a punch.

3. Fasten the connector to the circuit wire. Thread the connector into the hole, thread on a locknut and tighten it. There should be about 8 in. of wire in the box.

4. Strip the ends of the wire and form a hook on the end of each wire. Hook the black wire under the screw at the fuse socket. Put the white wire under the screw on the grounding bar. Tighten the screws (terminals).

5. Insert the main fuse in the box. The power is now on. Now screw in a 15-amp fuse or set the circuit breaker.

If the service entrance is a circuit breaker—not fuse—arrangement, you will have to pry out an escutcheon plate where a new circuit breaker toggle will be inserted. There are two types. One simply snaps into the space and is secured by friction of the toggle housing. The other type has a plug-in device. By turning off the power and removing an existing toggle, you can determine the type the circuit breaker utilizes.

1. Slip the white neutral wire and bare grounding wire into the slot in the box and fasten it to the neutral bar. Pull on it to make sure it is secure and the holding screw is properly tightened.

2. Hook the black power wire to the circuit

breaker. There is a screw on the toggle device for this.

3. Slip the toggle breaker in the appropriate slot so it "clicks" or is secure in the slot.

4. Turn on the main breaker toggle and check the circuit.

When the job is complete, and if you have complied with the electrical code in your community, have an inspector check your work. The inspector's okay means the work is satisfactory and the system probably complies with insurance regulations.

making wire connections

The wiring systems that may be used in residences usually consist of either flexible-armor type or non-metallic sheathed cable with a ground wire which may be insulated or bare. These wiring systems should not be intermixed. For example, if your home is wired with flexible armor type cable, stick with this cable. Regardless of the wiring type you use, the basic techniques for joining (splicing) these wires are the same.

• Stripping and cutting wire is best done with a combination tool that both cuts and strips clean the most common sizes of stranded and solid wire. A button on the handle lets you set the jaws to the desired wire gauge so you can remove the insulation without breaking the wires.

About ½-inch of insulation should be removed from the wire to expose this conductor. Try to shape the insulation like a sharpened pencil rather than a blunt cut. The nose of the stripping tool can be used to form the loop or hook on the wire so the wire may be properly fastened under the terminal screws on the outlet or switch you're wiring.

• After the wire is bared and bent into a hook, fit it around the terminal screw in the direction the terminal screw turns—usually clockwise.

This way, when the terminal screw is tightened it also tightens the wire under the screw. If the wire is installed backward, the wire is likely to back out as the screw is tightened down. This results in a poor connection.

• To join wire at prewired fixtures, such as a ceiling light, use solderless connectors. They often are called "wire nuts." The connectors are plastic caps with a threaded metal insert that let you "screw" the wires together in a connection.

After the wires are bared and inserted into the cap and twisted, give the wires a slight tug to make sure the connector won't slip off. It's also a good idea to wrap plastic electrical tape around the connector and wires for added strength.

• Ground wires are required by codes if the wire is nonmetallic cable.

Receptacles must be grounded from a green screw or a ground clip; both are mounted on the junction box.

To make this connection, the bared ground wire is looped under the green screw and then pushed through the ground clip.

It is important that all systems are grounded throughout. If you miss one ground connection, you break the entire connection.

working with cable

Wiring with plastic or metallic cable is just as easy as wiring with other types of wire. Here are several tips to help you do jobs easier and safer:

• There is no "multiple choice" question in wiring. If you have any doubts about which wire goes where, don't guess. Call in a professional.

• Always buy UI-approved, sheathed, copper wiring. It may be packaged in armored metallic cable (type AC) or thermoplastic cable (type TW or THW). These letter symbols are embossed on the cable's outer surface.

For 15-ampere circuits, use No. 14 gauge wire. For 20-ampere circuits, use No. 12 gauge wire. Each size should have a third grounding wire. This is specified in the store by "14/2 With Ground." Or "12/2 With Ground."

• Follow the color codes when you are joining new conductors to existing ones. Black wires are always connected to black wires; white wires go to white wires. Green or bare wires go to their counterparts.

The coding is very important since in house wiring the white always acts as the grounded neutral conductor, the black as the power wire, and the bare or green wire as the safety grounding conductor that protects you from electrical shock.

• If you plan to install a new junction box or take a new line out of an existing box, be sure to attach the grounding wire to the metal box. If two or more sets of conductors are connected in the box, connect the two grounding wires together in addition to attaching them to the metal frame. One break in the line can cancel out the safety factor along the entire circuit.

• Always run the black or power conductor (wire) through the switch, never the white wire. If you switch the white instead, the fixture on the circuit will be a permanent, hot, shock hazard—even when the switch is turned off.

• In three-way switching, controlling one light from two different locations, buy two three-way switches and cable specified as "14/3 With

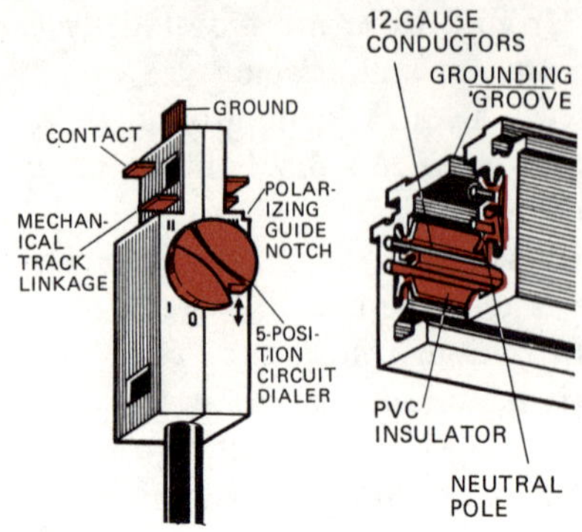

SINGLE AND triple-circuit track is manufactured by Swivelier, Nanuet, NY 10954. Dial settings on a three-circuit system will activate any combination of lamps.

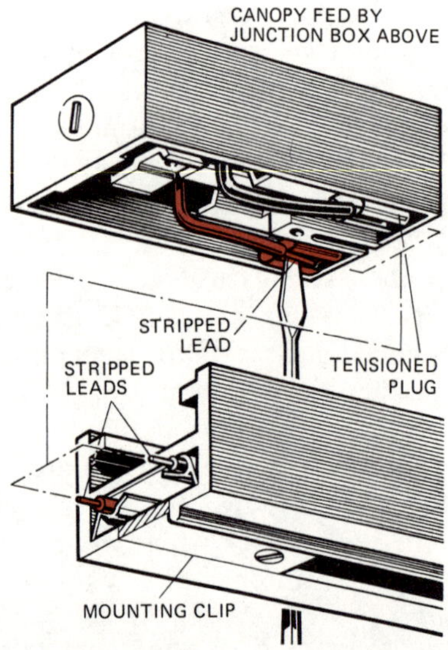

CANOPY BOXES, wired at the ceiling, serve as plugs for the different track sections. This snap-in wiring system is made by Lightolier, 346 Claremont Ave., Jersey City, NJ 07305.

Ground." All necessary wires are in the cable.

adding a wall outlet

Rooms in older homes never seem to have enough electrical outlets, and many times a long extension cord is used to plug in a lamp across the room.

Although it may look difficult, adding a new outlet is an easy job. Here are the steps:

1. Trace the outlet box on the wall between wall studs. The box should be the same height as the others above the floor. Use a 2½-in.-deep box; all boxes are the same width and height.

Use the box as a template and trace its outline on the wall. You can locate the wall studs by tapping on the wall and listening for a solid sound. Or use a magnetic stud finder.

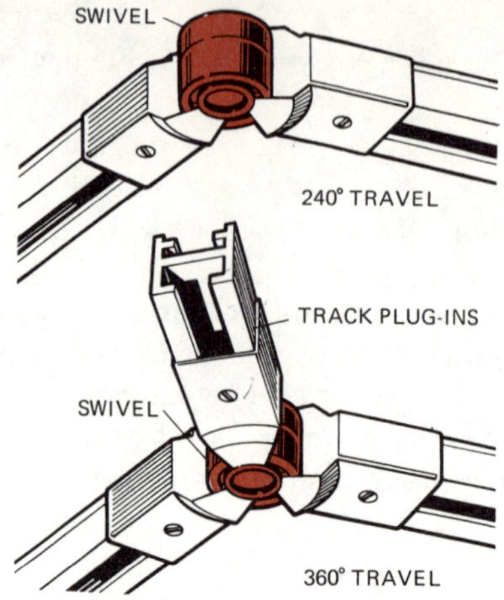

THESE CONNECTORS and a six-point swivel for track in any direction are the features of these connectors by Lightcraft, 5691 Rising Sun Ave., Philadelphia, PA 19120. The lights simply ride in the channels.

If the wall is lath and plaster, chip away a small hole in the center of the outline to expose a lath so the template can be centered over a full lath. This will provide better strength.

If the box will be fastened to paneling, you can buy a box with special clamps that grip the panels for support. If the wall is lath and plaster, the box is fastened to the wood lath with small screws. If the wall is plasterboard, the box is anchored in the hole with special metal supports.

2. For plasterboard walls, trace around the box and drill two ½-in. holes through the wall at the top and bottom half-round notches.

Then cut the opening with a hand-held hacksaw blade or a keyhole saw. You can protect your hands from the teeth of the saw blade by wrapping the grip with a couple of twists of plastic electrician's tape.

3. You may use armored cable or plastic cable to wire the new outlet. You must cut the armored cable with a hacksaw; the plastic cable may be cut with a sharp utility knife.

Codes require that the wire and box be grounded. If you use armored cable, the metal covering serves as the ground. If you use plastic cable, the third or "ground" wire inside the insulation must be connected to the outlet box with a screw and/or special clip made for this purpose.

4. Strip off the insulation about ½-in. from the black and white wires. Then form a hook on the ends of the bared wires and connect the hook to the terminals of the outlet. The black wire should be hooked to the brass terminal, and the white wire to the light-colored terminal. Also, the hooks should go onto the terminals the direction the terminal screws turn—usually clockwise.

If you are making any other connections inside

the box or along the circuit remember that black wires are always connected to black wires and white wires are always connected to white wires.

5. How you run the cable from an existing box to a new one depends on where the boxes are.

If they're on the same wall, remove the baseboard, notch each stud to accept the cable, and cover the wire with metal kickplates for protection.

If the boxes are on different walls and there is a basement or crawl space below, it's easier to bore up into the walls from underneath and run the cable across under the joists.

If the new outlet is on the other side of a doorway, the cable can be concealed behind the trim. You may have to chip out the plaster or wallboard and run up and over the door. When reinstalling the trim, be careful not to nail through the cable.

To connect the cable to an old box, punch open a knockout port and fish a thin wire through this hole to pull the cable into the box.

installing a surface switch

If you want to install a new wall switch but don't want to cut into the wall covering, you can use a surface switch, provided there is an existing receptacle nearby. The system is UL-listed.

The system has three adhesive-backed components that are pressed against the wall. A plug-in, solid-state relay transformer (power unit) is set next to an existing single-gang receptacle. The unit is connected with 15 feet of .005-in.-thick two-wire conductor tape, and a clear plastic, wafer-thin touchbutton switch completes the hook-up.

The power unit steps down 110-120v. power to a 2-v. level, claimed to be so safe that if you cut into the wire the extremely low voltage would not be felt as an electrical shock.

An alternate design, using the conductor tape and switch as before, has a separate power unit installed inside a double-gang wall receptacle or ceiling fixture outlet. Extra touchbuttons may be obtained for multiple switching.

tracking light where it's needed

Track lighting is the answer to illuminating an entire room without putting a 200-watt bulb in the middle of the ceiling. Track lights also may be used for spotlighting, depending on the fixture.

Installing track lighting is simple. One junction box, for example, can feed a series of tracks. You can hang fixtures from the tracks that will throw exactly the light you want.

Track lighting frees you from the limitation of having one outlet box near every source of light. It also lets you make a mistake or change your mind. When you sink a lot of money into an elaborate center-ceiling fixture, that's it. The light is going to stay there. But if you don't like the way your tracks look, just unplug them from the supply box and make a different arrangement. You can also slide fixtures along the track, bunch them at either end, or put different fixtures (throwing different kinds of light) on different tracks altogether. The possibilities are endless.

The system starts at the feed box.

This box is small, matching the contour and style of the track that sits on the ceiling and connects to the junction box above it. Once this is installed, wiring the rest of the system is easy.

Since conductors run the full length of the track, power is available at each end. There are caps (made to close off one end if you're hanging only one track) and connectors (elbows and straights) that let you plug one track into another and continue the system in any direction.

Measure from a side wall and snap a line where the track will be. Small mounting clips are screwed into the ceiling and tracks slip onto them. These clips make installation easy and space the track about ¼ in. off the ceiling to absorb the margin of high or low spots that could make the track uneven.

Two types of track are available. Most basic and easiest to install is a single-circuit track fed with a standard three-wire cable (hot, neutral, and ground). You can control it with two or three-way switches.

All lamps on this track will go off and on at the same time. But they also make three-circuit track with hardware to match. This system links three separately switched circuits with each length of track. It's ideal in a large room where you can install continuous tracks to cover the entire area.

A light you can't see? This sounds impossible, but it's a special effect from a newly developed fixture. You can look directly into this light from six inches away without squinting. It throws a wide beam of clean white light, but you can't see where the beam is coming from.

The effect is both dramatic and mystifying.

Objects appear to be lighting themselves. The light source is a clear bulb with a silver bowl covering half its outer skin. Light bounces up into a mottled, high-purity, aluminum bowl and is diffused down onto the room. The fixture is generally referred to as "no-glare" lighting.

Crimp-on connectors

By SHELDON M. GALLAGER

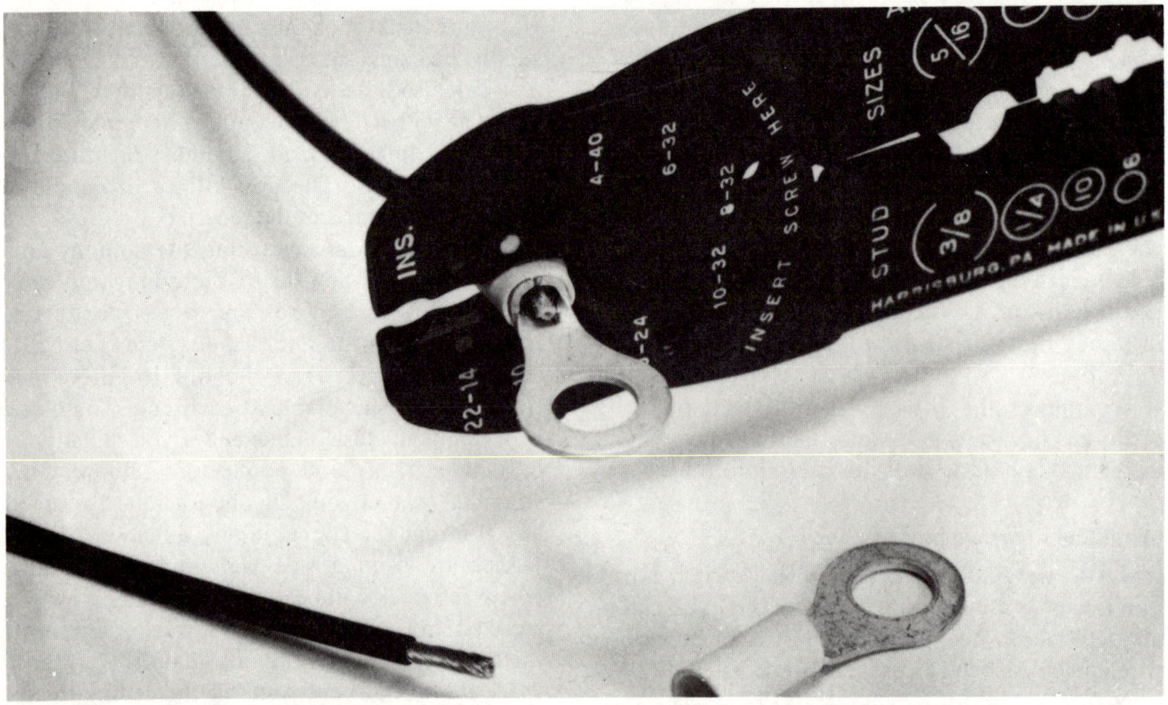

A QUICK SQUEEZE and you've permanently fastened an eye-type connector to a wire end without any soldering. This tool has an extra-large crimping notch near the center for auto-ignition cables.

■ THE FASTEST WAY to join two wires or attach a connector is with a crimping tool. If you don't believe it, try one of these handy, inexpensive aids the next time you install a light fixture or hook up speaker leads to your hi-fi set.

Crimp-on connectors not only save time over soldering, but handle jobs where soldering could be difficult. When working with heavy wire, for instance, the metal draws heat away so fast it's hard to make a good soldered connection with a light-duty iron. Crimped connectors eliminate the problem. They come in a variety of types and sizes. Many have color-coded insulation sleeves for quick identification of wire gauge. Yellow is used for heavy 10 to 12-gauge wire, blue for medium 14 to 16-gauge wire and red for light 18 to 22-gauge wire. Some crimping tools have similarly color-coded crimping notches so you can tell at a glance which notch to use depending on the wire diameter you're working with.

TWO TYPICAL CRIMPING TOOLS are Vaco's at the top below and Api's Super Champ at the bottom. Both handle wire gauges from 10 to 22, and cut and strip ends.

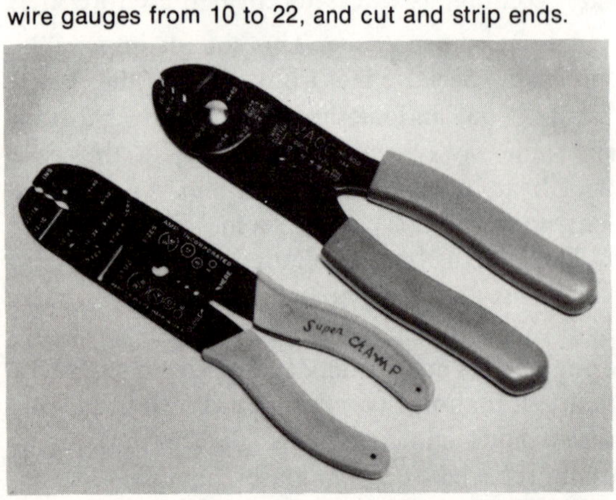

Open-ended spade lugs are good for making quick connections to screw terminals since they can be slipped on or off with only a few turns of a screwdriver. Closed-ended eyes can't pull off accidentally, but take a little longer to install since the screw must be removed completely and

SEE ALSO

Lighting . . . Soldering . . . Testers, continuity . . . Wiring, electrical

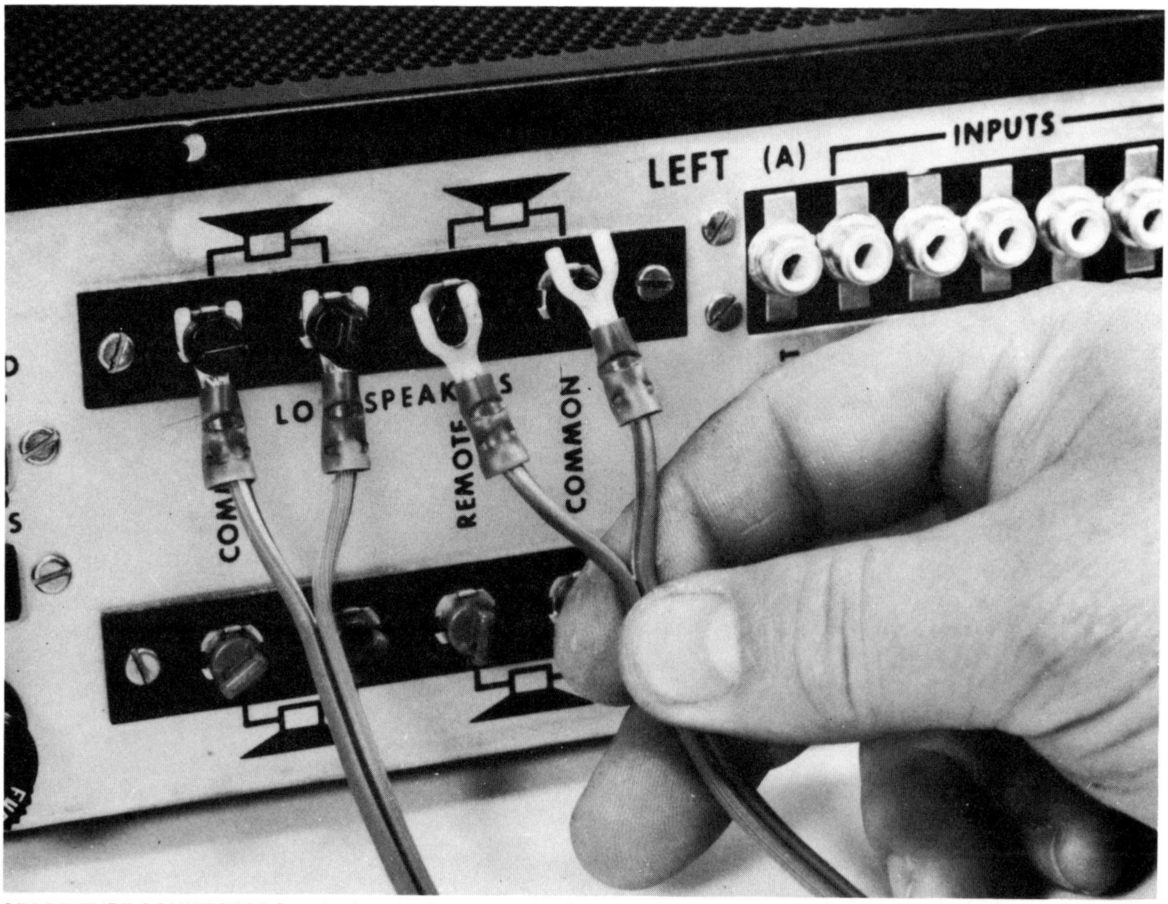

SPADE-TYPE CONNECTORS make fast work of attaching speaker or antenna leads to a hi-fi set. Note the double crimp marks—one to lock the connector to the wire and one to anchor the sleeve to the insulation.

inserted through the hole. Spades are best for connections that may be changed frequently, eyes for those likely to be more permanent. There are also several types of end-to-end connectors for splicing wires together.

Crimping tools all perform basically the same function, but vary slightly in design. Most types cut and strip wire ends in preparation for attaching connectors. In addition to crimping notches for standard wire sizes, some incorporate an ex-

3 TYPES OF CRIMP-ON CONNECTORS FOR EASY WIRE SPLICING

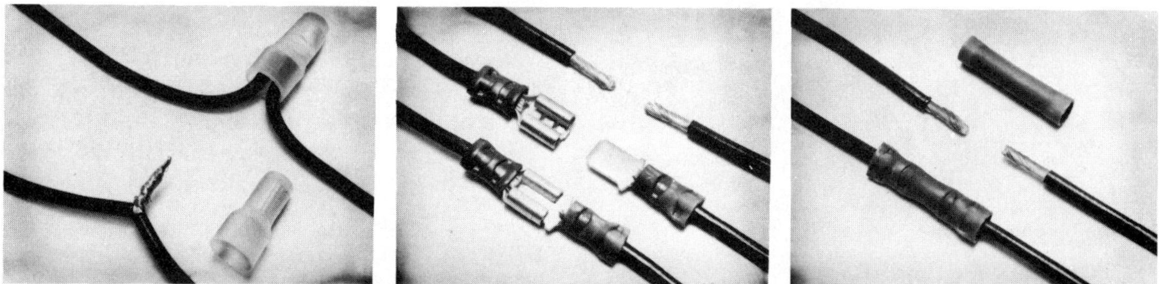

THE BELL-SHAPED SPLICER at the left works like a wire nut except you crimp it on tightly instead of just screwing it on. All you do is twist the wires, slip on the connector and squeeze. At the center, a slip-together coupling can be quickly disconnected if necessary. At the right is a permanent end-to-end splice.

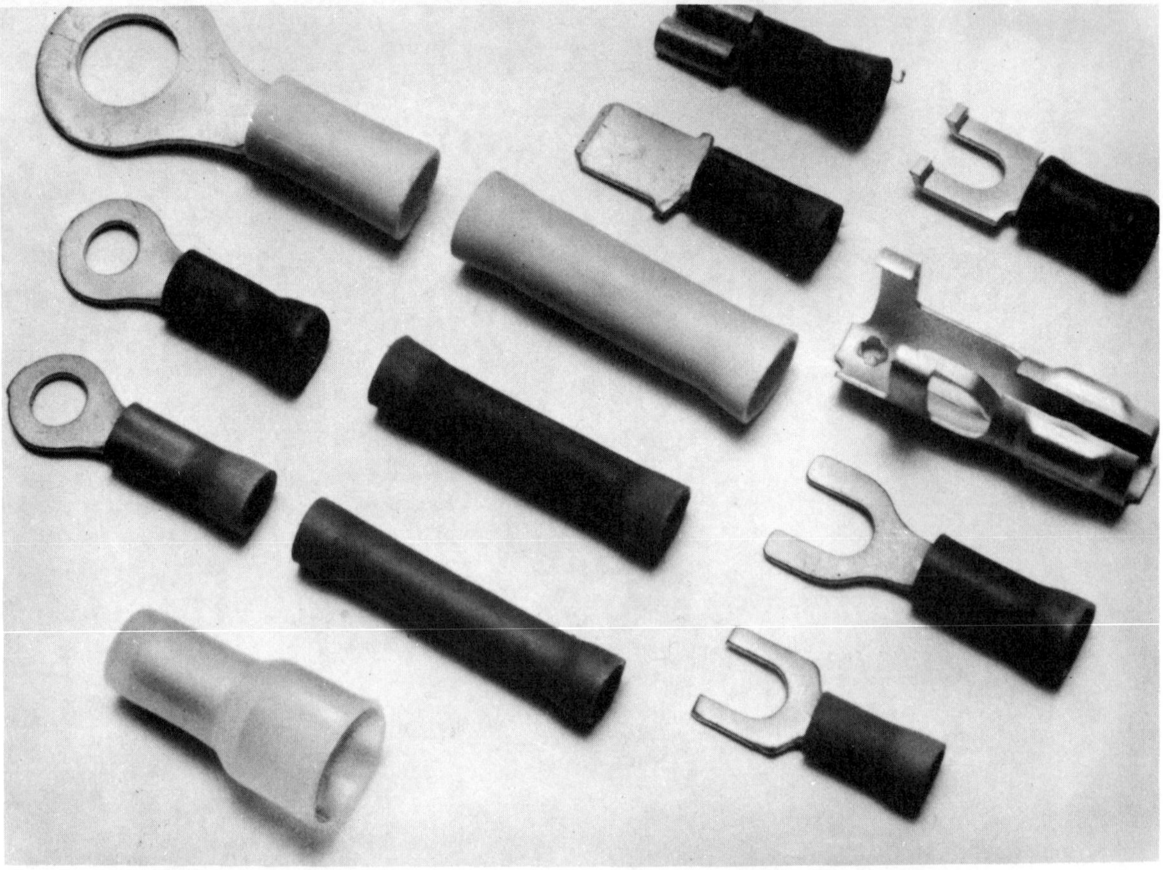

SOME CONNECTORS are shown above. Most common are round eyes, straight end-to-end couplers and slotted spade lugs. At the top right is a bent-tip spade lug designed to hook under a screwhead. Below this is an auto ignition-cable connector. At the lower left: the bell-ended type for joining wires twisted together. At the upper center: quick-disconnect slip-fit couplings.

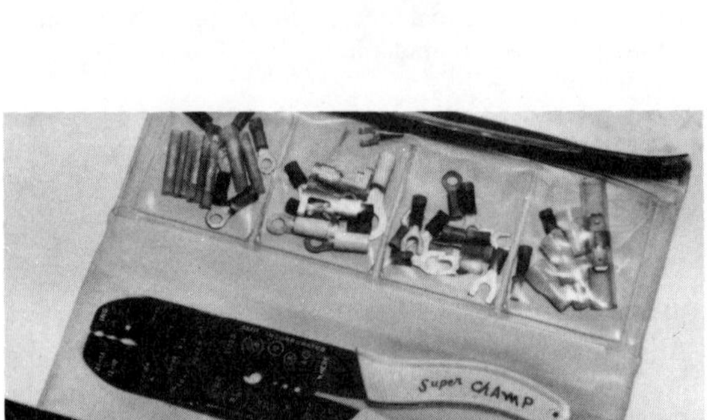

HANDY KITS include the crimping tool, assorted connectors and instructions in a plastic carrying case.

BOLT-SHEARING SLOTS are helpful when you don't have the right length on hand and can't get to a store.

tra-large notch for fastening connectors onto heavy auto-ignition cable. If you do a lot of car work, this is a good feature to look for. The better models also have bolt-cutting blades that will shear a bolt to exact length—a welcome aid if you need a non-standard size.

Recommended crimping techniques vary slightly so follow the instructions that come with the particular tool you buy. Some call for a single crimp; others advise a double crimp—one around the bare wire end and a second around the insulating sleeve. Prices range from about $5 for a tool alone to $10 for kits that include a tool and assortment of connectors.

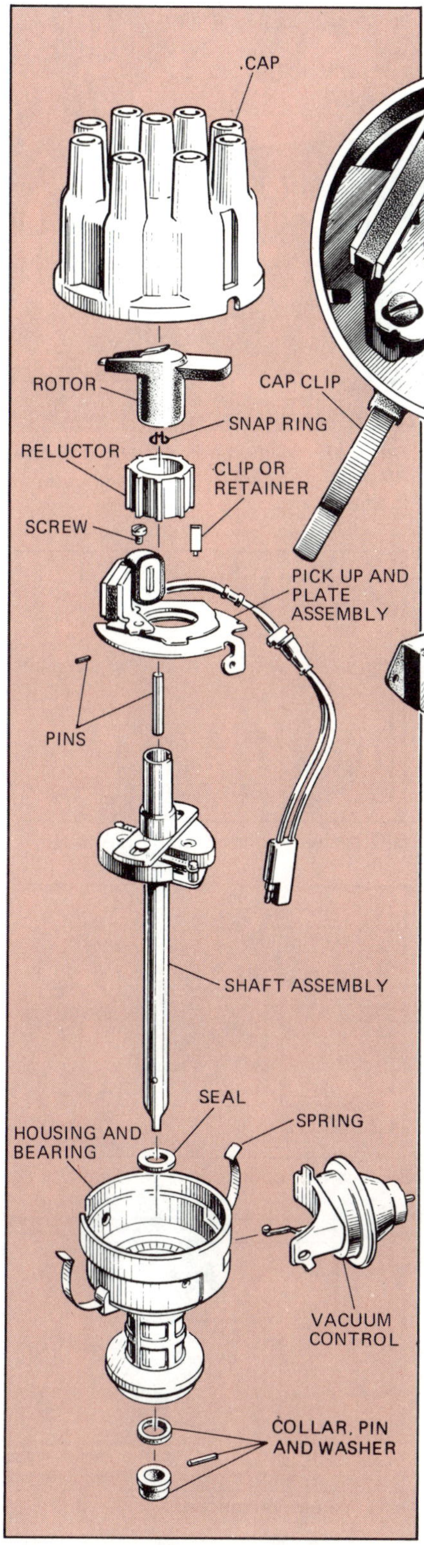

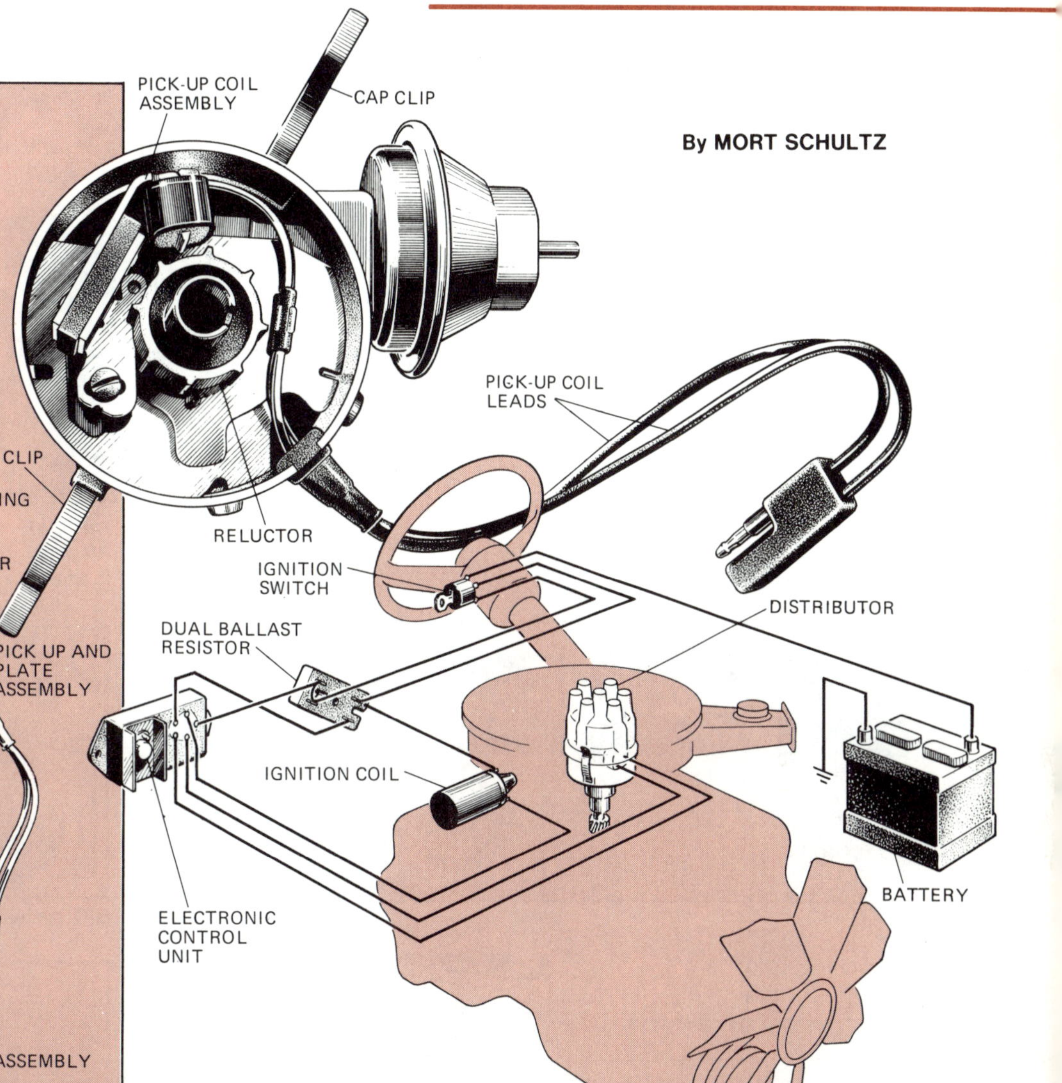

By MORT SCHULTZ

CHRYSLER electronic ignition system with connections between components is shown above. At top is the distributor, which is exploded at left.

How to troubleshoot an electronic ignition system

■ ALTHOUGH original-equipment electronic ignition systems have been with us for several years, they remain a mystery to most people.

The electronic principles involved are pretty much the same from one system to another. However, each system has its own unique design and requires special tests to diagnose problems.

As this is written there are five different electronic ignitions employed by American manufacturers on most cars and many trucks. They are

SEE ALSO

Alternators, auto . . . Autos, maintenance . . . Cables, auto . . . Differentials, auto . . . Distributors, auto . . . Ignition systems, auto . . . Misfiring, auto . . . Sparkplugs . . . Tune-up, auto

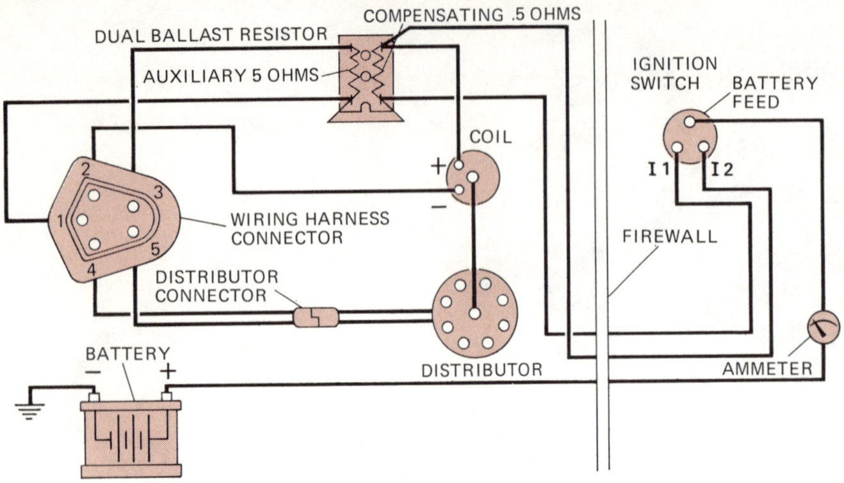

CHRYSLER system schematic diagram which you'll need to make test connections with voltmeter and ohmmeter. Troubleshooting procedure is outlined in text.

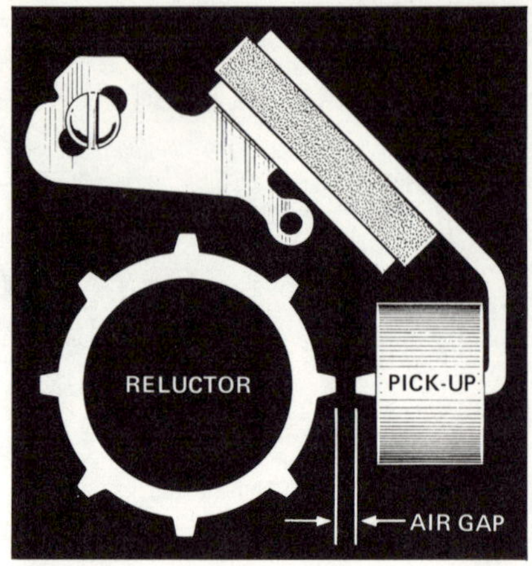

AIR GAP between reluctor and coil corresponds to point gap in conventional ignition.

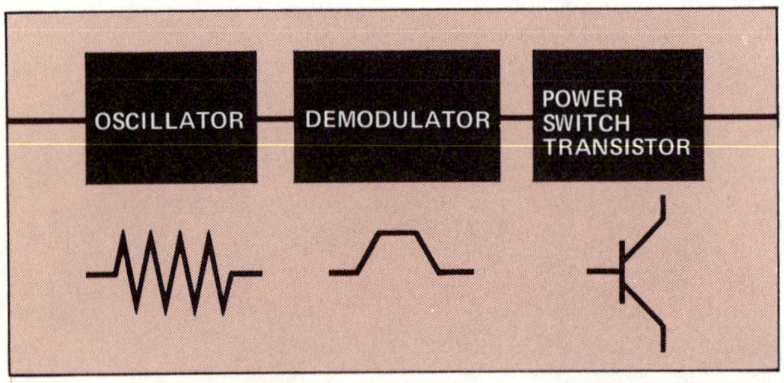

AMC'S breakerless inductive discharge system (BID) uses an electronic control unit containing the circuit block diagrammed at left. Action of power switch transistor cuts off coil primary circuit so that high voltage is induced in secondary.

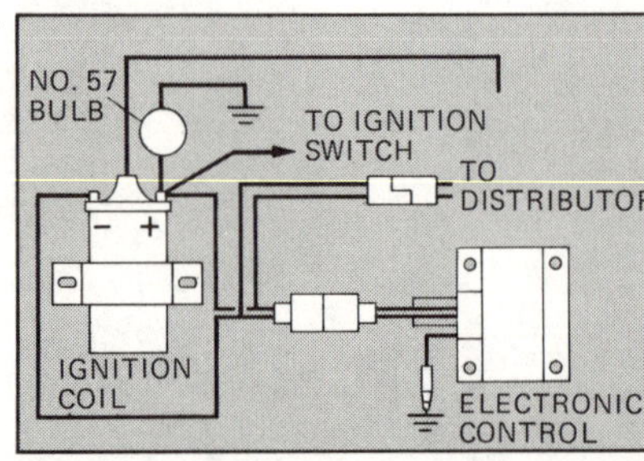

BID system: connections for Test No. 1.

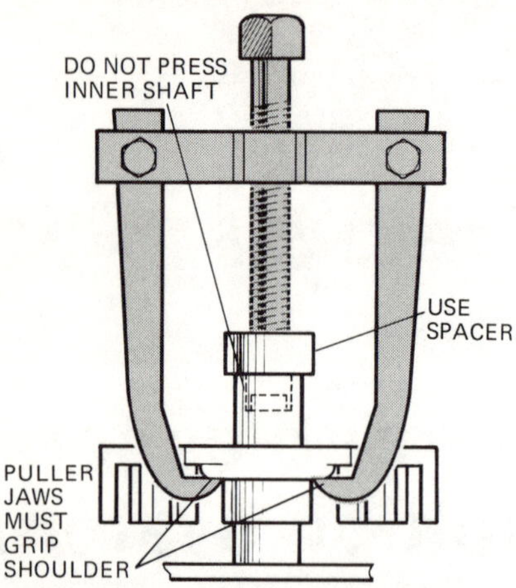

REMOVING the trigger wheel of BID system requires care as pointed out above.

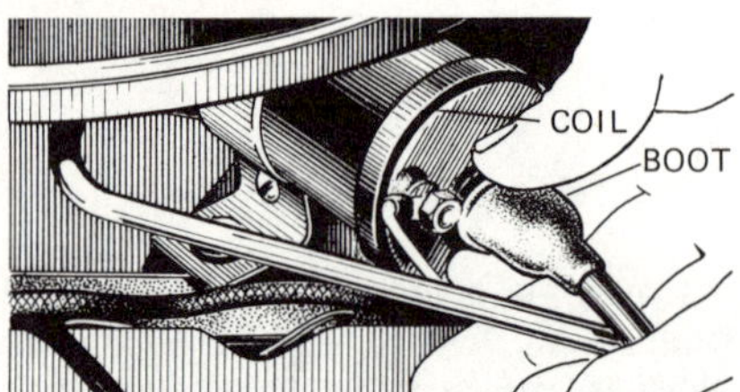

COIL-TO-DISTRIBUTOR cable is too frequently overlooked when checking out a problem. Make sure it's in contact.

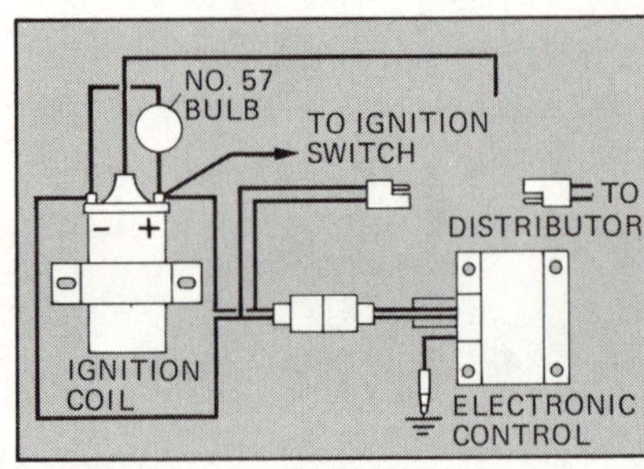

BID system: connections for Test No. 2.

A 0.050-IN. wire gauge is used to set distance between wheel and sensor.

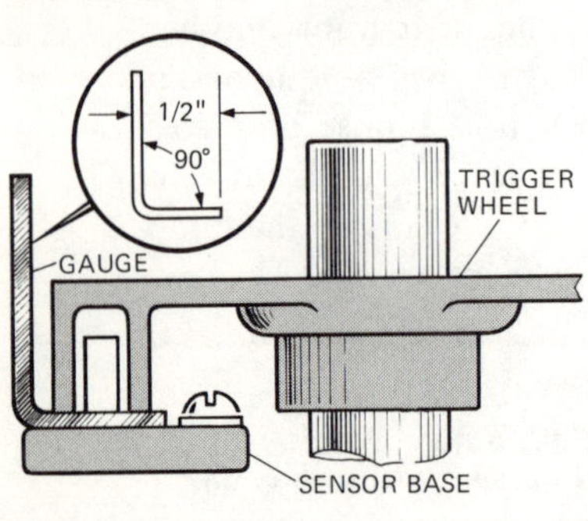

REMOVING and installing sensor assembly requires lead routing as shown.

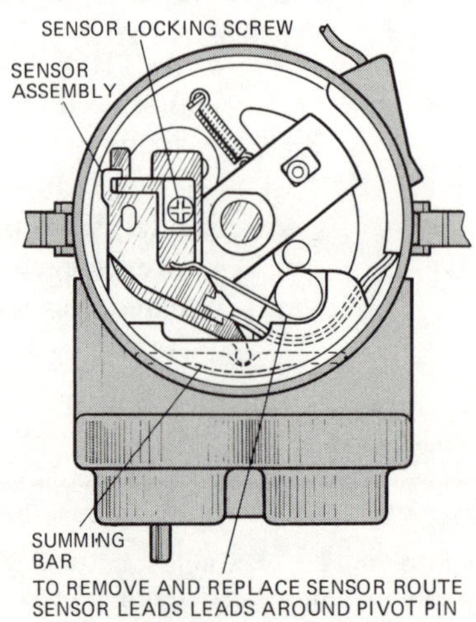

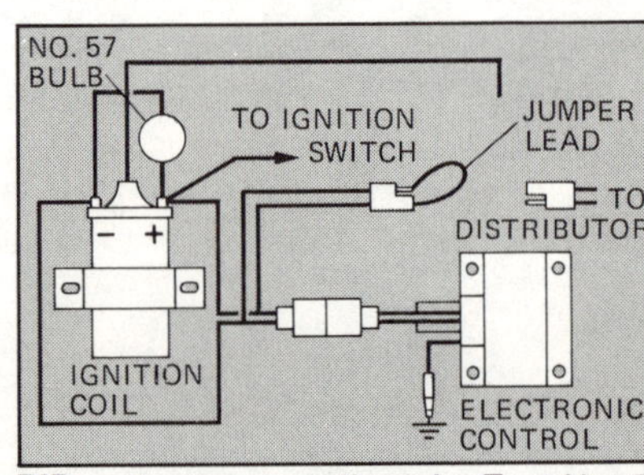

BID system: connections for Test No. 3.

BID system: connections for Test No. 4.

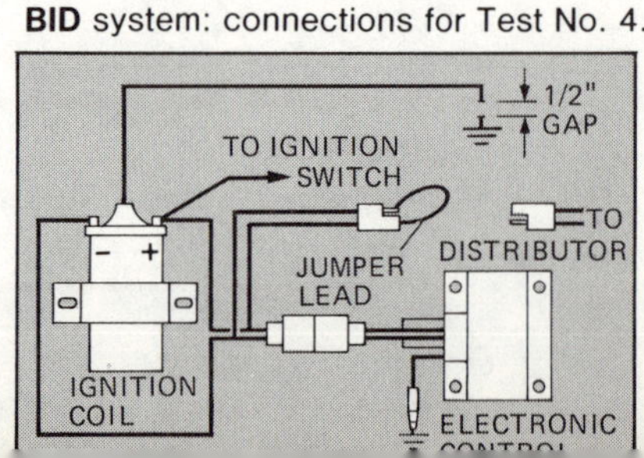

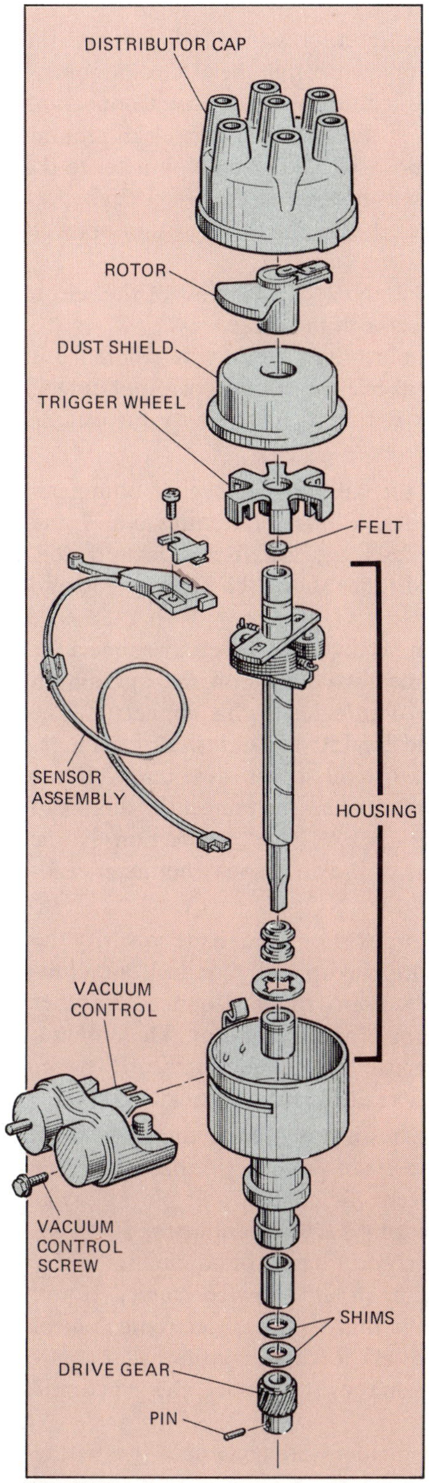

AMC BID system distributor is exploded above. Trigger wheel and sensor assembly are the heart of the system.

QUICK CHECK CHART—FORD S/S IGNITION SYSTEM

Test Condition	Test Voltage Between	Reading in Volts Should Be	Action to Take
Key On	Red wire socket and ground	Battery voltage ±0.1	Check red wire and connectors through ignition switch
	Green wire socket and ground	Battery voltage ±0.1	Check green wire to ignition coil and test coil
Cranking	White wire socket and ground	8 to 12	Check white wire and connectors through ignition switch
	Purple wire socket and orange wire socket	Any direct current fluctuation (0.5 minimum)	Test distributor components

Test Condition	Test Resistance Between	Reading in Ohms Should Be	Action to Take
Key Off	Purple wire socket and orange wire socket	400 to 800	Test magnetic pickup
	Black wire socket and ground	0	Test magnetic pickup
	Purple wire socket and ground	70,000 or more	Test magnetic pickup
	Orange wire socket and ground	70,000 or more	Test magnetic pickup
	Redwire socket and ignition coil tower	7000 to 13,000	Test coil
	Green wire socket and red wire socket	3.0 to 4.0	Check harness, ignition coil
	Red wire socket and ignition coil BAT terminal	1.0 to 2.0	Check resistance wire
	Iginition coil primary terminals	1.0 to 2.0	Test coil
	Orange wire socket and orange wire socket	0	Check wire and terminals
	Purple wire socket and purple wire socket	0	Check wire and terminals

the American Motors' Breakerless Inductive Discharge (BID) ignition system; Chrysler Corporation's electronic ignition system; Ford Motor Company's Solid State (S/S) ignition system; General Motors' High Energy Ignition (HEI) system; and International Harvester's electronic ignition system.

To put the Chrysler system into perspective, consider that it has a primary, a secondary and three additional circuits.

The primary circuit consists of a battery, ignition-switch side of a ballast resistor, primary windings of the ignition coil, power switching transistor (in the electronic control unit) and the car's frame.

The secondary circuit consists of the secondary windings of the ignition coil, distributor cap and rotor, sparkplug cables, sparkplugs and the car's frame. The three additional circuits are the auxiliary ballast resistor, electronic control unit feed and pickup.

The auxiliary ballast resistor and ignition-switch side of the ballast resistor are housed in one unit called the dual ballast resistor. The auxiliary resistor section is used to operate the circuitry of the electronic control unit. The normal resistor section helps maintain constant primary current with respect to engine speed.

During engine starting, this resistor is bypassed so that the full battery voltage will be applied to the ignition coil.

The electronic control unit feed works hand-in-hand with the auxiliary ballast resistor to operate the electronic control unit circuitry. The pickup circuit senses the proper timing for the power switching transistor.

In operation, a reluctor rotating with the distributor shaft produces a voltage pulse in the distributor's magnetic pickup coil assembly. This pulse is transmitted to the power switching transistor in the electronic control unit, thus allowing the transistor to interrupt the current flow through the primary circuit. This break in the primary current induces the high voltage in the secondary circuit.

Caution: Do not touch the power switching transistor while the car's ignition switch is on. You will get a shock.

The circuitry in the electronic control unit determines the length of time that the power switching transistor maintains the flow of current in the primary circuit. This determines dwell, which cannot be adjusted. Dwell affects ignition timing. Once basic ignition timing is set, further checks become unnecessary.

Chrysler: finding the trouble

The troubleshooting procedure is clear. When a problem that you think is ignition-caused occurs, start by visually inspecting secondary cables for defects, and the primary wire at the ignition coil and ballast resistor for tightness.

At this point, you have a choice. You can buy Chrysler's Electronic Ignition Tester (C-4166-A), or use a voltmeter rated at 20,000 volts, and an ohmmeter that employs a 1½-volt battery. Since the Chrysler tester comes with instructions, let's outline the other test procedure.

1. Turn off all accessories.
2. Check battery voltage first. It should be a minimum of 12 volts.
3. With the ignition switch off, remove the multiwiring connector from the electronic control unit. Turn the ignition switch to ON. Connect the negative lead of the voltmeter to a clean ground. Connect the positive lead of the voltmeter to the wiring harness connector at the No. 1 cavity.

The voltage reading should be within one volt of battery voltage.

Check No. 2 and No. 3 cavities of the wiring harness connector in the same way.

If there is more than a one volt difference in any reading, check the circuit corresponding to the particular wiring harness cavity for cleanliness and tightness.

4. Turn off the ignition. Connect an ohmmeter to wiring harness connector cavities No. 4 and No. 5. This tests the distributor pickup coil. Ohmmeter resistance should be between 150 and 900 ohms.

If the reading is higher or lower, disconnect the dual-lead connector coming off the distributor. Connect your ohmmeter to this connector. The reading should be 150-900 ohms. If it isn't, replace the pickup coil in the distributor. If the reading is 150-900 ohms, reconnect the dual-lead connector, tightly. A loose connection is the probable cause of the erroneous ohmmeter reading to begin with.

5. One other test should be made to verify the condition of the pickup coil. Connect one ohmmeter lead to a clean ground. Connect the other to the connector of the distributor. The ohmmeter should register an open circuit. If meter doesn't show a reading, replace pickup coil.

6. Continue testing by connecting one ohmmeter lead to a clean ground. Connect the other lead to the electronic control unit pin at cavity No. 5 of the wiring harness connector. This tests the electronic control unit ground circuit.

The ohmmeter should show continuity. If not, tighten the bolts that hold the electronic control unit to the firewall. Recheck continuity. If continuity still doesn't exist, replace the electronic control unit.

7. Remove meters and reconnect the wiring harness.

8. Check the air gap between a tooth of the reluctor and the pickup coil pole by aligning the two. Loosen pickup coil hold-down screw and insert a .008 nonmagnetic plastic feeler gauge between the two.

Align the air gap so contact is made between the reluctor tooth and the feeler gauge, and the pickup coil pole and the feeler gauge. Tighten the hold-down screw. You should be able to remove the feeler gauge without using force.

Double check the air gap by trying to insert a 0.010 feeler gauge between the two without using force. It should not fit.

9. Remove the vacuum advance hose from the source of vacuum. Put the end of the tube in your mouth and draw in, creating vacuum, and rotate the plate assembly.

If the pickup coil pole hits a reluctor tooth, the air gap is not adjusted properly.

If the pole hits the reluctor on the side, the distributor shaft is bent. Replace the distributor.

10. Remove the high-tension voltage cable from the center tower of the distributor. Hold it about 3/16 in. from ground with insulated pliers. Crank the engine. If the spark does not arc, you should replace the electronic control unit. Test again.

If spark still doesn't arc, put back the old electronic control unit and return the new one. Buy a new ignition coil instead.

Chrysler: replacing pickup coil

1. Remove the distributor cap and rotor.

2. Remove the screws and lockwashers that attach the vacuum control unit to the distributor housing. Disconnect the vacuum control arm from the plate. Remove the vacuum control.

3. Using two screwdrivers, pry up from the bottom of the reluctor. Be careful not to distort or damage the teeth.

4. Remove the screws and lockwashers holding the lower plate to the distributor housing. Lift off the lower plate, upper plate and pickup coil.

5. Reverse the procedure to reassemble the unit, making note of these points:

□ To replace the reluctor, position the reluctor keeper pin in place on the reluctor sleeve, slide the reluctor sleeve and press the reluctor firmly in place.

□ Lubricate the felt pad on top of the reluctor sleeve with a single drop of light engine oil.

□ Set the air gap between the pickup coil and reluctor.

BID: finding the trouble

As in a conventional ignition system, the job of the ignition coil is to transform relatively low voltage in the primary to the high voltage needed by the sparkplugs. In the BID system, this happens when the demodulator "orders" the power-switch transistors to switch off the coil primary circuit. A high voltage is induced in the ignition coil's secondary winding, which is distributed to the sparkplugs through the distributor cap, rotor and high tension ignition wires.

One thing *won't* happen when components of AMC's BID system go on the blink: no spark will be present at the sparkplugs, and the engine won't start. By components I refer to the electronic control unit, ignition coil and distributor parts.

To check the system when it fails, you could purchase the BID Electronic Ignition Pulse Simulator. The tester is available from Kent-Moore, 28635 Mound Rd., Warren, MI 48092, under part No. J-25331-01, for around $25.

However, the BID system can also be tested simply and quickly by using a No. 57 light bulb, a jumper lead and a pair of keen eyes. Cost: about 50 cents. Let's discuss the cheapie method here.

Find out if starting trouble is ignition-induced by disconnecting a high tension cable from a sparkplug. Using insulated pliers, hold the cable ½ to ¾ in. from a clean spot on the engine. Crank the engine. If there's no spark, start probing the ignition.

1. If backfiring takes place when the engine is cranked, maybe the distributor cap is wet, cracked or dirty, or its terminals are loose. Replace a damaged cap.

If backfiring accompanies cranking, it's also possible for ignition timing to be out of adjustment or for ignition wires to be incorrectly connected.

2. Inspect the distributor rotor for damage. Replace if necessary.

3. A defective distributor-to-coil secondary cable will prevent starting, and frequently goes unnoticed by a troubleshooting mechanic. Disconnect and check it with an ohmmeter. Allowable resistance is 5000 to 10,000 ohms.

4. Disconnect the distributor primary wires, which are black and dark green, from the control unit connector, which is blue and white. Spread male connector with a punch or awl, and crimp female connector slightly to insure a tight fit.

5. If spark is still not present as you try to start the engine, hook up your No. 57 bulb. Call this test 1. Connect one jumper to the coil positive and the other to ground. Turn the ignition switch to ON and then to START. If the bulb does not light with the switch in one or both positions, a problem exists between the battery and coil. Specifically, look to a defective ignition switch or wiring.

6. If the bulb lights with the switch in both positions, connect the bulb across the coil terminals. Unplug the distributor lead connector. With

FORD SOLID STATE (S/S) ignition system distributor is detailed here. The armature and stator perform the same switching function as points in a conventional system.

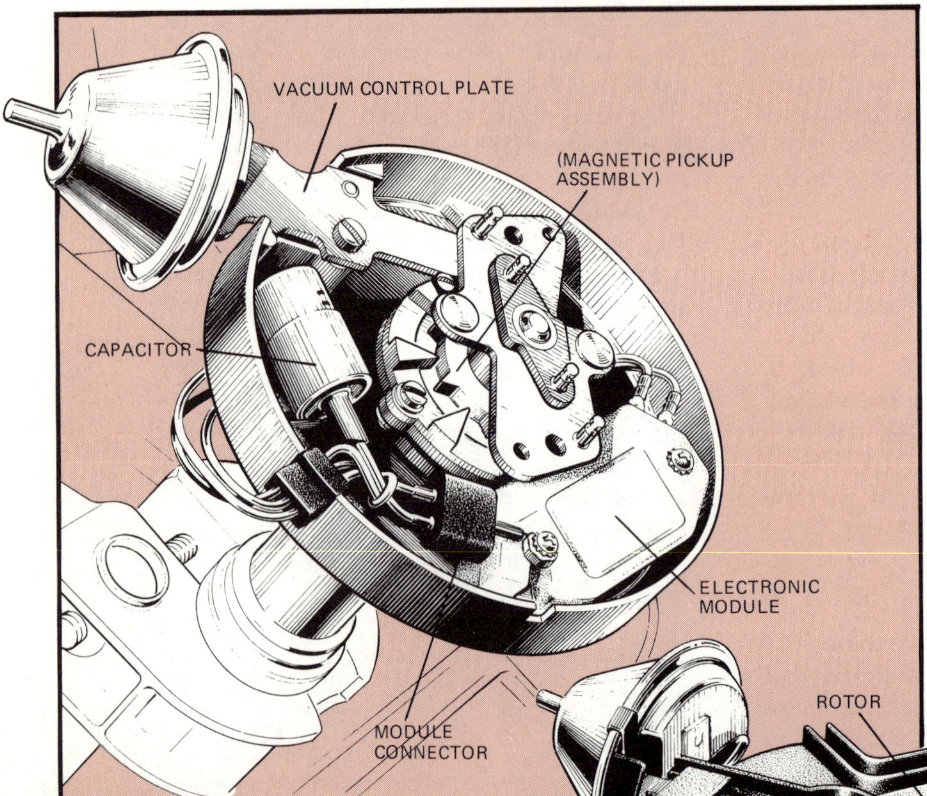

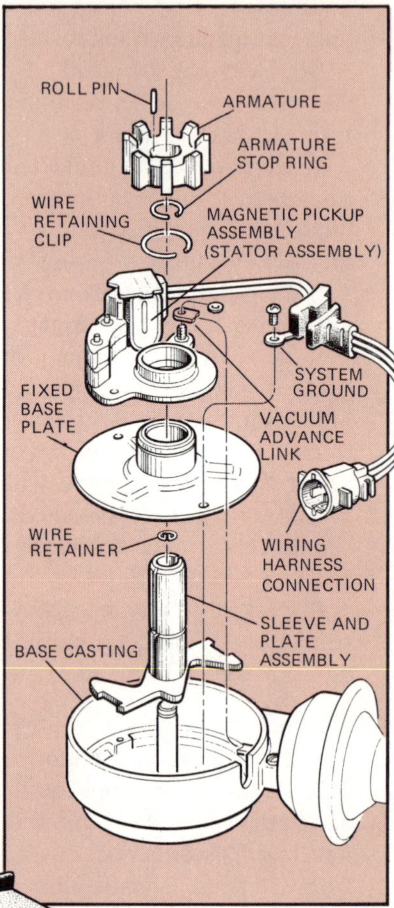

GM HIGH ENERGY Ignition (HEI) system for V6 and V8 engines. The HEI distributor contains all components, including the ignition coil. Two views, at right and above, show inside of distributor with rotor installed and rotor removed. Pickup coil leads are identified for testing HEI pickup. At right, below is inside of cap with test terminals marked.

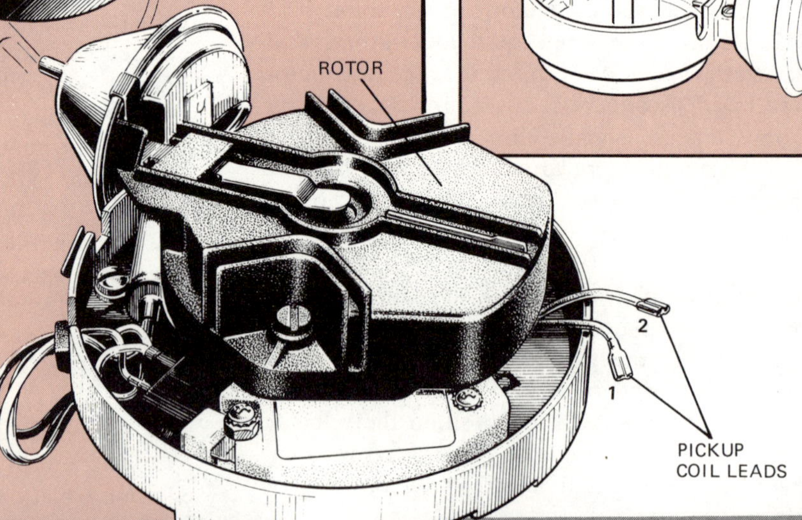

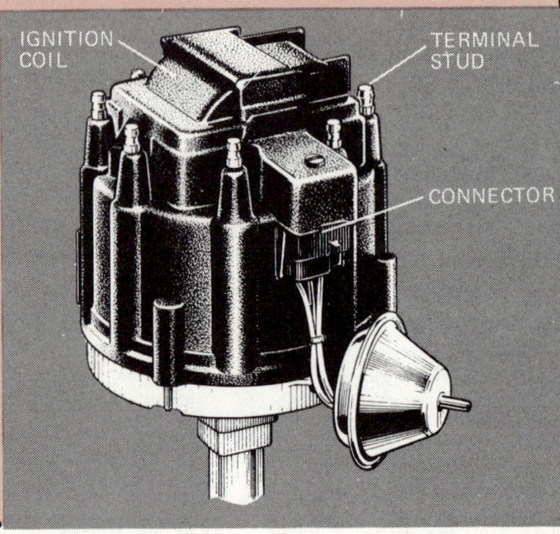

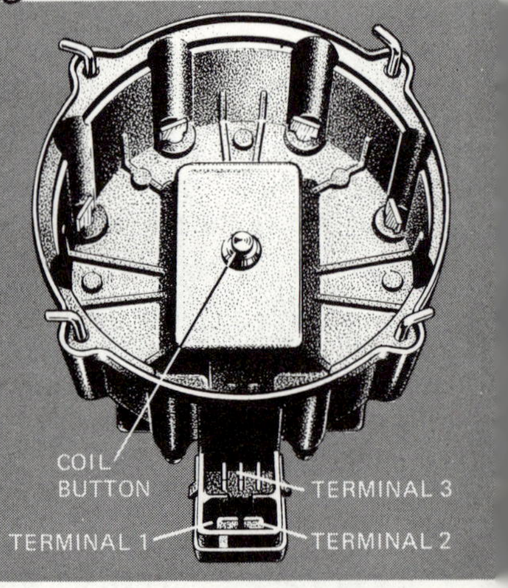

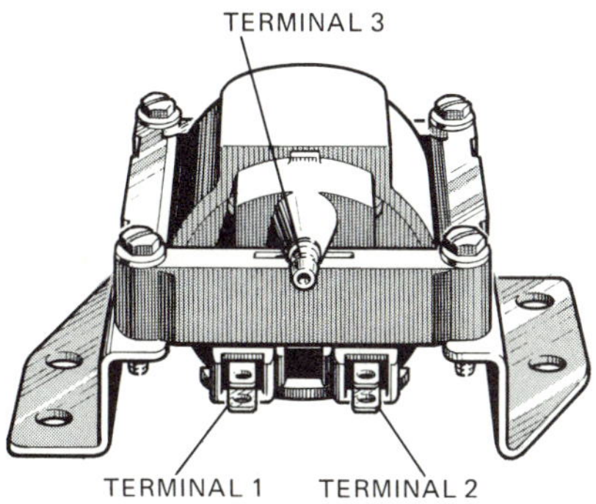

THE HEI external coil is tested with an ohmmeter at terminals marked.

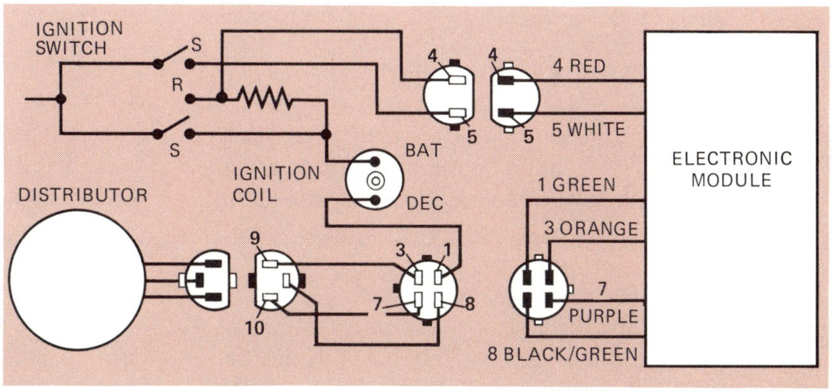

FORD S/S ignition schematic shows wiring for 1976–1977 models but can be used to pinpoint wiring connections for your car using the color code.

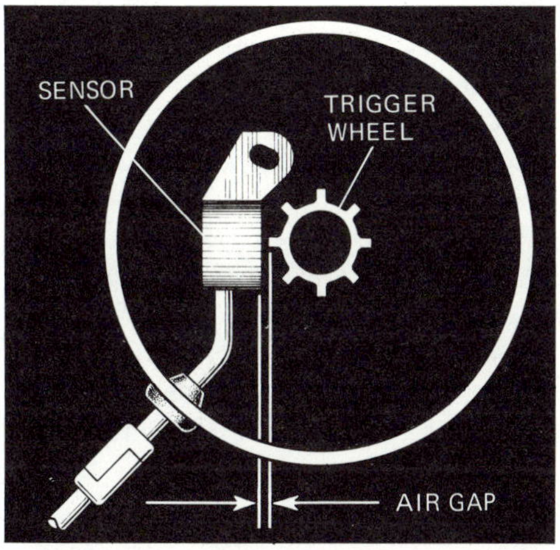

AIR GAP adjustment between sensor and trigger wheel of the International system.

INTERNATIONAL ELECTRONIC ignition system is in the top schematic. The hookup for checking the secondary circuit components is below. The bottom drawing shows connections for testing the sensor.

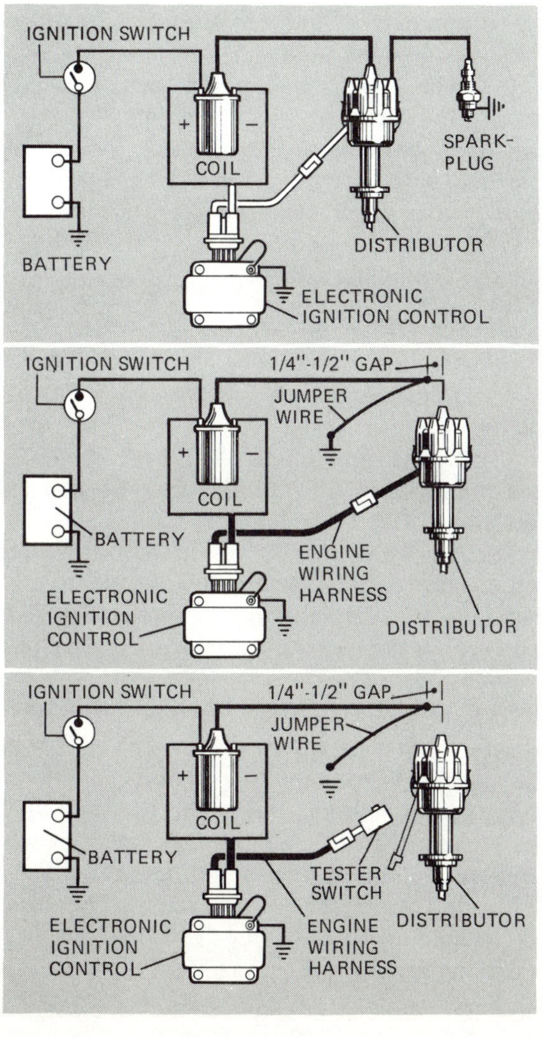

the ignition switch ON, the bulb should light. If it doesn't, replace the electronic control unit. Call this Test 2.

7. If the bulb does light, use a jumper lead to short across the electronic unit lead terminals. If the bulb stays on, replace the electronic control unit. This is Test 3.

8. If the bulb switches off, unhook the bulb from the ignition coil for Test 4. Disconnect one end of the jumper wire from across the electronic control unit lead terminals. Remove the coil-to-distributor secondary cable at the distributor, and hold its end ½ in. from ground. Be sure to use insulated pliers. Crank the engine and short out the electronic control unit lead terminals with the jumper.

If spark jumps the gap between the end of the cable and ground, the sensor in the distributor is causing the problem. Replace it.

If there is no spark, replace the coil.

BID: replacing the sensor

1. Remove the distributor cap, rotor and dust-shield.

2. Remove the trigger wheel. A small gear puller is needed. Use a thick flat washer or nut as

a spacer between the turn-down of the gear puller and the distributor's center shaft. Don't press directly on the shaft. Be sure the jaws of the puller grip the inner shoulder of the trigger.

3. Loosen the sensor locking screw about three turns. This screw has a tamperproof head design. Use a standard needle-nose pliers to remove the screw. Replacement sensors use standard slotted screws.

4. Lift the sensor lead grommet out of the distributor. Pull the sensor leads out of the slot around the sensor spring pivot pin. Lift and release the sensor spring. Slide the sensor off the vacuum chamber bracket.

5. To install a new sensor, place the sensor on the vacuum chamber bracket. Make sure the tip of the sensor fits in the summing bar. Place the sensor spring in position on the sensor, and route the sensor leads around the spring pivot pin. Install the sensor lead grommet in the distributor, and position the leads so they can't be caught by the trigger wheel.

6. You now need a sensor positioning gauge. It should have come with the new part. Place the sensor against the flat of the center shaft yoke, moving the sensor sideways until the gauge can be seated. Tighten the sensor retaining screw snugly.

7. Check the sensor's position by removing and installing the gauge. If the sensor is properly positioned, you will be able to remove and replace the gauge without the gauge demonstrating side movement. Tighten the sensor retaining screw and remove the gauge.

8. Set the trigger wheel in place on the shaft yoke. See that the sensor core is positioned about in the center of the trigger wheel legs. The legs should not be touching the sensor core.

9. Put trigger wheel on the yoke.

10. Bend a 0.050 wire gauge to the configuration shown and place it on the sensor. Press the trigger wheel in place until it just touches the gauge. Remove the gauge.

11. Apply three or four drops of SAE 30 oil to the felt wick on top of the yoke. Button up the distributor and time the ignition to specification.

Note: There is no dwell adjustment to make.

GM's HEI system: finding a problem

GM has a set troubleshooting procedure that is logical, simple and requires only a volt-ohmmeter. First, analyze the problem: Either the engine won't start or it will run rough. Then be sure the connector on the side of the distributor is secure and that all sparkplug cables are tightly connected. If this doesn't solve the problem, probe deeper:

(A) engine won't start

1. Connect a voltmeter between the BAT terminal lead on the distributor and ground. Turn on the ignition switch.

If the voltage reading is zero, there is an open circuit between the BAT terminal and the battery.

2. If the voltmeter records battery voltage, remove a sparkplug cable and hold it ¼ inch from ground using a pair of insulated pliers. Crank the engine.

If a spark occurs, the cause of the trouble is not inside the distributor. Look for bad sparkplugs or a fuel system breakdown. If there is no spark, distributor components should be tested (C, below).

(B) engine runs rough

1. Make sure fuel is reaching the carburetor.
2. Check vacuum hoses for leaks.
3. Start the engine. Look and listen to see if arcing is occurring. You can usually see or hear sparks jumping to ground through a defective cable. Replace the cable.
4. Check ignition timing and centrifugal advance with a stroboscopic timing light.
5. Remove sparkplugs and check for correct gap and other conditions that cause misfiring, such as fouled, glazed or damaged firing ends.

If the cause of the problem isn't found, test distributor components (C, below).

(C) testing distributor parts

1. Remove the distributor cap, which is held by four fasteners. Depress each fastener and twist one-half turn.

2. Examine cap terminals, ignition coil button and rotor pickup for burned areas, which indicate arcing. Replace a damaged component.

3. If the ignition coil is inside the distributor cap, connect an ohmmeter between terminals 1 and 2 in the distributor cap. The meter should read zero or nearly zero. If it doesn't, replace the ignition coil.

Now, connect one ohmmeter lead to the ignition coil button in the distributor cap. Connect the other lead first to the No. 2 terminal and then to the No. 3 terminal. Take both readings with the ohmmeter scale set on its high scale. If *both* readings are infinite, replace the ignition coil.

To replace the ignition coil, remove the three screws holding the coil to the distributor cap. Remove the ground wires from the coil, push the coil leads from the underside of the connectors and remove the coil.

4. If the ignition coil is an external unit, connect an ohmmeter between the No. 1 terminal and ground. With the ohmmeter on its high scale, the reading should be infinite. If it isn't, replace the coil.

Connect the ohmmeter leads between the coil's No. 1 and No. 2 terminals. With the ohmmeter on its low scale, the reading should be zero or nearly zero. If not, replace the ignition coil.

Connect the ohmmeter leads between the No. 2 and No. 3 terminals. With the ohmmeter on its high scale, the reading should *not* be infinite. If it is, replace the ignition coil.

5. Connect a vacuum source to the vacuum advance. If the vacuum advance doesn't move the vacuum control plate as vacuum is applied, replace the vacuum advance.

Disconnect the pickup coil leads to the electronic module and connect an ohmmeter to lead 1 and ground. Set the ohmmeter on the middle scale and operate the vacuum advance, using the vacuum source, to the full range of travel of the vacuum control plate. If the meter doesn't show an infinite reading at all times, replace the pickup coil.

Connect the ohmmeter to leads 1 and 2. Apply vacuum. If meter reads less than 500 ohms or more than 1500 ohms at any time, replace pickup coil.

You have to take the HEI distributor off the engine to replace the pickup coil. With the distributor out of the engine, drive the pin from the distributor shaft gear, remove the rotor, remove the shaft assembly from the housing, and take off the thin "C" clip to release the pickup coil.

6. If everything to this point checks out, there remains only the electronic module as the cause of your problem. It may be tested with HEI tester J-24642, which is available from Kent-Moore Tools, 1501 South Jackson St., Jackson, MI 49203.

However, the process of elimination has made it practically a sure thing that the electronic module is to blame, so you may want to replace it and avoid the cost of this instrument. The module is held by two screws, and you don't have to remove the distributor from the engine to remove the module.

Ford's S/S system: finding a problem

When an engine problem (hard starting, missing) occurs that may be ignition-caused, test the battery first. Then, make sure all harness connections are tight. A loose connection is the most common cause of a problem with the S/S system.

Disconnect the distributor connector and hook up a voltmeter between the two parallel blades. Place the voltmeter scale at 2.5 volts. Crank the engine.

The voltmeter needle should fluctuate. If it doesn't, look for damage inside the distributor, particularly a bad distributor cap and rotor, loose armature, broken armature teeth and misaligned roll pin. Make sure, too, that the armature rotates when the engine is cranked. If it doesn't, the sleeve and advance plate assembly are probably damaged. If visual distributor checks don't reveal the reason for the voltmeter needle not fluctuating, replace the magnetic pickup assembly.

If the voltmeter needle fluctuates during the test, check out the secondary circuit. Remove the high-tension coil lead from the distributor cap and hold it about 3/16 inch from ground as you crank the engine. Use insulated pliers to avoid shock.

Caution: Do not perform a spark intensity test at the sparkplugs. It may create an arcing condition inside the distributor that will cause damage.

If you get spark when doing this test, the cause of the problem you are having will be found in the secondary circuit. Check sparkplugs, cables, rotor and distributor cap.

If you don't get spark, the trouble is in the primary circuit. Turn your attention to the electronic module.

The easiest way to test the module is to borrow a module you know is good. Unplug the old module (don't remove it from the engine) and plug in the new one.

Do another spark intensity test. If spark occurs, it verifies that the old module is bad. Now you can take it off the engine and install the new one.

To install the new module, dip both ends of each connector in Lubriplate DS. Make the connections and wipe off excess lubricant.

If you have failed to uncover the cause of the trouble to this point, it is located at one of a number of wires or terminals, or the ignition coil. As you did with the electronic module, the coil may be tested by substituting a coil you know is good.

Testing primary circuit wires and terminals is done with a volt-ohmmeter. Use the quick check chart (page 1077) to make connections and check results.

Electronic modules from one year to another are different. Modules for 1974 and 1975 models have four-terminal connectors that plug into the ignition switch harness and three-terminal connectors that plug into the distributor harness. However, the arrangement of terminal pins differs. Thus, electronic modules used in 1974 and 1975 models are not interchangeable.

In 1976 and 1977 models, four-terminal connectors that plug into the ignition switch harness are also used. However, two-terminal connectors are used at the distributor harness. The 1978 models employ a variation of connectors. So *remember:* If you have to replace an electronic module, get the right one. The wrong one won't fit.

Although connector arrangement differs from year to year, each wire is color-coded, and color-coding is the same from year to year.

Therefore, the placement of the red wire, for example, in its connector will differ from one model to another. But the purpose of the red wire is the same, and it is tested the same way. This holds true for all wires, which have the following purposes:

- *Red wire*—The ignition switch supplies current to the electronic module through this wire when the engine is running.
- *White wire*—The ignition switch supplies current to the electronic module through this wire when the engine is being cranked.
- *Orange and purple wires*—These wires transmit signals from the distributor to the electronic module.
- *Green wire*—This wire receives primary ignition current from the ignition coil.
- *Black wire*—This wire is connected to the green wire inside the electronic module to complete the primary circuit.
- *Blue wire* (used only in seven-terminal setups)—This wire functions like a fuse to provide protection for the system.

trouble-shooting IH's electronic ignition system

Parts cannot be repaired. If tests uncover a malfunction, the part causing the trouble has to be replaced.

Make tests with a d.c. voltmeter, 12 to 18 inches of jumper wire with an alligator clip on each end, pair of insulated pliers, and SE-2503 tester switch which you can order from National Industries, Inc., 2745 Gunter Park Drive W., Montgomery, AL 36109.

Proceed as follows:

1. Check battery voltage. Recharge or replace a low battery.

2. Replace damaged primary and secondary wiring and make sure connections are tight and free of corrosion.

3. Connect the voltmeter between the coil positive terminal and ground. Turn on the ignition switch. The voltmeter should record battery voltage. If it doesn't, look for a high resistance condition between the battery and coil.

4. Disconnect a sparkplug cable. Using the insulated pliers, hold the cable's terminal end near ground while cranking the engine. If there is spark, check the sparkplugs. If there is no spark, reconnect the cable and proceed.

5. Disconnect the coil cable from the center tower of the distributor cap. Attach the jumper wire to the cable at a point ¼ to ½ inch from the metal terminal. Attach the other end of the jumper to ground. With the coil cable suspended away from ground, crank the engine. A spark should *not* jump between the cable terminal and jumper wire clip. If it does, the distributor cap or rotor is damaged.

6. Disconnect the distributor wire connector near the distributor and attach the tester switch. Turn the ignition on and press the tester switch. If a spark appears between the coil cable terminal and jumper wire alligator clip, replace distributor sensor and adjust trigger wheel-to-sensor air gap (see below).

7. Connect the voltmeter between the coil negative terminal and ground. With the ignition switch on, you should get a reading of 5 to 8 volts. A reading that is under 5 or over 8 indicates a bad ignition coil.

8. Press the tester switch. Voltage should increase to battery voltage and drop back to 5 to 8 volts when the tester switch is released. If not, replace the electronic ignition control unit. However, if voltage fluctuates as it should, but no spark appears between the coil cable terminal and jumper wire alligator clip, replace the ignition coil.

9. To adjust the air gap between the sensor and trigger wheel, loosen the sensor mounting screw and rotate the trigger wheel until one tooth is aligned with the center line of the sensor. The trigger wheel should be perpendicular to the flat surface of the sensor.

With a plastic feeler gauge of the correct size (see the vehicle's emission control decal), move the sensor in or out to set gap. Tighten the mounting screw and recheck the setting.

Connect a dwellmeter and start the engine. If dwell is not according to the specification on the emission control decal, move the sensor toward or away from the trigger wheel. Moving the sensor toward the trigger wheel decreases dwell; moving it away increases dwell.

Outdoor gear for indoor emergencies

By LEWIS PERDUE

During disaster or dimout, many items of camping equipment can do double duty. If selected carefully, these items can keep you going comfortably for days

FLOODS AND DISASTERS, fuel shortages, electrical brownouts and failures keep forcing millions of Americans to try to become as self-sufficient as their ancestors once were. Camping equipment intended for use for fun outdoors can be the answer for today's city and country dwellers when civilization gets jerked out from under our feet.

When heavy rains changed a placid river into a torrent that rose to within inches of their door, one family kept a written record of their plight. Their home was spared, although amphibious vehicles rescued neigbors from roofs of houses nearby. But the powerplant supplying electricity for the valley was under water so lights didn't light, the trash compactor wouldn't compact, the stove couldn't cook, dishwasher wouldn't wash, refrigerator no longer functioned and the freezer lost its battle against outside heat as melting ice cream oozed down the front. Their water pump wouldn't pump—but they couldn't use that water source anyway because a rising water table had overflowed their septic tank into the well. Their oil-burning furnace wouldn't heat because its control and circulating pump were electric. The family tried to boil water and cook in their fireplace but, like the ornamental fireplaces found in so many homes, it was ill-suited for utility. The charcoal barbecue grill was not much more help.

Fortunately the family had a camping stove that could serve for cooking food and boiling water plus a lantern to shed light on these essential chores. Both were fueled with gasoline and they were able to siphon enough from their car to keep both going until electric power was restored. Looking back afterward, they realized how lucky they had been.

When faced with a long-term power interruption, the basic requirements for most families are heat to cook and warm the kitchen plus light during the night. Non-electric camping gear powered with propane or gasoline can fill these bills. If the emergency occurs during warm months, keeping room temperature up is less serious. But during blizzard or ice-storm power shortages of winter, heat conservation and fuel economy are vital.

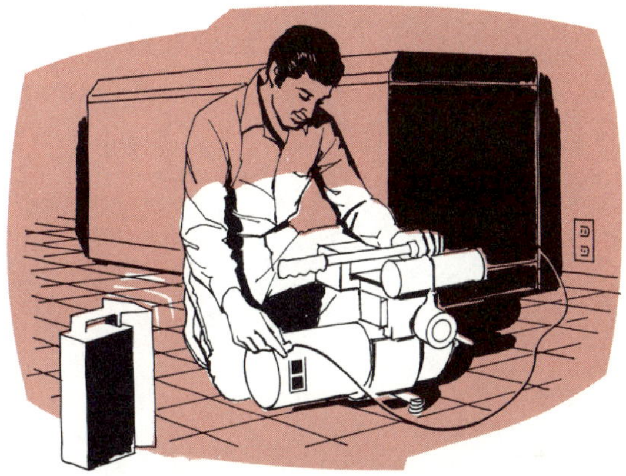

PORTABLE GENERATORS that provide such comfort around a campground can be both life and money-savers when used to power your appliances during dimout.

When the heating system fails during cold weather, the entire family should limit itself to one or two rooms, and not try to heat the entire house. The kitchen is best choice as a family room, since it can be partly or completely warmed by heat given off while preparing food. The kitchen should also be used for living and sleeping, with screened-off areas to give privacy for anyone too modest for communal living. Good sleeping bags will save fuel by allowing room heat to be drastically lowered at night. Down-filled bags are best, but are expensive. A bag with at least three pounds of polyester fill usually runs a close second. Remember that some ventilation must be provided for fresh air, particularly if a combustion heater is being used.

A first question by campers and homeowners alike when shopping for campstoves, heaters and lanterns is: propane or gasoline?

Propane is more expensive, but is more con-

SEE ALSO

Camping . . . Electrical wiring . . . Fire engines . . . Fire extinguishers . . . Generators, emergency

CAMPSTOVE COOKERY indoors will often prove a lot easier than preparing meals in a fireplace. The kitchen can be closed up into a family room for warmth or even emergency sleeping.

venient to use. When the demand is greatest, however, the supply of the standard 14.1-ounce propane cylinders may dwindle. If you decide on propane, it could be worthwhile to keep on hand a refillable bulk tank. It will cost more initially but allows long-term savings.

During an emergency, an adequate supply of white gasoline can also run short if filling stations cannot meet demand or power fails for their electric pumps. Regular gas can be used with some makes; with others it should be avoided except in emergencies. Additives in the gasoline can eventually clog orifices and valves, and possibly cause danger of lead contamination. It is best to keep on hand a supply of the recommended fuel, particularly for use with catalytic heaters where impurities can ruin the unit.

An advantage claimed for some liquid-fueled models is that, though they have to be pumped periodically, they can be made to work better in cold weather. Several bottled-gas LP lanterns, for instance, become dimmer as the temperature drops, and stove burners lose efficiency. Brightness levels of some propane lanterns will drop 20 to 80 percent as temperatures go from 70° to 35°. Extra pumping of gasoline models can prevent this. Coleman units use a patented LP regulator to keep temperature changes from lowering efficiency.

A single-mantle lantern will produce about as much light as a 75-watt light bulb and will burn about two ounces of propane or three of gasoline per hour. A double-mantle lantern can produce about 20 percent more light and uses about three ounces of propane or five ounces of gasoline an hour. A two-burner stove, using both burners, might need 11 ounces of gasoline per hour, while a similar propane stove should exhaust a 14.1-ounce cylinder in about 3½ hours.

Flame and catalytic heaters are available, with catalytic by far the safest in households with pets and small children. The flameless catalytic is less likely to start a fire or cause a burn. Propane-fueled catalytics are much more convenient than liquid-fueled models since no tall sooty flame is needed to prime LP heaters.

Some gasoline lanterns and stoves can burn LP gas when a converter is used. This may void the warranty, however, and like other emergency preparations should be experimented with in advance. Study instructions regarding ventilation, as well. Whether your appliances burn gasoline or propane, they use up oxygen, and their use indoors in a completely closed kitchen or bedroom could be dangerous.

Once you are prepared for emergency food, light and heat, give thought to the problems of a nonfunctioning water pump, defrosting freezer and refrigerator, and radios and TV with no power to give you reports of the disaster. When your home freezer stops running, keep it closed. Food will usually stay frozen for two days in a fully loaded freezer and at least a day in a half-loaded one. If it's winter and the temperature is

Generator wattage required

Add up items you use to determine approximate portable generator capacity you need.

APPLIANCE	AVERAGE POWER USED (WATTS)
Electric blanket	200
Broiler	1350
Coffeemaker	800-1100
Furnace fan	270
Oil burner	270
Water pump	340
Frying pan	1200
Hot plate	1250
Radio	80
Color television	325
Sump pump	400
Range (per element)	1250
Refrigerator/freezer	350-450
Freezer	300
Space heater	750-1500
Iron	900-1200
Water heater	1500
Light bulbs	Indicated on bulb

not likely to rise above freezing outdoors, some of the food can be placed there before it starts to thaw, but be sure it is placed where it is protected from animals, both domestic and wild. In some areas of the flood-ravaged Northeast a few years ago, freezer trucks were available where people could store food from powerless home freezers. In other parts of the country, commercial frozen-food lockers have been borrowed or rented during similar emergencies. Local police or Red Cross units can sometimes advise if these are available, once the initial emergency has passed but power lines are still down.

Many campers own small hand-carried gasoline-powered generators. These small powerhouses often pack 1100 to 1500 watts of power into a 60 to 100-pound package. They can be stowed easily in a car trunk or back of a station wagon and can be carried by one or two men. These portables can bring convenience and comfort to a campsite with little effort and cost, but if selected for suitable use during a home emergency as well, they can switch from pinch-hitter role to that of star performer.

A typical 1100-watt plant, 19 by 17 by 16 inches, may cost $150 and provide a great deal of camping satisfaction and emergency aid for the money. A typical freezer may use about 300 watts of power, a furnace fan 270, TV 300 and a radio 80. One burner of an electric stove can consume about 1250 watts, so you'd need either a bigger generator (1500 watts at about $200 weighing 75 pounds), or a smaller hot plate. An electric frying pan would not be a good substitute; many use about 1200 watts.

Care must be taken not to overload your generator. Most motors will draw from it an extra amount of power (surge current) when they start and could overload the generator even though your constant operation load current is within the unit's limits. One rule of thumb is to hook up appliances which use power equal to no more than 75 percent of the generator's maximum operating capacity.

Most appliances have wattage requirements stamped or embossed on them. Some carry only current ratings, but these can be converted into watts since wattage equals current (amperes) times voltage (120 volts). Many generators can be run on either gasoline or natural gas and have designs that make conversion simple for the camper or homeowner.

cars serves as generator

Another source of emergency electrical power is your car's generator or alternator. A temporary 12-volt automotive extension trouble lamp can be plugged into a car's cigaret-lighter socket, and several companies sell converters that will supply enough current to power lights, radios and small appliances. These converter kits, however, will not run the induction motors found in refrigerators, freezers, pump and furnace motors and other large appliances. But auxiliary alternators from many of these same companies, designed for use in addition to your car's standard alternator, can power induction motors. Since a car engine is not primarily intended for producing electricity, however, it will be less efficient than a small portable auxiliary 1100-watt generator that's priced only about twice as much as the auto modifications or additions and is much less expensive to run.

Many other camping items, of course, can become very useful indoors, especially if resumption of electrical power is delayed over several days. Candles, flashlights, water-purification equipment, first-aid gear, warm clothing, foul-weather gear and extra camp bedding will be put to excellent use if additional disaster victims must move in temporarily with you. With luck, the situation will be cleared up quickly, but the camper who has chosen his outdoor gear with a thought for indoor use as well will never regret it.

How to service emissions controls

SEE ALSO

Autos, maintenance . . . Carburetors, auto . . .
Catalytic converters, auto . . . Chokes, auto . . .
Distributors, auto . . . Exhaust systems, auto . . .
Ignition systems, auto . . . Lubrication, auto . . .
Sparkplugs . . . Tune-up, auto

■ IT MAKES GOOD sense to maintain emissions controls periodically from the time a car is new. In addition to increasing air pollution levels, neglected emissions control devices cause poor gasoline mileage, hard starting, stalling, hesitation on acceleration, and dieseling. Dieseling is engine run-on after the ignition is turned off.

Servicing the following emissions control units falls within the skills of a Saturday mechanic:

- Fuel-evaporation canister.
- Positive crankcase ventilation (PCV) valve, hoses and filter.
- Thermostatic control valve in the air cleaner snorkel.
- Exhaust gas recirculation (EGR) valve.

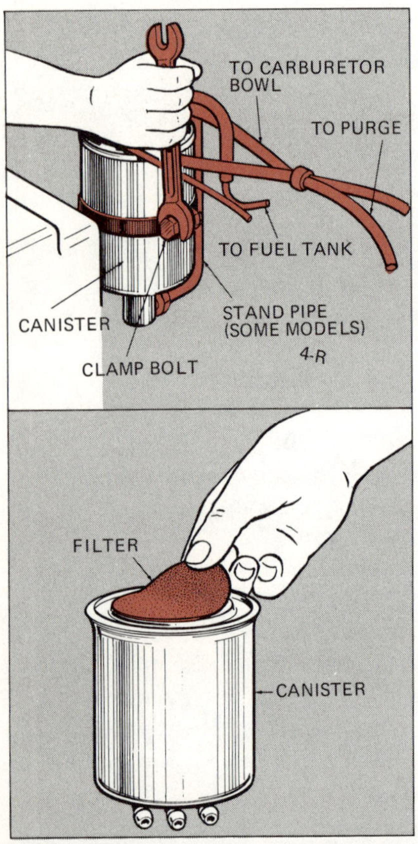

THE FUEL CANISTER is often forgotten. To replace it, remove canister and turn filter upside down. Tag lines so that you know which goes where.

How to service the fuel-evaporation system

The fuel-evaporation-control system prevents gasoline vapors from entering the atmosphere. Vapors coming from the fuel tank and carburetor are stored in a charcoal canister when the engine is off, and are burned when the engine is running.

The only part of the system requiring service is the charcoal canister. In some cars, imports particularly, the canister should be replaced at 50,000 miles.

In other cars, usually domestic, canisters are fitted with a filter that should be inspected and replaced if covered with dirt. If the filter is blocked, gasoline vapors escape into the air. A gasoline odor is one sign that the filter requires servicing.

To service the filter, do this:

1. Find the canister, which is mounted either at the right or left front of a car engine compartment. In a light truck or van, the canister may be in a different location.

2. Remove the bracket or strap holding the canister. Turn the canister upside down.You may have to remove the hoses attached to the canister. If so, mark hoses with tags to assure proper reconnecting. Such designations as "left," "center" and "right" may be used.

3. Slip the filter from the canister housing. In some cases, the filter is held by a spring wire.

4. Inspect the canister housing which, if cracked, should be replaced. If the canister is not damaged, slip in a new filter.

5. Reinstall the canister.

6. Examine hoses. Replace those that have cracked or hardened. Fuel-evaporation-control system hoses are made to withstand fuel vapor. If replacement is necessary, buy only fuel-resistant hoses.

This service should be done when you have an engine tune-up.

How to service the PCV system

If the PCV system gets blocked, pressure builds up in the crankcase and may force oil out of the oil filter tube and past the engine oil seals. The result is loss of oil. Naturally, a clogged PCV system also contributes to air pollution.

The heart of the PCV system is the PCV valve, which controls the rate at which vapors in the engine crankcase are allowed to return to the intake manifold. If the PCV valve sticks on the vacuum side of the valve, the flow of air through the valve is restricted. This enriches the air/fuel mixture entering the cylinders, reducing fuel mileage.

If the PCV valve sticks in mid-position, too much air passes through the valve. This makes the fuel mixture too lean and causes rough engine idling. If the valve sticks so it can't move back to close the crankcase port, an engine backfire may cause an explosion in the crankcase.

A combination of shaking and checking for vacuum usually reveals whether a faulty PCV valve exists. When you tune up the engine, do this test:

1. Pull the PCV valve from its position in the valve cover or intake manifold. Shake the valve. If it rattles, it generally indicates a functioning valve. However, this is not a foolproof test.

2. Start the engine and cover the end of the valve with your thumb. If there is no vacuum ("pull" on your thumb), the valve may be plugged or the PCV system hoses may be blocked.

3. Remove and clean out the hoses. This can be done by ramming a cloth wad through them. If hoses are cracked or have hardened, replace them.

4. Test for vacuum after the hoses

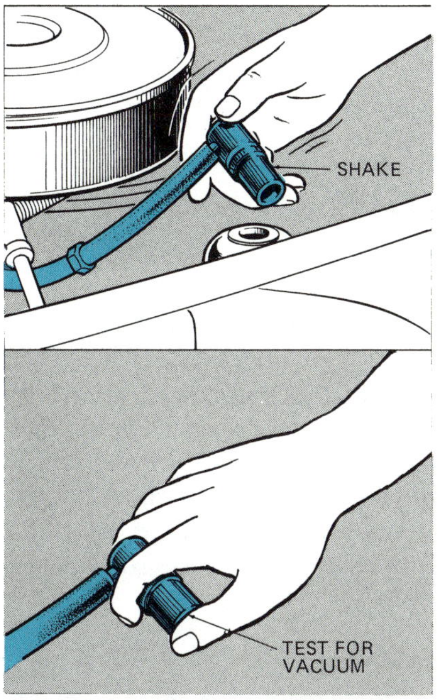

AN EASY WAY to test a PVC system is to shake the valve to see that it rattles and (engine running) check for vacuum by covering valve end with your thumb.

are reconnected. If there is still no vacuum, replace the PCV valve.

Sludge can be cleaned from a PCV valve by shooting in PCV cleaner. However, there is no way to determine accurately if the spring inside the valve is weak and no longer metering out the proper volume of air. For this reason, car manufacturers recommend replacing the valve every year.

A part of the PCV system often overlooked is the PCV inlet filter, which is generally positioned in the side of the main body of the air cleaner. This filter cleans the air before it enters the crankcase and should be replaced at the same time as the air cleaner filter.

In some cars, the filter pad may be lifted out of a small pocket in the air cleaner. With most installations, the following procedure is necessary:

1. Snap out the retaining clip that holds the PCV filter container to the air cleaner. This clip is at the end of the PCV hose connected to the filter.

2. Remove the container.

3. If possible, take the filter pad from the container. Discard the filter. In some cases, the entire assembly has to be replaced.

4. Wash the container and let it stand until dry.

5. Oil the new filter pad sparingly with your engine oil and then place it into the container.

6. Attach the container to the air cleaner with the retaining clip.

Testing thermostatic control valves

The thermostatic control valve in the air cleaner snorkel controls the temperature of air entering the carburetor during cold weather. Maintaining temperature within tight limits makes it possible to calibrate the carburetor on the lean side. This reduces hydrocarbon emissions, improves engine warm-up and cuts down on the chance of carburetor icing during the warm-up period.

This system, which is sometimes referred to as the heated inlet air system, consists of a vacuum diaphragm that sits on top of the air cleaner snorkel, a temperature sensor which is located inside the air cleaner and a control valve installed in the snorkel. These are the steps to follow:

1. Check the functioning of the system with the engine cold and the air temperature below 50° F. Remove the

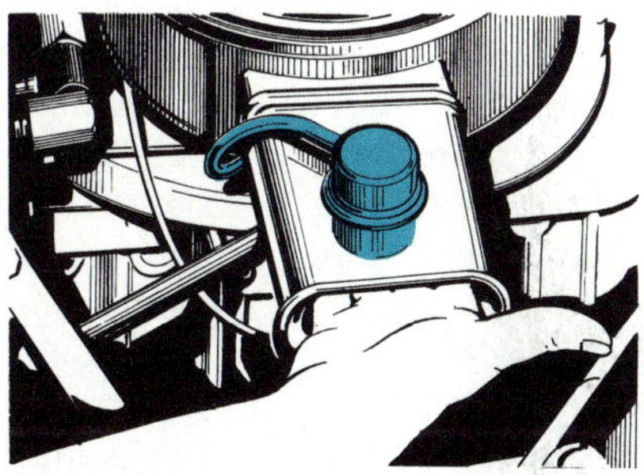

ONE WAY to see if the snorkel valve is working properly is by hand-testing. The valve should be closed when the engine is started and open thereafter.

duct connected to the snorkel, If there is one, and put your hand inside the snorkel. See that the control valve moves freely.

2. Start the engine. As the engine warms up, the valve should move in the direction opposite to that when the engine was cold.

3. If the control valve doesn't operate in this way, test the vacuum diaphragm with a vacuum pump. If the vacuum diaphragm functions properly when tested, replace the sensor.

4. Test control-valve action once a year.

How to service the EGR valve

American Motors Corp.:

1. Remove the EGR valve from the engine.

2. Scrape deposits from the valve base using a wire brush.

3. By hand, compress the valve diaphragm to determine if the poppet valve is functioning. This is established by the valve moving freely. If the poppet valve sticks, discard the EGR valve.

AMC recommends this service every 30,000 miles.

Chrysler Corp.:

1. Remove the EGR valve from the engine.

2. Inspect the poppet valve and seat for carbon. If any deposits are discovered, continue servicing as detailed below. If not, reinstall the valve.

3. Apply manifold heat-control valve solvent to the poppet valve and seal, but be careful not to spill solvent on the valve diaphragm. Allow solvent to loosen deposits. If solvent is spilled on the diaphragm, replace the EGR valve. Solvent causes irreparable damage.

4. With a vacuum pump, apply vacuum to the valve vacuum nipple to open the valve. Then, use a knife to scrape off carefully all deposits from the seat and poppet valve.

Chrysler recommends this service every 15,000 miles.

Ford Motor Co.:

1. Remove EGR valve from the engine.

2. Outfit an electric drill with a short piece of speedometer cable. Insert the end of the cable into the valve cavity located between the poppet and the seat.

3. Turn on the drill. Employing a circular motion, loosen deposits.

Ford recommends this procedure when one of the following engine problems occurs: rough idling, stalling, rough acceleration under light throttle application, excessive fuel consumption, stalling under deceleration and detonation.

General Motors:

1. Remove the EGR valve.

2. Hold the valve diaphragm down and plug the vacuum tube.

3. Release the diaphragm. The poppet valve should not close until 20 seconds or more have elapsed. If it does, replace the EGR valve.

4. Check for deposits on the poppet valve and seat. If they are present, tap the end of the poppet valve with a plastic hammer and shake deposits from the unit.

5. Look for deposits in outlet holes. Clean them out carefully with a knife or screwdriver.

6. Scrape mounting surfaces of the EGR valve and the engine with a wire brush.

GM recommends this procedure when one of the following engine problems occurs: rough idling, stalling, rough acceleration under light throttle application, excessive fuel consumption, stalling under deceleration and detonation.

Build an energy-saving house

By HARRY WICKS

■ BUILDING A HOUSE that will conserve as much energy as possible isn't particularly difficult. Our ancestors knew how to do it, and so do we. But until recently, we did not consider it necessary to be concerned with how much energy we consumed—or how much we wasted through lack of planning. The energy crunch changed that outlook.

Though a new house with energy-conservation features generally costs more than one without them, your initial cash outlay—and more—will be returned in the form of savings on heating bills. For example, once the house has been closed in, you can provide insulation in exterior walls only by chopping holes in the walls around the house perimeter and blowing in the material. The time, therefore, to think of saving energy is in the planning stage.

In broad terms, there are five planning steps you can take to save as much energy as possible:

1. Position house on the site with regard to exposure and all the elements.
2. Design the home for efficient energy use.
3. Select materials and workmanship that will conserve energy.
4. Plan the use of insulation.
5. Get top efficiency from appliances, mechanical equipment and fireplaces.

position your house with care

The basic idea is to use the natural terrain to protect the house from the elements. For example, can your house be built in a valley instead of on top of a hill? Can you locate it on the protected side of a hill or on the sunny side of a slope? Remember, you can obtain some insulation by building partly *into* a hillside.

SEE ALSO

Furnaces . . . Heating systems, home . . . Home improvement . . . Insulation . . . Remodeling . . . Solar energy . . . Solar water heaters . . . Winterizing, homes

And don't make the mistake of arbitrarily clearing all rocks and vegetation from the site. Look for this fault particularly if buying a contractor-built or vacation community home. Many builders and developers find it cheaper to build if just about all trees are knocked down and the land is leveled.

allow for sun and wind

Always keep sun and wind in mind when locating your house on a site. In cold-weather areas, winter winds usually come from the North, so it makes sense to face the walls with maximum insulation and minimum glass area that way. If the house design and property layout permit, the shortest wall should face north.

In much of today's architecture, especially in leisure-home designs, large areas of glassed walls seem almost mandatory. By siting your house so the glass walls face south, the low winter sun will shine into them during most of the daylight hours and ease the load on the heating system. In warmer areas, where cooling is of primary concern, the glass areas should also face south. With properly designed overhangs (often called "eyebrows"), little or no sun comes in during the summer when the sun is high. By contrast, if these windows are on the east or west sides, they pick up heat almost half the day, thus putting a burden on the house cooling system.

You can get protection as well as beauty from landscaping, too. A row of evergreens planted to the north or northwest of a house can be an effective wind barrier.

Tall deciduous trees should be retained or planted to the south, west or east of the house to provide cooling shade in the summer. In winter, after the leaves have fallen, these trees do not block the roof and walls from the warming rays of the sun.

design a functional house

Use plain common sense when picking your house—don't be guided by esthetics alone. If you

Here are 10 things you can do to help keep fuel bills down

1. Use double-glazed windows throughout to reduce heat transmission up to 50 pecent.

2. When choosing a house style, favor multilevel designs over ranch homes. Their proportionately smaller roof areas for a given amount of space cut down heat loss.

3. Insulate exposed walls with material having an R-value at least 11 (3½-in. mineral wool batts or equivalent); ceilings with material having an R-value at least 19 (6 in. thick).

4. Use light-colored shingles on the roof to reflect sunlight and thus assist cooling equipment.

5. Adequately ventilate attic to lessen solar heat gain.

6. Use à minimum of 1-in.-thick perimeter insulation for on-grade slabs and footings.

7. Accept only tight installations of windows and doors. Cracks existing between frames and rough openings should be packed with insulation and sealed with an appropriate vapor-barrier material.

8. Caulk around all joints between windows, doors and siding with a high-quality latex or butyl caulk compound.

9. In extra-cold climates, use storm windows. When tightly fitted, they can reduce infiltration of air by 30 to 50 percent.

10. Preserve as many trees as possible for reasons explained in the text.

question your knowledge in this area, an architect should be consulted.

First, make sure your house is designed for the climate it will be exposed to. For example, a house with a sprawling layout and large areas of glass walls might suit the climate perfectly in the southwest United States. But park the same house in the northern reaches of Maine, and it becomes an energy-guzzling monster to heat.

The house should be practical to heat and cool. The design feature to key in on is the ratio of roof area to floor area (see sketch): The lower the ratio, the easier it will be to heat or cool the house. Though the drawing shows that a round house is most efficient in this regard, that shape is difficult to build and live in. Next best is a square house; after that in decreasing efficiency, the rectangular, L, H and T shapes.

In colder climates, a two-story house makes good sense. Since most heat is lost through the roof, a two-story house saves money because it has a lower proportion of roof to floor area. You can save as much as 15 percent in fuel consumption by having living areas on two levels instead

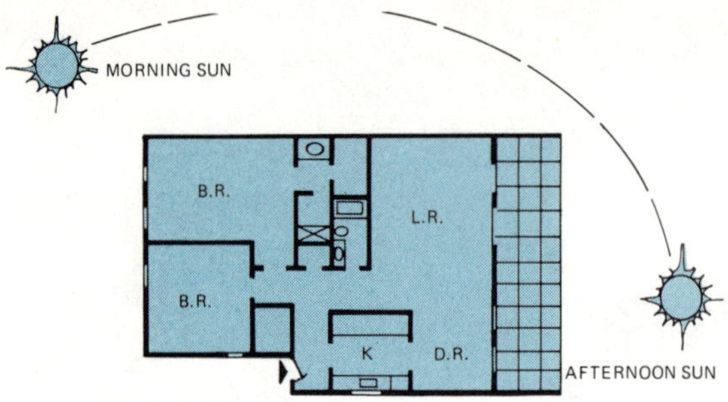

CONSIDER YOUR floor plan: Keep common (or active) living space confined to one part of the house and sleeping (or inactive) rooms in another for zoned heating and cooling. Active rooms may be warmed by facing them toward the afternoon sun.

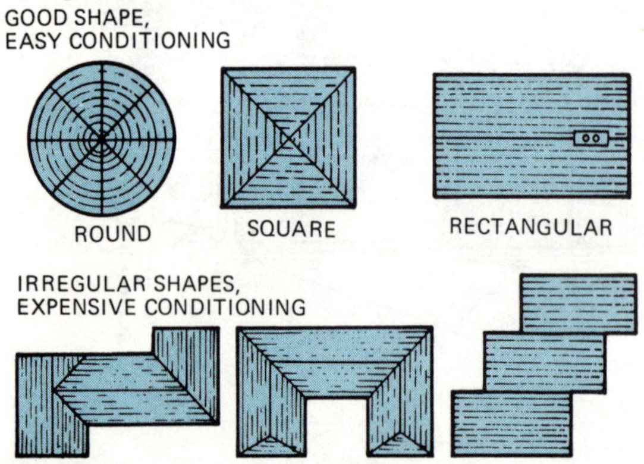

THE KEY to efficient heating and cooling is the ratio of roof to floor areas—the less roof area, the better. A two-level house has a lower proportion of roof to floor area and can save up to 15 percent on fuel.

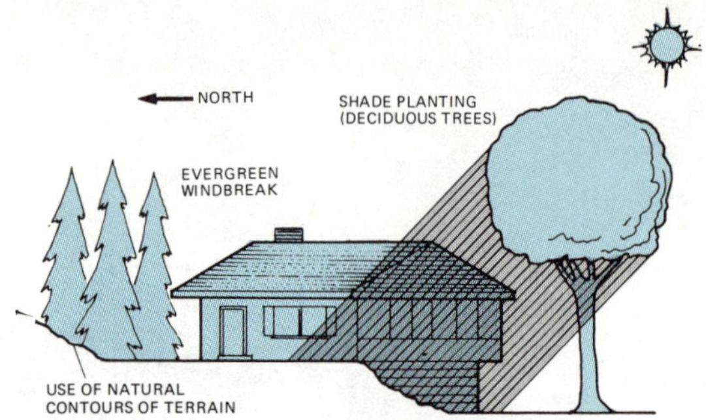

LANDSCAPING SHOULD protect your property as well as beautify it. A row of evergreens north of your house breaks the wind, while deciduous trees on the other sides provide shade in the summer and allow warming sunlight through in the winter when they are bare. Use of terrain is also helpful.

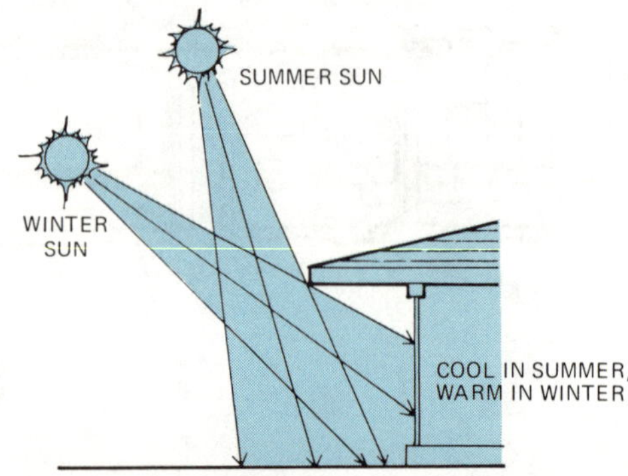

CORRECTLY DESIGNED roof overhangs shield walls from the higher summer sun, yet expose the same walls to the winter sun which is at a lower angle. An attached porch, carport or patio roof also serves to protect the walls.

of sprawled out on one level.

Give careful attention also to your floor plan. Grouping common living space in one part of the house and sleeping quarters in another facilitates zoned heating and cooling (dual thermostats, one for each area) and allows the closing off of a section when not in use. If possible, family rooms, kitchens and dining rooms should face south and west so they are warmed by the afternoon sun. Bedrooms should be oriented to the morning sun so they can be cooled easily for comfortable sleeping.

Well-planned ventilation can reduce the need for home cooling. In fact, many architects agree that in some regions, airconditioning is totally unnecessary if the house is properly ventilated. Along these lines, a courtyard or atrium (enclosed or open) can be used to create better ventilation; even though an atrium adds wall area, it may cut the cooling load.

Don't automatically opt for large expanses of glass—the major cause of heat loss. Windows should be positioned and located with more than a view in mind. Too often, they are included for esthetic reasons only and are not operable for ventilation. Often, when the cooling system is spinning the meter at dizzying speed, the house could be cooled by merely opening and closing the right windows.

high ceilings waste heat

Cathedral ceilings are dramatic and currently in vogue. But be aware that such ceilings can bring with them serious heating problems. Energy is wasted in conditioning a large volume of air in high unused spaces. And, since warm air rises, it is especially difficult to heat high-ceilinged rooms.

Old architectural standbys can still save a lot of energy. Attached porches, carports and decking can also protect windows and doors from the direct rays of the sun if they are carefully laid out. If your architectural design allows, consider using operable shutters over windows to screen out direct rays of the sun and cold wind blasts.

When you compromise function, you're almost certain to compromise good design.

101 ways to cut home energy costs

"**THERMOSTAT:** check; fireplace damper: check; radiator covers: check; lint trap . . ."

THE ENERGY CRISIS is hardly news, and few doubt its seriousness. It's grimly reflected every month when bills arrive. The news is full of grandiose plans for the year 2000, and entrepreneurs keep devising systems for homeowners that would cost nearly as much as the house itself—with little hope of amortizing such expense in a normal lifetime. So far, there's been little useful information about how the average homeowner can beat soaring utility and heating bills.

Are there any ways to beat the system? You bet there are! The first step is to take a look at where energy goes in a normal American home. The figures are well established. Some 70 percent goes to heat and/or to cool the house; 20 percent heats water; 10 percent runs lighting and appliances.

With that for starters, here are 101 *practical* things you can do *right now* to slash the local utility company's bite, and soaring home fuel bills, by up to half or more. Many cost nothing at all; others involve minor expense for simple projects, most of which you can build or install yourself; a few require sensible investment that will pay for itself over a few years of use. All have been tested and proven for the Federal Energy Administration (FEA) or the Energy Research and Development Administration (ERDA), by scientific laboratories in universities or in industrial labs.

THINGS TO DO WITHOUT BUILDING OR INSTALLING ANYTHING

■ Keep daytime thermostats at 65° F. in winter and (if you have central airconditioning) at 78° in summer. Both limits fall within a good health range. "People who insist they're pneumonia bait at anything below 75° in winter," say ERDA scientists, "are the same ones who cry 'heat prostration' in summer if the airconditioner is set above 65°." You'll save 3 percent of fuel costs for every degree the *average* house temperature is cut.

■ Drop your 'stat to 55° when you retire in winter. The fuel bill will drop one percent for every degree dialed down at night.

■ Remove radiator covers (or use perforated tops) if your system is steam or hot water. Radiators create special convection currents in front of windows and outside walls. Covers decrease their efficiency.

■ For maximum efficiency, use flat paint on radiators and dust them regularly. Dust and metallic paints are insulators.

■ Protect your thermostat from drafts. If it's near a frequently used fireplace, move it to a more distant inside wall. Fireplace heat will keep it from triggering the furnace and distant rooms will get too cold, wasting fuel to get them back to proper temperature.

■ "Zone control" your home manually by closing off unused rooms and turning off their radiators (or shutting registers). Use self-sticking foam weatherstrip to seal such doors to prevent air exchange either way. Similar zone control can be realized with central airconditioning in summer.

■ In hot-air systems, replace the filter monthly during the heating season. A dirty filter reduces efficiency.

■ Check ductwork for leaks and tape any loose seams or joints.

■ Have your furnace serviced annually by a professional and make sure he checks—and adjusts if necessary—the burning rate.

■ Hang drapes on all windows where practical; close them at night in winter months.

■ Double-hung windows with storm sash on an unshaded south wall can serve as solar collectors in the winter.

SEE ALSO
Furnaces . . .
Heating systems, home . . .
Home improvement . . . Insulation . . .
Remodeling . . . Solar energy . . .
Solar water heaters . . .
Winterizing, homes

Open the inside window a few inches (no more than three or four) from top and bottom. The greenhouse effect of the storm sash will warm air between the panes and set up a chimney that heats low-lying room air coming in at the bottom and sends it back through the open top 20° or more warmer.

■ Turn off ventilating fans in kitchen or bath when they've done their job. They can empty a house of warm air in one hour.

water heaters

■ Repair leaky faucets. One drop per second wastes 60 gallons of expensively heated water per week.

■ Set hot water tank at 120°—"medium" on some heaters—not the usual 140°. It will be plenty warm, and you'll cut 20 percent from the cost of hot water—which accounts for 20 percent of your total heating bill.

■ Flush sediment from the bottom of the heater tank at least yearly. A buildup will insulate water from the heat source. If you hear water gurgling when the heater's on, you have sediment.

■ Use cold water to flush away food in the sink garbage disposer. It works better than hot water; grease particles flush out and there's no buildup in pipes.

■ Home cleaning (woodwork and so forth) works as well with cold water and proper detergents.

fireplaces

Does an open fire on the hearth add warmth to a house or suck more furnace-warmed air up the flue than it replaces? There are no simple answers. Much depends on the type of fireplace, flue-size and efficiency, controls and so on. Some researchers claim open hearth fires produce only (or mostly) radiant heat that warms bodies, not air. This may not necessarily be wholly true.

Last winter two fireplaces in a *Popular Mechanics* house were put to work to find out. With the hot-air furnace thermostat set at 65°, and an outdoor reading of 28°, a packaged fireplace in a den sent a thermometer in that room from 55° to 68° in two hours—with the room's door open. The furnace kicked in twice during that period—less than normal under the weather conditions.

In a separate experiment, an open fire in a bigger living-room fireplace (with built-in heat vents), a room thermometer went from 55° to 73° in less than an hour in the same weather. Doors to adjacent rooms were open and the furnace never went on while the fire burned. Our conclusion: *Some* fireplaces *do* increase ambient temperature with the furnace "on line" and, obviously, without a deficit of heated inside air up the flue. Until the turn of the century, that's how most country homes were heated.

Add-on fireplace devices will increase fireplace efficiency and sensible fireplace practices can help!

■ With a fireplace going, keep doors to other rooms closed—or keep the furnace turned off until you need it.

■ If the thermostat faces a frequently used fireplace, or is close by, move it to the far end of an inside wall or to another room with no alternate heat source.

■ Keep the fireplace damper closed when no fire is burning. An open flue from a 48-inch-square fireplace opening will remove 8 percent of furnace-warmed air from the house continually.

■ Fasten a metal handle to the bottom of a five-gallon enamel canning pot and (wearing an asbestos glove) use it as a snuffer to extinguish a live-embers (not blazing) fire when you leave the fireplace. *Be sure all live coals* are extinguished before you close the damper.

airconditioning

■ Set your thermostat at 78°, which can be comfortable if you dress lightly. If your usual setting was 72° you'll save between 12 and 14 percent (depending on your area) of the annual bill for cooling.

■ Don't set the thermostat colder "to get it started" on the theory that it will cool the room sooner. It won't.

■ Change your airconditioner's filter monthly during the cooling season. Dirt slows movement of cool air into the house.

■ Keep the airconditioner's fan on "high" except in humid weather. The compressor works just as hard whether the fan is high or low. On high, more cooled air is brought into the house and the compressor will shut itself off sooner.

■ Spread cooled air around your room with a small portable fan. It keeps the cooled air from "layering" and settling to the floor.

■ Turn off a room airconditioner when you leave the room. You'll use less current bringing the temperature down again when you return than if you left it running.

■ Don't locate lamps, TV or radio near enough to affect the airconditioner's thermostatic control, which is highly sensitive.

■ Keep direct sunlight from entering an airconditioned room. This is readily achieved by drawing drapes and closing blinds or shades. Such simple measures can reduce the sun's heat input into a room by up to 80 percent.

■ Keep windows and outside doors shut when temperature outside is higher than inside.

■ If you use storm windows in winter, leave them up in summer. The double glass has an insulating effect that can cut heat infiltration by more than half.

■ Keep lights off whenever possible while the airconditioner is running, and use lamps with as low wattage as possible when you need light. Incandescent lamps add considerable heat for the airconditioner to get rid of.

■ Do all cooking and baking possible in early morning and late evening during hot weather.

lighting

■ "Light zone" your house to provide good illumination for reading, writing, sewing or sketching, with wattage as low as possible elsewhere. Wattage saved in this simple manner can add up to almost three figures in a year.

■ Use one large bulb in preference to three smaller ones where bright light is needed. A 100-watt lamp will provide better reading light than three 40-watt bulbs.

REMOVE radiator covers to let heat convection function more efficiently.

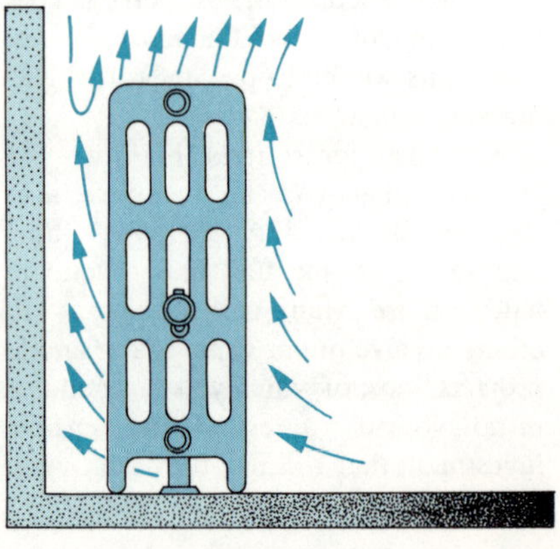

■ "Long life" incandescents use more energy than standard bulbs. Enough said.
■ Turn off all but one or two low-watt lamps when watching TV. You only need enough light to balance TV brightness and avoid eyestrain.
■ Specify 4-watt clear night-light bulbs. They use half the energy of the 7-watters and provide almost the same light.
■ Keep all bulbs and shades clean. Dirt absorbs light.

■ Use outdoor spots, floods and driveway illumination only when necessary.
■ Use fluorescent bulbs whenever possible. A 40-watt fluorescent will use 140 watts less than a 60-watt incandescent in a seven-hour period—and provide more than five times the amount of light.

kitchen

■ Never boil water in an open pan. It boils sooner and over less heat in a covered vessel. Once boiling, keep it rolling with as low a flame as possible. Unpressurized boiling water gets little hotter, no matter how high the flame.

UNPLUG the coffee warmer and use a Thermos bottle to keep the coffee hot.

■ Kept clean, range-top burners and reflectors produce more heat with less energy.
■ Don't put small pans on large heating elements or (on gas stoves) let flame exceed diameter of the pan. Heat missing the pot bottom is lost to the air.
■ Turn off heating elements of electric stoves shortly before cooking time is up. They'll stay hot long enough to finish the job without using more electricity.
■ Don't open the oven door to "peek and poke." It wastes heat. Use a timer for baking and roasting.

■ Small electric fry pans and grills use less energy than a range or oven for small meals. A toaster uses less power than the oven or grill for family toast.
■ Keep the refrigerator food compartment at 40°; freezer compartment at 5°. A thermometer will give you the proper setting for the unit's dial control.
■ Manual-defrost refrigerators and freezers should be defrosted regularly. More than a ¼-inch buildup of frost puts an extra load on the compressor motor.
■ Check seals on refrigerator and freezer doors. If you can slip a piece of paper under them anywhere, have them replaced.
■ Don't wash dishes under hot running water or you'll be throwing away gallons of costly heated water. Close the drain, fill the sink with warm water and detergent, and rinse with a hot spray in the dish drainer.
■ Never run your dishwasher until it has a full load.
■ If your washer has no "air-dry" switch, turn the control to "off" position after the last rinse, crack the door and let the dishes air-dry by themselves. You'll save a third of the energy cost of automatic dishwashing.
■ The "rinse-hold" control on dishwashers uses three to seven gallons of hot water each time used. Avoid using it.

laundry

■ Don't wash partial loads. Wait until you can fill the machine—unless it has a "small load" attachment.
■ Always presoak badly soiled clothes, or use the soak cycle to avoid having to run a wash twice.
■ Clothes can be cleaned successfully in warm water rather than "hot" water, and can be rinsed well in cold water. You'll save half the demand on the water heater with these easy steps.

■ Don't let lint build up in the dryer's collector screen. It blocks airflow and takes more time and heat to do the job.
■ Don't forget the old-fashioned clothesline. Outdoors in fine weather clothes get a fresh sunshine smell. On bad winter days, hang them in a basement area warmed by the furnace. That dryer—gas or electric—uses a phenomenal amount of energy.
■ Dry heavy and lightweight laundry separately if there's enough wash for two loads. Light clothes dry faster, use less energy. They may even dry with residual heat left from the first batch.

bathroom

■ Try five-minute showers instead of 30-minute tub baths. You'll use 25 percent less hot water. In a year it can amount to nearly $50 for a family of four in water heating cost.
■ Don't scrub nails or wash hands under a running stream. Fill sink for washing and rinsing. You'll use half as much heated water.

INSULATION

ATTIC CALLS for R-30 insulation (see chart). Add more to bring it up.

■ The FEA estimates that some 40 million single-family homes in this country are inadequately insulated. By bringing them up to par, the heating and cooling load for each home could be reduced by 20 to 30 percent. That means that if your home heating bill runs to $400, a $300 investment in insulation could pay for itself in three to five years.

Check where and how much insulation your house may need. Local building materials dealers can provide the insulation "R-values" recommended for your area. The "R" stands for resistance to heat loss (or heat gain, in summer). The amount of resistance provided by the thickness of any particular insulating material is expressed by a number; the higher the number, the higher the insulating, or resistance, value. All building materials have *some* insulating value, including walls with no insulation at all. But such R-values are quite low (see the chart for the thickness required in different types of insulation to produce a given R-value).

R-VALUE	STANDARD WOOD FRAME WALL UN-INSULATED	REFLECTIVE SHEET	BLANKET OR BATTS		LOOSE (POURED IN)			FOAMED** PLASTICS (RIGID PANEL OR FOAM IN PLACE)		EXPANDED** MINERALS LOOSE
		SHEET	GLASS FIBER	ROCK WOOL	GLASS FIBER	ROCK WOOL	CELLULOSE FIBER	POLY-STYRENE	POLY-URETHANE	VERMICULITE OR PERLITE GRANULES
UP TO R-3		1 SIDE	1″	1″						1″
R-4		2 SIDES						1″		
R-6	*								1″	
R-11			3½″	3″	5″	4″	3″			
R-19			6″	5¼″	8″	6″	5″			
R-22			6½″	6″	10″	8″	6″			
R-30			9½″	9″	13″	11″	8″			
R-38			12″	10½″	17″	14″	11″			

*AVERAGE WALL OF 2 x 4 STUDS, ½″ PLYWOOD SHEATHING, ¾″ CLAPBOARD SIDING, 15-LB. FELT VAPOR BARRIER, ½″ PLASTERBOARD
**R-VALUE IS CALCULATED PER INCH OF MATERIAL USED

IN COLD basements or crawl spaces, blanket-type insulation should be used to wrap metal ducting as shown above. In heated basements, or in areas where water pipes may freeze, don't wrap the ducts.

BLANKET-TYPE insulation is used as shown in basements and crawl spaces, with a strip against the header joist between the floor and sill, and strips cleated to the sill and draped down the wall.

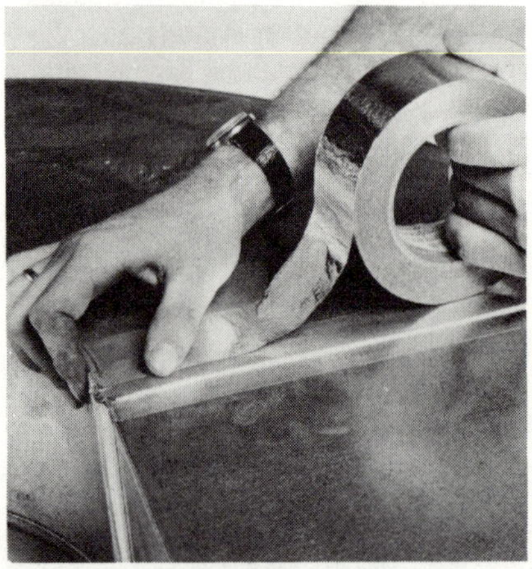

HOT-AIR DUCT TAPE, a product of companies like 3M, is used to seal every seam and gap in metal work. Installers frequently miss a lot of places.

FOUNDATION WALLS can be insulated outside. Wall is exposed to frost line, then covered with insulation such as Dow's Styrofoam panels; hole is then backfilled.

■ Check attic insulation, where most heat loss occurs in a house. ERDA recommends R-30 (9 to 10 inches of batts or blanket type). It's best installed between ceiling joists, and can be layered if you already have some but not enough. It can cut 5 percent from your heating bill if you add 3 or 4 inches to bring it up; up to 30 percent if you're starting from scratch.

■ As for walls, ERDA tests show that electrical gear, braces and firestops block blown-in insulation, leaving huge voids, and that blow-in and foaming types are too expensive for dollar payback in a reasonable time. It will cut some heat loss if you retrofit exterior walls. If you do, R-11 to 13 is recommended. Be sure to have the installer put vents in the wall for moisture control. Insulated walls can save you 16 to 20 percent in heating costs.

■ Insulate basement or crawl-space walls—it's worth a 5 to 25-percent saving, depending on weather-tightness of your home's underpinnings, and will also protect water pipes against frost. This can be done outside by digging trenches and laying in one-inch foam panels, as shown, against the exterior side of the basement or crawl-space wall, or on the wall's interior side with blanket-type insulation. While the foams have a much higher R-value per inch of thickness, they are not often used inside due to the combustible properties of most. Urethanes are very flammable. Ureas are less so, but their insulating value drops somewhat with time.

■ Insulating a water heater can save another 5 to 12 percent in heating cost. Johns-Manville puts out special blanket kits for electric or gas-type heaters. Keep all gas-heater vents exposed.

CAULKING AND WEATHERSTRIPPING

Up to 70 percent of heat loss in poorly built homes can be due to infiltration of outside air through window and door frames. Caulking and weatherstripping materials for an average three-bedroom home may cost as little as $25. Savings in costs for heat can run to 10 percent or more per year.

■ Insulate ducts and pipes. Long runs of sheet-metal ducting and hot-water pipe can lose more heat on the way to destinations than they deliver there. Special two-inch blanket-type insulation is made for ductwork; asbestos sleeve sections are available for all water-pipe diameters. Together, they can cut from 5 to 10 percent of your yearly heating bill.

■ Run a lighted candle around the inside of all window and door frames. If the flame dances, you need caulking. If it leans away from window sash edges, and if you can slide heavy paper under the door, you need weatherstripping.

All joints where two different materials, or sections of the house, meet should be caulked.

■ Caulk along window and door tops between the drip caps and siding . . .

■ Caulk along the joints between window and door frames and siding . . .

■ Caulk along the underside of windowsills where they butt the siding . . .

■ Caulk all inside and outside corner joints that are formed by the siding . . .

■ Caulk along the underside of the siding, where it laps the foundation wall . . .

■ Caulk around hose bibs and other outside wall penetrations by pipes, electrical service conduits, dryer vents, ventilator housings and so forth. (A new

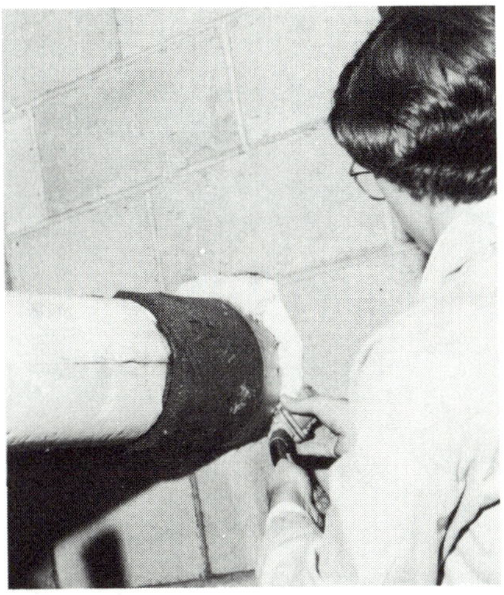

NEW TYPE of seal is foamed in place, above, insulates the spaces it fills. Process requires a pressure gun.

A QUICK and easy Seal Patch can be pressed in place at wall openings.

Seal-Patch made by the Duro Div. of Woodhill can be pressed in place for a tight, instant seal on the sort of small openings described) . . .

■ Caulk where pipes and wires penetrate ceilings from an unheated attic . . .

■ Caulk along joints where chimney and other masonry meet siding . . .

■ Caulk along joints where the porch decks and roofs meet the siding . . .

■ Caulk along joints where the gable ends meet the roof eaves.

■ Check all window panes and apply glazing compound where old putty has hardened and cracked or broken off.

■ Weatherstrip all outside windows and doors. Cheapest and easiest to install is the self-sticking foam strip, but it should be replaced every couple of years. It won't stand up, either, along the sides of double-hung windows where friction of raising and lowering the sash induces

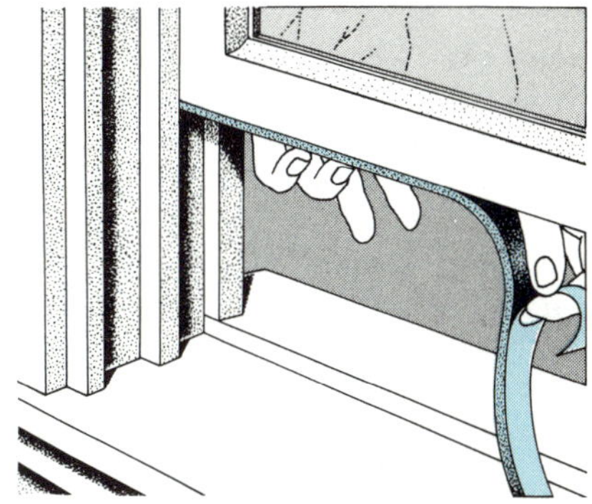

SELF-STICKING foam rubber weatherstrip installs easily, wears out fast.

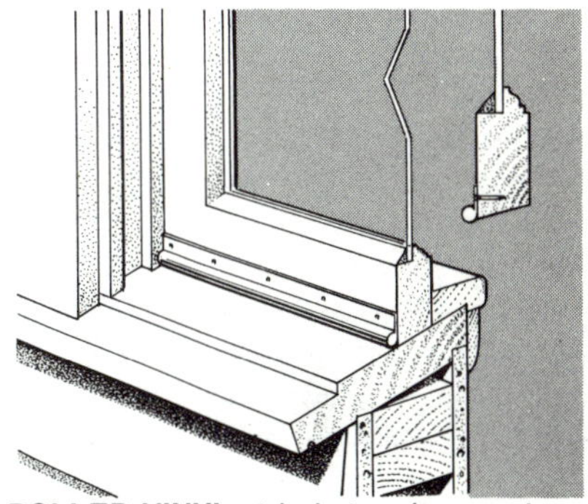

ROLLED VINYL strip is tough, easy to install, but highly visible.

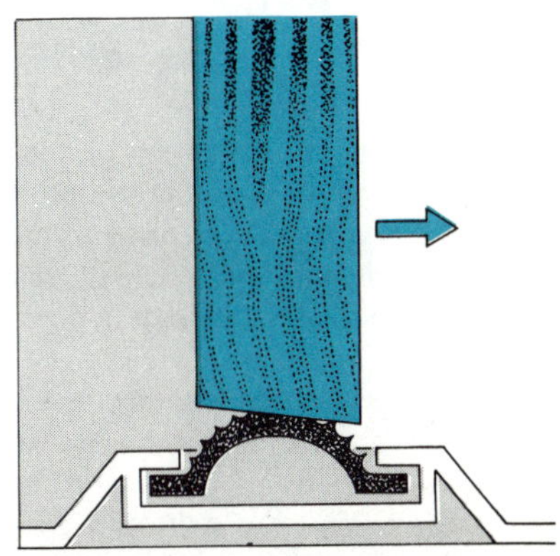

VINYL BULB threshold for exterior doors is efficient and replaceable.

TUBE CAULKING applied by gun does a quick job at all exterior joints.

heavy wear. Rolled vinyl stops are readily tacked in place by do-it-yourselfers for a longer-lasting seal. Spring metal makes a snug, durable seal, but calls for precise placement and handling. Metal J-stripping is the best of all, but requires removal of doors and windows and highly critical alignment; it's really a job for a professional.

■ Install sealed thresholds under outside doors. "Sweep" types are easily tacked in place on the outside surface of the door bottom by anyone who can swing a hammer, but may wear the carpet where they rub across it when you open and close the door. Vinyl bulb types are better, but tougher to install; interlocking metal units are excellent, but need critical alignment. The latter two types require removal of the door and refitting its bottom.

■ Weatherstrip the attic door if you have one, or icy air from up there will pour down in a continuous stream to chill expensively warmed rooms below.

QUICK AND EASY RENOVATIONS

■ Install a doorway at the top of your stairway, and keep it closed in winter. It will prevent warm air from rising to the bedrooms (where less is needed), and cooled air upstairs from cascading down the stairwell into the living areas.

■ Build a false dropped ceiling in the stairwell to prevent the warm air in downstairs rooms from collecting in the "heat trap" against the stairwell's two-story-high ceiling—where it does no one any good.

■ Install doors to all rooms (including dining room, if possible), so that seldom-used areas can be closed off when unoccupied for reasonable lengths of time, and their heating units shut down.

■ Fill in unnecessary or unused windows—remove frame, insulate cavity and finish off the exterior and interior to match their respective wall surfaces.

■ If your house roof provides the proper exposure and area, or if there is open space exposed to the southern sun in winter, consider installing solar collectors to provide water-heating energy. A number of good systems are now available.

UNNECESSARY WINDOWS should be removed and closed in permanently.

DOOR installed at top of a stairwell prevents heat from going upstairs.

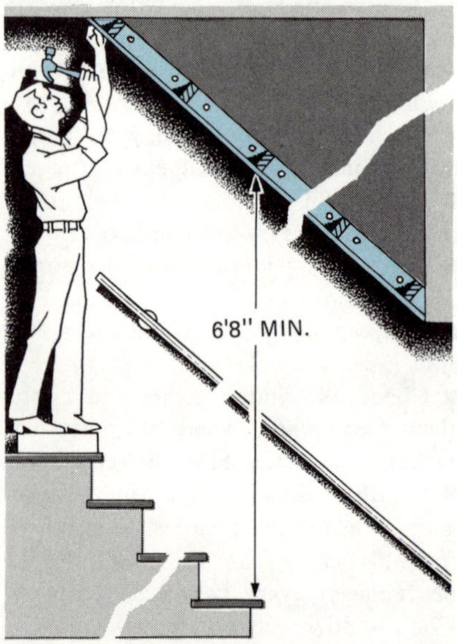

FALSE CEILING over stairway eliminates a second-floor heat pocket.

ADD-ON INVESTMENTS THAT CAN PAY OFF

■ Install a clock thermostat. It will automatically turn down the heat when you retire and back up in the morning before you awake, to preset temperatures of your choice. It can pay back its cost (about $70 to $140) in fuel saving in one or two years. It should be installed professionally. Clock-timer units that trigger heating elements beneath the thermostat and "fool" it into not activating the furnace switch until a desired time, are cheaper ($30 to $50). Not all are dependable, however. Consult your local heating specialist for the best system for you, and insist on a binding warranty.

■ Don't overlook similar clock timers to control central airconditioning, if you have it. It's far cheaper to re-cool the house than to let the unit run for hours when you're not there.

FOAM-FILLED steel door seals out weather with a magnetic rubber strip.

■ New flue-pipe heaters that fit in the metal flue section leading from your furnace to the chimney, pick up waste heat that normally would go up the stack and put it to use where you direct it. They're available through most large heating supply outlets. They can salvage up to five percent of heat that normally would be lost to the outdoors.

■ Automatic dampers that cut off the flue when the furnace kicks off prevent

CLOCK THERMOSTAT made by Honeywell turns heat up and down automatically.

firebox heat from disappearing up the chimney. They can save a lot of heat, but must be installed by experienced professionals. Improper installation can back up exhaust gases into the furnace room. If you're about to buy a new furnace, however, consider getting one with a built-in automatic flue damper.

■ If you heat by electric furnace, it may be well worth your while to switch to a heat pump—an airconditioning-type device that draws heat from outside air (even when it's below zero) to warm the house, and reverses in summer to provide cooling. "Whole house" units cost about $2000 but can cut consumption of the energy required by an electric furnace as much as 40 percent.

■ A less expensive energy-saver is a new add-on heat pump from York Air Conditioning. The "Maximizer" indoor coil fits on any type furnace to provide heat in winter and airconditioning in summer at considerable savings.

■ Another interesting energy-saver is a

ECU'S WASTE-HEAT device uses air-conditioner exhaust to heat water.

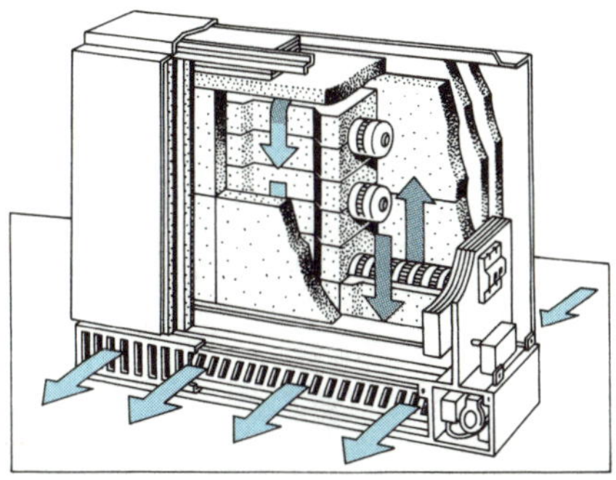

CONTROL ELECTRIC'S Storage Heat unit saves warmth for off-peak use.

heat-recovery device the size of a large metropolitan telephone book. The unit, made by Energy Conservation Unlimited in Longwood, Fla., hooks up to the hot-air exhaust of central airconditioners and uses the waste heat for hot water production.

■ Add a hot-water circulator to the fireplace to blow heat into the room that otherwise would be lost up the chimney.

■ If you have no fireplace damper, install glass doors in the opening. They'll not only serve as a damper when the fireplace is not in use, but can be shut to snuff out the fire when you retire or leave the house.

■ Put in an attic fan if you have none, and use it to bring outside air in through open windows on the shady side when it's 78° or less outdoors in summer. The airconditioner is wasting kilowatts when it's that cool outside. The fan uses far less energy.

■ Heat loss via the exterior entry door to your home can be substantial. Now it

BRONZE reflective Solarcool glass by PPG makes a storm sash for summer.

FLUE RADIATOR from Stoneberg uses furnace-flue heat to warm a basement.

can be cut up to 16 percent by a new steel door with a honeycomb and foam core. The unit is designed to replace your combination storm door and exterior wood door. It's made of 24-gauge steel and has an insulating value more than two times that of wood. ERDA engineers used it with magnetized rubber weatherstrip for a perfect seal.

■ Buy lamps with three-way switches and use the lowest wattage until you *need* more light. Better yet, install solid-state dimmers to control all of the lighting in the house. They can cut your lighting bill by up to one-third if properly used.

■ If you cook with gas, make your next stove one with piezoelectric ceramic starters instead of a pilot light. They'll save you the 30 percent extra gas that those pilot lights consume.

■ Make sure your next refrigerator has a power-saver switch to cut out the heating elements in the walls and doors (when not needed) to prevent condensation in humid weather. Also insist on manual defrost. Automatic uses more energy.

■ If your TV has an "instant on" feature, it's never really turned off. Use the "vacation" switch. And when you buy a new set, insist on one without the "instant on" gadget. It's costing you money.

■ Even if you have storm windows, a third pane of glass will cut the window heat loss in your home by a measured third. If you have central airconditioning, you may want to consider PPG's bronze glass, which cuts solar penetration in the summer.

How to solve starting, stalling and hesitation problems

■ HARD STARTING describes an engine which fails to start promptly or does not start at all. The condition may occur all the time or only when a particular set of circumstances is present. For example, the engine may start promptly when cold, but not when warm. On the other hand, it may not start in cold weather, but may kick-off in hot weather at the touch of the starter.

Stalling defines an engine that starts, but fails to keep running. The condition is often referred to erroneously as hard starting if the engine stalls immediately after it starts. Some conditions that cause hard starting cause stalling. In fact, an engine that stalls may become an engine that's hard to start if the condition is allowed to continue.

Hesitation describes a letdown in engine response as the vehicle is accelerated. There is a noticeable pause, and the engine may seem about to stall: Sometimes it does. Several malfunctions that cause hesitation also cause stalling.

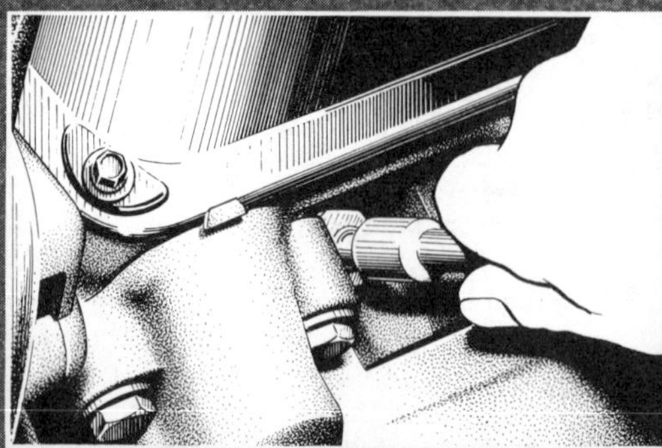

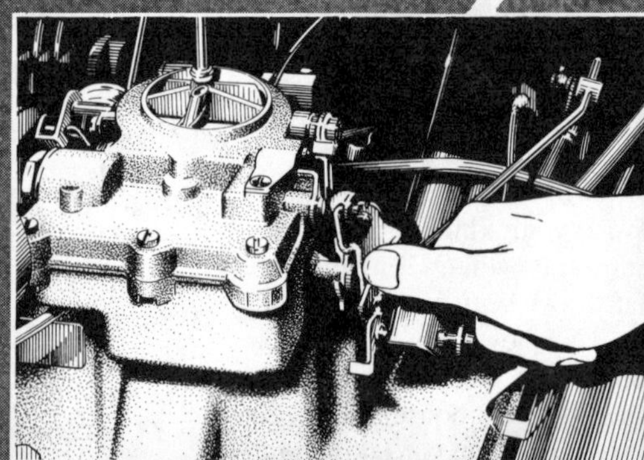

HARD STARTING problem? Check first for spark and fuel. As shown above, pull sparkplug boots, not cables. Work throttle lever, right, to see if fuel is entering carb. Check tightness of coil-to-distributor and sparkplug cables, below. Also inspect terminals in distributor cap; if corroded, you won't start.

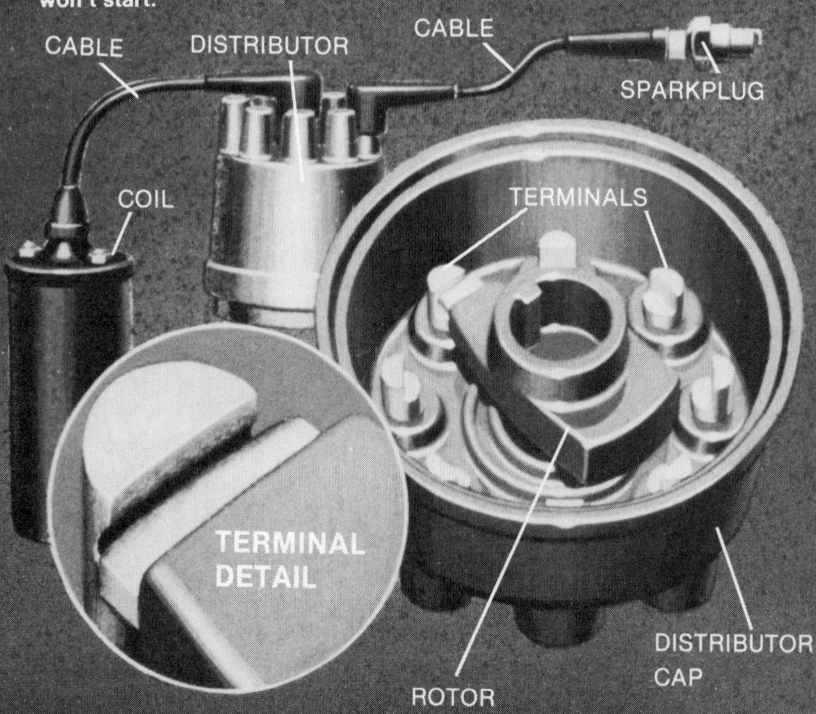

HARD STARTING

Tracking down the cause

Why don't engines start? The causes are summarized under the following conditions:

Condition 1—When the engine (cold or hot) cranks, but fails to start promptly or does not start at all.

■ Improper starting procedure.

Ignition system

■ Damaged distributor cap or burned terminals.

■ Broken rotor contact.

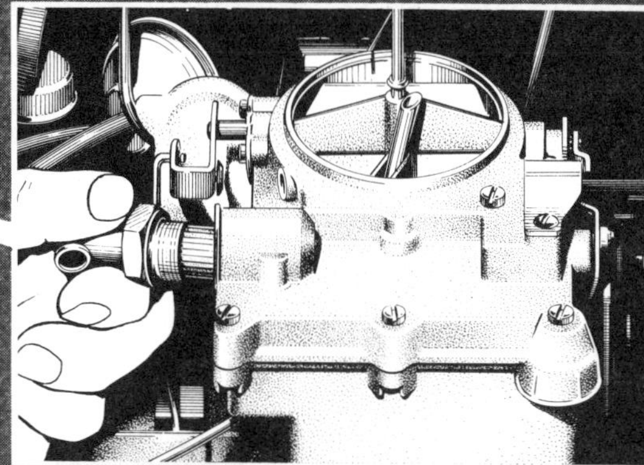

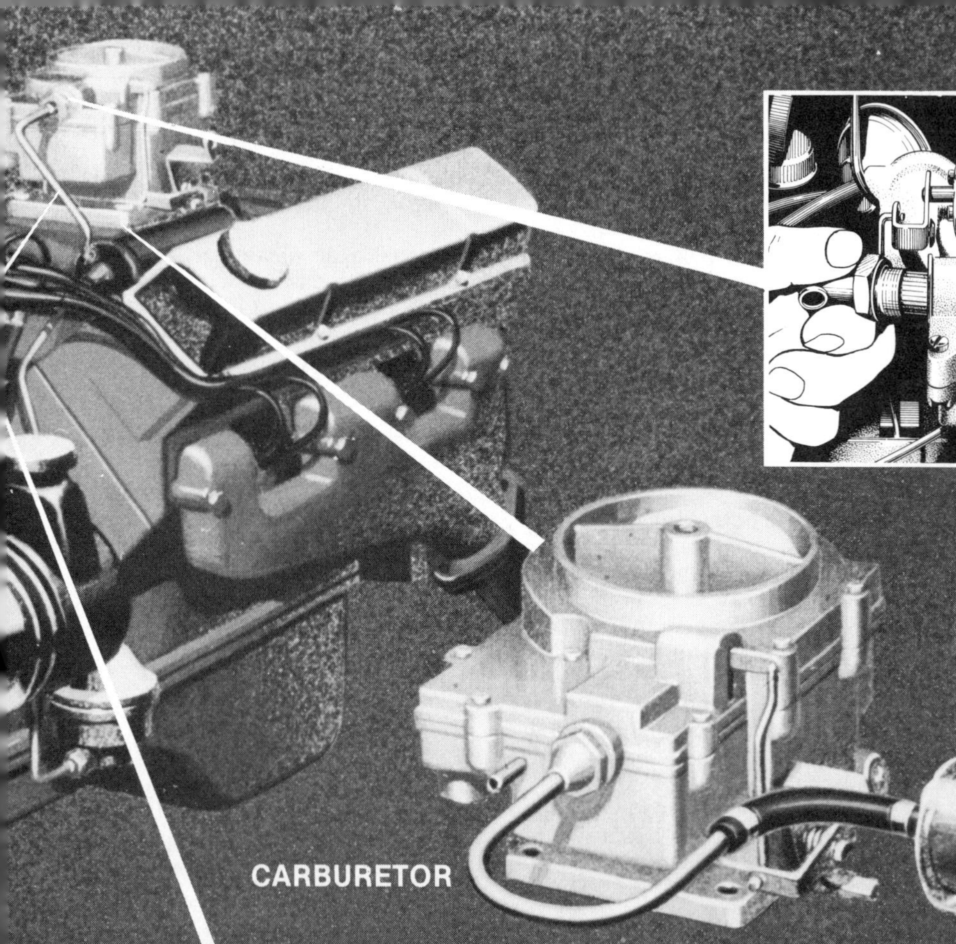

FUEL STARVATION may have one or more of several causes, including blockage at the fuel filter. Internal-type fuel filter is installed in the carburetor body as shown above. Remove, examine and clean or replace as necessary. Filter shown below is installed in the fuel line between fuel pump and carb.

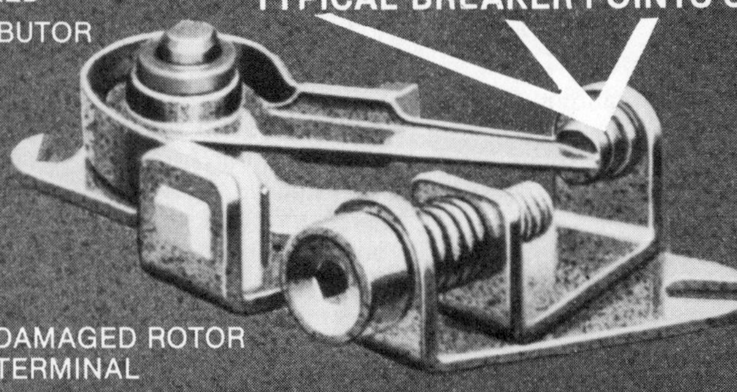

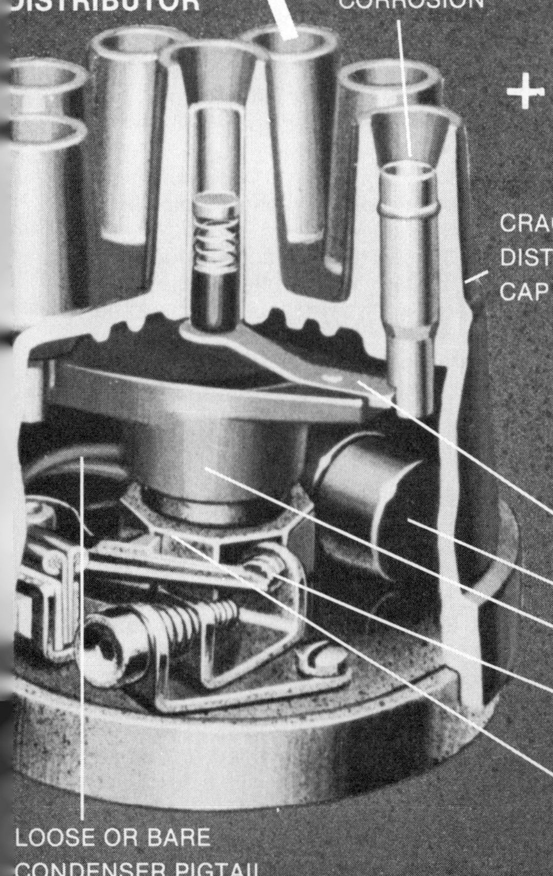

DISTRIBUTOR PROBLEMS that may cause hard starting are shown at left. Shown above is a set of breaker points which may have to be removed from the distributor for close examination. Details of the points shown left to right, above, are eroded points which are the results of a bad condenser and oxide-coated which make poor contact.

■ Bad ignition coil.
Conventional ignition
■ Worn or damaged distributor points.
Electronic ignition
■ Faulty component, such as pickup coil, electronic control module, ballast resistor.
■ Worn distributor shaft.
■ Broken or loosely connected primary wire.
■ Defective ignition switch.
■ Cracked, worn, improperly adjusted sparkplugs.
■ Bad sparkplug (secondary) cables.
Fuel systems
■ No gas.
■ Clogged fuel filter or fuel line.
■ Malfunction in carburetor.
■ Defective fuel pump.
■ Fuel system vacuum leak.

Condition 2—When the engine barely cranks if warm, but starts promptly if cold.
■ Excessive carbon in the engine.
■ Carburetor percolation.

Condition 3—When the engine cranks, but fails to start in wet weather; starts promptly in dry weather.
■ Cracked distributor cap.
■ Cracked coil.
Electronic ignition
■ Damaged electronic control unit.
■ Bare primary or secondary wires.
■ Brittle, cracked sparkplug boots (covers).

Condition 4—When the engine doesn't crank or only emits surly growls.
■ Corroded, loose or damaged battery cables.
■ Weak battery.
■ Bad starter switch, relay or motor.

Zeroing in on Condition 1

In the case of hard-starting Condition 1, determine if the engine is being started properly. People have a tendency to flood engines, especially in cold weather.

Consult your owner's manual for proper starting procedure. If the manual is not available, depress the gas pedal to the floor once (to set the automatic choke), let the pedal up all the way and then position it halfway to the floor. Crank the engine. If the engine doesn't start in 15 seconds, let it rest for 20 seconds. Keep your foot away from the gas pedal and the ignition key off. Then, try again. If the engine doesn't start now, forget it. Don't add a dead battery to your problem.

Tackle ignition system testing next:

1. Disconnect a cable from a sparkplug. Use a pair of sparkplug cable pliers so you don't damage the cable. If pliers aren't available, pull the cable free by twisting and pulling the sparkplug boot—not the cable.

2. Insert a screwdriver having a nonconductive handle inside the sparkplug cover, so the tip of the screwdriver touches the cable terminal.

3. Place the screwdriver shank ¼ to ½ inch from a clean ground on the engine block. Hold the screwdriver by the handle to avoid shock.

4. Have someone crank the engine momentarily. The ignition system is not causing hard starting if a blue spark jumps the gap between the screwdriver and ground. A yellow or orange spark, or no spark, signals a malfunction.

Don't continue cranking, which may damage the ignition system. One spark is all that's needed to judge ignition performance.

A fuel-system problem will result in an engine getting little or no fuel, or too much fuel.

To see if little or no fuel is reaching the engine, remove the carburetor air cleaner. If the choke plate is closed, open it by tripping the choke lever. Move the throttle linkage back and forth once or twice as you look down the carburetor throat. If the fuel system is working, strong gas jets will stream into the carb.

If an engine gets too much gas, you will probably smell it. If you aren't sure, remove a sparkplug or two after trying to start the engine. If sparkplug tips are wet, the engine is flooding.

Pinpointing ignition failure

If the reason for hard starting is in the ignition system, this orderly troubleshooting procedure will help you find the cause:

1. Tighten primary wire connections at the coil if they are loose.

2. Examine the coil. Replace, if cracked.

3. Examine and test sparkplug cables, including the cable from distributor to coil. If one cable is bad, the engine will start, but misfire. If more than one cable is ineffective, starting becomes difficult.

If the distributor-to-coil cable is bad, the engine won't start since high voltage can't reach sparkplugs. The cable allows the coil to feed voltage to the distributor cap, rotor and plugs.

A visual examination may reveal a bad cable. Cracks and brittle insulation are conditions to look for. However, a visual examination doesn't always reveal faulty cables, since wires inside the insulation may be damaged.

The most accurate way of testing cables is with an ohmmeter. Each cable is rated at a particular resistance, depending upon the length of the cable. Short cables are rated at a lower resistance than longer cables.

If you have an ohmmeter, do this with the ignition *off:*

A Remove the distributor cap.

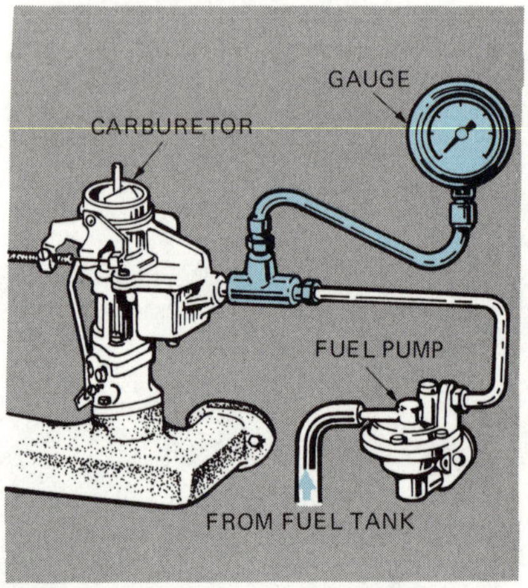

MEASURE fuel pump pressure with a gauge to manufacturer's specifications.

B Disconnect one cable at a sparkplug.

C Insert the ohmmeter probe in the sparkplug end of the cable so it touches the terminal. Hold the other ohmmeter probe against the electrode inside the distributor cap that the cable serves. Be sure ohmmeter probes make solid contact.

D If the meter shows that cable resistance is more than the ohm rating given in the car's shop manual, detach the cable from the distributor cap. These instructions do not apply to the distributor-to-coil cable (see below).

E Test the suspicious cable again. If the cable still fails to meet specification, replace it. However, if cable resistance falls into line, there's a defect in the distributor cap. The terminal is probably corroded or burned, so clean cap towers with a distributor cleaning tool, polishing contacts. Also polish terminals on the distributor side of the cap.

F Reconnect the cable and test resistance again. If resistance is still too high, replace the distributor cap.

G Start the engine and let it warm up; then shut it *off.* Disconnect the distributor cap and connect the ohmmeter between the center contact of the cap and one of the primary terminals at the coil. Resistance should not exceed the ohms rating in the shop manual.

If resistance is greater, remove the distributor-to-coil cable at the coil and test resistance by touching a probe to the cable terminal and a probe to the distributor contact. If resistance is still greater than specification, replace the cable. If resistance falls into line, tighten all connections and test overall resistance again. If overall resistance still exceeds service manual specifications, the coil is probably faulty. Replace it.

4. Examine the distributor cap for physical damage. A carbon track is damage indicating a hairline crack. Look also for burned or eroded terminals.

If you have to replace a distributor cap, make sure each cable is installed in its proper tower. Line up the replacement cap so distinguishing marks parallel the old cap's distinguishing marks. Transfer one cable at a time from one cap to the other.

5. Remove the rotor. Replace a broken rotor, or one having a broken, burned or eroded metal contact.

6. Conventional ignition: It is usually difficult to examine distributor contact points with points mounted in the distributor. You may have to remove them.

Spread points apart. A silver-gray finish (smooth or slightly rough) is acceptable. Replace pitted, burned or eroded points. Also replace the condenser.

Note: A bad condenser allows electrical surges to destroy points. A faulty resistor or excess lubricant splashing from the cam also leads to premature failure of points.

7. Electronic ignition: Unlike conventional ignition systems, electronic ignition systems differ from one car to the next. Testing electronic ignition systems, therefore, differs from car to car.

Note: Beginning with 1978 models, AMC adopted a solid-state electronic ignition system for V8 engines that is similar to Ford's.

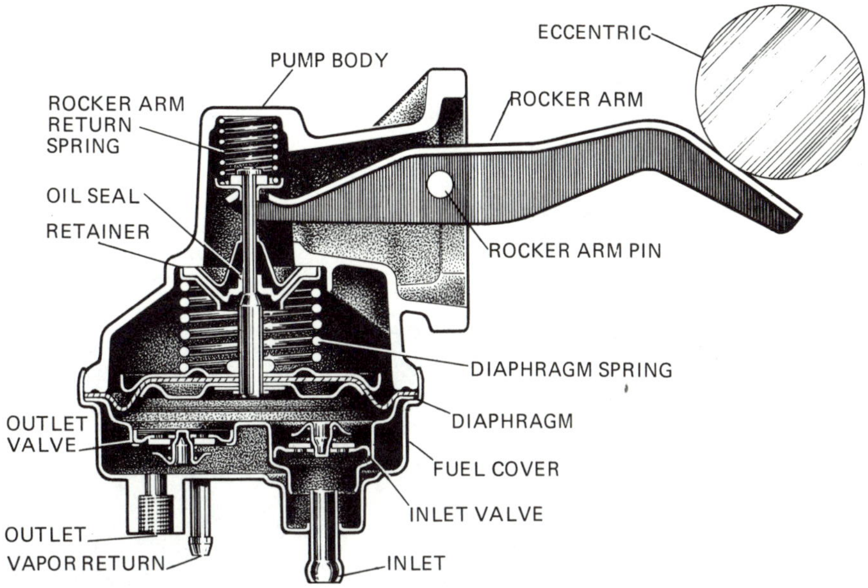

NOTE HOW the rocker arm strikes the eccentric; also the vapor-return fitting.

8. Ignition failure can also result because of a malfunction in the ignition switch circuit. This circuit unit consists of an ignition switch and an ignition wire that plugs into a wire junction box on the firewall before passing on to the coil. Make sure the connection at the junction box has not worked loose. See that the wire at the coil and ignition switch are tight. Check the switch.

Sparkplugs are special

The only way to determine if hard starting is caused by bad sparkplugs is to remove plugs from the engine for examination. Look for damaged or worn electrodes, in particular.

Pinpointing fuel system failure

Suppose little or no gas reaches the carburetor during the fuel system "squirt" test (see *Zeroing in on Condition 1*). The cause of the trouble is one of the following:

- Clogged fuel filter.
- Defective fuel pump.
- Clogged fuel line.
- Vacuum leak.
- Blockage in the fuel tank.
- Trouble in the carburetor bowl (clogged internal fuel filter, sticking float needle, binding float, clogged circuits).
- No gas.

To trace fuel starvation to a particular point, disconnect the fuel line at the carburetor bowl.

Caution: No smoking! Keep the engine off. The engine should be cold. Disconnect the battery ground cable. Place a small plastic container under the fuel line fitting to catch gas that may drip.

With the line disconnected, face its end toward a container. Have someone briefly crank the engine. If no gas, or only a dribble, flows into the container, look for a fuel filter in the

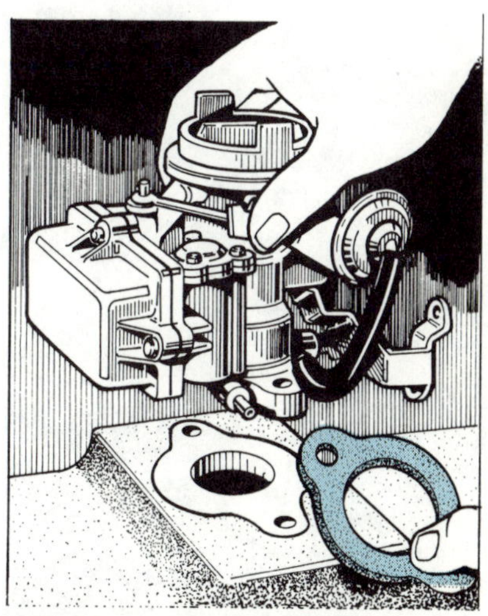

THICKER gasket between carb and intake manifold may eliminate percolation.

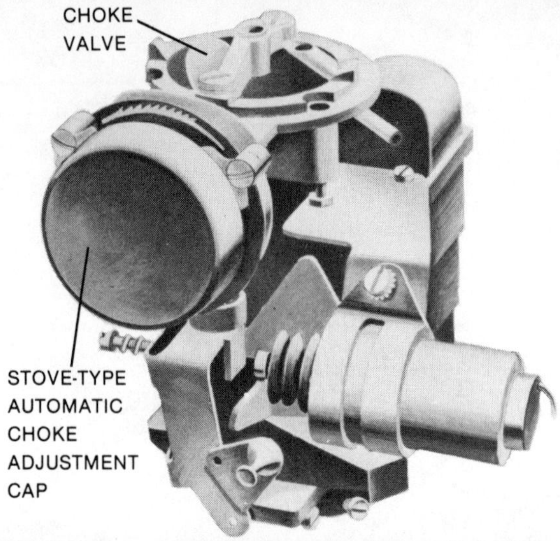

CARBURETOR DETAILS show stove-type automatic choke (left), well-type (below), and idle-adjustment screws (bottom). Automatic choke provides proper fuel/air mixture for stall-free cold starts. Fast-idle screw, which rides on stepped cam, selects ideal engine speed in relation to choke-valve opening.

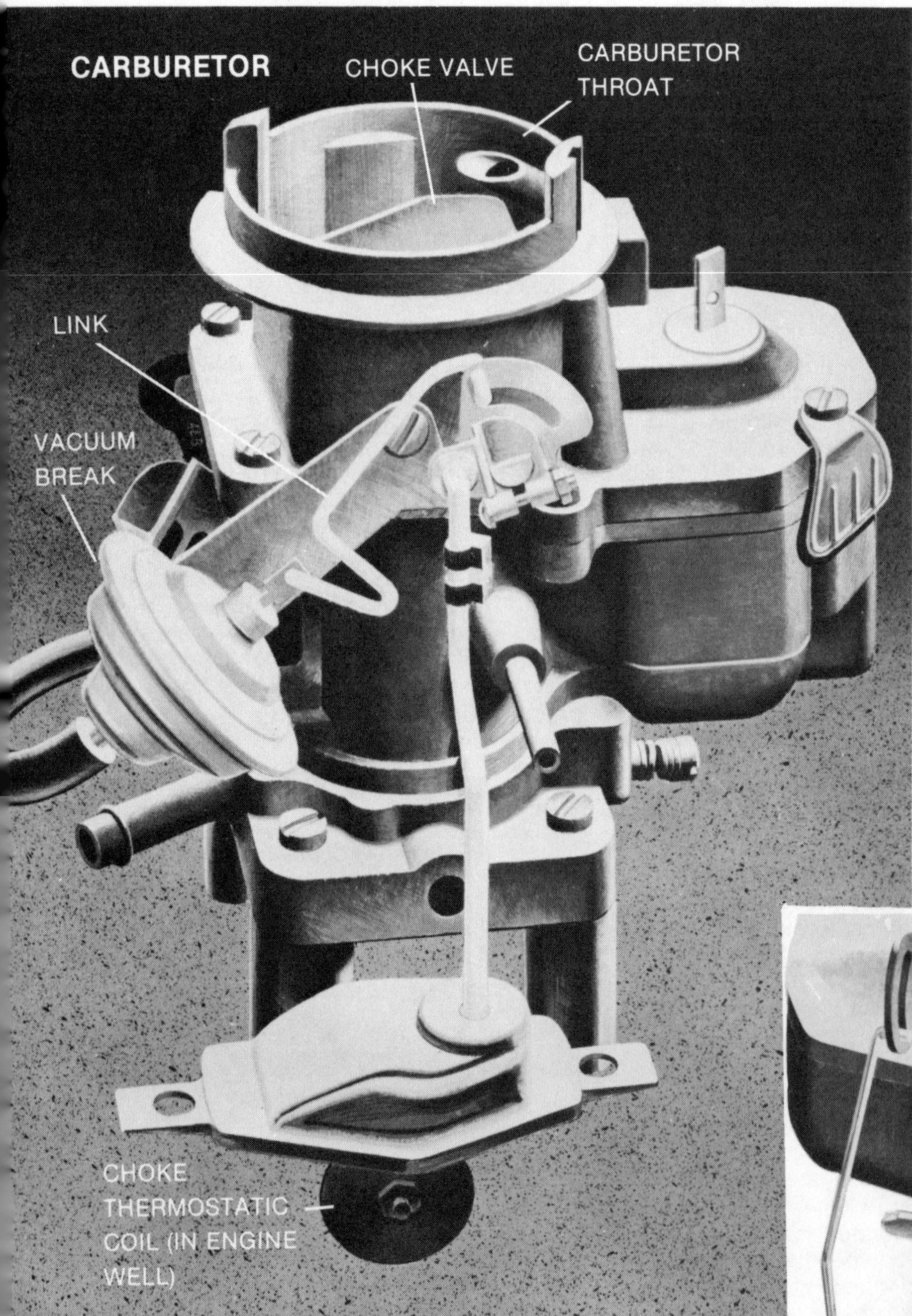

fuel line between the carburetor and fuel pump. This metal or plastic cylinder is called an in-line fuel filter. Most Chrysler Corp. and AMC models have one. Replace it.

Ford and GM models usually have fuel filters in the carburetor inlet. If this filter gets blocked, gas will get to, but not through the carburetor. There will be no jets of gas when you activate the throttle linkage (see *Zeroing in on Condition 1*).

Remove this filter, reconnect the fuel line and check starting. If the engine starts, the filter is clogged. Replace it.

After the fuel filter, the next component to test if fuel isn't getting to the carburetor is the fuel pump. Before doing this, make sure fuel system fittings are tight. Inspect for gas leaks at all connections from fuel tank to carburetor.

A loose fitting allows air to enter the fuel system. Air disrupts vacuum, which is necessary to get gas to the carburetor. Also, make sure fuel hoses aren't flattened, kinked or clogged. Disconnect the fuel line at both the carburetor and fuel pump. Blow through the line to make sure it's not clogged. Reconnect the line. If fuel still doesn't flow from the fuel line, test the fuel pump:

1. Connect a fuel pump pressure gauge to the disconnected end of the fuel line at the carburetor (see drawing).

2. Start the engine and check fuel pump pressure as you rev the engine from idle to moderate speed.

Note: If the car is equipped with a fuel evaporation emission control system, as most 1970 to present models are, squeeze off the fuel

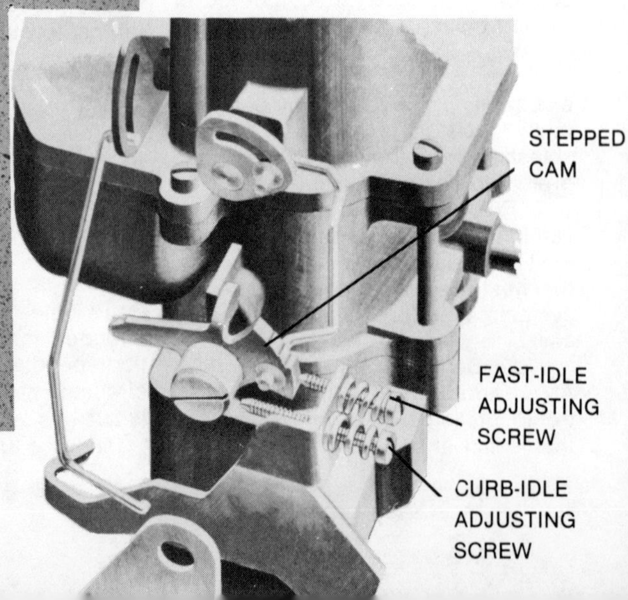

pump vapor return hose to get an accurate reading.

3. Fuel pump pressure should remain constant at engine idle and throughout the acceleration range. Pressure should be on target with the fuel pump pressure specification in the service manual. This specification varies from car to car.

If fuel pump pressure is too low, too high, or shifts significantly at different engine speeds, replace the pump.

4. Equip yourself with a graduate marked off in pints and a watch with a second hand.

5. With the fuel line disconnected at the carburetor, aim the line into the graduate.

6. Start and idle the engine. Watch your watch. The fuel pump should deliver one pint of gas in 30 seconds or less. If the flow is below this, check again for a loose connection or restricted line.

Replacing a fuel pump

Replacing a fuel pump is no big deal. Here's how:

1. If you can't reach the fuel pump from beneath the hood, raise and support the car.

2. Disconnect the fuel tank-to-fuel pump gas line at the inlet side of the fuel pump. Plug the line. A golf tee or short pencil makes a suitable plug. Fold a cloth over the pump connection to absorb fuel that leaks.

Caution: Where possible, use two wrenches to avoid damage. Hold one fitting with one wrench and use the other to loosen or tighten. Use the same technique to connect and disconnect the fuel line at the carburetor.

3. Disconnect the fuel vapor return hose from the fuel pump fitting and plug the hose.

4. Disconnect the fuel pump-to-carburetor gas line at the fuel-pump outlet. Plug the end of the line.

5. Remove the fuel-pump mounting bolts.

6. Tipping the pump up, pull it straight back from the engine.

7. Clean the fuel-pump mounting flange on the engine using a brush with kerosene. Be sure loose gasket material and other dirt doesn't remain.

8. Coat a new gasket with gasket cement. Put the gasket in place.

9. Install the new pump. If you have trouble getting the pump into the engine, remove the pump and crank the engine until the shaft's fuel pump eccentric (cam) is at a low point. The eccentric must be in contact with the fuel-pump rocker arm, as shown in the drawing.

10. With pump in place, install hardware, but don't tighten until you lift up on the pump. Tighten screws to 13-15 foot-pounds.

11. Reconnect all lines. Start the car, run the engine and check for leaks.

SAFETY FIRST, always. Use strong supporting tool for carrying battery.

TROUBLESHOOTING STALLING

CAUSES TO CHECK	CORRECTION	REFER TO
☐ Sticking automatic choke, including inoperative vacuum break.	Repair and adjust.	
☐ Incorrect slow and fast-idle speeds.	Adjust.	
☐ Bad sparkplugs and/or sparkplug cables.	Replace.	Sect. 1: *Sparkplugs Are Special.*
☐ Damaged conventional or electronic distributor parts, including loose or bare primary wire.	Replace.	Sect. 1: *Pinpointing Ignition Failure.*
☐ Carbon inside engine, especially at exhaust manifold ports.	Treat with carbon solvent, such as GM Top Engine Cleaner.	Sect. 1: *Zeroing In on Condition 2.*
☐ Dirt-clogged carburetor air filter.	Replace.	
☐ Partially clogged fuel filter.	Replace.	Sect. 1: *Pinpointing Fuel System Failure.*
☐ Contaminated fuel.	Drain fuel system, including fuel tank, and flush with cleaner.	
☐ Clogged PCV valve.	Replace.	
☐ Carburetor repairs.	If carburetor has not been serviced in 30,000 miles, clean and overhaul it, using parts in the carburetor repair kit for your model carburetor.	
☐ Weak fuel pump.	Replace.	Sect. 1: *Pinpointing Fuel System Failure.*
☐ Inoperative thermostatic air cleaner.	Replace.	
☐ Vacuum loss through loose or split vacuum hose.	Repair or replace.	
☐ Vacuum leak from carburetor-manifold area.	Repair.	
☐ Inoperative manifold heat-control valve or vacuum-controlled fuel vaporization valve.	Free or replace.	
☐ Bad EGR valve.	Replace.	

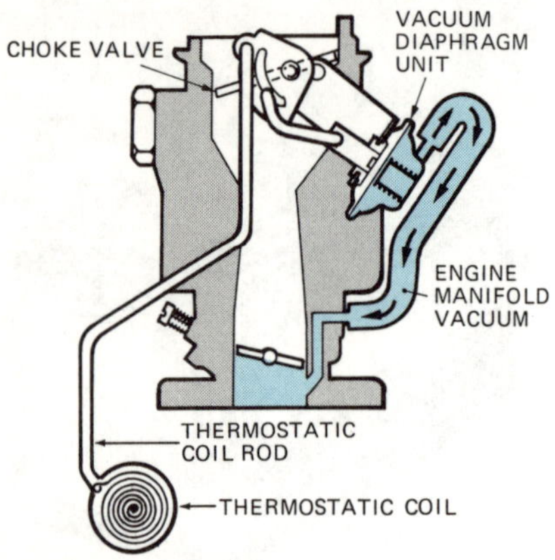

AUTOMATIC choke gives engines the right mixture for stall-free starts.

Zeroing in on Condition 2

Carbon buildup is the trouble in most cases involving older engines that are hard-starting only when warmed up. Carbon, when it gets hot, has the effect of increasing an engine's compression ratio, which makes it difficult for the starter motor to crank the engine. In fact, many people blame the battery or starter motor since the engine sounds the same as it would if the battery were weak or the starter motor were defective.

To check for carbon, do a compression test with the engine warmed to operating temperature. If the test shows overall compression in excess of normal specification (consult manufacturer's specification in your shop manual), carbon exists. The engine may have to be disassembled and cleaned.

Try the simple, inexpensive way first. Get GM Top Engine Cleaner, or equivalent, and use as directed. If you're lucky, you may get rid of carbon and your problem.

Carburetor percolation also causes hard starting when the engine is warm. However, the engine will crank more briskly than if it were loaded with carbon.

Percolation refers to gas in the carburetor bowl boiling over and flooding the cylinders. Heat is the cause.

To cure the problem, reduce heat. One way is to discard an underhood insulating pad. Another is to use a thicker gasket between the carburetor and manifold. This raises the carburetor off the hot engine, maybe just enough to eliminate the trouble.

Hard-starting Conditions 3 and 4

The ignition system is usually at fault if an engine won't start in wet weather but may start in dry weather. Check for cracked distributor cap or coil and replace either or both if they are defective.

Another hard-starting condition occurs when the engine may growl or be silent but won't catch at all. This signals a defect in the starting system, which consists of the battery, battery cables, starter relay and/or switch (solenoid) and starter motor. The engine will barely turn over, if it cranks at all.

Examine battery cables and terminals first. Cables must be tightly connected and have no breaks in insulation. If terminals and battery posts are corroded, clean them since such foreign matter hampers the flow of current.

Use a battery hydrometer to test battery electrolyte for specific gravity. This test, which determines the percentage of sulphuric acid in electrolyte, will pinpoint a weak battery. In a battery that is losing charge, plates absorb sulphuric acid from the electrolyte, consequently causing a drop in specific gravity. (The specific gravity of some maintenance-free batteries cannot be tested, because the battery seal cannot be broken. It is, therefore, necessary to test a maintenance-free battery with a battery tester.)

Test specific gravity of a conventional battery as follows:

1. Add water, if necessary, to bring electrolyte in each cell to proper level. If water is added, run the engine at fast idle for 15 minutes before testing, so fresh water mixes with electrolyte.

2. Remove battery vent caps.

3. Draw electrolyte from one cell into the hydrometer. Make sure that the hydrometer float is riding freely in the hydrometer tube.

Caution: A battery emits highly explosive gas. Do not smoke when near a battery. Disconnect the ground (negative in most cases) cable to prevent sparks. If electrolyte gets on your skin, flush with water immediately. If electrolyte splashes in your eye, flush with water and get to a physician immediately. Electrolyte is an acid that can result in burns and blindness.

4. Hold the hydrometer at eye level. Note the reading. Return electrolyte to the cell and take readings, one at a time, of all other cells.

(Specific gravity varies with electrolyte temperature. Each reading has to be interpolated to 80° F. If your hydrometer doesn't have a built-in temperature compensator, which automatically gives direct readings, insert a thermometer in electrolyte to obtain its temperature. For every 10° that this temperature is above 80° F., add .004 to the specific gravity reading. For every 10° that the temperature is below 80° F., subtract .004 from the reading.)

5. Compare readings. A difference of .050 or more points between readings reveals a shorted cell or cells. Replace the battery.

If overall specific gravity is below 1.225 points, slow-charge the battery and retest. You're looking for a minimum overall reading of 1.225 either before or after charging. If the battery doesn't attain this, replace it.

If the battery and battery cables are sound, test the starter system to determine if the cause of hard starting is in the starter switch, starter relay or starter motor.

Inherent starting problems

Some service bulletins covering hard starting which have been issued are as follows:

Chrysler Corp.

■ 1974 models with 318 cu.-in. engines and 1¼-in. BBD carburetors—hard starting when hot. *SB 14-08-74T.*

■ 1975 models with 318 cu.-in. engines and automatic transmissions—hard starting after partial cool-down. *SB 14-10-75.*

FoMoCo

■ 1973–74 models with 4300 4V carburetors—hard cold starts. *SB 59.*

■ 1976, all models—hard starting with slow cranking speed. *SB 111.*

■ 1976 models with 351-cu.-in. engines—hard starting at temperatures below 32° F. *SB 119.*

■ 1977 models with 2.3L engines and automatic transmissions—hard starting during sub-zero temperature conditions. *SB 129 and 133.*

STALLING

Tracking down the cause

An engine can start and then stop running when idling or cruising whether it's cold or warmed up. The chart at left summarizes causes of stalling and the cures. Where the same problem causes both stalling and hard starting, you are referred to the cure already discussed.

Driver's role

One cause of stalling not listed in the chart is driver impatience. According to the National Highway Traffic Safety Administration, "A vehicle's engine operates at maximum efficiency when the engine is warmed to operating temperature. Trying to get a lot of speed or acceleration from a cold engine, especially today's more sophisticated engines, invites stalling."

In other words, don't expect to start a cold engine and drive immediately at freeway speeds. The engine probably won't take it.

Still, don't let a cold engine idle excessively in an attempt to warm it up, especially if the car has a catalytic converter. Idling causes unnecessary wear and leads to damage.

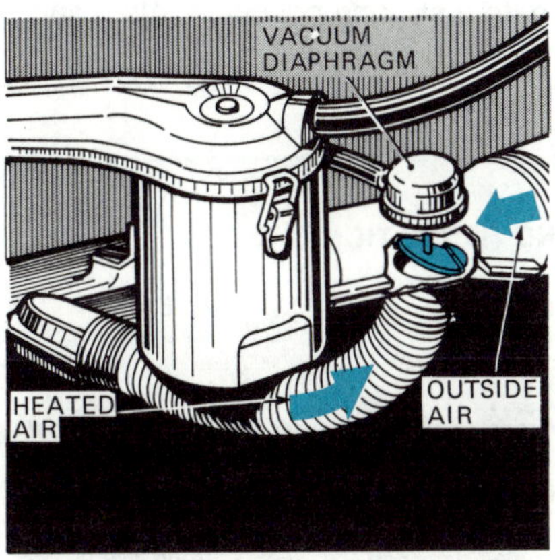

DIAGRAM of Omni air cleaner depicts control damper door has over inlet air.

The key word is *moderation.* Start the engine and drive slowly for a few minutes.

What you should know about chokes

A malfunctioning automatic choke is high on the list of causes that lead to stalling. Before working on a choke, you have to know how and why chokes act as they do.

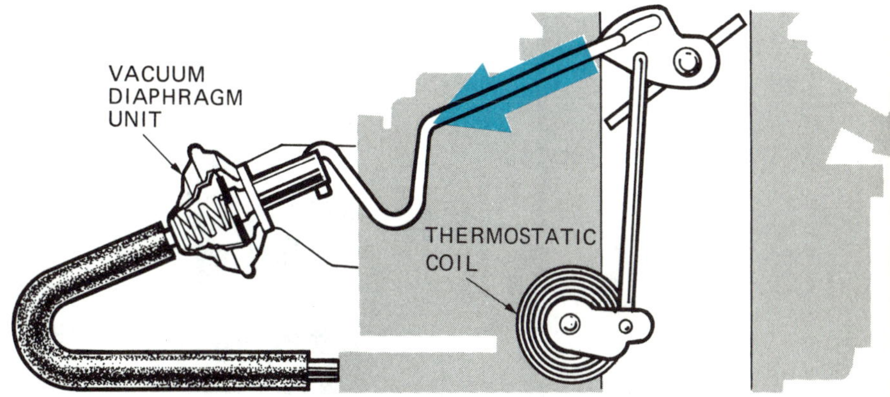

VACUUM BREAK pulls the choke plate open to let air mix with gas for combustion.

A choke provides the right fuel mixture for quick cold-engine starting and warm-up. When the engine is cold, thermostat coil tension holds the choke valve closed over the carburetor throat so the engine gets a mixture rich in gas. The thermostat coil is usually located in a choke cap on the carburetor or in a well in the engine.

The thermostatic coil is connected to the choke valve in the carburetor throat. If the coil is housed in the choke cap, it is connected to the choke valve by a piston and shaft. If the coil is housed in a well in the engine, it is connected to the choke valve by a long rod.

Chokes having the thermostat coil in a choke cap are called stove-type chokes. You will find stove-type chokes on carburetors used on AMC, Ford and GM engines. Chrysler Corp. engines generally use well-type chokes. Let us use a stove-type choke to explain how chokes work.

As you crank a cold engine, air pressure against the offset choke valve and the action of a choke piston cause the valve, which is closed tightly over the carburetor throat because of thermostat coil tension, to open slightly. A thermostat coil is at maximum tension when it is cold and releases tension as it gets warm.

As for the action of the choke piston, intake manifold vacuum pulls the piston down in its cylinder, which helps to pull the choke valve open slightly when the engine is cold. All this action is to make sure that even when a cold engine is cranked, it won't get a fuel mixture consisting of 100 percent gasoline. Pure gas can't burn. It needs air.

When the engine starts, continued pull on the piston by engine vacuum and the force of air against the choke valve overcome thermostat coil tension to allow the choke valve to assume a partially open position. As the piston moves down in its cyclinder,

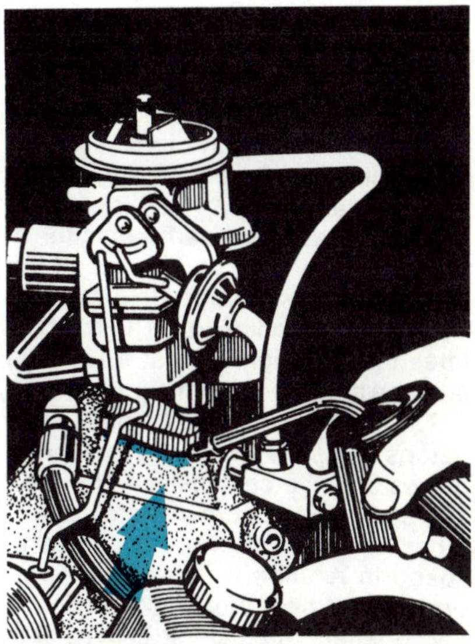

VACUUM LOSS from leak around carburetor is pinpointed with oil-kerosene.

slots in the sides of the cylinder open so heated air from the exhaust manifold enters the thermostat coil housing. This warm air causes the thermostat coil spring to gradually lose tension, and the coil releases its hold on the choke valve. Within a minute or so after a cold engine is started,

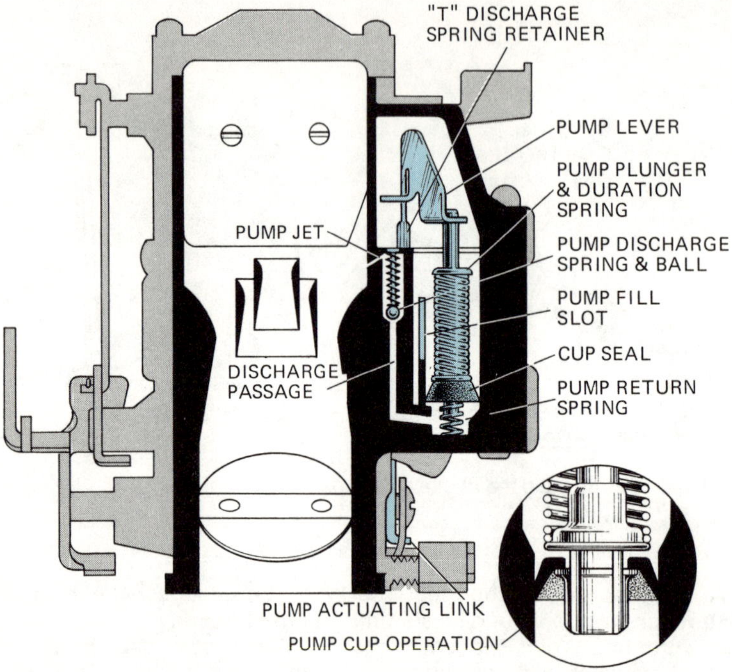

ACCELERATING circuit's pump injects gas for rapid engine response on step- down.

the choke valve attains a fully open position.

Other cold-engine assist-starting mechanisms

The automatic choke works hand-in-hand with the carburetor fast-idle mechanism to prevent stalling during engine warm-up. A fast idle cam, which activates the carburetor throttle plate, is located on the side of the carburetor. It is attached to the choke valve shaft by a linkage. The cam rotates into position against a fast idle screw when the shaft moves.

On the cam are indentations called "steps." As the choke valve shaft moves and the cam rotates, the fast-idle screw skips from one step to another to provide the ideal engine speed in relation to the choke valve opening. When the choke valve is fully opened, the fast-idle cam rotates free of the fast-idle screw, which allows the carburetor throttle plate to return to curb-idle position.

Most models produced recently also have a vacuum break and electric assist unit to increase the efficiency of automatic chokes. These components open the choke plate as quickly as possible to provide the leanest fuel mixture needed for starting. Getting the plate open quickly reduces the richness of fuel the engine consumes and, therefore, cuts down on exhaust emissions. If either the vacuum break or the electric-assist unit malfunctions, the air to gas ratio is upset and stalling can occur.

Note: If an engine floods during starting, you can clear fuel from the intake manifold by slamming the gas pedal to the floor and keeping it there as you crank the engine. With the accelerator in this position, a tang on the throttle lever hits against the fast-idle cam, which causes the choke rod to move up. This opens the choke valve allowing air into the carburetor, which helps clear the flooding condition.

Testing chokes

Testing an automatic choke is done by observing.

1. Remove the carburetor air cleaner while the engine is cold. The choke valve should be closed tightly over the carburetor throat. If it isn't, have an assistant press the accelerator pedal to the floor and let it up. The valve should close. If not, the choke mechanism probably needs servicing.

2. Crank the engine. As this is being done, the choke valve should open slightly. As the engine starts and begins warming up, the valve should continue opening and engine idle should gradually drop from fast to normal speed.

3. Clean linkage (if the choke mechanism needs servicing) to eliminate a sticking condition. Also, apply carburetor cleaner around the choke

TROUBLESHOOTING HESITATION

CAUSES TO CHECK	CORRECTION	REFER TO
Fuel System		
☐ Binding throttle cable.	Repair.	
☐ Choke too lean (hesitation occurs with engine cold).	Test; adjust or repair if defective.	Sect. 1: *What You Should Know About Chokes.*
☐ Malfunctioning vacuum break or choke electric-assist unit.	Test; replace if defective.	Sect. 1: *Testing a Vacuum Break.*
☐ Dirty carburetor air filter; damaged thermostat air cleaner.	Replace filter; repair damaged air cleaner.	Sect. 1: *Troublesome Thermostat Air Cleaner.*
☐ Contaminated fuel.	Drain fuel system, including fuel tank, flush with cleaner.	Sect. 1: *Contaminated Fuel.*
☐ Partially clogged fuel filter.	Replace.	Sect. 1: *Pinpointing Fuel System Failure.*
☐ Low fuel pump pressure.	Test; replace if defective.	Sect. 1: *Replacing a Fuel Pump.*
☐ Damaged accelerating pump.	Replace if defective.	
☐ Dirty carburetor circuits or damaged parts.	Clean and overhaul, or replace the carburetor.	
Engine		
☐ Leaking valves.	Repair.	
☐ Restricted exhaust system.	Clear or replace clogged part.	
☐ Vacuum leak.	Repair.	Sect. 1: *Vacuum Loss.*

valve. If this doesn't solve the problem, you may have to disassemble the choke mechanism to replace the thermostat coil and free a binding piston, but first test both the vacuum break and the electric-assist unit.

Testing a vacuum break

If the choke valve doesn't open and there is a vacuum break on the carburetor, verify that the vacuum break is working. Start engine, and alternately pull and push the vacuum hose off and on the vacuum break. If vacuum break linkage doesn't move, replace vacuum break.

Testing an electric-assist unit

The procedure for testing an electric-assist unit varies from one car to another. The following explanation applies to a single-stage control, consisting of a control switch and ceramic heating element, which is used on many Chrysler Corp. engines. The procedure is offered as an example to demonstrate that testing the mechanism is not difficult.

To test the control switch:

1. Remove BAT electric terminal from the control switch.

2. Connect a 12-volt testlight to the switch's load terminal, which is the small terminal, and to ground.

3. Start the engine.

4. Reconnect the BAT electric terminal. The testlight should light. It may stay lit for a few seconds or longer, but it must not stay on for more than five minutes. If the testlight doesn't work this way, replace the control switch.

To test the heating element:

1. Remove BAT electric terminal from the control switch.

2. Connect an ohmmeter to choke housing and touch the other lead to a bare spot on the choke wire connector of the control switch, but do *not* touch the ohmmeter to the BAT terminal. A reading of 4 to 12 ohms means that the heating element is working. If you don't get this reading, replace heating element.

Handling a troublesome thermostat air cleaner

Thermostatically controlled air cleaners have been used since the early 1970's to reduce the amount of carbon monoxide generated by cold engines. A thermostat air cleaner does this by regulating the temperature of air entering the carburetor.

A damper door in the air cleaner inlet (snorkel) closes when the engine is cold. No cold air can enter. Instead, warm air from the exhaust manifold is diverted through a tube to the carburetor. This cuts down on carbon monoxide, since less carbon monoxide is produced when gasoline is mixed with warm air.

If the damper door in the snorkel fails to close when a cold engine is started, stalling occurs, because the engine isn't calibrated to accept cold air. To determine if the thermostat air cleaner is causing a stalling condition as a cold engine is being started, check the air cleaner by observing the damper door.

If you can't see the damper door by looking into the nose of the snorkel, remove the air cleaner cover and filter element, and check damper door operation from the backside. You now have a chance to also examine the filter element, which has to be clean and unclogged to prevent a stalling problem. A dirty air cleaner chokes off air entering the engine, forcing the engine to run on a richer-than-normal fuel mixture.

If the damper door is not closed as you start the engine (cold), look for:

■ Split or loose hot air tube from the manifold to the air cleaner. Replace or reconnect.

■ Defective vacuum motor. Unhook the vacuum hose that is connected to the vacuum motor *at the engine end.* Draw in on the hose by mouth or with a vacuum pump. If the damper door does not close, replace the vacuum motor.

■ Defective sensor. If applying vacuum to the vacuum motor closes the damper door, the sensor is bad. Replace the part by straightening the tangs holding it to the air cleaner housing.

A thermostat air cleaner malfunction causes warm-engine as well as cold-engine stalls. As the engine starts and warms up, the damper door should open. If it stays closed, the engine will stall. A defective sensor is usually to blame for the damper door staying closed when it should open.

Other causes of stalling

■ Carburetor idle speeds—Correct slow and fast idle-speed adjustments are basic to a properly running engine. Adjust to the specifications of the car manufacturer.

The propane-assisted method of setting carburetor idle has been endorsed by manufacturers of domestic cars. According to Chrysler Corp., "The method of propane idle set is the only effective and approved procedure to properly set the curb idle speed on all domestic engines. This procedure is absolutely essential to assure proper performance of a vehicle as well as emission reliability."

The propane method of adjusting the carburetor can help engines that experience not only stalling, but also hesitation, surge and rough idling.

■ Contaminated fuel—Contaminated fuel refers to gasoline that contains water, dirt or other foreign material. Disconnect the fuel line at the carburetor. Let some gas drop in the palm of your hand. If gas contains water, drops will remain after the gas evaporates.

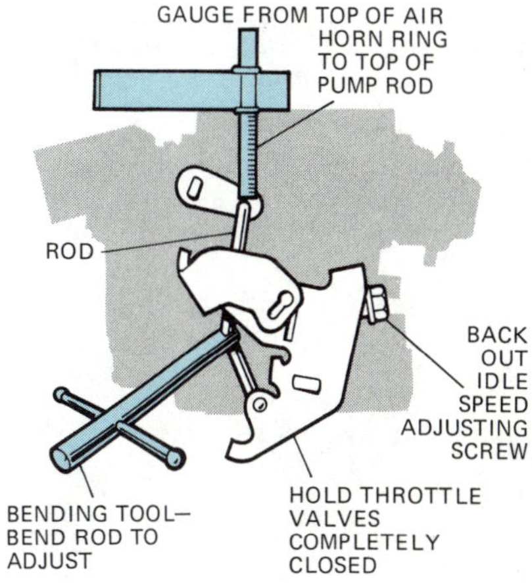

ADJUSTING accelerating pump operating rod of GM Rochester 2GC carburetors.

Contaminated gasoline requires draining of the fuel system and replacing both the pick-up filter in the fuel tank and the fuel line filter. Drop the fuel tank, dump contents, wash the tank with kerosene and replace the pick-up filter.

■ Clogged PCV valve—A clogged PCV valve, or hose, upsets the air to gas ratio. Stalling results.

Start the engine and remove the PCV valve from its seat in the engine. Hold your finger tightly over the tip of the valve. Lack of suction indicates a clogged system.

Replace the PCV valve, which is the likely suspect, but don't overlook the possibility of a clogged, loose or kinked PCV hose.

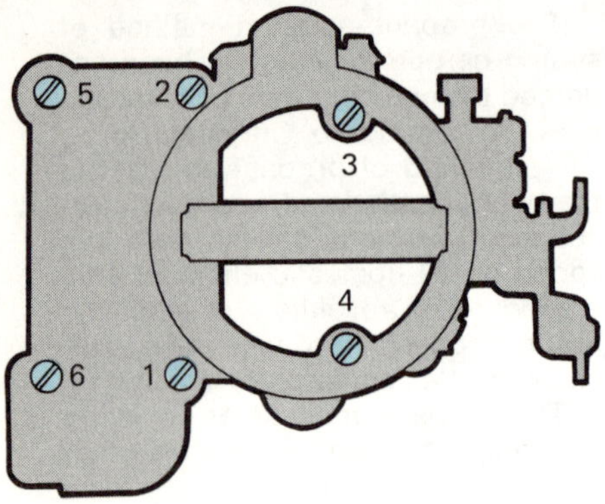

AIR HORN tightening sequence, 1V carb.

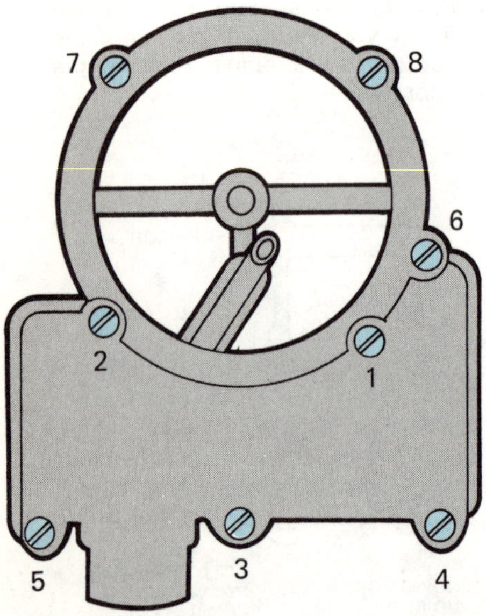

AIR HORN tightening sequence, 2V carb.

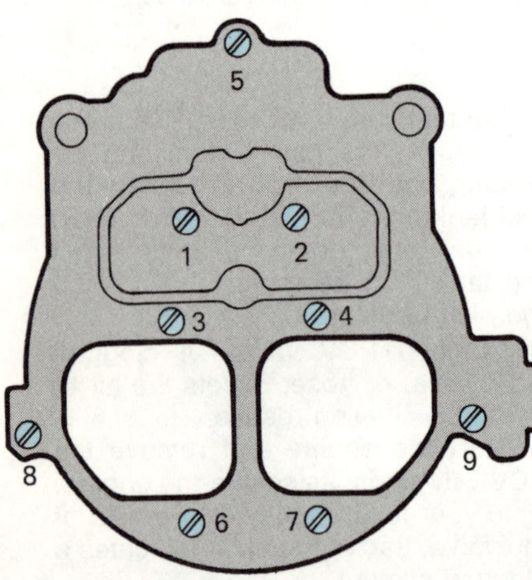

AIR HORN tightening sequence, 4V carb.

■ Vacuum loss—The engine must maintain vacuum to keep from stalling and/or idling rough. The engine can lose vacuum if a vacuum hose serving a vacuum-operated component loosens or splits. Vacuum is also lost if carburetor fittings loosen or the carburetor-intake manifold gasket ruptures.

Connect a vacuum gauge to a vacuum port on the engine. Start the engine and let it run at idle speed. If the vacuum gauge shows a reading below normal specification, which is generally 17-21 inches of mercury (less for some engines), examine hoses. Then, check for vacuum loss around the carburetor and intake manifold by spreading an oil-kerosene mixture around joints. An increase in vacuum on the vacuum gauge signifies that the mixture has sealed a leaking area. Tighten bolts or replace the gasket.

■ Inoperative heat valve—If your engine has a manifold-heat-control valve, there is a counterweight under the exhaust manifold. With the engine cold, try moving the counterweight. If it is stuck, the valve is stuck.

Lubricate the valve shaft by poking the nozzle of a can of manifold-heat-control-valve lubricant on the engine side of the counterweight. Tap the counterweight with a hammer. If this doesn't free the manifold-heat-control valve, consider replacing the manifold.

Some engines use a vacuum-operated vaporization valve, which is controlled by a thermostat vacuum switch. This unit will malfunction if a vacuum hose loosens or splits, if the thermostat vacuum switch fails or if the valve binds because of corrosion or dirt.

This device directs heated air to the intake manifold so fuel vaporizes as a cold engine warms up. If vaporization doesn't occur, the fuel mixture will be too concentrated, causing the engine to flood and stall. The same thing occurs when a manifold-heat-control-valve fails to function.

■ Bad EGR valve—The exhaust gas recirculation (EGR) valve should not leak. If it does, vacuum is lost and the engine will stall.

If the type of valve on your engine allows you to feel the rubber diaphragm, test as follows (other EGR valves have to be taken from the engine for testing):

1. Set the transmission in PARK or NEUTRAL and apply the parking brake. Run the engine at between 1400-1600 rpm. Let the engine warm up a minute or two.

2. Place a finger under the EGR valve and disconnect the vacuum hose. Engine speed should increase and the diaphragm should move down.

3. Reconnect the hose. The diaphragm should move up as engine speed decreases.

If these things don't happen, put your finger over the end of the hose. You should feel pulling. If you do, vacuum is present at the hose. The EGR valve should be serviced or replaced.

If you don't feel vacuum, check the hose and carburetor port for a blockage. As a last resort, replace the thermostatic vacuum switch that controls the EGR valve.

Inherent Stalling Problems

The Department of Transportation has issued several recalls to cure stalling problems. Two in particular involve 1974–76 AMC passenger cars and Jeeps with electronic ignition systems, and 1975–77 Chrysler Corp. cars. See your dealer.

Some service bulletins that have been issued by manufacturers to eliminate inherent stalling problems are as follows:

Chrysler Corp.

■ 1975 models with Holley 2245 carburetor—a repair to allow the vehicle to get a correct idle adjustment. *SB 14-06-75.*

■ All models—fuel system contamination cleaning procedure. *SB 14-11-75.*

■ 1976 California models with 400-4V engines—stalls and/or sags at medium to heavy acceleration before engine is warmed up. *SB 14-13B-76.*

■ 1976 models with electronic lean burn engines—idling and/or stalling. *SB 14-16-76.*

■ 1977–78 models—propane assisted curb idle speed and mixture setting procedure. *SB 14-12-78.*

FoMoCo

■ 1973 six and eight-cylinder engines with air cleaner valve and duct vacuum motor assembly—stalling on cold engine driveaway. *SB 30C.*

■ 1974 Mustang and Pinto with 2300-cc engines and manual transmission—stalling on cold engine driveaway. *SB 71.*

■ 1974 Mustang II with 2800-cc engines—stalling on cold engine driveaway. *SB 76.*

■ 1975 models with 351W engines—stalling on cold engine startup. *SB 83.*

■ 1975 models with 460-cu.-in. engines—stalling on cold engine driveaway. *SB 91.*

■ 1976 Granada, Maverick, Monarch and Comet with 302-cu.-in. engine and automatic transmission—stalling on heavy acceleration after cold start. *SB 112.*

■ 1976–77 models with 460-cu.-in. engines—stalling on stopping and turning. *SB 130.*

■ 1977 Granada and Monarch with 250-cu.-in. engines and automatic transmission—stalling with airconditioner operating. *SB 125.*

HESITATION

Tracking down the cause

Engine hesitation on acceleration, which is also called flat-spot acceleration, is usually caused by one of the conditions outlined in the "Troubleshooting Hesitation" chart.

The cause of hesitation is usually found in the fuel system. Causes listed under this heading in the troubleshooting chart are in order of difficulty. The least difficult to troubleshoot is first. What follows is an explanation of tasks to do in an attempt to resolve hesitation. Procedures discussed previously are listed in the chart's "Refer To" column. After making each adjustment or repair, road-test your car to determine if the hesitation problem has been alleviated.

Testing throttle cable

1. Check throttle-cable movement by removing the air cleaner and observing throttle cable action as an assistant depresses and releases the accelerator pedal.

2. Clean off dirt if the cable binds. Use carburetor cleaner. See that the throttle lever is also dirt-free.

Hesitation in some models has been caused by a plastic retainer at the throttle lever end of the accelerator cable slipping and catching. If this is happening, try to reposition and secure the retainer with wire, or replace the cable.

Testing the accelerating pump circuit

A damaged accelerating pump is the No. 1 cause of hesitation. The purpose of this pump is to inject a quantity of gasoline into the carburetor through a special accelerating circuit when rapid acceleration takes place. This quick spurt of gas compensates for the rapid rush of air into the carburetor that takes place during step-down acceleration.

Without an accelerating pump in the carburetor, the air-to-gas ratio would be thrown off, and the engine would starve for gas until the flow of fuel caught up with the rush of air. In other words, engine hesitation on acceleration would take place.

To test the accelerating pump and circuit, warm up the engine. Turn off the engine and remove the carburetor air cleaner. Activate the throttle lever rapidly two or three times. If full streams of gas aren't ejected from the jets, the accelerating circuit needs work.

Working on the accelerating pump

The external rod that operates the accelerating pump can usually be adjusted. Check this adjustment first. You may not have to open the carburetor.

The adjustment procedure and specification for each carburetor differ, so consult your car's shop manual. The following procedure, which applies to late model Rochester 2GC carburetors on GM cars, gives you an idea of how the job is done. The pump-rod specification for the 2GC carburetor is either $1^{11}/_{16}$ or $1^{21}/_{32}$ inch.

1. Back out the idle-speed adjusting screw. Hold the throttle lever so the throttle valve is completely closed.

2. Place a gauge from the top of the air horn to the top of the accelerating pump rod. Measure.

3. If the distance is not to specification, bend the accelerating pump rod to attain the specified distance.

4. Set curb-idle speed to specification.

If the accelerating-pump-rod adjustment is correct, a damaged accelerating pump is probably causing hesitation. To replace the part, do this:

1. Remove the air horn.

2. Check the cup in the end of the accelerating pump. If it is cracked, split or distorted, replace the accelerating pump. The accelerating pump is usually held by a clip-pin type retainer that is removed with needle-nose pliers.

3. Replace the air horn, using a new gasket.

4. Make sure the air horn is tightened correctly. An air leak will affect engine performance. Use the applicable air-horn-screw-tightening sequences.

If replacing the accelerating pump fails to bring about a substantial discharge of gas from the accelerating pump circuit, the circuit is probably blocked or there is other carburetor damage. In any case, remove the carburetor from the engine. Disassemble, clean and overhaul the carburetor with parts contained in a specific rebuild kit for the particular model. If you don't wish to bother with rebuilding, install a new carburetor. A local parts dealer can help you get the right overhaul kit or carburetor.

Engine causes of hesitation

You can determine if a leaking valve or restricted exhaust system is causing hesitation by hooking up a vacuum gauge. The following vacuum-gauge needle movements are significant:

■ The needle drops to a low reading, returns to normal, drops, returns and keeps doing this. A leaky valve exists. If your car is equipped with mechanical valve lifters, a valve adjustment to specification may solve the problem.

■ The needle drops slowly to zero as engine speed is increased. There is a restriction in the exhaust system. Look for mud clogging the tailpipe. Check for a kinked pipe. A restricted catalytic converter can also cause the trouble. Replace damaged parts.

Toyota recall

The National Highway Traffic Safety Administration warns owners of 1971, 1972 and 1973 Toyota Corolla and Carina models with 1600-cc engines that throttles can stick suddenly in the open position, causing loss of control. The cause of the problem has been traced to a cracked heat tube from the exhaust manifold to the choke chamber.

Cracking allows exhaust contaminants to enter the choke chamber. An accumulation of sludge in the chamber can bind the throttle linkage, which causes the throttle to stick.

Throttle sticking is frequently preceded by hard starting, rough idling, stalling or hesitation. If you experience any of these with a 1971–73 Toyota Corolla or Carina, have the heat tubes checked.

How to cure missing, surging and lack of power

MISSING OCCURS under two operating conditions: at idle and under way. An engine that misses at idle runs unevenly and feels as if it's skipping. If the condition is bad enough, the car shakes.

Under way, a missing engine gives a steady pulsating or jerk that usually becomes more pronounced as load on the engine is increased. The sensation is not normally felt above 30 mph. Under way and at idle, a missing engine often causes the exhaust to produce a steady spitting sound.

Surging describes an engine that delivers a pronounced variation in power although the accelerator pedal and, thus, the throttle is kept steady. To the driver, it seems as if the car is speeding up and slowing down.

Lack of power (or sluggishness) defines an engine that is not delivering the power it should at high speed or when put under load. In other words, the car doesn't accelerate to the speed it should, it loses speed going uphill, and it has less-than-normal top speed for the position of the throttle.

MISSING

Tracking down the cause

What causes stalling can also cause missing. Proceed as follows to zero in on your particular problem:

1. Check for vacuum loss through loose or split vacuum hoses.

2. Make sure no leak exists at the carburetor-to-intake manifold mounting.

3. Examine primary ignition wires at the coil and distributor. Replace wires that have cracked insulation, and see that the wires are tightly connected.

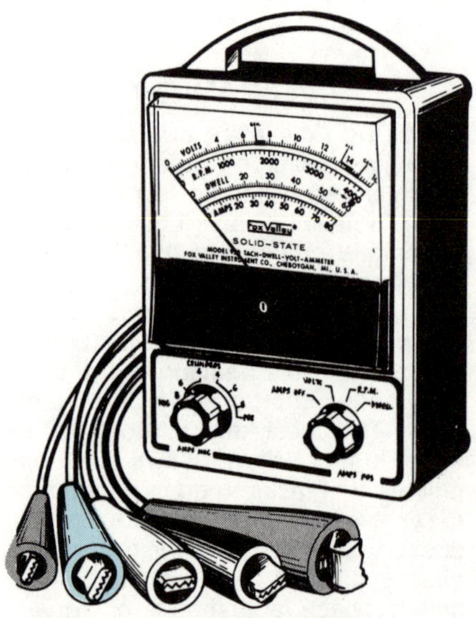

DWELL/TACH/volt/ammeter can be combined in one instrument.

IN THIS carb, disconnect tube at clamp (arrow), blocking snorkel.

DISCONNECT EGR hose at near end and plug hose to sustain vacuum.

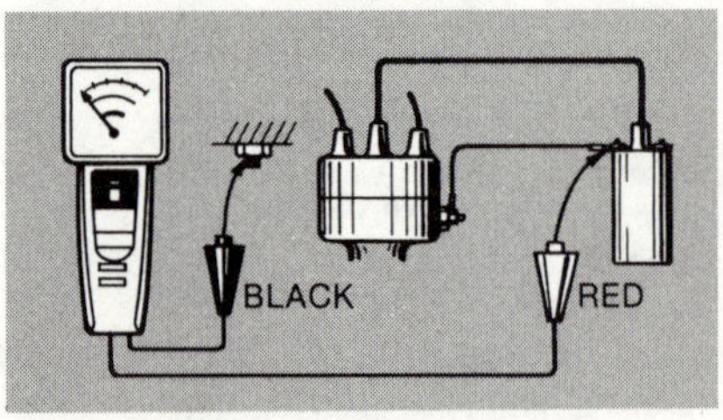

DWELLMETER is connected to the ground (black wire) and coil (red).

SEE ALSO

Carburetors, auto . . . Dieseling, auto . . . Electronic ignition, auto . . . Fuel systems, auto . . . Ignition systems, auto . . . Misfiring, auto . . . Motor oil . . . Sparkplugs . . . Stalling, auto . . . Tune-up, auto

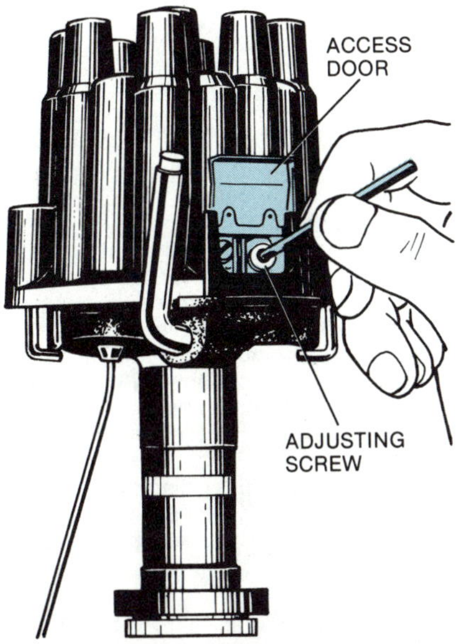

SOME distributors have access door for adjusting the contact points.

4. Disconnect carburetor air cleaner vacuum tube, if one is present. Plug the tube opening or the opening in the air cleaner or manifold so vacuum is not lost.

5. Disconnect vacuum hose of the exhaust gas recirculation (EGR) valve. Plug end of the hose so vacuum is retained.

6. Disconnect and reconnect cables from each sparkplug in turn, while the engine is running, using insulated pliers to avoid a shock. There should be a drop in engine revolutions per minute (rpm) as each plug is disconnected. If there is a drop in rpm, check the following to find the cause of missing:

- Thermostatic air cleaner.
- Distributor and distributor points of a conventional ignition system (see below).
- Engine timing and carburetor mixture and idling speed (see below).
- Positive crankcase ventilation (PCV) system (refer to Stalling).
- EGR valve operation.

7. Remove sparkplugs if there is no rpm drop in one or more cylinders as each plug is disconnected (see No. 6 above), and look for cracks, wear, improper gap, burning or fouling. Recondition or replace plugs, whichever is necessary (see below).

8. If missing continues, test each sparkplug cable. Then examine the distributor cap and rotor for damage or moisture and dirt. If the parts aren't damaged, wipe them clean and dry. Retest engine performance.

9. Suspect a problem in the engine if the above procedure fails to uncover the cause of missing (see below).

Look in the distributor

This discussion assumes that the engine is equipped with breaker-point (conventional) ignition. Missing can occur if breaker points are corroded, dirty or incorrectly adjusted, or if the distributor shaft assembly (bushing, shaft, breaker plate and cam) is damaged.

After replacing distributor points and/or setting gap with a feeler gauge to the specification in the manual or on the vehicle emission control decal, set the point dwell with a dwell meter and tachometer. Dwell refers to the duration of time that the points are closed. The measurement and subsequent resetting of point gap, if necessary, establishes point spacing precisely. Proceed as follows:

1. Connect dwell meter and tachometer (usually combined as one instrument). Follow hookup instructions in the booklet accompanying

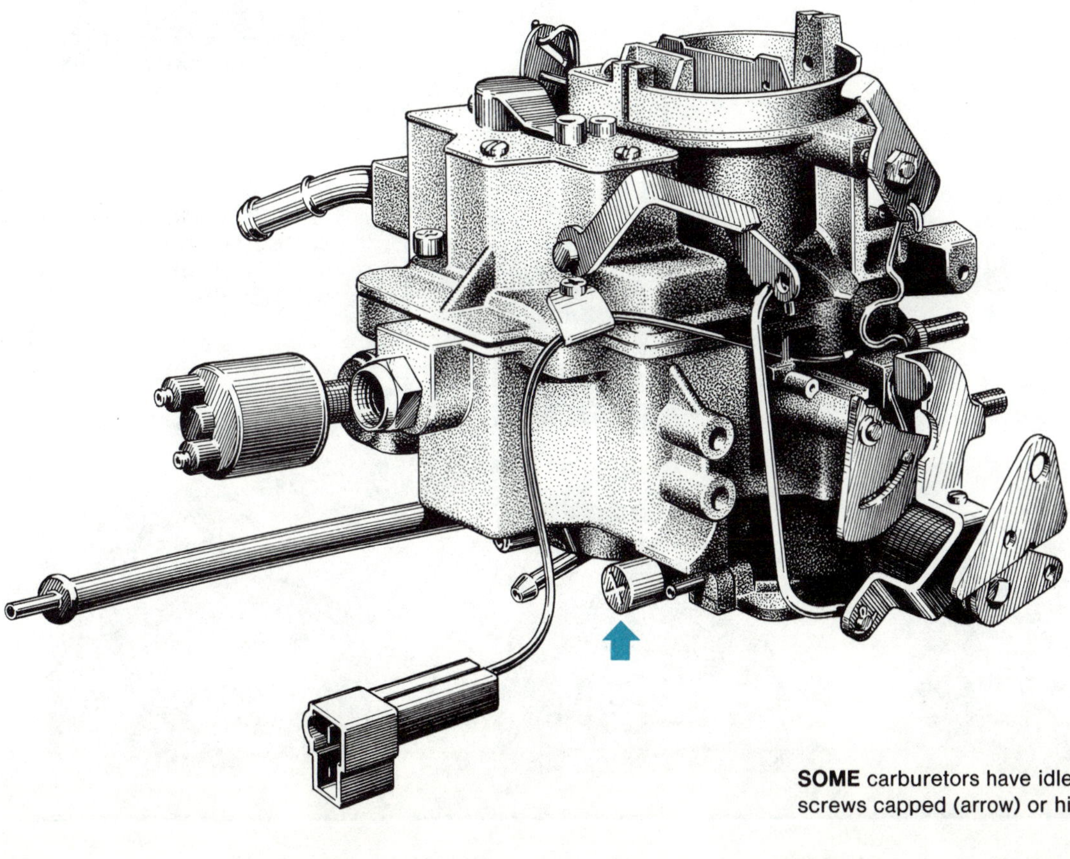

SOME carburetors have idle mixture screws capped (arrow) or hidden.

the instrument. Usually, the meter is connected so the ground lead (usually black) is attached to a clean metal part of the engine, while the other lead (red, yellow or any color other than black) is attached to the primary wire terminal at the coil. The primary wire is the thin wire (not the secondary cable) extending from the coil to the distributor.

2. Place instrument switches at proper settings. For example, if you are working on an eight-cylinder engine, set the selector to "8." Place the function switch on "Tach."

HOW TO 'READ' YOUR PLUGS

Shown here are sparkplugs taken from 15 different engines. Here's how to "read" them.

1. Almost white, fluffy gray deposit on insulator tip and side electrode is normal for emission-controlled engines using lean mixtures and no-lead fuels. This plug has high mileage and should be replaced.
2. White with light tan tint: The soft deposits on center electrode and darker deposit on side electrode indicate proper heat range for the way this engine is being used—at moderate speeds and loads.
3. Light tan deposits on a well-used plug. The yellow deposit on the side electrode is normal and comes from metallic additives.
4. Yellowish, soft white deposits on the center electrode and insulator are normal for an engine using fuel containing certain metallic additives. Shell deposits are normal, not signs of wrong fuel mixtures.
5. Classic example of a normal plug with fluffy, chocolate brown deposit on the insulator. Note slightly lighter color on side electrode showing that it's running a bit hotter. Sooty black deposit on shell suggests rich mixture, perhaps new air filter needed.
6. Fluffy red deposits are normal in engines using fuels with MMT additives. Slightly oily deposit on the shell may be due to an engine not yet fully broken in. In an older engine it might indicate the beginning of wear on piston rings, valve guides/seals.
7. Detonation damage: The firing end of the insulator is broken and metal transferred from center electrode to the side electrode. Possible causes: a. Overadvanced ignition timing. b. Fuel too low in octane. c. EGR system malfunctioning.
8. Preignition damage. White deposits on a blistered insulator, along with burned electrodes, reveal extreme heat condition. Possible causes: a. Sparkplug too hot. b. Overadvanced ignition timing. c. Glowing deposits in combustion chamber. d. Cooling system clogged. e. Exhaust system blocked.
9. Soot fouling. Fluffy, black soot deposits on insulator and electrodes. Possible causes: a. Excessively rich

SPARKPLUGS THAT INDICATE NORMAL ENGINE OPERATION

1

SPARKPLUGS THAT INDICATE THE NEED FOR TUNE-UP OR REPAIR

5

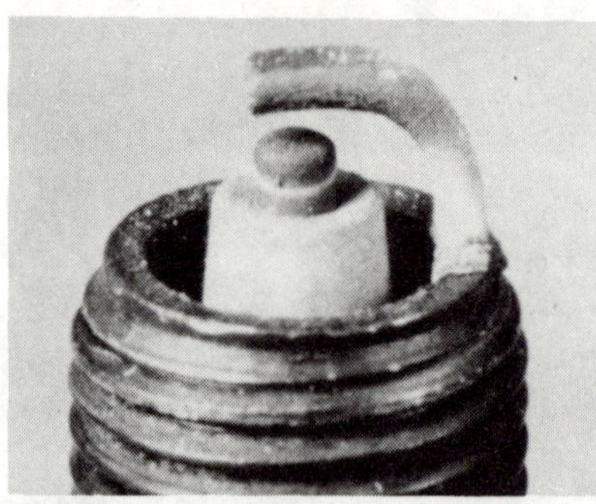
6

10

11

12

3. Start engine and let it idle. Read the tachometer. It should show that the engine is idling at the specified carburetor idle speed. If it isn't, set the idle (see below).

4. Switch dwell meter/tachometer to the dwell function. The meter should record the dwell specified on the vehicle emission-control decal or in the manual. This specification is given in degrees, such as 28–32°. Set dwell, if necessary. If the distributor has an access door, slide the door open and engage the distributor point adjusting screw with an Allen wrench.

mixture due to sticking choke or defective carburetor. b. Faulty ignition primary circuit or defective sparkplug wires. c. Excessively cold starting without engine warm-up.

10. Oil fouled. Oily, usually black deposit covering insulator and electrodes. Possible causes: a. Excessive passage of engine oil into combustion chamber due to piston ring or valve guide seal leakage. b. Defective PCV system.
11. Carbon fouled. Hard, black carbon deposits on insulator and electrodes. Possible causes: a. Moderate amount of oil passing rings or valves. b. Defective PCV system. c. Sparkplug too cold. d. Sparkplug not correct type for engine.
12. Dirt fouling. Carbonized and sometimes granular deposits on and around the insulator and electrodes. Possible causes: a. Air cleaner missing. b. Defective air-cleaner mountings.
13. Bridged gap. Carbon particles are lodged in the sparkplug gap. Possible cause: Combustion chamber deposits accumulated during low-speed, light-load use break loose during demand for full power.
14. Glazed insulator. Glassy surface on the insulator as a result of deposits melting on plug. Possible causes: a. Sparkplug too hot. b. Local overheating due to cooling system blockage or similar defect.
15. Splashed insulator. Splotches of black, almost paint-like deposits on the insulator. Possible cause: Delayed correction of an engine miss allows soft, oily deposits to accumulate in cylinder. After tune-up these deposits break loose and foul plug.

2

3

4

7

8

9

13

14

15

IDLE SPEED of some engines is adjusted by idle speed screw on carb.

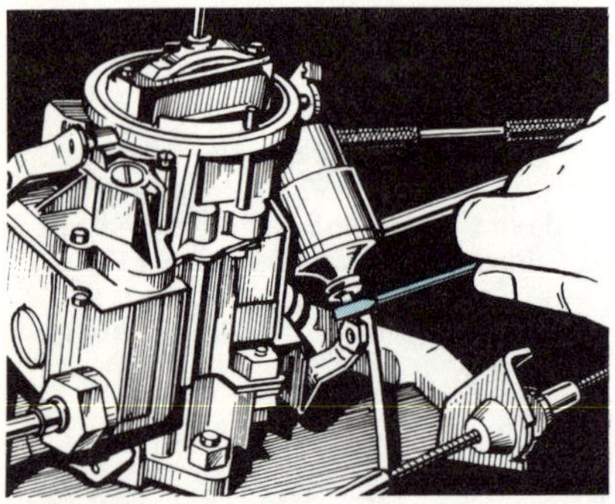

IDLE SPEED of other engines is adjusted by turning idle solenoid plunger.

With the engine idling, turn the screw until correct degrees of dwell are recorded.

Caution: Make sure the sliding door is closed tightly after making the adjustment. If dirt enters the distributor, the points will fail prematurely.

If the distributor doesn't have an access door, turn off the engine, remove the distributor cap and rotor, and reset breaker-point gap.

Bring points closer together if dwell angle is below specification and farther apart if dwell angle is excessive. With a smaller dwell angle, points begin opening farther from the crest of the cam lobe. Thus, they stay open for longer periods and closed for shorter periods. Conversely, with a larger dwell angle, points begin opening closer to the crest of a cam lobe and stay open less and closed longer.

5. Accelerate engine slowly with dwell set correctly, until the tachometer shows a reading of 1500 rpm. Note the dwell reading. Then let the engine return to idle and check the dwell reading again. If the dwell readings vary more than 3°, the distributor shaft assembly is damaged. Repair or replace the distributor.

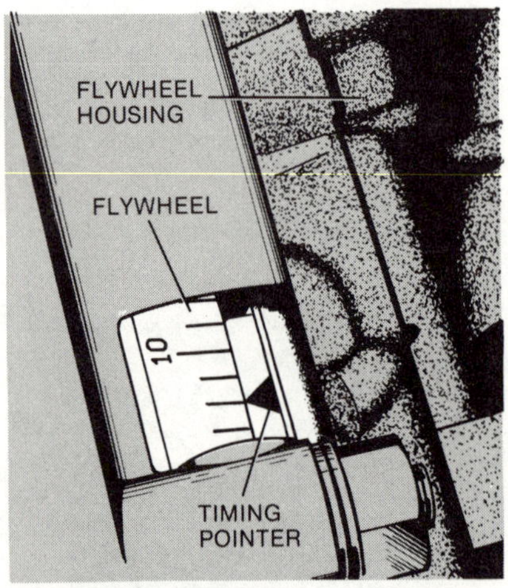

IMPORTED CARS, in particular, have timing marks on engine flywheel.

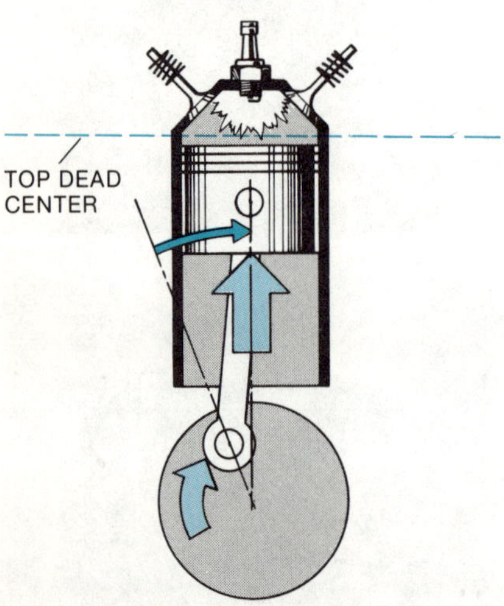

TIMING IS SET at predesignated spot in piston travel—at TDC, BTDC or ATDC.

Setting the carburetor

Stringent emission control standards have made the carburetor mixture tricky to adjust. From one year to the next and from one manufacturer to another, there are differences in procedure. You cannot, therefore, accurately set fuel mixture without specific manufacturer service instructions.

Furthermore, on most modern cars, the carburetor fuel mixture was set at the factory. The main reason for this setting going awry is a malfunction in the carburetor which would require overhauling or replacing the carburetor.

As for idle-speed adjustment, which establishes how fast or slow the engine idles when it is warmed up, the procedure is:

1. Be sure the engine is warm, so the choke is released.

2. Check the vehicle emission control decal or service manual for conditions that establish an accurate adjustment. For instance, some engines require airconditioners and headlights off. Others require airconditioners and/or headlights on.

3. Obtain your engine's specified idling speed setting from the decal or manual. This may be referred to as curb idle rpm, slow idle speed or slow idle rpm.

4. Note under what conditions you have to adjust idling speed if the carburetor is equipped with a curb-idle solenoid (also called an idle-stop or throttle solenoid). The purpose of this part is to close the throttle valve(s) simultaneously with the ignition shutoff, so fuel can't get past the valve(s) into cylinders. Fuel leaking into the cylinders after the ignition is turned off can cause dieseling—that is, engine run-on.

5. Connect a tachometer and check engine idling-speed rpm.

6. Make the adjustment if rpm is not to specification. In the absence of a curb-idle solenoid, turn the curb-idle screw until the tachometer records the specified idling speed.

If your car has a curb-idle solenoid, the manufacturer will specify, on the decal or in the service manual, how idle speed is to be adjusted. It

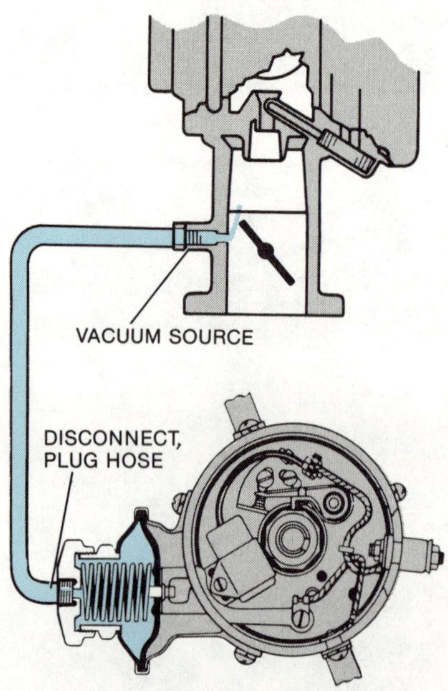

DISCONNECT, plug vacuum advance to adjust timing to specifications.

OBSERVE the timing mark and pointer to see if adjustment is right.

may be done by turning the solenoid plunger or de-energizing the solenoid (by disconnecting its wire and turning the idle-speed screw).

Setting timing

Timing is the firing of a sparkplug at the instant the piston in the cylinder the plug serves is in position to deliver maximum power. To determine if spark is being delivered at the proper time, you need a stroboscopic timing light. This is aimed at the timing marks, which are located on the crankshaft pulley or flywheel.

Marks correspond to the piston's position in the first cylinder of an engine. The timing light is connected to this cylinder and flashes when spark is delivered. You can tell if ignition occurs at the proper moment in the piston's cycle by the relationship of the flashing light to the position of the timing marks. If timing is not correct, as established by the engine manufacturer, bring it into synchronization by loosening and turning the distributor.

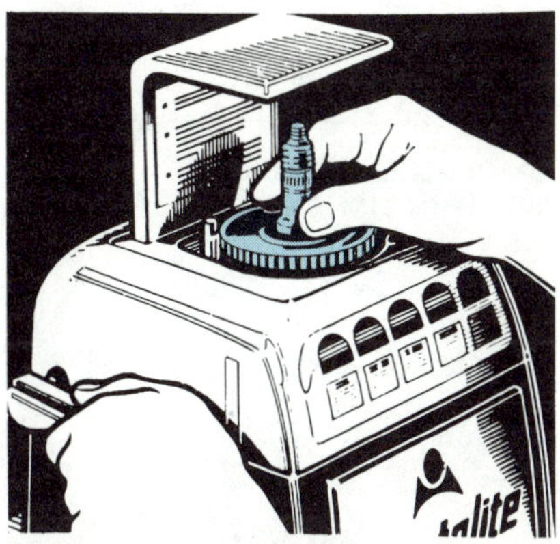

SANDBLAST sparkplugs before reusing for good performance.

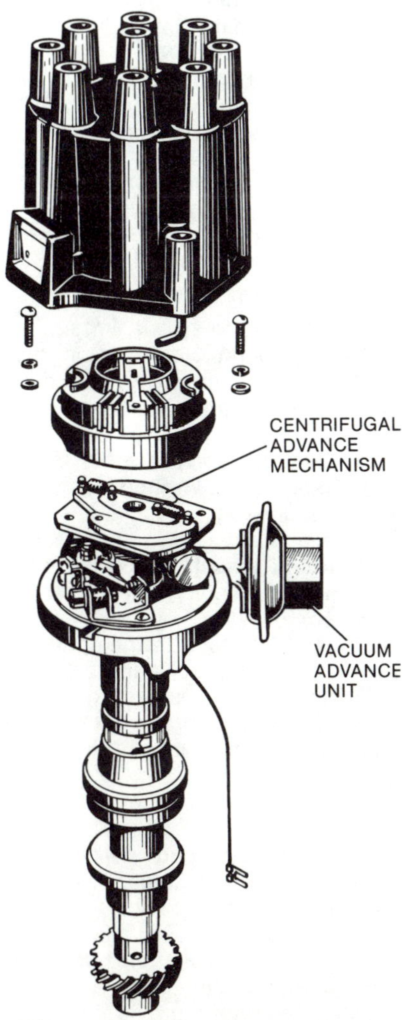

TIMING light checks condition of centrifugal and vacuum advance units.

To set ignition timing, first consult the emission control decal to establish necessary conditions. In most cases, warm up the engine and disconnect the vacuum advance hose from the vacuum advance unit. Plug the end of the hose to prevent vacuum loss.

The vacuum advance is a chamber normally attached to the distributor. Its purpose is to advance and retard ignition timing, according to the demands of acceleration and deceleration put on the engine. The action of the vacuum advance depends on the presence of engine vacuum delivered to the vacuum advance unit from the engine through the vacuum hose.

When you check the emission control decal, also determine the ignition timing specification. It's given in degrees, such as so many degrees BTDC, ATDC or TDC (0°).

USE SPARKPLUG feeler gauge to obtain accurate setting.

BTDC stands for Before Top Dead Center. This means that ignition should take place when the piston is the specified number of degrees before it reaches the top of its compression stroke.

ATDC stands for After Top Dead Center. This means that ignition should take place when the piston is the specified number of degrees after it has passed the top of its compression stroke and is on the downstroke.

TDC (10°) stands for Top Dead Center and means that ignition should take place when the piston is at the peak of its compression stroke.

Timing is normally adjusted as follows:

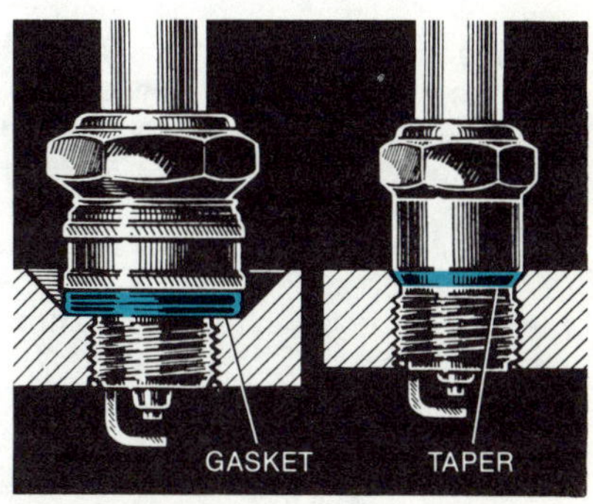

SQUARE-SHOULDERED plug, left, needs gasket; tapered plug, right, doesn't.

1. Locate the timing marks. In most cars, they are on the crankshaft pulley, which is at the front of the engine. In some cars, timing marks are located on the flywheel, which is at the rear of the engine. In this case, the marks are visible through a peephole in the flywheel housing.

2. Note the way timing marks are laid out. There is a 0° mark, designations indicating BTDC and ATDC, and a degree scale of numerals and index marks denoting various degree positions. There is also a pointer. The degree scale moves as the engine runs, but the pointer remains stationary.

3. If you have difficulty seeing the degree scale and pointer, clean them with kerosene. Find the mark that coincides with the specified timing of the engine and outline that mark with white paint. Also paint the pointer.

4. Identify the No. 1 plug. In four- and six-cylinder engines, the No. 1 plug is the first one at the front of the engine, closest to the radiator.

No. 1 plug of V8 engines, other than Ford, Mercury, Lincoln and Cadillac, is the first plug at the front of the engine, closest to the radiator, on the left (driver) side. Ford, Mercury, Lincoln and Cadillac have the No. 1 plug at the front of the engine, closest to the radiator, on the right (passenger) side. Check the service manual to determine the No. 1 plug if you have a make different from those mentioned here.

5. Connect the timing light according to the manual that comes with the instrument. There are two general kinds of lights. One uses an a.c. power source and is connected to a wall outlet. The other uses a d.c. power source and is connected to the car battery.

Whichever light you use, it has a lead that is connected to the No. 1 sparkplug. Usually, it is necessary to remove the cable from the sparkplug and insert an adapter between the cable terminal and plug. Then attach the timing-light lead to the adapter.

6. If you haven't checked point dwell and engine idling speed before as described earlier in this section, connect a dwell meter/tachometer and do it now.

7. If, according to the emission control decal, it is necessary to disconnect and plug the vacuum advance hose, use a pencil, golf tee or suitable-size screw.

8. With the engine idling, aim the timing light directly at the timing marks as if you were pointing a pistol. Sight straight down the center of the barrel and pull the switch trigger. In a car with timing correctly set, the timing mark and pointer will line up with each other and appear to be stationary. If the pointer and mark don't coincide, and you see the index scale moving, adjust the timing as follows:

9. Shut off the engine. Loosen the distributor hold-down bolt until you can turn the distributor. Use a distributor wrench (offset type), if necessary, to gain access to the bolt. Do not remove the bolt.

If the distributor sticks in the engine, give it a shot of carbon dioxide from a CO_2 fire extinguisher. Put on gloves to turn the distributor.

10. Restart the engine and aim the timing light at the timing marks as you slowly turn the distributor by grabbing the vacuum advance chamber. When timing mark and pointer line up, turn off the engine and tighten the distributor hold-down bolt. Be careful not to disturb the distributor position. Then check the adjustment.

PLUG SIZE	WITH TORQUE WRENCH (ft.-lbs.) Cast-Iron Head	Aluminum Head
10 mm	8–12	8–12
12 mm	10–18	10–18
14 mm, gasket seat	25–30	18–22
14 mm, tapered seat	7–15	7–15
18 mm, gasket seat	32–38	28–34
18 mm, tapered seat	15–20	15–20

SPARKPLUG TORQUING SPECIFICATIONS

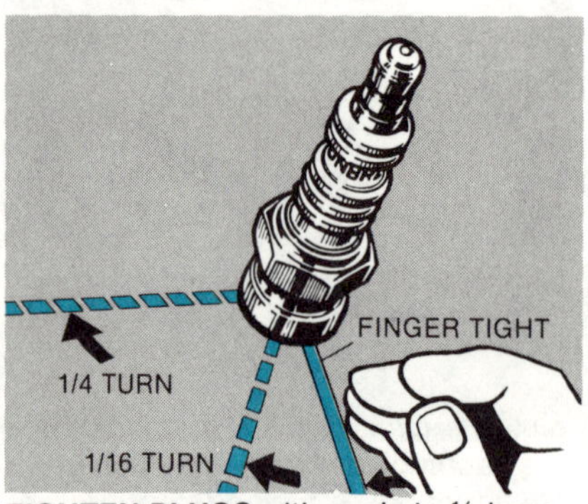

TIGHTEN PLUGS with gaskets ¼ turn; tighten tapered seat plugs ¹⁄₁₆ turn.

11. With timing set use the timing light to test the centrifugal advance and vacuum advance mechanisms. The centrifugal advance, a spring-and-weight component in the distributor, changes ignition timing by means of centrifugal force as engine speed varies.

12. To check centrifugal advance, aim the timing light at the timing scale as you increase engine speed slowly, from idle to 1500 rpm. The timing mark should advance as engine speed increases, and return to its original setting when engine speed decreases. If this does not happen, the distributor needs repair.

13. To check the vacuum advance, unplug and reconnect the vacuum hose to the vacuum advance chamber. Aim the timing light at the timing scale and run the engine at 1500 rpm. The timing mark should advance to a position that is farther than the position it assumed when you tested the centrifugal advance. If this doesn't happen, the diaphragm in the advance chamber is probably leaking, and the vacuum advance chamber should be replaced.

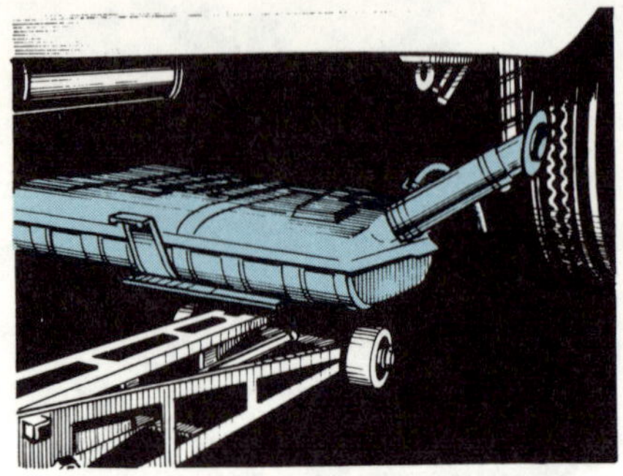

IF FUEL system is contaminated, tank should be removed and cleaned.

How to replace sparkplugs

Faulty sparkplugs are the main reason engines miss when the car is rolling. Here is the correct procedure for removing plugs:

1. Use the correct tools for the job. Usually, a ¹³⁄₁₆-inch or ⅝-inch hex sparkplug socket, ratchet wrench and an extension are needed.

2. Identify each sparkplug cable with the engine cold. Write identifying numbers on strips of masking tape and attach the tape to the sparkplug cables. This will facilitate correct reconnecting of cables to plugs.

3. Grasp and rotate each sparkplug boot, pulling it from the sparkplug.

4. Loosen each sparkplug, with one turn only.

5. Blow dirt and carbon from around each sparkplug. Use compressed air, if possible. If compressed air is not available, aim the end of a length of vacuum hose at the area around the plug and blow through the other end.

6. Remove each plug and examine its tip for any unusual condition.

TROUBLESHOOTING SURGING

CAUSES TO CHECK	CORRECTION
☐ Inoperative thermostat air cleaner.	Repair.
☐ Vacuum loss through loose or split vacuum hose.	Repair or replace.
☐ Vacuum leak from carburetor-manifold area.	Repair.
☐ Defective or loose primary ignition wires at coil and distributor.	Tighten or replace.
☐ Incorrect ignition timing.	Adjust.
☐ Malfunctioning centrifugal advance and vacuum advance units.	Repair or replace.
☐ Dirty fuel filter.	Replace.
☐ Defective sparkplugs.	Service or replace.
☐ Weak fuel pump.	Replace.
☐ Split, leaking or kinked fuel line or hose.	Replace.
☐ Clogged fuel tank strainer and dirty fuel tank.	Replace strainer; clean fuel tank.
☐ Dirty carburetor; damaged parts.	Overhaul.

The photos and captions on page 1114–1115 will help identify plug conditions and indicate what needs to be done in each case.

Incidentally, if a plug binds in the engine, but a few threads are exposed, drip some light oil on the threads and screw the plug back into the engine. Let the oil soak the threads before you try to remove the plug again.

7. Do a compression test (see below), with sparkplugs out of the engine, if you suspect that engine missing is being caused by an engine problem.

Suppose the plugs you remove are not worn, just dirty. They can be restored to service if you have a sparkplug cleaner (one for home use is available from a parts and accessories dealer). If you don't have a cleaner, take plugs to a service station for cleaning.

Wipe plugs to get rid of dirt, moisture and oil. Clean wet deposits from the firing tips by washing plugs in kerosene. Use a brush to work the solvent inside insulators.

Dry the plugs with an air hose—even if you have to pay a service station attendant a dollar or two to use his. Sparkplug tips have to be thoroughly dry so solvent doesn't cake inside the plug. This will cause misfiring.

Clean the plugs in a service-station cleaning machine, but do not blast them for longer than five seconds. Longer blasts wear down insulators and electrodes.

Using the gap adjusting tool of a sparkplug feeler gauge, open the outside electrode of each plug enough to slip a sparkplug file between the electrodes. Do not use pliers or any tool other than a sparkplug tool or you will damage the plug.

File the center and outside electrodes clean. This requires only a pass or two with the file.

Use a small wire brush to clean threads, but don't touch the electrodes with the brush. You can cause damage.

Use a sparkplug feeler gauge—no other type—to gap plugs. Be sure you have the correct specification for your engine. You will find it on the emission control decal or in the service manual.

Insert the correct-size wire gauge and move it in and out. If the gauge is too loose or too tight between electrodes, use the adjusting tool to close or open the gap by bending the side electrode. Bending the center electrode will damage the plug. Gap is set properly when you feel a slight resistance on the feeler gauge as you move the gauge between electrodes.

It is important to remember that electrode gaps of new plugs are not preset at the factory. You must set gap before installing new plugs.

To install plugs correctly, do this:

1. If the car has an aluminum-head engine, coat the first two or three threads of each sparkplug with a thin layer of graphite to prevent seizing.

2. Use a small brush or thread-chaser to clean the threads of sparkplug ports.

3. If you are installing used plugs, examine the seat. Plugs with square seats use gaskets, and new gaskets should be used. If you can't get replacement gaskets, replace the plugs. Using old gaskets causes compression loss. Plugs with tapered seats do not use gaskets.

4. Screw the plugs into the engine by hand until they are finger-tight. If plugs use gaskets, thread gaskets on plugs, so they are flush against the base of the shell, before installing the plugs.

5. If you have a torque wrench, torque plugs to the specifications in the shop manual. If you don't have a torque wrench, tighten plugs finger-tight, then with a wrench—¼-turn for plugs with gaskets, 1/16-turn for tapered-seat plugs.

Overtightening plugs make them difficult to remove the next time around. Not making them tight enough causes compression loss. Get it right.

Testing engine compression

Low compression in one or more cylinders will cause an engine to miss. Compression refers to the process by which pistons reduce volume within a cylinder, thus increasing pressure of the fuel mixture within the cylinder.

Low compression can be caused by several factors, but whatever the cause, the solution requires engine dismantling. Reasons for low compression include worn piston rings, leaking or sticking valves, and leaking head gasket.

Compression is tested with a compression tester. Readings are compared with manufacturer specifications to determine if there is a compression loss. To test compression, proceed as follows (the task is easier if someone is inside the car to crank the engine and hold the throttle open):

1. Warm up the engine.

2. Remove all sparkplugs.

3. Disconnect the distributor-to-coil secondary cable (that's the thick wire).

4. Screw or push the compression gauge securely into the first cylinder. The seal between the gauge and engine block has to be tight to prevent compression loss and an inaccurate reading.

5. Have an assistant hold the accelerator pedal to the floor as he or she cranks the engine using the ignition key. The engine should be cranked the same number of revolutions (at least eight) as each cylinder is tested to obtain an accurate comparison of compression readings between cylinders.

6. Note the highest compression reading. If it seems low, go on to the

TROUBLESHOOTING LACK OF POWER

CAUSES TO CHECK	CORRECTION
☐ Dirty air cleaner filter.	Replace.
☐ Inoperative thermostatic air cleaner.	Repair.
☐ Incorrect ignition timing.	Adjust.
☐ Malfunctioning centrifugal advance and vacuum advance units.	Repair or replace.
☐ Defective sparkplugs.	Service or replace.
☐ Malfunctioning automatic choke.	Adjust or repair.
☐ Bad EGR valve.	Replace.
☐ Dirty carburetor or defective part.	Repair or replace.
☐ Sticking valves.	Test compression; repair.

next cylinder and afterward retest the low-reading cylinder. Record readings on paper.

To judge compression accurately, you have to know the manufacturer's specification. This is available in the shop manual and in some owner manuals.

Compression obtained for each cylinder does not have to conform exactly to specification. Manufacturers give a leeway. For example, American Motors, Chrysler and General Motors allow that the lowest reading obtained may be 80 percent of the highest-reading cylinder. Ford allows a 75 percent edge. However, any cylinder that shows compression lower than 100 pounds per square inch (p.s.i.) indicates a defect.

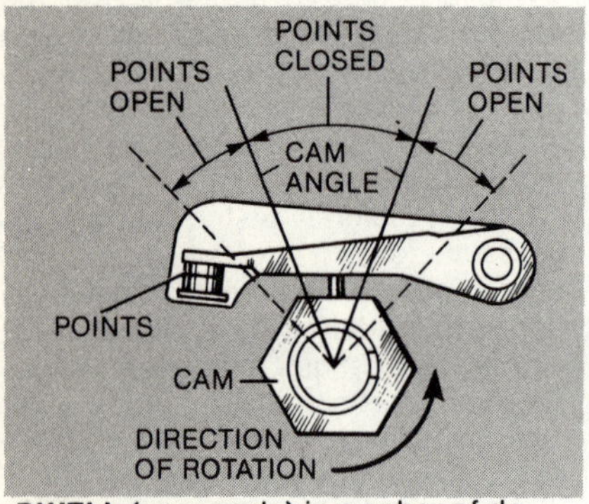

DWELL (cam angle) is number of degrees of rotation points stay closed.

SURGING

Tracking down the cause

The accompanying chart summarizes the causes of surging.

Working on the fuel system

You can check fuel lines visually to establish if a malfunction is causing engine surge. Surging can occur if there is a loose connection or leak allowing air to enter the line and inhibit gas flow, or if a kink or other obstruction in a line is curtailing the flow of gas.

Seldom will a fuel line cause trouble. It is more likely that a fuel tank, which builds up sediment or rust over the years, is reducing the flow of fuel and causing surge. Foreign matter may be clogging the strainer in the tank or some other part of the system, restricting gas flow.

Fuel-system contamination is apparent if you have to replace the fuel filter often. If your car has an in-the-carburetor fuel filter, verify its condition by removing and examining the filter. Particles on the filter signal a fuel-system contamination.

To verify the condition in cars with in-line fuel filters, disconnect the fuel line at the fuel pump end of the filter and allow fuel to drip into a container. Examine the fuel for contaminating particles.

Cleaning the fuel tank and fuel system is not a job for the ordinary home mechanic. If you want to give it a try or know what a mechanic should do, the general procedure follows:

Cleaning fuel systems

1. Disconnect the battery.

2. Siphon fuel from the fuel tank into a clean container.

3. Disconnect the fuel line and vapor return hose, if the car is equipped with one, at the fuel tank.

4. Disconnect the ground wire and unplug the wire from the fuel tank sending unit.

5. Disconnect the vent hose.

6. Unhook the support strap and lower the fuel tank.

7. Loosen and unscrew the fuel tank sending unit cam ring and remove the sending unit assembly, which probably contains the fuel tank strainer. Install new strainer.

8. Remove the fuel filter in fuel line or carburetor. Leave fuel line disconnected.

9. Place the tank away from flame and heat. Remember, you are dealing with components that store and carry gas.

10. Finish draining the fuel tank by rocking it back and forth, letting gas run out the sending unit hole. If rust comes out, get a new gas tank. Rusted tanks can't be salvaged.

11. Clean the inside of the tank with steam or running hot water for at least five minutes. If you use water, make sure none remains in the tank.

Caution: Despite cleaning, fuel vapors remain in the fuel tank. Do not bring flame or heat near the tank.

12. Disconnect the fuel tank-to-fuel pump line at the fuel pump. Introduce air pressure into the line at the fuel tank end to blow the line clean. Pipes on the fuel-tank sending unit should be cleaned out with low air pressure.

13. Install the fuel-tank sending unit, using a new gasket.

14. Install the new tank and connect wires and lines, including the fuel line at the fuel pump. However, do not reconnect the fuel pump-to-carburetor fuel line. Instead, connect a 3-foot-long vacuum hose to the end of this fuel line.

15. Reconnect the battery, but disconnect the coil-to-distributor secondary (heavy) cable.

16. Put several gallons of clean gas into the fuel tank. Direct the vacuum hose at the end of the fuel line into a container. Operate the car's starter until two quarts of gas flow into the fuel can. This flushes the fuel pump and fuel lines. Discard the gas in the container since it has probably become contaminated.

17. Remove the vacuum hose and reconnect the fuel line. Hook up the coil-to-distributor cable. Start the engine and check all connections for leaks.

As far as cleaning the carburetor is concerned, try one of the products that permit cleaning with the carburetor remaining in the car.

If dirt has built up to an extreme point, remove and disassemble the carburetor. Clean parts individually and rebuild the carburetor, using a carburetor rebuild kit.

LACK OF POWER

Tracking down the cause

The chart included with this article summarizes the causes of lack of power.

METRIC CONVERSION

Conversion factors can be carried so far they become impractical. In cases below where an entry is exact it is followed by an asterisk (*). Where considerable rounding off has taken place, the entry is followed by a + or a - sign.

CUSTOMARY TO METRIC

Linear Measure

inches	millimeters
1/16	1.5875*
1/8	3.2
3/16	4.8
1/4	6.35*
5/16	7.9
3/8	9.5
7/16	11.1
1/2	12.7*
9/16	14.3
5/8	15.9
11/16	17.5
3/4	19.05*
13/16	20.6
7/8	22.2
15/16	23.8
1	25.4*

inches	centimeters
1	2.54*
2	5.1
3	7.6
4	10.2
5	12.7*
6	15.2
7	17.8
8	20.3
9	22.9
10	25.4*
11	27.9
12	30.5

feet	centimeters	meters
1	30.48*	.3048*
2	61	.61
3	91	.91
4	122	1.22
5	152	1.52
6	183	1.83
7	213	2.13
8	244	2.44
9	274	2.74
10	305	3.05
50	1524*	15.24*
100	3048*	30.48*

1 yard =
.9144* meters
1 rod =
5.0292* meters
1 mile =
1.6 kilometers
1 nautical mile =
1.852* kilometers

Fluid Measure

(Milliliters [ml] and cubic centimeters [cc or cu cm] are equivalent, but it is customary to use milliliters for liquids.)

1 cu in = 16.39 ml
1 fl oz = 29.6 ml
1 cup = 237 ml
1 pint = 473 ml
1 quart = 946 ml
= .946 liters
1 gallon = 3785 ml
= 3.785 liters
Formula (exact):
fluid ounces × 29.573 529 562 5*
= milliliters

Weights

ounces	grams
1	28.3
2	56.7
3	85
4	113
5	142
6	170
7	198
8	227
9	255
10	283
11	312
12	340
13	369
14	397
15	425
16	454

Formula (exact):
ounces × 28.349 523 125* =
grams

pounds	kilograms
1	.45
2	.9
3	1.4
4	1.8
5	2.3
6	2.7
7	3.2
8	3.6
9	4.1
10	4.5

1 short ton (2000 lbs) =
907 kilograms (kg)
Formula (exact):
pounds × .453 592 37* =
kilograms

Volume

1 cu in = 16.39 cubic centimeters (cc)
1 cu ft = 28 316.7 cc
1 bushel = 35 239.1 cc
1 peck = 8 809.8 cc

Area

1 sq in = 6.45 sq cm
1 sq ft = 929 sq cm
= .093 sq meters
1 sq yd = .84 sq meters
1 acre = 4 046.9 sq meters
= .404 7 hectares
1 sq mile = 2 589 988 sq meters
= 259 hectares
= 2.589 9 sq kilometers

Kitchen Measure

1 teaspoon = 4.93 milliliters (ml)
1 Tablespoon = 14.79 milliliters (ml)

Miscellaneous

1 British thermal unit (Btu) (mean)
= 1 055.9 joules
1 calorie (mean) = 4.19 joules
1 horsepower = 745.7 watts
= .75 kilowatts
caliber (diameter of a firearm's bore in hundredths of an inch)
= .254 millimeters (mm)
1 atmosphere pressure = 101 325* pascals (newtons per sq meter)
1 pound per square inch (psi) = 6 895 pascals
1 pound per square foot = 47.9 pascals
1 knot = 1.85 kilometers per hour
25 miles per hour = 40.2 kilometers per hour
50 miles per hour = 80.5 kilometers per hour
75 miles per hour = 120.7 kilometers per hour